# Plays

The Seagull, Uncle Vanya, Three Sisters, The Cherry Orchard
*with* The Evils of Tobacco, Swan Song, The Bear
*and* The Proposal

'The critical clamour for a Complete Chekhov in Michael Frayn's translation
has borne fruit' . . . *Sunday Times*

In the past ten years, since the National Theatre commissioned and staged
his translation of *The Cherry Orchard*, Michael Frayn's translations of all four
of Chekhov's late masterpieces have been performed to great acclaim.

For Frayn, who is both proficient in Russian and a notably successful
playwright himself, translating Chekhov is a labour of love and homage
fuelled by a complex understanding of Chekhov the writer and of the
characters he created. All this is evidenced in Frayn's substantial introduction.

For this volume Frayn has added four of Chekhov's short plays to make
this the most comprehensive, accurate and playable one-volume Chekhov
selection.

ANTON CHEKHOV (1860–1904) first turned to writing as a medical
student at Moscow University, from which he graduated in 1884. Among his
early plays were short monologues (*The Evils of Tobacco*, 1885), one-act
farces such as *The Bear*, *The Proposal* and *The Wedding*, (1888–89) and the
'Platonov' material, adapted by Michael Frayn as *Wild Honey*. The first three
full-length plays to be staged, *Ivanov* (1887), *The Wood Demon* (1889) and
*The Seagull* (1896) were initially failures. But the Moscow Arts Theatre's
revival of *The Seagull* two years later was successful and was followed by his
masterpieces, *Uncle Vanya* (1889), *Three Sisters* (1901), and *The Cherry
Orchard* in 1904, the year of his death.

*The front cover shows a detail from* Humdrum ('Zhiteyskaya proza') 1982–1893
*by V. Baksheyev and is reproduced by courtesy of the Tretyakov Gallery,
Moscow.*

# ANTON CHEKHOV
# Plays

The Seagull
Uncle Vanya
Three Sisters
The Cherry Orchard

*together with four of the Vaudevilles:*
The Evils of Tobacco
Swan Song
The Bear
The Proposal

*Translated and introduced by Michael Frayn*

Methuen Drama

**METHUEN WORLD CLASSICS**

This collection first published as a Methuen paperback original
in Great Britain in 1988 by Methuen London Ltd
and in the United States of America by
Routledge, Chapman and Hall Inc, 29 West 35th Street, New York, NY 10001
Revised and reprinted in 1991 by Methuen Drama,
an imprint of Reed Books Ltd,
Michelin House, 81 Fulham Road, London SW3 6RB
and Auckland, Melbourne, Singapore and Toronto

Reprinted 1991, 1992
Reissued with corrections and a new cover design 1993
Reprinted 1993, 1994 (three times), 1995

*The Evils of Tobacco* first published in this translation in 1988. Translation copyright ©
1988, 1991 by Michael Frayn. Original work entitled *O vrede tabaka*

*Swan Song* first published in this translation in 1988. Translation copyright © 1988,
1991 by Michael Frayn. Original work entitled *Lebedinaya pesnya*

*The Bear* first published in this translation in 1988. Translation copyright © 1988,
1991 by Michael Frayn. Original work entitled *Medved*

*The Proposal* first published in this translation in 1988. Translation copyright © 1988,
1991 by Michael Frayn. Original work entitled *Predlozhenie*

*The Seagull* first published in this translation in 1986 by Methuen London Ltd.
Translation copyright © 1988, 1991 by Michael Frayn. Original work entitled *Chaika*

*Uncle Vanya* first published in this translation in 1987 by Methuen London Ltd.
Translation copyright © 1988, 1991 by Michael Frayn. Original work entitled *Dyadya
Vanya*

*Three Sisters* first published in this translation in 1983 by Methuen London Ltd. Revised
for this edition 1988. Translation copyright © 1983, 1988, 1991 by Michael Frayn.
Original work entitled *Tri sestry*

*The Cherry Orchard* first published in this translation in 1978 by Eyre Methuen Ltd.
Reprinted 1982, 1984 and 1986 by Methuen London Ltd. Revised for this edition
1988. Translation copyright © 1983, 1988, 1991 by Michael Frayn. Original work
entitled *Vishnyovy sad*

British Library Cataloguing in Publication Data

Chekhov, A. P.
    Chekhov: plays.——(Methuen's world dramatists).
    I. Title II. Frayn, Michael
    891.72'3          PG3456.A19

ISBN 0–413–18160–X

Printed and bound in Great Britain by
Cox & Wyman Ltd, Reading, Berkshire

CAUTION

# Contents

# Anton Pavlovich Chekhov

1860    Born the son of a grocer and grandson of a serf, in Taganrog, a small port on the Sea of Azov, where he spends his first nineteen years, and which he describes on a return visit in later life as 'Asia, pure and simple!'

1875    His father, bankrupt, flees from Taganrog concealed beneath a mat at the bottom of a cart.

1876    A former lodger buys the Chekhovs' house and puts the rest of the family out.

1879    Chekhov rejoins his family, who have followed his father to Moscow, and enrols at the university to study medicine.

1880    Begins contributing humorous material to minor magazines under the pen-name Antosha Chekhonte.

1882    Begins contributing regularly to the St Petersburg humorous journal *Oskolki* – short stories and sketches, and a column on Moscow life.

1884    Qualifies as a doctor, and begins practising in Moscow – the start of a sporadic second career which over the years brings him much hard work but little income.

1885    Begins writing for the *St Petersburg Gazette*, which gives him the opportunity to break out of the tight restrictions on length and the rigidly humorous format in which he has worked up to now.

1886    Another step up the journalistic ladder – he begins writing, under his own name and for good money, for *Novoye vremya*. Alexei Suvorin, its millionaire proprietor, an anti-Semitic reactionary who had the concession on all the railway bookstands in Russia, becomes Chekhov's close friend.

1887    Is a literary success in St Petersburg. Writes *Ivanov* as a result of a commission from a producer who wants a light entertainment in the Chekhonte style. The play is produced in Moscow (his first production) to a mixture of clapping and hissing.

1888    Begins to publish his stories in the 'thick journals'; has survived his career in comic journalism to emerge as a serious and respectable writer. But at the same time begins writing four one-act farces for the theatre.

1889    *The Wood Demon* (which Chekhov later uses as raw material for *Uncle Vanya*) opens at a second-rate Moscow theatre, and survives for only three performances.

1890    Makes the appalling journey across Siberia (largely in unsprung carts over unsurfaced roads) to visit and report on the penal colony on the island of Sakhalin. Sets out to interview the entire population of prisoners and exiles, at the rate of 160 a day.

1892    Travels the back country of Nizhny Novgorod and Voronyezh provinces in the middle of winter, trying to prevent a recurrence of the previous year's famine among the peasants. Is banqueted by the provincial governors. Moves to the modest but comfortable estate he had bought himself at Melikhovo, fifty miles south of Moscow. Becomes an energetic and enlightened landowner, cultivating the soil and doctoring the peasants. Spends three months organizing the district against an expected cholera epidemic.

1894    Starts work on the first of the three schools he builds in the Melikhovo district.

1896    *The Seagull* opens in St Petersburg, and survives only five performances after a disastrous first night. Chekhov tells Suvorin he won't have another play put on even if he lives another seven hundred years.

1897    Suffers a violent lung haemorrhage while dining with Suvorin, and is forced to recognize at last what he has long closed his eyes to – that he is suffering from advanced consumption. (Is also constantly plagued by piles, gastritis, migraine, dizzy spells, and palpitations of the heart.) Winters in Nice.

1898    Moves his headquarters to the Crimean warmth of Yalta. Stanislavsky revives *The Seagull* (with twelve weeks rehearsal) at the newly-founded Moscow Arts Theatre, and it is an immediate success.

1899    Sells the copyright in all his works, past, present, and future, to the St Petersburg publisher A. F. Marks – a contract which is to burden the rest of his life. *Uncle Vanya* produced successfully by the Moscow Arts Theatre.

1901    *Three Sisters* produced by the Moscow Arts Theatre, but rather poorly received. Chekhov marries his mistress, Olga Knipper, an actress in the Moscow Arts company, the original Arkadina in *The Seagull*, Yelena in *Uncle Vanya*, Masha in *Three Sisters* and Ranyevskaya in *The Cherry Orchard*.

1904    *The Cherry Orchard* is produced in January; and in July, after two heart attacks, Chekhov dies in a hotel bedroom in the German spa of Badenweiler.

# Introduction

Chekhov's reputation now rests chiefly upon the four oblique
and haunting plays he wrote in the last ten years of his life. In
fact he was not really a natural dramatist. The page, not the
stage, was his element. The skits and spoofs with which he
began his literary career while he was still a medical student
matured seamlessly into stories of the most exquisite restraint
and insight, and his reputation no less seamlessly with them;
even if he had never written a single line for the theatre he
would still be one of the most marvellous writers ever to have
lived. His sporadic parallel career as a playwright followed a
quite different pattern. For the greater part of his life it
remained a source of frustration, anguish, and self-doubt.
Again and again he renounced it; again and again he
discovered that he was 'absolutely not a dramatist'. He went
through bouts of defensive cynicism, when he announced
that the theatre bored him, that it was 'the venereal disease of
the cities', and when at last he had a little success in the
commercial theatre he made it clear to his friends that he was
only doing it for the money. But then the transition he was
trying to make, from page to stage, is one that remarkably
few major writers in the whole history of literature have
managed at all. And his struggles to understand and master
the recalcitrant medium of the theatre changed forever its
nature and possibilities.

The two careers were oddly out of step with each other
from the very beginning. While he was still only starting out
as a humorist in the comic journals he was already writing a
serious and substantial work for the theatre – the huge
untitled drama most usually known as *Platonov* (and as *Wild
Honey* in my adaptation of it). This was followed in 1885 by a
long one-act play, based on one of his stories, entitled *On the*

*Highroad*, which is melodramatic in tone, but which attempts a striking picture of society's lower depths. Neither of these was performed during his lifetime. The former was supposedly torn up after its rejection by the actress to whom Chekhov offered it, and did not resurface until sixteen years after his death, while the latter he seems to have abandoned after it was forbidden by the censor as being 'too gloomy and sordid', and also, to judge by the underlining in the censor's report, because it showed a member of the landowning classes in a drunken and destitute condition. His first seriously-intended work of any length to come before the public (leaving aside his detective novel, *The Shooting Party*, which, for all its delicious brilliance, was written as a potboiler) was also a play – *Ivanov*, in 1887. It was written (in ten days, according to Chekhov) at the suggestion of the theatremanager Korsh. Korsh specialised in light comedy, and Chekhov's sister Masha said he threw out his proposal – rather casually, during a conversation in the foyer of the theatre – because of Chekhov's reputation as a humorist. The play is not a humorous work, however – in fact it is possibly the most lowering thing that Chekhov ever wrote. Korsh apparently did not blench when he received the script; though Chekhov did when he saw Korsh's production of it. There were four rehearsals instead of the promised ten, and on the opening night only two of the cast knew their parts; the rest got through, said Chekhov, 'by prompter and inner conviction'. The reviews were decidedly mixed. So were the reactions of the first-night audience, with clapping, hissing, whistling, stamping, and 'absolute carnage' up in the gallery.

In the following year, 1888, Chekhov began the long and well-documented struggle (which we will examine when we come to look at each of the plays in detail later) with the material that was to become first *The Wood Demon* and then *Uncle Vanya*. But by this time his two careers had undergone a curious reversal. With the publication in that year of his long story, *The Steppe*, the successful boulevard journalist

became accepted as a writer of serious fiction – while with
Korsh's production of first *Swan Song* and then *The Bear* in
the same year the unsuccessful serious dramatist emerged as a
writer of popular boulevard comedies. In fact a number of his
early comic pieces had been in dialogue form, so that one-act
'vaudevilles' were a more natural bridge into the theatre than
four-act dramas. It still took him a long time to break out of
the bridgehead he had established. When he attempted to
relaunch his career as a serious dramatist with *The Seagull*
eight years later it was an even worse disaster than *Ivanov* –
such a disaster that he swore off playwriting once again. It
was not until 1897, and the second production of the play at
the Moscow Arts Theatre, that he at last managed to get
is two careers in step.

What finally enabled Chekhov to succeed, where so many
other writers have failed, in working both these apparently
similar but fundamentally different modes, is something that
goes very deep in his character: his elusiveness. It is the loss
of their authorial voice that so often bewilders writers who
turn from books to plays. How many Government ministers,
on permanent display to the public, could adapt to being civil
servants, operating out of sight? Chekhov's strength was that
he had no authorial voice to lose. Various critics have
remarked upon the 'colourlessness' of his language. It is
colourless in the same way that glass is colourless; we look
straight through it without ever noticing it. We find ourselves
seeing not Chekhov's world, but the world of his characters.
We inhabit them, as they inhabit themselves, completely and
without surprise. We find ourselves inside peasants – inside
an old peasant woman, in one amazing story, to live shut up
in her hut with her all the long winter among a family of
peasants; inside a little boy, in the story that first made his
literary reputation, as he travels across the hot summer
steppe on his way to start school, moving with him out of his
childhood into a huge world that stretches away to the
horizon and beyond. We find ourselves inside doctors,

certainly – but never one who bears much resemblance to Chekhov himself. In fact we find ourselves inside everyone except Chekhov. And yet we remain at the same time somehow detached from these people. Chekhov's other extraordinary power – which also helps to make his characters playable by actors – is to show us these new selves from outside even as we live inside them, with entirely unsentimental coolness and irony. It's like the experience one has in dreams, where one is both taking part in the action and looking down upon oneself as a dispassionate observer.

Chekhov's absence from his work, and his extreme detachment from his characters, must be fully grasped if we are to understand these plays. This has proved as difficult in the past as it has to accept the absence and inscrutability of God, and the plays have become obscured by the authorial intentions which people have read into them. Chekhov, like God, is sometimes seen as full of loving-kindness towards his characters, the only expression of which seems to be his supposedly wistful and elegiac view of the world. An impression lingers that the plays are about impoverished gentry with nothing to do all day but watch their fortunes decline; 'Chekhovian' is a synonym for a sort of genteel, decaying, straw-hatted ineffectualness. There are such characters, it's true – Gayev and his sister in *The Cherry Orchard*, and Telegin, the ruined neighbour who is living on Uncle Vanya's charity – but they are few in number. What we forget, when we are not face to face with them, is that most of the people in these plays are not members of the leisured class at all. They have to earn their living, and earn it through hard professional work. We catch them at moments of leisure, because this is when they can stand back and look at their lives, but their thoughts are with their jobs. The memory that remains with us from *The Seagull* is of people sitting in a garden and enjoying their 'sweet country boredom'. Who are these idle folk? They are two actresses, two writers, a doctor, a teacher, a civil servant, and a hard-pressed estate manager.

Some of them have time to sit down because they are only at the beginning of their careers, some because they are at the end; the others are simply on holiday. The idleness of Masha and Andrey, in *Three Sisters*, is remarkable because it is in such contrast to the drudgery of Masha's husband and her other two sisters; the idleness of the fading landowners in *The Cherry Orchard* is being swept aside by the industrious energy of the new entrepreneurs and activists. At the centre of *Uncle Vanya* is a woman so drugged with idleness that she can't walk straight; but the corrupting effects of this are felt in the lives around her, and they are lives of hitherto unceasing toil – whether the pedantic labours of her husband, or the agricultural stewardship of Vanya and Sonya, or the sleepless rural medicine of Astrov. At the end of the play Astrov departs to his practice, and Vanya and his niece resume their drudgery on stage, in front of our eyes. This is surely remarkable. It's not the first time that work has been shown on stage. In *The Weavers*, first produced in Berlin three years earlier, Hauptmann had shown the wretched weavers labouring at their looms. For that matter we see the gravediggers briefly at work in *Hamlet*, and we have seen plenty of servants serving, soldiers soldiering, and actors rehearsing. But this is surely the first great theatrical classic where we see the principals set about the ordinary, humdrum business of their lives. Why is it the feckless Gayevs and the dozing Sorin who spring to so many people's minds first? A bizarre combination of nostalgia and condescension, perhaps – nostalgia for a lost world of servants and rural leisure, easy condescension from the moral superiority of our own busy lives. In fact work is one of the central themes in these harsh plays. Work as the longed-for panacea for all the ills of idleness; work as obsession and drudgery and the destruction of life; work as life, simply. What Sonya looks forward to in heaven for herself and her uncle at the end of *Vanya* is not finding peace, as some translations have it; what she says, five times over, in plain everyday Russian, is that they will *rest*.

A very different view of the plays has gained ground more recently – the idea that, far from being gentle expressions of regret for a vanishing world, they are declarations of faith in progress. It's not surprising that Soviet producers and critics should want to claim Chekhov as a herald of the Revolution. But the somewhat similar views of the late David Magarshack, one of the most distinguished of Chekhov's translators, have had a good deal of influence upon English directors. Magarshack concedes, in his book *The Real Chekhov*, that the playwright 'was never impressed by the facile optimism of the revolutionaries who believed that by sweeping away the old order they would establish peace and harmony on earth.' But he argues that 'in all his plays Chekhov gives expression to his own social and political views by putting them into the mouths of his characters. He was very conscious that a writer's duty was to show an active interest in the social and political problems of his day.'

The only evidence that Magarshack offers for this assertion (apart from the interest shown by Astrov, in *Uncle Vanya*, in the destruction of the environment) is that he makes Trigorin say in *The Seagull*: 'As a writer I must speak of the common people, of their sufferings, of their future.' But even the most cursory glance at the passage in question makes it plain that, far from announcing a manifesto, what Trigorin is doing is complaining about the *miseries* of being a writer. Indeed, he concludes that in spite of this feeling that he ought to be dealing with the social questions of the day, all he can really write is descriptions of landscape, and that 'in everything else I'm false – false to the marrow of my bones'.

Trigorin, plainly, is labouring under the obligation he felt to do what was expected of the professional writer in Russia at the time. It was an obligation that Chekhov himself resisted. He gave an enormous amount of his time and energy to practical work for others (free medical treatment for the local peasantry, organizing against famine and cholera, building schools, reporting on the penal colony on Sakhalin), but he notoriously failed to be a progressive. As Simon Karlinsky shows, in the admirably combative glosses he offers in his edition of Chekhov's letters, the one section of Russian society that Chekhov consistently failed to please was the powerful progressive critical establishment; he lacked an ideology, he lacked social relevance. Chekhov himself put the matter beyond all reasonable doubt, because he did in fact issue what amounted to a manifesto of his beliefs; and it is very different from Trigorin's. It comes in a letter he wrote to the poet Alexei Pleshcheyev (and can scarcely have been intended to flatter Pleshcheyev's prejudices, since he most certainly *was* a progressive, and had in fact spent ten years in Siberia for his political activities). 'The people I fear,' wrote Chekhov, 'are those who seek to read tendencies into what one writes, and who want to see me as straightforwardly liberal or conservative. I am not a liberal – not a conservative – not a gradualist – not an ascetic – not an indifferentist. I should like to be a free artist, and nothing else, and I regret that God has not given me the power to be one. I hate lies and violence in all their forms . . . Pharisaism, stupidity, and arbitrariness reign not only in jails and merchants' houses; I see them in science, in literature, and among young people . . . That's why I nourish no particular predilection for security policemen or butchers or scholars or writers or young people. Signs and labels I account mere prejudice. My holy of holies is the human body, health, intelligence, talent, inspiration, love, and the most absolute freedom, freedom from force and lies, in whatever form these last two might be expressed. That is the programme to which I should adhere were I a major artist.'

What makes this absolute detachment so difficult to accept is the eloquence and passion with which various characters in each of these last four plays present their own beliefs. Magarshack, as we have seen, implausibly picks Trigorin in *The Seagull* as Chekhov's mouthpiece. In *Three Sisters* he plumps for Vershinin, with his vision of the 'astonishingly, unimaginably beautiful life' that will be lived in two or three hundred years' time. He could equally well have chosen Tusenbach, in the same play, who also has his eyes fixed on the future. He is predicting (with some accuracy, as it turned out) a 'great healthy storm' that will blow society clean of idleness and boredom in twenty or thirty years' time. But he is also saying precisely the opposite to Vershinin, insisting that human life will *never* fundamentally change, because it follows its own laws. Trofimov, in *The Cherry Orchard*, believes that mankind is marching towards 'a higher happiness,' to which he is showing others the way, even if he never sees it himself; but once again it's a different belief, because this 'march' is for him plainly a process of political struggle, not of natural evolution. There is a remark in Chekhov's notebooks, it's true, which faintly echoes the optimism of Vershinin and Trofimov – 'Man will become better when we have shown him to himself as he is' – and the writer Vladimir Tikhonov remembered him as saying that once people had seen themselves as they were 'they will surely by themselves create a different and better life. I shall not see it, but I know that everything will be changed, that nothing will be like our present existence.' It is difficult, though, to evaluate a remark which has been filtered through someone else's recollections. In the written record of the notebooks there is another entry that distances Chekhov from Vershinin and Trofimov almost as sharply as the Plescheyev letter does from Trigorin: 'We struggle to change life so that those who come after us might be happy, but those who come after us will say as usual: it was better before, life now is worse than it used to be.'

The most impassioned and moving visions of the future in these plays, however, are both expressed by women – by Olga at the end of *Three Sisters*, and by Sonya at the end of *Uncle Vanya*. These two heartbreaking speeches are quite different from Trofimov's secondhand rhetoric and Vershinin's obsessive 'philosophising'. They come from characters of such integrity, and are so powerfully placed, that we cannot help wondering, once again, whether they reflect some deep beliefs of this nature in Chekhov himself. But, once again, the beliefs are not consistent with each other. The forms of redemption that the two women expect are as different as the futures foreseen by Vershinin and Tusenbach; Olga, like Vershinin, expects the sufferings of the present to purchase happiness in this world – but a happiness which will be experienced only 'by those who live after us'. Sonya looks forward to some kind of personal recompense to herself and her uncle, but one which will be paid only in the next world. If Chekhov's views about the possibilities of happiness on earth are hedged by a faint ambiguity, his views on its likelihood in the next world are not. In a letter to the writer Shcheglov he states categorically that he had no religion.

On a number of occasions, in fact, Chekhov specifically dissociated himself from the ideas of his characters. 'If you're served coffee,' he says in a letter to Suvorin, his closest friend, 'then don't try looking for beer in it. If I present you with a professor's thoughts, then trust me and don't look for Chekhov's thoughts in them.' For him as author, he says in the same letter, his characters' ideas 'have no value for their content. It's not a question of their content; that's changeable and it's not new. The whole point is the nature of these opinions, their dependence upon external influences and so on. They must be examined like objects, like symptoms, entirely objectively, not attempting either to agree with them or to dispute them. If I described St Vitus' dance you wouldn't look at it from the point of view of a choreographer, would you? No? Then don't do it with opinions.' In another letter to Suvorin he took up the latter's complaint that one of his stories had not resolved the question of pessimism. 'I think that it's not for novelists to resolve such questions as God, pessimism, etc. The novelist's job is to show merely who, how, and in what circumstances people were talking or thinking about God or pessimism. The artist must be not the judge of his characters and what they are talking about, but merely an impartial witness. I heard a confused conversation, resolving nothing, between two Russian people about pessimism, and I have to pass on this conversation in the same form in which I heard it, but it will be evaluated by the jury, i.e., the readers. My job is merely to be talented, i.e., to be able to distinguish important phenomena from unimportant, to be able to illuminate characters and speak with their tongue.' The truth is that living characters in living fiction rarely parrot their author's opinions; nor do they speak nonsense. They speak for themselves, and their opinions are likely to have the same oblique and complex relationship to their author's opinions as their emotions do to his emotions, and their actions to his actions.

This same detachment of Chekhov's has led to another difficulty in understanding the plays which is much harder to resolve, and which is indeed likely to go on puzzling directors and actors, not to mention translators, as long as they are performed: whether or not they are to be taken as comedies. He designates the first of them, *The Seagull*, as a comedy; and so, on the whole, it is, for all its cool ambiguity. The difficulties really begin with the second, *Uncle Vanya*, where he refused to commit himself either way on the title-page – he describes it merely as 'Scenes from country life'. It is an overwhelmingly painful play. And yet there is plainly something ridiculous about Vanya himself – particularly in his effort to murder Serebryakov, and his failure to hit him at point-blank range. Are we to laugh or are we to cry? Both, no doubt. But this is easier to achieve in theory than in practice, and on the page than on the stage. An audience is a large, corporate creature with large, corporate emotions. It can stand close to the sufferer and feel his pain, or it can hold him at arm's length and see the absurdity of his helplessness; it finds it very difficult to be in both places at once. The ambiguity of the text gives the people who have to perform it genuine practical difficulties, and they must always be tempted to resolve them by pushing the tone in one direction or the other.

With the next play, *Three Sisters*, Chekhov joined in the debate himself. On the title-page he called it a drama, and it must surely be one of the most heartbreaking plays ever written. But Stanislavsky in his memoirs recalls Chekhov at the first read-through of the play as being 'certain he had written a light-hearted comedy,' and as being convinced, when the cast wept, that the play was incomprehensible and destined to fail. Nemirovich-Danchenko remembers him at the same occasion as struggling with a sense of embarrassment and repeating several times that he had written a 'vaudeville'. These protestations should perhaps be taken with some caution. Allowance must probably be made for the awkwardness of this first reading. Olga Knipper, who played Masha and was soon to become Chekhov's wife, recalls the cast not as weeping but as muttering discontentedly that it wasn't a play, that it was unactable, that there were no parts, while the author 'was smiling in embarrassment and walking about amongst us, coughing tensely'. Stanislavsky evidently conceded a little to Chekhov's view in the end. After the production had been running for three years, he wrote later, the audience 'began to laugh and grow quiet where the author wanted'.

The problem is most acute with the last play, *The Cherry Orchard*, where the tone is more ambiguous. Chekhov and Stanislavsky came to open disagreement about it. Chekhov not only described it on the title-page as a comedy; he insisted from first to last, as we shall see, that it was humorous. In his letters he called it a 'vaudeville'. He said it was 'not a drama but a comedy, in places even a farce . . . The whole play will be cheerful and frivolous . . .' He was not using these terms in some arcane private sense; the short plays are after all quite unambiguously cheerful and frivolous, quite straightforwardly comedies, farces, and vaudevilles. Stanislavsky's reaction to all this was to tell Chekhov bluntly that he was wrong. 'It's not a comedy, it's not a farce, as you wrote,' he informed him, after everyone had wept in the last act during the read-through at the Moscow Arts, 'it's a tragedy . . . I wept like a woman. I tried to stop myself, but I couldn't. I can hear you saying, "Excuse me, but it is in fact a farce . . ." No, for the plain man it is a tragedy.'

In the past most directors seem to have agreed with Stanislavsky. More recently the pendulum has swung the opposite way, and it has become fashionable to establish the comic nature of all these four plays by presenting the characters as ludicrously self-obsessed grotesques, and by supplying sight-gags that the author overlooked. This may be another result of Magarshack's eccentric influence. In his book *Chekhov the Dramatist* he urges the view that *The Cherry Orchard* is simply a funny play in its entirety. He even manages to find the last scene funny, where Firs is left locked into the empty house for the winter. He argues that the stage-direction says merely that Firs is lying motionless, not dying, and that someone will shortly realise what has happened, and come back and release him. This seems to me frankly preposterous. No doubt Firs is not clinically dead at the fall of the curtain, but anyone who believes he has a serious chance of emerging from that room alive has clearly never considered the practicalities of play-writing, let alone the effects of extreme cold upon extreme old age. In the course of the last act Chekhov establishes not once but three times, in a brilliantly escalating confirmation of misunderstanding, that the family believes Firs to have been taken off to hospital already; not once but four times that the house is to be closed up for the winter; and even twice that the temperature is already three degrees below zero. If you can believe that after all this there remained in Chekhov's mind some unexpressed hope that Gayev, say, might get the next train back from town, or that Yepikhodov might for some reason suddenly take it into his head to unlock the house again and inspect its contents, then you can believe that Wagner hoped the local Boy Scouts might put out the fire at the end of *Götterdämmerung* and give Siegfried and Brunnhilde artificial respiration.

Nor will the text as a whole support Magarshack's view. It is truly not possible to read the play in Russian without being moved, as Stanislavsky and his company were, to tears as well as to laughter. Some of Chekhov's references to the play's comicality have a characteristically teasing or self-mocking air – he was deeply shocked when Stanislavsky was said to be thinking of staging one of his actual vaudevilles at the Arts Theatre. He was also engaged in a running battle with Stanislavsky over the ponderousness of his staging. The trouble began from the very first moment of their first production together. This was how Act One of Stanislavsky's *Seagull* started, according to his prompt copy: 'Glimmer of lantern, distant singing of drunk, distant howling of dog, croaking of frogs, cry of corncrake, intermittent strokes of distant church bell . . . summer lightning, barely audible far-off thunder . . .' All this before the first two characters had even got on stage. Chekhov, grateful as he was for the success which Stanislavsky had at last given him with a serious play, was ungratefully cool about the production. He greatly disliked the slowness of Stanislavsky's tempo, and according to Nemirovich-Danchenko he threatened to put a stage-direction in his next play saying: 'The action takes place in a country where there are no mosquitoes or crickets or other insects that interfere with people's conversations.' Nothing about Stanislavsky's productions of the next two plays reconciled him. All the notes he gave about *Vanya*, when he finally saw it, were directed against the overtness of the action. With *The Cherry Orchard* he evidently feared the worst from the very beginning. 'I should very much like to be around at rehearsals to have a look,' he wrote anxiously to Nemirovich-Danchenko. 'I am afraid that Anya might have a tearful tone of voice (you for some reason find her similar to Irina) . . . Not once in my text does Anya weep, and nowhere does she speak in a tearful voice. In the second act she has tears in her eyes, but her tone of voice is cheerful and lively. Why in your telegram do you talk about there being a lot of

people weeping in the play? Where are they? The only one is
Varya, but that's because Varya is a crybaby by nature, and
her tears are not supposed to elicit a feeling of gloom in the
audience. In my text it often says "on the verge of tears", but
that indicates merely the characters' mood, not tears. There
is no cemetery in the second act.'

But even these quite specific comments can't be taken too
literally, because they are at variance with Chekhov's own
text. According to the stage-directions, Gayev is 'wiping away
his tears' in Act Three. Ranyevskaya, at the end of the act, is
'weeping bitterly'. Both of them, at the end of the last act,
'sob quietly'. Part of what Chekhov wanted when he insisted
on the comedy in his plays was surely a different style of
playing; he was looking for lightness, speed, indifference,
and irony; something that suggested not the inexorable
tolling of fate but the absurdity of human intentions and the
meaninglessness of events.

There are a number of common themes that weave their
way in and out of these four last plays. One of them, as we
have seen, is work. A more obscure one is the unacknowledged and unmentioned mysteries at the heart of all these
families. In *The Seagull* there is an entirely unexplained and
unremarked discrepancy between Arkadina's surname and
her son's. It suddenly becomes clear, too, without a word
being said, that it is Dorn, not Shamrayev, who is Masha's
father. There is another suggestion of a similar relationship
(first pointed out, I think, by Ronald Bryden) in *Three Sisters*,
where Chebutykin – the doctor again – cherishes an intense
attachment to Irina, whom he remembers carrying in his
arms as a baby, and whose mother had been the love of his
life. In *Uncle Vanya* the old nurse recalls – again without
comment or explanation – that Serebryakov's first wife, who
had loved him with all her heart, 'couldn't sleep at night for
grieving . . . did nothing but weep'. This had been when
their daughter, Sonya, was still little, and 'didn't understand'. And why, in *The Cherry Orchard*, has Ranyevskaya

adopted Varya? There is no mention of her background or parentage. Is she known (to everyone but us) to be the illegitimate daughter of Ranyevskaya's drunken late husband?

In all the plays, too, something is being lost. All attempts at forward motion – all the brave forays into the world of work and endeavour – are counterbalanced by the undertow of regret; there is some loss that will never be made good, even if all the bright prophecies of the optimists were to come true tomorrow. In *The Seagull* it is the innocence and hopes of Konstantin and Nina. In *Vanya* it is Vanya's life – sacrificed, as he comes to realise, to a worthless object, wasted through his own timidity and diffidence. In *Three Sisters* it is the lives of all three women that drain away in front of our eyes. In *The Cherry Orchard* the trees that begin in blossom and end beneath the axe are everything that can ever be lost by mortal man – childhood, happiness, purpose, love, and all the brightness of life.

But Chekhov's technique and ideas develop over the course of the four plays. Although *The Seagull* (as we shall see later) represents something entirely new in the history of the theatre, there are still one or two elements which Chekhov has not completely succeeded in accommodating to his new aesthetic. Konstantin's account in the last act of what has happened to Nina over the past two years is awkwardly and belatedly expository, dramatically inert, and curiously old-fashioned in tone – though it might be argued that it is only natural for him, as a writer of the time, to talk like a nineteenth-century short story. The soliloquies, too, have the air of survivals from an earlier convention. Elsewhere in the play we are left, as we are in life, to work out for ourselves what people are thinking and feeling from what they actually choose or happen to say to each other. It jars when we are suddenly given direct access to Dorn's thoughts about Konstantin's play, or to Konstantin's assessment of his own stories. Arkadina, after she believes she has broken Trigorin's will to leave her, even gives us an aside ('Now he's mine'); though again it could be argued that, since she is an actress, it may be she rather than Chekhov who has imported the line from the theatre. He is still relying heavily upon soliloquy in *Uncle Vanya*, but by the time he came to write the last two plays he had abandoned it. Andrey, in *Three Sisters*, delivers his disquisitions unheard to the deaf Ferapont. Firs, locked into the house alone at the end of *The Cherry Orchard*, is an old man talking to himself, as he has earlier even in other people's presence. The abandonment of soliloquy is part of Chekhov's developing naturalism. In *The Cherry Orchard*, however, he was plainly beginning to move on again. It is more dependent upon mood and symbolism than the first three plays, and some of the symbols – notably the breaking string – remain unexplained and oblique in their significance. He may have been planning to go further in this direction with the extraordinary new departure he was contemplating at the time of his death – a play about Arctic exploration.

There is another, even more fundamental, development over the course of the plays, and that is in the way they are resolved. All Chekhov's previous full-length plays culminate in the shooting of the central character. Platonov, in the untitled play, is shot by his rejected mistress. Ivanov, in the play that bears his name, and Voynitzky, in *The Wood Demon*, shoot themselves. The technique survives into *The Seagull*, where there is no one central character, but where it is still the suicide of a principal that brings the play to a close. But in *Vanya*, as we shall see, Chekhov finally thought his way past this tidy convention. Two more characters will die, it is true. Tusenbach's death in *Three Sisters*, though, is the result of a meaningless quarrel. It is shown not as *his* tragedy – the imminence of it gives him his first real awareness of the world and his first real pleasure in it – but as one more of the losses which empty the sisters' future of meaning. Firs is left dying at the end of *The Cherry Orchard*, but the sale of the

estate, which finally destroys any hopes the Gayevs have had
in life, has already occurred at the end of Act Three, so that
the last act is left once again to show life continuing. The
tragedy in these last plays is not death but the continuation of
life; the pain of losing the past, with all the happiness and
wealth of possibilities it contained, will always be compound-
ed by the pain of facing the future in all its emptiness. 'The
ability to endure' had already been identified by Nina at the
end of *The Seagull* as the most important quality in life. In
*Uncle Vanya* Sonya takes it up as her watchword – 'Endure,
uncle! Endure!' – as she coaxes Vanya through his despair at
the prospect of living for another dozen years, and as the
future dwindles to a 'long, long succession of days and
endless evenings' illuminated by neither any sense of purpose
nor any prospect of alteration. The three sisters, after all their
hopes have gone, understand that they 'have to live'.

   The courage to endure which is called upon at the end of
*Vanya* and *Three Sisters* is connected by both Sonya and Olga
with the passionate hopes they express for some remote
future in this world or the next. These hopes, as I have
argued, do not imply any similar faith on Chekhov's part.
This makes them no less moving; nor does our own unbelief.
Indeed it is surely the very impossibility of their visions, of
Sonya's sky all dressed in diamonds and Olga's peace and
happiness on earth, that makes the speeches so poignant.
And yet the force and insistence of the idea, in the two
successive plays, is very striking. I suspect that for once we
do get some insight into Chekhov himself here – not into his
beliefs or opinions, certainly, but into some much deeper and
less coherent feeling, some similarly poignant yearning for a
future whose unattainability he was just beginning to grasp.
It is a common experience for people in early middle age,
which is where Chekhov was when he wrote these plays, to
come over the brow of the hill, as it were, and to see for the
first time that their life will have an end. But the end with
which Chekhov came face to face in mid-life was suddenly

much closer still. It was not until six months after he had finished *Vanya* that he had his first major haemorrhage, and that his tuberculosis was finally diagnosed. But he had been spitting blood for a long time. He insists over and over again in his letters that this is the most normal thing in the world; but the more he insists the more one wonders. As Ronald Hingley puts it in his biography: 'Can Anton really have been unaware, still, that he suffered from tuberculosis? It seems incredible that a practising doctor could continue to ignore symptoms of which the possible purport might have struck any layman. On the other hand, as Chekhov's own works richly illustrate, human beings have an almost infinite capacity for self-deception. Did the man who deluded others about the desperate condition of his health also delude himself? Or did he hover between self-deception and self-knowledge?'

It was at some point in that final year before the diagnosis was made that he was writing *Vanya* and giving up the idea of death as a dramatic resolution. Perhaps somewhere inside himself he had begun to recognise what was happening to him. Perhaps, now that he was suddenly so close to it, death seemed a little less neat, a little less of an answer to the equation; perhaps it began to seem more like something you could look as far as, or beyond, but not at. And even if Chekhov hadn't yet seen the truth about his condition, perhaps Sonya and the others had in a sense seen it for him. A writer's characters, particularly when they are not forced to represent his conscious thoughts, can be appallingly well-informed about his unconscious ones. It is ironical. Chekhov most sedulously absented himself from his works. Sonya's passionate invocation of an after-life in which he did not believe may be one of our rare glimpses of him – and of an aspect of him that he couldn't even see himself.

\*

The first four plays in this collection (*The Evils of Tobacco, Swan Song, The Bear,* and *The Proposal*) are a selection from the one-acters with which Chekhov first made his reputation in the theatre. They are in a different mode from the four great dramas that follow; offered not as art but as entertainment. *The Evils of Tobacco*, in 1885, was his first attempt at the form. He intended it, he said, 'in the secrecy of his heart' for performance, but in the event it was published in a collection of his stories, and seems not to have been performed until fifteen years later. It was the next one, *Swan Song*, that gave him his first small success in the theatre. He adapted it from one of his stories (*Calchas*), and it was produced at Korsh's in 1888, just after the débâcle with *Ivanov*. It was merely part of a mixed bill, but it was a vastly more suitable piece for the house, and it was well enough received for proposals to be made for remounting it at the Maly, one of the imperial theatres. It must have seemed clear where his future in the theatre lay, and in the same month he was already writing *The Bear*. This was an original, not an adaptation. He subtitled it 'a joke in one act,' and it is indeed a comedy pure and simple, with none of the pathos of *Swan Song*. Chekhov complained that he and his sister could have acted better than the cast at Korsh's, but it made the audience laugh non-stop, and by the following year another commercial management, Abramova's, was fighting Korsh for the rights. It went on to cause a 'furore' at the Alexandrinsky, the imperial theatre in St Petersburg, and then to take the provinces by storm. Chekhov found it being played in several of the Siberian towns he passed through on his way to Sakhalin in 1890. It became such a favourite of amateur dramatic groups that Chekhov was complaining a decade later that 'practically every lady I meet begins her acquaintance with me by saying: "I've acted in your *Bear*!" ' And Tolstoy, who thought all Chekhov's later plays were even worse than Shakespeare's, was reported by Olga Knipper to have laughed until he could laugh no more.

Chekhov followed this up the same year with another one-act 'joke' in much the same vein, *The Proposal*. He expressed some doubts about this one. In a letter to the writer Shcheglov he said that he had 'knocked it together specifically for the provinces'. It would pass muster there, he thought, but he did not intend to put it on in the capital. It was in fact successfully performed in Moscow at the Maly, and given in St Petersburg before the Tsar, who was moved to send the author his compliments.

There are four more short plays, not included here, that Chekhov wrote over the next few years. The most interesting of them, to my mind, is *Tatyana Repina*, a parody of a drama by his wealthy publisher friend Suvorin. It seems to have been intended purely for Suvorin's amusement, and it makes insufficient sense without a knowledge of Suvorin's original. It is nevertheless striking in the way it counterpoints an endless Orthodox marriage service with the scandalised comments of the congregation when they realise that the bridegroom's abandoned mistress, who has supposedly poisoned herself, is present in the church. There is also a good comic character in the sceptical old watchman at the church, who dismisses the whole idea of weddings. 'Every day they go marrying and christening and burying, and there's no sense in any of it . . . They sing, they burn incense, they read, and God never listens. Forty years I've worked here, and not once did God ever listen . . . And where this God is I don't know . . . There's no point in any of it . . .'

The other three one-act plays from this period, *The Reluctant Tragedian*, *The Wedding*, and *The Anniversary* (together with a fourth, *The Night before the Trial*, which he left unfinished) were all adapted from his old stories. They seem to me notably weaker than the earlier plays, and they had a less striking success at the time. Even so, *The Wedding* made Tolstoy 'collapse with laughter' (as reported by Olga Knipper, at any rate), and *The Anniversary*, when it was finally performed in St Petersburg over a decade later, to mixed notices, still had the audience, according to one critic, 'not so much laughing as simply rolling with laughter'.

Chekhov designated most of the one-act comedies on their title-pages as 'jokes', and consistently disparages them all in his letters. *The Proposal*, he said, was 'a mangy little vaudeville'. *The Bear* was 'a piffling little Frenchified vaudeville' which he had written because he had nothing better to do, having used up so much 'sap and energy' on his novella, *The Steppe*, that he was incapable of doing anything serious for a long time afterwards. When, in later years, Olga Knipper reported that Stanislavsky was interested in the rewritten version of *The Evils of Tobacco*, Chekhov was so appalled at the idea of 'doing a vaudeville at the Arts Theatre' that he wrote back to her saying she had gone mad, and adding three exclamation marks. He claimed to have dashed these wretched 'vaudevilles' off at odd moments. He had ruined *The Evils of Tobacco*, he said, because he had only two-and-a-half hours to write it in. *Swan Song* he claimed to have written in one hour five minutes. The work on the latter, of course, involved mostly just transcription from an existing story, but even so it at least challenges the record playwriting speeds credited to Noël Coward and Alan Ayckbourn, each of whom is said to have written a full-length original play in three days. If Chekhov could have maintained his claimed rate with original material over the full course he would have completed *Hay Fever* or *Absurd Person Singular* inside a single working day.

Still, at the time he wrote most of these plays he was going through a phase of hating the theatre altogether. It was in his letter to Shcheglov about *The Proposal*, urging him to give up his love-affair with the stage, that he diagnosed the modern theatre as 'the venereal disease of the cities'. In fact a letter to another writer, Bezhetzky, suggests that he regarded 'vaude-villes' as a slightly less pathological manifestation than other types of play. 'I don't like the theatre,' he told him, 'I quickly get bored – but I do like watching vaudevilles.' With characteristic self-mocking jauntiness he said he also believed in vaudevilles as an author, and that 'anyone possessing fifty acres and ten tolerable vaudevilles I reckon to be a made man – his widow will never die of hunger.' If a vaudeville turned out badly, he urged Bezhetsky, 'don't be bashful – just stick a pen-name on it. The provinces will swallow anything. Just try to see there are good parts. The simpler the setting and the smaller the cast, the more often the vaudeville will be done.' The cynical tone is no doubt all part of the flippant pose, but the content is hard-headed, practical advice (as true now, of course, as it was then) that he was following himself. It was offered only a month before urging Shcheglov to flee the theatrical pox; and only a month after *that* he was telling Suvorin that he was going to turn to vaudevilles when he had written himself out in other directions. 'I think I could write them at the rate of a hundred a year. Ideas for vaudevilles pour out of me like oil from the Baku wells.' He even wondered whether he shouldn't donate his 'stake in the oilfield' to Shcheglov.

Chekhov may well have taken his vaudevilles more seriously than his offhandedness about them suggests. He was, as we shall see, notably flippant about *The Seagull*, too. And the four in this collection, at any rate, have solid theatrical virtues. *The Evils of Tobacco* and *Swan Song* both touch upon some deeper desolation than boulevard plays normally care to show; the old actor gazing forlornly into the blackness of the empty theatre, and the wretched lecturer who is not so much hen-pecked as hen-eaten and left as droppings, have something in common with Gogol's Poprishchin and Akaky Akakiyevich. And *The Bear* and *The Proposal* are classics of the comic theatre, full of energy, invention, and actors' opportunities. They are larger than life, certainly, but splendid in their magnification.

Chekhov's designation for them both, 'joke', is usually translated into English as 'farce'. The term is of course a capacious one, but there is a considerable difference between these plays and most French or English farces. As we know the form it usually depends upon panic, and the panic is usually generated by guilt and the prospect of some kind of social disgrace. The panic leads in its turn to deceit, which produces further and yet more alarming prospects of disgrace, from which grows ever greater panic, in a spiral known to scientists as positive feedback. There is no panic in *The Bear* or *The Proposal*, no deceit or threatened disgrace. What drives these characters is a sense of outrage – of anger at the failure of others to recognise their claims, whether to money or to land or to a certain status. In their anger they lose the ability to control their destinies or even to recognise their own best interests, just as the characters of traditional farce do in their panic. This is what these plays have in common with English and French farces – that their characters are reduced by their passions to the level of blind and inflexible machines.

This reduction is precisely what Bergson thought was the defining factor in all comedy. But if the other four plays in this collection are in any sense comedies, as Chekhov claimed, Bergson's explanation will not do for them. When Vanya in his rage and despair shoots at Serebryakov he is comic, but he is not in any way like a machine. This is surely one of the distinctions between the vaudevilles and what is to come.

'A comedy – three f., six m., four acts, rural scenery (a view over a lake); much talk of literature, little action, five bushels of love.'

Chekhov's own synopsis of *The Seagull*, in a letter to Suvorin written a month before he finished it in 1895, is characteristically self-mocking and offhand. (His cast-list is even one f. short, unless he added the fourth woman only during that last month, or when he revised the play the following year). He says in the same letter that he is clashing with the conventions of the theatre, but no one could have begun to guess from his flippant résumé how extraordinary an event was being prepared for the world. No doubt Chekhov took the play more seriously than the letter suggests, but even he can scarcely have realised quite what he had on his hands: a catastrophe so grotesque that it made him swear never to write for the theatre again; a triumph so spectacular that it established him as a kind of theatrical saint; and the first of the four masterpieces that would redraw forever the boundaries of drama.

He was 35 by this time, and had still had no real success as a serious playwright. For all his apparent casualness, as he finished *The Seagull* and read it through he had a moment of fundamental doubt. 'I am once again convinced,' he wrote to Suvorin, 'that I am absolutely not a dramatist.' Then there were prolonged difficulties in getting the play past the theatrical censor (see A Note on the Translation), which almost made him despair of the whole enterprise. But once this hurdle was behind him Chekhov's apparently offhand mood returned. The play was to be performed at the Alexandrinsky Theatre in St Petersburg, where *Ivanov* had been well received seven years earlier after its disputed opening in Moscow, and his letters in September 1896, as rehearsals approached, have the same cheerful flippancy as his original account of the play to Suvorin. They read with hindsight as ironically as the banter of some doomed statesman as he goes all unknowing towards his assassination. To his brother Georgi: 'My play will be done in the Alexandrinsky Theatre at a jubilee benefit [for the actress Levkeyeva]. It will be a resounding gala occasion. Do come!' To Shcheglov: 'Around the 6th [of October] the thirst for glory will draw me to the Palmyra of the north for the rehearsals of my *Seagull*.' To his brother Alexander: 'You are to meet me at the station, in full dress uniform (as laid down for a customs officer retd.) . . . On the 17th Oct. my new play is being done at the Alexandrinsky. I would tell you what it's called, only I'm afraid you'll go round boasting you wrote it.'

The seventeenth, when it came, was indeed a resounding gala occasion. 'I have been going to the theatre in St Petersburg for more than twenty years,' wrote a correspondent in a theatrical journal afterwards, 'and I have witnessed a great many "flops" . . . but I can remember nothing resembling what happened in the auditorium at Levkeyeva's 25th jubilee.' The trouble started within the first few minutes of Act One. Levkeyeva was a popular light-comedy actress, and even though she had no part in the play the audience were minded to laugh. The first thing that struck them as funny was the sight of Masha offering a pinch of snuff to Medvedenko, and thereafter they laughed at everything. Konstantin's play – Konstantin with his head bandaged – it was all irresistible. By Act Two, according to the papers next day, the dialogue was beginning to be drowned by the noise and movement in the audience; by Act Three the hissing had become general and deafening. The reviewers struggled for superlatives to describe 'the grandiose scale' of the play's failure, the 'scandalous' and 'unprecedented' nature of 'such a dizzying flop, such a stunning fiasco'. The author, they reported, had fled from the theatre.

According to his own accounts of the evening Chekhov had escaped from the theatre only when the play ended, after sitting out two or three acts in Levkeyeva's dressing-room, had eaten supper at Romanov's 'in the proper way,' then slept soundly and caught the train home to Melikhovo next day. Even Suvorin, though, accused him of cowardice in running away. All he had run away from, he protested in a letter to Suvorin's wife, was the intolerable sympathy of his friends. He told Suvorin: 'I behaved as reasonably and coolly as a man who has proposed and been refused, and who has no choice but to go away . . . Back in my own home I took a dose of castor oil, had a wash in cold water – and now I could sit down and write a new play.'

But Suvorin, with whom he was staying, recorded in his diary that Chekhov's first reaction had been to give up the theatre. He had not come back until two in the morning, when he told Suvorin that he had been walking about the streets, and that 'if I live another seven hundred years I shan't have a single play put on. Enough is enough. In this area I am a failure.' When he went home next day he left a note telling Suvorin to halt the printing of his plays, and saying that he would never forget the previous evening. He claimed to have slept well, and to be leaving 'in an absolutely tolerable frame of mind'; but he managed nevertheless to leave his dressing-gown and other belongings on the train, and the accounts he subsequently gave of the evening in various letters to friends and relations make it clear how painful the experience had been. 'The moral of all this,' he wrote to his sister Masha, 'is that one shouldn't write plays.

Things at the Alexandrinsky improved somewhat after the first night. 'A total and unanimous success,' wrote Komissar-zhevskaya, who was playing Nina, in a letter to Chekhov after the second performance, 'such as it ought to be and could not but be.' There were encouraging reports from other friends, too, but Chekhov remained sceptical. 'I couldn't help reflecting,' he replied to one sympathiser, 'that if kind people find it necessary to comfort me then my affairs must be in a bad way.' In fact the play was withdrawn after five performances, and was subsequently attacked by reviewers even when it appeared in published form, clear of the shortcomings of the production. Still, within a month or so his theatrical hopes had revived again, and he was telling Suvorin of the existence of a new play 'not known to anyone in the world' – Uncle Vanya. And two years later, in a stunning reversal of fortune of the kind that occurs in plays (though never in Chekhov's own), The Seagull triumphed in Moscow as noisily as it had failed in Petersburg.

In fact the event went rather beyond anything one might find in a play; it was more like something out of a backstage musical – particularly as recounted by Stanislavsky (who was both directing and playing Trigorin) in his memoir of

Chekhov. For a start the fate of the newly-founded Moscow Arts Theatre depended upon it. The other opening productions had mostly either failed or been banned by the Metropolitan of Moscow, and all hopes were now riding aboard this one salvaged wreck. There was a suitable love interest depending upon the outcome of the evening – the leading lady (Olga Knipper, playing Arkadina) and the author had just met, and were to marry two plays later – provided there *were* two more plays to allow their acquaintance to develop. Moreover, the author had now been diagnosed as consumptive and exiled to Yalta. The dress rehearsal was of course a disaster. At the end of it Chekhov's sister Masha arrived to express her horror at the prospect of what another failure like the one in Petersburg would do to her sick brother, and they considered abandoning the production and closing the theatre.

When the curtain finally went up on the first night the audience was sparse, and the cast all reeked of the valerian drops they had taken to tranquillise themselves. As they reach the end of Act One Stanislavsky's paragraphs become shorter and shorter:

We had evidently flopped. The curtain came down in the silence of the tomb. The actors huddled fearfully together and listened to the audience.

It was as quiet as the grave.

Heads emerged from the wings as the stage staff listened as well.

Silence.

Someone started to cry. Knipper was holding back hysterical sobs. We went offstage in silence.

At that moment the audience gave a kind of moan and burst into applause. We rushed to take a curtain.

People say that we were standing on stage with our backs half-turned to the audience, that we had terror on our faces, that none of us thought to bow and that someone was even sitting down. We had evidently not taken in what had happened.

In the house the success was colossal; on stage it was like a second Easter. Everyone kissed everyone else, not excluding strangers who came bursting backstage. Someone went into hysterics. Many people, myself among them, danced a wild dance for joy and excitement.

The only person who remained completely calm seems to have been Chekhov himself, since he was 800 miles away in the Crimea, exiled by his consumption. But when after Act Three the audience began to shout 'Author! Author!', as audiences do in this kind of script, and Nemirovich-Danchenko explained to them that the author was not present, they shouted 'Send a telegram!' In the event he was informed of his triumph not only by telegram, but in shoals of letters from everyone present. Judging by how rarely he referred to it either beforehand or afterwards in his own letters from Yalta, however, he had kept this production at a distance emotionally as well as geographically, and the Moscow success was considerably more remote from him than the Petersburg failure.

There were of course external reasons for the play's extraordinarily different reception in the two capitals. The choice of Levkeyeva's benefit night in St Petersburg, on the one hand, and the fact that it had been produced there at nine days' notice; the thorough preparation in Moscow on the other hand, with twelve weeks' rehearsal. But the play would almost certainly have elicited a passionate response of one kind or another. Its influence has been so widespread and pervasive since that it is difficult now to realise what a departure it was. The traditional function of literature in general, and of drama in particular, has always been to simplify and formalise the confused world of our experience; to isolate particular emotions and states of mind from the flux of feeling in which we live; to make our conflicts coherent; to illustrate values and to impose a moral (and therefore human) order upon a non-moral and inhuman universe; to make intention visible, and to suggest the process by which it takes effect. *The Seagull* is a critical survey of this function. For a start two of the characters are writers. One of them is using the traditional techniques without questioning them, the other is searching for some even more formalised means of expression; and what interests Chekhov is how life eludes the efforts of both of them. Konstantin cannot even begin to capture it, for all the seriousness of his intentions; Trigorin feels that in the end all he has ever managed to do without falsity is landscapes, while his obsessive need to write drains his experience of all meaning apart from its literary possibilities. The extraordinary trick of the play is that all around the two writers we see the very life that they are failing to capture. What Chekhov is doing, in fact, is something formally impossible – to look behind the simplification and formalisation by which the world is represented in art and to show the raw, confused flux of the world itself, where nothing has its moral value written upon it, or for that matter its cause or its effect, or even its boundaries or its identity.

The most obvious characteristic of this approach is the play's ambiguity of tone. Chekhov calls it a comedy, but does not give us any of the stylistic indications that are customary when events are to be seen as comic. Indeed, what we are watching has not even been clearly organised into *events*; a lot of it bears a striking resemblance to the non-events out of which the greater part of our life consists. Then again, the play is to a quite astonishing extent morally neutral. It displays no moral conflict and takes up no moral attitude to its characters. Even now, after all these years, some people still find this difficult to accept. They talk as if Arkadina and Trigorin, at any rate, were monsters, and as if the point of the play were to expose her egotism and his spinelessness. It is indeed impossible not to be appalled by Arkadina's insensitivity towards her son, or by the ruthlessness with which she attempts to keep Trigorin attached to her; moral neutrality is not moral blindness. But Konstantin continues to find good in her, for all his jealousy and irritation, and she remains capable of inspiring the love of those around her. Konstantin's assessment is just as valid as ours; the devotion of Dorn and Shamrayev is just as real and just as important as our outrage. There is moral irony, too, in her manipulation of Trigorin; had she succeeded more completely in blackmailing him to remain with her she might have saved Nina from the misery that engulfs her. It is hard to respect Trigorin as we see him crumble in Arkadina's hands, harder still to like him when we know how he has treated Nina. But Masha likes and respects him, and for good reason – because he listens to her and takes her seriously; no grounds are offered for discounting her judgment. And when Trigorin wanders back in the last act, makes his peace with Konstantin, and settles down to lotto with the others, he is once again neither good nor bad in their eyes, in spite of what he has done; he is at that moment just a man who always seems to come out on top, whether in lotto or in love. We are perfectly entitled to find against him, of course – but that is our own verdict; there has been no direction to the jury in the judge's summing-up; indeed, no summing-up and no judge.

But then nothing is fixed. Everything is open to interpretation. Are we, for instance, to take Konstantin seriously as a writer? Impossible, after Nina's complaint that there are no living creatures in his work. But then it turns out that Dorn likes it, and he is a man of robust good sense (though not good enough to prevent his ruining Polina's life). And in Act Four we discover that Konstantin is at any rate talented enough to be able to make a career as a professional writer. But even then Trigorin's judgment remains the same as Nina's, and Konstantin comes round to much the same view himself.

No one is valued for us; nothing is firmly located or fully explained. Why is Arkadina called Arkadina? She is Sorina by birth and Trepleva by marriage. It could be a stage-name, of course, or she could have married more than once. The people around her presumably know. They do not trouble to tell us. Has Dorn had an affair with Arkadina in the past? Is this why Polina is so relentlessly jealous of her? Is it what Arkadina is referring to when she talks about how irresistible he had once been? (In an earlier draft Polina begins to weep quietly at this point; but that may of course be for the lost early days of her own love.) In an astonishing moment at the end of Act One we do in fact stumble across one of the unexplained secrets of this world, when Dorn snatches Masha's snuff-box away from her, admonishes her for this 'filthy habit', and flings it into the bushes. From that one gesture of licensed impatience we understand why Masha feels nothing for Shamrayev, her father, why she sees herself as being 'of dubious descent', and why she feels so close to Dorn; because Dorn is her father, not Shamrayev. But who knows this, apart from us and Dorn? Not Masha herself, apparently. Does Shamrayev? Arkadina? Medvedenko? We are not told; the clouds that have parted for a moment close in again.

But then which of them knows about Dorn's relationship with Masha's mother in the first place? Perhaps everyone; or perhaps no one. We can only speculate. In any case it is characteristic of the relationships in the play; overt or covert, they are all one-sided, unsatisfactory, anomalous, and unlikely ever to be resolved. Medvedenko loves Masha who loves Konstantin who loves Nina who loves Trigorin who is supposed to love Arkadina, but who doesn't really love anyone, not even himself. No one's life can be contained in the forms that marriage and family offer. Konstantin's dissatisfaction with the existing dramatic forms is only a special case of this general condition. Plainly Chekhov is not advocating new social forms, in the way that Konstantin is calling for new literary ones. In the end even Konstantin comes to think that it is not a question of forms, old or new –

the important thing is to write from the heart; nor are there any social forms suggested in the play which could ever contain the great flux of life itself.

Is there any trace of Chekhov himself for once in either of the two professional writers in the play? Konstantin is scarcely likely to be a self-portrait, overwhelmed as he is by an artistic family, obsessed by questions of literary theory, and unable to create a living character; Chekhov's parents, after all, ran a provincial grocery, he displayed no interest in theory, and life is the very quality in which his stories and plays abound. But Trigorin is another matter. He is a celebrated and successful author, in much the same way that Chekhov was. His passion is fishing; so was Chekhov's. His modest estimate of his place in Russian letters is very much the kind of thing that Chekhov might have said mockingly about himself. More importantly, it seems at any rate plausible that his painful memories of beginning his career, and the terrible compulsion to write which is eating his life, reflect something that Chekhov felt about himself – particularly since the only palliative for his obsession is the fishing. The passage in Trigorin's works to which Nina's inscription on the medallion refers ('If ever you have need of my life, then come and take it') is a line from one of his own stories. Then again, the little tricks of style that Konstantin identifies in Trigorin's stories, as he despairingly compares them with his own in Act Four – the short cuts that he believes make things easy for Trigorin – are Chekhov's own. The two details he quotes that Trigorin uses to set up his moonlit night – 'the neck of a broken bottle glittering on the bank of the millpool and the shadow of the water-wheel black beside it' – are almost precisely the ones that Chekhov had used a decade earlier, with similar economy, to establish the moonlit night in a story called *The Wolf*. It is a compelling piece, full of the life that evaded Trigorin, and Chekhov can scarcely have been mocking his own technique, because a month or two after he wrote it he gave his brother Alexander a lesson by post in short story writing in which he quoted variants of the same two details to illustrate how to breathe life into descriptions of nature by the use of specific concrete details.

There would be something characteristically self-mocking, of course, in choosing a second-rate author to represent himself, but the parallel breaks down soon enough. When Trigorin confesses to Nina that all he can write is landscapes we realise that the picture which has been built up deliberately excludes the very essence of Chekhov's literary identity. Nor do any of the other biographical details fit. Arkadina is indeed based in part upon an actress, Yavork-skaya, who seems from her letters to have been very briefly his mistress. But Chekhov, unlike Trigorin, had no difficulty in disentangling himself from her, and in keeping women at arm's length generally. One of the women who were in love with Chekhov, Lika Mizinova, he kept at bay so successfully that she provided a model for not one but two of the characters in *The Seagull*: first Masha, with her life ruined by the unquenchable but unreciprocated love she has for Konstantin, and then Nina. To forget the Masha-like feelings she had for Chekhov, Lika threw herself into a disastrous affair with a friend of his, the Ukrainian writer Potapenko, who left his wife and went off to Paris with her, where he made her pregnant and then abandoned her. Potapenko, ironically, having provided Chekhov with a model for the more dubious aspects of Trigorin, was then called upon by him, after the play was finished, to undertake on his behalf all the endless negotiations with the censor.

Nina was also contributed to by another of Chekhov's admirers, the writer Lidia Avilova, whom he treated even more high-handedly. She gave him a charm for his watch-chain with a page reference inscribed upon it, exactly as Nina does Trigorin with the medallion, and referring to the same passage. Meeting her later at a masked ball, Chekhov promised to give her the answer to this from the stage in his new play. Ronald Hingley, in his biography of Chekhov, recounts how she went to the catastrophic first night in St Petersburg and struggled to hear the promised answer through the uproar all around her. She noted the page-reference given by Nina, and when she got home looked up the same page and line in a volume of her own stories. It read: 'Young ladies should not attend masked balls.' By this time, anyway, says Hingley, Chekhov had passed Avilova's fervently inscribed charm on to Komissarzhevskaya, the actress playing Nina, and it was being used on stage as a prop. If Chekhov had modelled Trigorin's behaviour with women on his own the play would have ended after Act Two.

There are, as I have suggested earlier, some slightly awkward survivals in *The Seagull* from the existing dramatic conventions of the day. The other complaints which are sometimes made against the play, however, seem to me to stem from misunderstandings. The symbolism, for instance, is occasionally disparaged as a portentous device to be outgrown by Chekhov in the three later and even greater plays. In fact there is rather less symbolism in *The Seagull* than in the others. The only symbol is the seagull itself, and this is set up not by Chekhov but by Konstantin, as Nina immediately recognises when he lays the bird accusingly at her feet. It is part of the portentousness and inertness of Konstantin's art, not of Chekhov's – and it is then taken up by Trigorin and absorbed into the machinery of *his*, when he discovers the dead bird and outlines his story of the girl who is destroyed with the same wilfulness and casualness. Between them they burden Nina with an image for herself and her fate that comes to obsess her. One of the themes of the play, as I have argued, is the way in which art warps and destroys the life that it draws upon. The message of the seagull, as it stands there stuffed and forgotten at the end of the play, is precisely of the deadness of the symbolic process.

Many people, too, have had difficulty in the past with the scene in the last act between Nina and Konstantin. The difficulty has arisen because it has often been regarded, and played, as a version of the traditional mad scene, where the pathos of the heroine who has lost or been rejected by her love is demonstrated by her retreat from reality into a world of illusion. This is plainly not the case with Nina for the greater part of the scene; she gives an entirely clear, calm, and sane account of her experiences. The problem comes when she says, as she does in all the English translations of the play that I have come across, 'I am a seagull'. The poor girl thinks she is a bird; her mind is plainly going. Now, there is a much more reasonable construction to place upon her words here, but it is obscured by a difficulty in the translation of the Russian which may at first sight seem quibblingly small. In the Russian language there is no such thing as an article, either definite or indefinite. No distinction can be made, in speech or thought, between what English-speakers are forced to regard as two separable concepts – 'a seagull' and 'the seagull'. So when Nina signs her letters 'Chaika' (Seagull), it is perfectly open to Konstantin to regard this as a sign of distraction, of the sort suffered by the grief-stricken miller in Pushkin's *The Water Sprite*, who tells people he is a raven. But what Nina herself means, surely, when the distinction has to be made in English, is not that she is *a* seagull but that she is *the* seagull. In other words, she is not identifying with the bird but with the girl in Trigorin's story, who is the Seagull in the same way that Jenny Lind was the Swedish Nightingale, or Shakespeare was the Swan of Avon. This is the idea that has seized hold of her – not that she has white wings and a yellow beak – but that she has been reduced to the status of a manipulated character in Trigorin's fiction – a character whose fate can be summed up in a single image. This is an obsessive thought, and she makes repeated efforts to throw it off, but it is not in any sense a deluded one. She *has* been manipulated; she is another victim of the distorting and deadening process of art. One can't help wondering if Avilova and Lika Mizinova ever came to feel that they had this in common with Nina, as well as everything else.

If her picture of herself as being the seagull of Trigorin's projected story is sane and sober, so is her claim to have found her way at last as an actress. We have no way of judging whether her hopes are well-founded; but her feeling that she is on the right path at last is an entirely rational one. Konstantin takes it seriously, anyway – seriously enough to realise that he by comparison is still lost, and to shoot himself in despair as a result. Faced with that testimony to the seriousness of his judgment we are scarcely in a position to dissent.

And this in fact is the final irony of the play – that in the end the Seagull herself escapes, wounded but still flying. It is the shooter who is shot, the writer who is written to death. Konstantin, not Nina, turns out to be the real victim of Trigorin's story, the true Seagull; Konstantin, who first brought the creature down to earth and declared it to be a symbol, is the one who ends up symbolised, lying as inert and irrelevant in the next room as the poor stuffed bird is in this. Perhaps Mizinova and the others found some symbolic comfort in that.


No one knows exactly when *Uncle Vanya* took its present form. It was most probably in the summer of 1896, between the completion of *The Seagull* and its disastrous première in St Petersburg. It was first produced in the following year, as the second of the four last plays. But in its origins it goes back to a much earlier period than *The Seagull*. It is substantially a reworking of *The Wood Demon*, which was conceived nearly a decade before, at the time when Chekhov was still only just emerging as a serious writer. Its development can be followed with unusual closeness, partly because of the existence of this earlier version, and partly because it started out, bizarrely, as a collaboration with Suvorin, the early stages of which are recorded in their correspondence. Its progress towards its final form was tortuous and painful, and it is the story of

Chekhov's own development as a dramatist. It was many times nearly abandoned; so was Chekhov's new career. At an early point both play and career nearly took off in a startlingly different direction, when Chekhov proposed changing the subject to the story in the Apocrypha of Holofernes and his decapitation by Judith, or else Solomon, or alternatively Napoleon on Elba, or Napoleon III and Eugénie. The possibilities are as extraordinary to consider as Vanya's own missed alternative career as a Schopenhauer or a Dostoyevsky.

The first work on the proposed collaboration seems in fact to have been done by Suvorin rather than Chekhov. Suvorin, Chekhov's closest friend, was a publisher by trade, and a man of great wealth, but he had literary ambitions of his own – he wrote *Tatyana Repina*, the play which Chekhov parodied, and stories which he submitted to Chekhov's practical and often devastating criticism. The earliest reference to their joint venture is in a letter Chekhov wrote to him in November 1888, where he acknowledges receipt of 'the beginning of the play', and congratulates Suvorin on the creation of one of the principal characters – Blagosvetlov, who was to become Serebryakov in the final version. 'You've done him well: he's tiresome and irritating from the very first words, and if the audience listens to him for 3–5 minutes at a stretch, precisely the right impression will be produced. The spectator will think: "Oh, dry up, do!" This person, i.e., Blagosvetlov, should have the effect on the spectator of both a clever, gouty, old grouser and a dull musical comedy which is going on for too long.' It was a little ironical that this tedious character was Suvorin's contribution to the enterprise, because some people thought later that Chekhov had *based* him on Suvorin.

In the same letter Chekhov goes on to remind Suvorin of 'the bill of our play' – a list of eleven characters, with a description of each of them. Of these eleven, four can be recognised as the precursors of characters in the final version of *Uncle Vanya*. One of them, Blagosvetlov's daughter, bears little resemblance to the plain, hard-working Sonya she eventually became, and is more like Yelena, her lethargic and beautiful stepmother. But the other three are already the substantial originals of Serebryakov, Astrov, and Vanya himself. Blagosvetlov is a retired government official, not an academic, but he is 'of clerical origins, and was educated in a seminary. The position he has occupied was achieved through his own efforts . . . Suffers from gout, rheumatism, insomnia, and tinnitus. His landed property he got as a dowry . . . Can't abide mystics, visionaries, holy fools, poets, or pious Peters, doesn't believe in God, and is accustomed to regard the entire world from the standpoint of business matters. Business matters first, last, and foremost, and everything else – nonsense or humbug.' Astrov, at this stage, is still a landowner rather than a doctor. But he already has his amazingly prescient concern for the ecology (and is already nicknamed the Wood Demon because of it). He already believes that: 'The forests create the climate, the climate influences the character of the people, etc., etc. There is neither civilisation nor happiness if the forests are ringing under the axe, if the climate is harsh and cruel, if people are harsh and cruel as well . . .' Blagosvetlov's daughter is attracted to him, as Yelena is in *Vanya*, 'not for his ideas, which are alien to her, but for his talent, for his passion, for his wide horizons . . . She likes the way his brain has swept over the whole of Russia and over ten centuries ahead . . .'

His account of the proto-Vanya is brief, and contains characteristics which were later discarded ('Drinks Vichy water and grouses away. Behaves arrogantly. Stresses that he is not frightened of generals. Shouts.') But in outline Uncle Vanya is already there – and in describing him Chekhov is also laying down the first outline of the plot: 'The brother of Blagosvetlov's late wife. Manages Blagosvetlov's estate (his own he has long since run through). Regrets he has not stolen. He had not foreseen that his Petersburg relations would have such a poor appreciation of his services. They don't understand him – they don't want to understand him – and he regrets he has not stolen.'

Chekhov says in his letter he will sketch out the rest of Act One himself and send it to Suvorin. He undertakes not to touch Blagosvetlov, and suggests sharing the work on Blagosvetlov's daughter, because 'I'll never be able to manage her on my own.' The great arborealist will be Chekhov's up to Act Four, then Suvorin's up to a certain scene where Chekhov will take over because Suvorin will never manage to catch the right tone of voice. Then he will leave Suvorin to start Act Two, as he did Act One.

It is difficult to believe that this strange two-headed beast would have been any substitute for the *Vanya* it would presumably have displaced. Fortunately, perhaps, Suvorin seems to have backed down, and left Blagosvetlov as his sole contribution, because a month later Chekhov was writing to ask him why he was refusing to collaborate on *The Wood Demon* (as it was by this time called), and offering to find a new subject altogether if Suvorin would prefer it. This was when he proposed switching to Holofernes or Solomon, or one of the two Napoleons. (Chekhov himself did in fact start on the Solomon project; a fragment of a monologue for the king was found among his papers. See A Note on the Translation.) But not even the attractions of a biblical or historical subject could tempt the literary-minded magnate back into harness, and the following spring Chekhov reluctantly began to struggle with the material on his own.

There were some moments of elation in the weeks that followed, judging at any rate from the bulletins to Suvorin. 'Act III is so scandalous that when you see it you'll say: "This was written by a cunning and pitiless man" . . .' 'The play is terribly strange, and I'm surprised that such strange things are emerging from my pen.' There were also more or less simultaneous moments of discouragement, when he informed other correspondents that he was not going to write plays, and that he was not attracted by the idea of fame as a dramatist. By the end of May, with only two acts written, he had given up, and in September he had to start all over again from the beginning.

Then, when it was at last finished, the play was rejected out of hand by both the Alexandrinsky Theatre in St Petersburg, which had just successfully staged *Ivanov*, and by the Maly in Moscow. An unofficial meeting of the Petersburg section of the Theatrical-Literary Committee, which vetted all plays submitted for production in the imperial theatres, judged it 'a fine dramatised story, but not a drama'. Lensky, the actor for whose benefit performance the play had been offered to the Maly, returned the manuscript to Chekhov with a particularly crushing dismissal. 'I will say only one thing: write a story. You are too contemptuous of the stage and of the dramatic form, you have too little respect for them, to write drama. This form is harder than that of the story, and you – forgive me – are too spoiled by success to study as it were the basic ABC of the dramatic form, and to learn to love it.' Even Nemirovich-Danchenko, another member of the committee, who was later to be a co-founder with Stanislavsky of the Moscow Arts Theatre and one of Chekhov's most important patrons, thought that Lensky was right in diagnosing ignorance of the demands of the stage (though he thought Chekhov could easily master them). 'Say what you like,' he wrote, 'clear, lifelike characters, an interesting conflict, and the proper development of the plot – these are the best guarantee of success on the stage. A play cannot succeed without a plot, but the most serious fault is lack of clarity, when the audience can't possibly grasp the essence of the plot. This is more important than any stage tricks or effects.' Chekhov swore again – not for the last time – to give up playwriting. But in the end he rewrote once more, and did a completely new version of the last act, with which he had been having difficulties from the beginning. The play was then produced, in December 1889, by

Abramova, one of the Moscow commercial managements. It was dismissed by the critics not only as untheatrical, but also as 'a blind transcription of everyday reality,' and was taken off after three performances.

With hindsight, the most remarkable thing about *The Wood Demon* is how much of *Uncle Vanya* is already there – often word for word. All the essential material of Act One, including most of the big speeches; almost the whole of Act Two; and in Act Three the entire scene in which Serebryakov proposes to sell the estate. It seems amazing that this wealth of brilliant scenes was not enough to alert even the most sluggish producer and the most jaded critic to Chekhov's powers in the theatre. But it is true that they fail to make the impact they should because he had not yet overcome certain faults recognisable from his two earlier full-length plays, *Ivanov* and the play without a title. The characters are too simple: too noble and Tolstoyan in the case of the Wood Demon himself, too coarsely comic in the case of Orlovsky, the debauched son of a local landowner. The setting of the first and last acts has wandered in pursuit of the picturesque; and there is something unsettling about the tone of the whole. It may have seemed offensively naturalistic to contemporary critics, but to the modern reader it veers more towards the facetiousness of Chekhov's early comic journalism, and towards a certain bucolic jollity, which sit oddly with the story that is beginning to emerge. At the end of Act Three all resemblance to the later version ceases. Vanya attempts to shoot not Serebryakov but himself, and succeeds. So the last act is left without a Vanya, and instead proceeds by way of a sunset picnic alongside an old watermill to a happy ending, with the Serebryakovs more or less reconciled, the Wood Demon and Sonya paired off, and even the debauched Orlovsky settling down with a nice girl. Nemirovich-Danchenko's assessment of the play is shrewd; the story is not clear. And the reason is that Chekhov has not yet recognised the story he is trying to tell.

After its failure in Moscow the play was abandoned again, and might well have remained so for good. It seems to have been Prince Urusov, a jurist and well-known literary figure, who provoked Chekhov into starting work on it again – somewhat ironically, because Urusov admired the earlier version so much that he persisted to the end in believing that Chekhov had ruined it by turning it into *Uncle Vanya*. It was Urusov's request for permission to reprint the text of *The Wood Demon*, in fact, that made Chekhov re-read it. He evidently did not like what he saw (years later he was still telling the loyal Urusov: 'I hate that play and I try to forget about it') and it was presumably this reawakened dissatisfaction that made him set to work on it again. The internal evidence, at any rate – the dates of the diaries and notebooks which were the provenance of some of the material in the new version – suggests that the reworking was done the following year, in 1896. The letter that he wrote to Suvorin that December, a month after the debacle with *The Seagull*, seems to refer to *Vanya* as a finished text. If this dating is correct then the project was probably only just completed in time, since his experience with *The Seagull* had made him swear off playwriting once again.

The play in its new form still faced one final rebuff. The Maly Theatre asked for it, which gave the Theatrical-Literary Committee the chance to produce an even more magisterial rejection and scheme of improvement than before. Its report identified a number of 'unnevennesses or lacunae' in the play, and complained of 'longeurs', such as 'the extended eulogy of forests, shared between Sonya and Astrov, and the explanation of Astrov's theory of arboriculture'. The committee was worried about the distressing frequency with which it believed Vanya and Astrov were shown suffering from hangovers, and the unfortunate effect that would be produced if this were thought to be the cause of Vanya's attempt to shoot Serebryakov. It felt that Vanya and Astrov 'as it were merge into a single type of failure, of superfluous man,' and it complained that 'nothing prepares us for the powerful outburst of passion which occurs during the conversation with Yelena'. It reserved its greatest concern, though, for Vanya's treatment of Serebryakov. 'That Vanya could take a dislike to the professor as Yelena's husband is understandable,' it conceded; 'that his sermonising and moralising cause irritation is also natural, but the disillusionment with Serebryakov's academic stature, and indeed more precisely with him as an art historian, is somewhat strange . . . nor is it a reason for his being pursued with pistol shots, for his being hunted down by someone who is no longer responsible for his actions.' The unfairness of shooting professors because you have a low opinion of their academic achievements seems to have spoken deeply to the committee's learned members.

This time, however, Chekhov declined all suggestions for rewriting. By now, in any case, the play had been successfully produced in a number of provincial theatres, and it was finally established in Moscow by being produced at the Arts Theatre – though its reception there was initially more muted than the hysterical success which *The Seagull* had just enjoyed. With hindsight we can see that Chekhov's reworking of the material from *The Wood Demon*, whenever it was done, has shifted it across the crucial divide that separates the four last plays from all his earlier ones, and indeed from all the earlier ones in the world.

Some of the changes he has made are straightforward improvements in dramatic technique. He has concentrated the setting of the play on the place where the real events of the story actually happen – the Serebryakovs' estate – and he has stripped out the superfluous characters. But in the course of doing this he has had an idea of genius. He has elided the debauched young neighbour, Orlovsky, with the Wood Demon. The most upright and selfless character in the original play is now the one who also indulges in periodic drinking bouts; instead of being in love with Sonya he is now, like Orlovsky, first coarsely knowing about Vanya's relations with Yelena, and then ready to propose a passing liaison with her himself; he has become Astrov in all his dark, self-contained complexity. And Yelena, a figure of uncompromised virtue in the original version, has become fascinated by him, so that, engaged as she is to advance poor Sonya's cause with him, she has become touched by the same characteristic ambiguity. With these changes the whole tone of the play has been modified. The mood has changed from one of comfortable idleness to one of uncomfortably interrupted work. The bucolic geniality and the facetiousness have gone, and left exposed the sense of wasted life at the heart of the story.

Chekhov's second masterstroke in the rewriting, even more fundamental and consequential than the new ambiguity of the characters, is his alteration to the aim of Vanya's revolver. All his full-length plays up to this point, as we have seen, have resolved with the death of one of the central characters. Now, instead of letting Vanya likewise tidy himself away after his confrontation with Serebryakov, he has had the idea of making him turn murderer instead of suicide – and of failing.

In the first place this is simply a more interesting development. For the pacific and long-suffering Vanya to have been driven to attempt murder tells us much more about the intensity of his anger and of his sense of betrayal; and his missing the target is something he at once recognises as bitterly characteristic. This is slightly obscured by the traditional translation of his line. 'Missed again!' sounds as if it refers only to the two shots. The word he uses in Russian, however, refers not only to a missed shot but to any kind of mistake (see A Note on the Translation). What he is thinking of is surely all the missed opportunities in his life, and in particular his failure to have made advances to Yelena when she was still free. Then again, the fact that he misses at point blank range opens up a whole series of questions about the nature of these mistakes. Perhaps they are not serious attempts at all; even as he pulls the trigger he *says* 'bang!', like a child with a toy revolver. And even if he sees them as seriously intended, are they examples of what a modern psychiatrist would call self-sabotage? And if they are, is the unconscious objective to protect himself from the consequences of success? Not only from being tried for murder, but from being tested as lover and husband, from having the chance (as he at one moment believes he could have done if only he had lived 'normally') to become a Schopenhauer or a Dostoyevsky – and *then* failing, with no possibility of concealing his own responsibility for it?

In the second place, the failure of this dramatic gesture to have dramatic consequences destroys the drama; or rather it destroys the neatness with which the slow and confused changes of the world we inhabit are concentrated theatrically in simple and decisive events. The world of *Vanya* is the ambiguous and unresolved world of *The Seagull* – stripped of even the final note of resolution suggested by Konstantin's suicide. Most of the relatively few notes Chekhov gave to the director and actors were to do with this dislocation and diffusion. Exiled in Yalta, he missed the Moscow production, but when he saw it on a tour the Arts Theatre made to the Crimea in 1900 one of the actresses in the company remembered his telling them afterwards that Sonya shouldn't kneel and kiss her father's hand on the line 'You must be merciful, father' at the end of Act Three, because 'after all that wasn't the drama. All the sense and all the drama of a person is on the inside, and not in external appearances. There was drama in Sonya's life up to this moment, there will be drama afterwards – but this is simply something that happens, a continuation of the shot. And the shot, in fact, is not drama – just something that happens.'* In a similar spirit

---

*There is something askew – and perhaps this is in keeping with the obliqueness of the play – about either Chekhov's note or the actress's memory of it, because his own stage direction calls for Sonya to kneel, if not to kiss her father's hand, while the line can hardly be construed as a 'continuation of the shot' because it occurs before it.

he deprecated Stanislavsky's direction that Astrov should make his pass at Yelena, in Act Four, 'like a drowning man clutching at a straw'. By then, says Chekhov in a letter to Knipper, who was playing Yelena, Astrov knows that nothing is going to come of his attraction to her, 'and he talks to her in this scene in the same tone of voice as he does about the heat in Africa, and kisses her in the most ordinary way, quite idly.' Stanislavsky remembered him as saying, after the performance in the Crimea, ' "He kisses her like that, though." – And here he planted a brief kiss on his own hand. – "Astrov has no respect for Yelena. In fact when he leaves the house afterwards he's whistling." '

More important even than the nature of the failed murder are the consequences it has for the last act. Chekhov, as we have seen, had already tried various versions of this. What had caused the problem was his odd insistence, in all the variants of *The Wood Demon*, on placing Vanya's suicide at the end of Act Three, so that this traditional dramatic resolution still left everything unresolved for everyone else. But he had been feeling his way towards *something* with this arrangement, and now that Vanya remains alive it becomes clear what it is: precisely that – remaining alive. He has given dramatic expression to the theme first broached by Nina in *The Seagull*, which dominates all the last three plays – survival itself, the tragedy not of death, but of continuing to live after life has been robbed of hope and meaning.

Chekhov does not name the town where the Prozorov family lives in *Three Sisters*, but we discover its spiritual identity soon enough; its name is Exile.

Like so many others for so many reasons in Russian life and literature, they find themselves in a place which they see not as *here* but as *there*. In their hearts they inhabit Moscow, where the spring comes early and there is love and fame. In the flesh they find themselves resident in some dull town in the north of Russia, where the winter lingers and no one has ever been heard of. In a letter to Maxim Gorky, Chekhov said it was a town like Perm, which gives some geographical scale to their plight. Perm is 700 miles from Moscow, in the northern Urals, and at that time there was no direct railway line to Moscow. The 1914 Baedeker lists a twice-weekly express to St Petersburg, taking about two days, while the ordinary train to the next nearest town of any size along the line, Yekaterinburg (where the imperial family were shortly to be murdered) took 23½ hours. The great Russian distances dominate the Prozorovs' lives. They watch the cranes flying overhead on their huge autumn journeys to the south. They welcome the other birds of passage in the play, the soldiers, as they arrive from the ends of the Empire with their baggage of new ideas and old quarrels and boredom and desperate wives; and they watch them depart again, bound maybe for the Chita garrison in Siberia, 2,000 miles to the east, or for the Kingdom of Poland, 1,400 miles to the west, to live in yet more lodgings with 'two chairs and one sofa, and stoves that always smoke'; permanent exiles. The play was written in exile, too – in Yalta, where Chekhov had been banished by his doctors, 1,300 miles away to the south-west. In his letters he refers to Yalta as his prison. He complains about the cold, the heat, the cruel wind. He longs for Moscow – and, like the Prozorovs, puts off his planned visit from week to week, and day to day, while he finishes the play. When he finally took it to Moscow to copy it out, in October 1900, he must have felt he was escaping from his own text.

The characters in the play – the Prozorovs and the soldiers alike – are exiles in time as well as in place. The sisters look wistfully back towards their Moscow childhood, longingly forward to their Moscow future. Tusenbach is waiting for the 'great healthy storm' that will blow society clean of idleness and boredom in twenty or thirty years time. Vershinin has his eyes fixed on the 'astonishingly, unimaginably beautiful' life that will be lived in another two or three hundred years.

Solyony lives in the past; he identifies himself with Lermontov, who died fifty years before. Chebutykin wonders if he has ceased to exist entirely. The only time that none of them regards as home is the one they actually inhabit, somewhere in the last decade of the nineteenth century. Tusenbach finds his way back to the present briefly in the last act, when he notices the beauty of the world around him as if for the first time in his life. But then he is on his way to be killed; he has no future to distract him.

This sense of the difficulty that human beings have of living in the present lies at the very heart of the play. It has been much misunderstood. The play was written, it is true, at the beginning of a new and hopeful century, when belief in progress was high, and when the pressures upon the archaic despotism of imperial Russia were plainly becoming irresistible. Many people shared with Vershinin and Tusenbach the vision of a future in which everything would in one way or another be totally changed. Some influential commentators have argued that Chekhov was one of them. (Magarshack, for instance: '. . . He makes the idealist Vershinin his mouthpiece on the future of mankind, taking, as usual, great care that the expression of his views should be strictly in character.') But he made it abundantly clear in his letters, as I have shown earlier, that the characters in his plays express their own views, not his. And even if we knew nothing of Chekhov's general attitude, it is obvious from the internal evidence of the play that Vershinin and Tusenbach are not the author's spokesmen. For a start they disagree totally with each other about the nature of the changes they expect. Then again all hopes for the future – particularly the utopian ones of Vershinin – are parodied by the fatuous optimism of Andrey in Act Four, after he has comprehensively denounced the town's sordid record up to now: 'The present is loathsome, but then when I think about the future – well, that's another story. It all becomes so easy and spacious; and in the distance there's a gleam of light – I can see freedom, I can see me and my children being freed from idleness, from roast goose and cabbage, from little naps after dinner, from ignoble sponging off others . . .'

And really the whole structure of the play is designed to undercut Vershinin. He insists that life is already becoming 'steadily easier and brighter.' But more than three years go by in the course of the play, and *nothing changes* – not at any rate for the better – nothing even begins to change. Vershinin philosophises on regardless – obsessively, never interested in anyone else's views, plainly seeking some rationalisation for the unhappiness of his own life. He is a bore on the subject. What's marvellous, though, in Chekhov's understanding of him – and of his hearers – is that, although he threatens boredom each time he returns to the question, he never does in fact bore – he rides boredom down, he becomes eloquent, he captures the imagination. Olga, at the end of the play, is even more compelling when she justifies her courage in facing life after the destruction of all the sisters' hopes by a rather similar appeal to the future: 'We shall be forgotten – our faces, our voices, even how many of us there were. But our sufferings will turn to joy for those who live after us. Peace and happiness will dwell on earth, and people living now will be blessed and spoken well of.' I have shown earlier why I think that this last speech of Olga's, like the apparently similar speech by Sonya at the end of *Uncle Vanya*, is no more a direct expression of Chekhov's own hopes or beliefs than the visions of Vershinin or Tusenbach. It is also immediately undercut by Chebutykin. From the very beginning of the play, as David Magarshack notes in his book *The Real Chekhov*, the separate upstage conversations of Chebutykin and the other officers are used as an ironic counterpoint to what is being said downstage. And there at the end of the play sits Chebutykin, upstage and alone, the last remaining member of this chorus. 'Anyway, it doesn't matter,' he says to himself after Olga's speech, 'it doesn't matter.' Not that his view is any more authoritative. He sees life one way, because he's Chebutykin, and he's given up, and she sees it another way, because she's Olga, and she hasn't. And if it's Chekhov speaking through Olga, then it's equally Chekhov replying to himself through Chebutykin; the drama is within Chekhov exactly as it is within all of us.

Chebutykin's comment is an apt one, too. Because whatever happens to future generations, even if some benefit accrues to them from the sufferings of the three sisters – and there is no suggestion as to how this might happen – it still won't matter as far as *these* people are concerned, and *they* are the ones whose fates we have been invited to examine. Drama makes the generalities of the human condition specific in particular men and women; the fate of those who remain offstage is beyond representation or consideration.

'It doesn't matter.' The phrase is on everyone's lips throughout the play. Masha tries to hush Vershinin's declaration of love, then concedes that it doesn't matter. It doesn't matter to Andrey whether the mummers come or not. Even Vershinin, dejected at the anomie of military and civilians alike, uses it. Indifference is the mode of the play, not optimism; indifference to a world that offers only indifference in return.

With hindsight, we might possibly think that Tusenbach has proved the best of the three prophets, not only because the storm he was predicting did in fact occur – and in almost exactly the twenty years he estimated – but because of his suggestion that the time they live in might be remembered with respect. His assertion that there were no executions then is not quite right – there were no civil executions in Russia then, but, according to the 1900 Brockhaus, general cases could still be transferred to the military courts for disposal by military law. All the same, a Russian today might look back, if not with respect, then at least with affection, as Andrey does, to evenings out at the Grand Hotel on Resurrection Square, or at Testov's on the corner of Theatre Square. Anyone who knows Moscow today might feel a pang for the incorporation of Resurrection Square itself into the great barren plain now known as the Square of the Fiftieth Anniversary of the October Revolution. And if you happen to be walking along the Sadovoye Ring now, and you come to a street turning off it to the north-east that starts out as Karl Marx Street and ends up as Bakunin Street, you might feel something more than a pang to realise that this is Old Basmannaya Street, where the sisters lived their happy days as children. (They couldn't have lived in a more Muscovite-sounding street; *basman* was a kind of bread, and *basmannik* was a colloquial name for an inhabitant of the city.) Perm has in fact gone back to being Perm, after leaping to the unfortunate conclusion that it was really called Molotov. And what happened to the Prozorovs when Tusenbach's good healthy storm broke? They would all have been in their forties by then; so would Tusenbach himself. Did they survive their good healthy wetting? Did they flee to Paris or New York, into yet deeper exile? Or did they remain, to be scattered at some point in the next few decades into camps still further north, still further east? And did they, as they laboured there, recall Tusenbach's other successful prediction, that in twenty or thirty years' time everyone would be working?

If the play is about one thing then it is not about the hopes held out by Vershinin, or by Olga, or by any of them. It is about the irony of those hopes – about the way life mocks them. Irina's hopes of redemption by work are betrayed by the actual experience of it; Andrey's hopes of academic glory are betrayed by Andrey; the sisters' hopes of Moscow are deferred and deferred and then shelved forever. Even, conversely, Anfisa's fear of being put out into the street is vain – she finds herself better housed and better off than she has ever been before. The only character whose hopes seem likely to be realised is Natasha, and then because hers are so small and concrete and piecemeal – another baby, another room of the house to put it in, another little triumph.

This is the future as it's actually going to be – not an unimaginable beauty on earth, but Protopopov in the sitting-room.

But the irony goes deeper than this. It wouldn't make any difference even if their hopes *were* realised. As Vershinin says, if the sisters actually did live in Moscow they would cease to notice it. Perhaps in their hearts they understand this. Even Irina. She has no ties – she could leave for Moscow at any time. But she doesn't. And Vershinin's objection is valid not only against the sisters' hopes but his own as well. 'Happiness,' as he says, 'is not for us and never can be. All we can do is long for it.'

Even more ironically, one of the things that destroys their chance of happiness is their hope of achieving it, which alienates them from the life they actually lead. And the final irony of the play is its demonstration that we cannot live without the hopes that cut us off from life. We are both poisoned and nourished by the act of hope itself. And when all hopes for ourselves have been destroyed – as the sisters' have been at the end of the play – then we summon whatever dogged courage we can muster to confront the rest of our lives – and we start to tell the old consoling story once again; only this time not about ourselves, but about another people, living under quite different laws, on the far side of the storms.

By the time Chekhov came to write *The Cherry Orchard*, in 1903, he was dying. This final play gave him one of the hardest struggles he had ever had. For a start he was increasingly exhausted by his illness, while his waning strength was further eroded by the discomfort of his life in Yalta, and by travelling back and forth to Moscow because of disagreement between his doctors about which climate would suit him best. There was tension in the household, too, between his sister, Masha, and his new wife, Olga Knipper;

while the short hours of his working day were wasted by the perpetual stream of visitors that his fame attracted. In the end the play was a triumph, and at the first performance, on 17 January, 1904, his forty-fourth birthday, he was brought up on stage between acts three and four for lengthy speeches and presentations. But by this time he was visibly failing; he had only another four months to live.

It was the play itself that presented the greatest problems. He had been thinking about it for two years before he began to write, and it had been conceived from the very first as a comedy. 'The next play that I write,' he said in a letter to Knipper in March, 1901, 'will definitely be a funny one, a very funny one, at any rate in conception.' In another letter he described it as 'a four-act vaudeville', and in the autumn of that year, according to Stanislavsky, he gave the actors at the Moscow Arts a kind of oral trailer for what he had in mind. Three of the four disconnected details he produced were essentially comic: a servant who went fishing; a cheerful billiards enthusiast with a loud voice and only one arm; and the owner (male or female) of a country estate who kept borrowing money off the servant. This list may have been more in the nature of a whimsical camouflage for his intentions than a serious exposition of them – it would have been very much his style. He may even have been joking when he included as the fourth item an even smaller and more disconnected detail: 'a branch of cherry blossom sticking out of the garden straight into the room through an open window.'

From this one tiny visual flourish, however, came the real play – and all his difficulties with accommodating it to his original comic conception. During the course of the next two years he must have traced that branch back out of the window – back to the orchard in which the tree was rooted, back to the social history and economic forces which explained why that orchard had been planted and why it was now about to be felled. The trail took him not only outwards through

Russian society and across the Russian landscape, but backwards in time through his own writing and his own life. From where he now stood, on the brink of his last work, and at the end of his life, he found himself returning to themes he had touched upon in his stories over his entire professional career, and going back further still, to his childhood. As a schoolboy in Taganrog he had heard stories told by the mother of one of his friends about her life as a landowner before the Emancipation (on an estate where there was an ancient serf like Firs) in Poltava province, which was famous for its cherry orchards. He had spent summer holidays as a child on a rural estate out in the steppe to the north of Taganrog, where his grandfather (a manumitted serf himself) was steward. He had heard the distant sound of a breaking cable in the mines while he was staying with a boyhood friend on another property in the steppe. His own modest family home had been sold off to pay his father's debts – and bought by the wealthy friend who had promised to save it. By the time he began to write the play, that single branch at the window had led him to a world which was remarkably difficult to accommodate in a 'four-act vaudeville'.

In fact *The Cherry Orchard* is the most elusive and difficult of all these four last plays. It is noticeably less naturalistic than the first three, and more dependent upon mood and symbolism. It is also even less directly dramatic. The conflict from which the play springs is intense; the Gayev family is being broken apart by powerful forces – forces rooted deep in history and in the society around them. But in the whole course of the play only one dramatic event is thrown up by this conflict – the crisis itself, the announcement by Lopakhin that he has bought the estate. There is a curious air of detachment about some of the episodes. Charlotta Ivanovna's musing about her past, and the irruption of the Passerby, seem like side-eddies at the edge of the main river. For the whole of this second act, in fact, the narrative comes to a halt. Life hangs suspended for a while in the old mode before everything finally changes, like water scarcely moving in the depths of the millpool before it plunges down the race.

Chekhov confessed to Knipper that he had been 'scared' himself by the 'lack of movement' in Act Two. So was Stanislavsky when he saw it in rehearsal. 'For a long time the play was not working,' he wrote later. 'Particularly the second act. It contains no action, in the theatrical sense, and at rehearsals seemed very monotonous. It was essential to show the boredom of doing nothing in a way that was interesting.' He asked for cuts. Chekhov did more than cut; he rearranged and rewrote. (The material that came out can be found in A Note on the Translation.) The cuts were restored in Mike Alfreds's 1986 production of the play at the National Theatre, London, but this seems to me quite wrong. The alterations went into the original production a month after it had opened, when it was already an established success. It is difficult to believe that Chekhov would have made them at that stage if he had not fully concurred in them himself. But they shed a little more light on several of the characters. Charlotta Ivanovna has a good line about Ranyevskaya – 'She's perpetually mislaying things. She's mislaid her life, even.' And Firs is more plainly seen as what he is – a peasant, an ex-serf, rather than a kind of Russian Jeeves.

Two other characters have in the past been much misunderstood by directors. Natural sympathy for the Gayev family and their feckless charm has sometimes obscured the qualities of Lopakhin and Trofimov, the representatives of economic and political progress who are in their different ways pushing them to the margins of life. ('Suddenly no one needs us any more,' as Gayev sadly discovers in Act Four, when the money has gone.) They both feel genuine love for their unintended victims, and Chekhov's letters make it clear that he took a characteristically objective view of both of them. 'Lopakhin is a businessman, it's true,' he wrote to Stanislavsky, conscious of the way in which progressive prejudice was likely to work, 'but he is in every sense a decent person. He must behave with complete decorum and propriety, without pettiness or trickery . . . In casting this part it must be kept in mind that Lopakhin has been loved by Varya, a serious and religious young lady; she wouldn't have fallen in love with some grasping peasant.'

Trofimov has suffered in different ways. In the past he has sometimes been portrayed in English productions as an inadequate and immature personality who is afraid to emerge from university and face the real world. This view has been given currency by the translation which has become traditional for his ironic description of himself – 'the eternal student', a phrase that suggests in English not only the correct primary meaning of remaining a student forever, but also (as in 'the eternal schoolboy' or 'the eternal triangle') the idea of his being the unchanging student *type*. The Russian phrase, *vyechniy studyent*, has quite a different overtone; it is a variant of *vyechniy zhid*, literally 'the eternal Jew', but in English the Wandering Jew, who was condemned to wander the earth for all eternity without shelter. Chekhov makes the implication of this clear in the same letter to Knipper in which he admits to his worries about Act Two. His other anxiety, he says, is '. . . the somewhat unfinished state of the student, Trofimov. The point is that Trofimov is perpetually being exiled, perpetually being thrown out of the university – and how do you show things like this?' Exiled, of course, for his political activities; and the difficulty of showing things like this being the censor (who, even as it was, cut two passages from Trofimov's speeches – about the condition of the workers and about the effect that the ownership of serfs has had upon the Gayev family). Chekhov plainly takes Trofimov seriously as a man who holds sane and genuine convictions for which he is prepared to suffer. But then to go to the opposite extreme, as was done in Trevor Griffiths's adaptation of the play, and to turn him into a 'positive hero' in the Socialist Realist sense, is also an absurdity. Even if we had not discovered by now that Chekhov's characters are never puppets, Trofimov and his beliefs, like Vershinin and his, are obviously being held at some slight ironic distance. He is plainly ridiculous when he claims to be 'above such things as love'. Even his sincerest speeches topple into rhetoric about mankind marching towards higher truth and higher happiness. (His excited outburst to Anya at the end of Act Two – 'On, on, on! We are going to that bright star that blazes from afar there, and no one can hold us back! On, on, on! In step together, friends!' – echoes a famous revolutionary ode by Pleshcheyev, the writer to whom Chekhov addressed his disclaimer of all political and religious enthusiasm – 'On, on, with neither fear nor doubting/To great and valorous feats, my friends . . .!/And like a guiding star on high/Let blaze for us the sacred truth . . .'). He complains about people doing nothing but talk even as he stands there doing nothing but talk. Lopakhin and Trofimov, in fact, like all Chekhov's characters, speak out boldly and sincerely in their own voices. Each rises to his heights of magnanimity and understanding, and each comes up against his own particular limitations.

The greatest problem, though, in playing and understanding *The Cherry Orchard* is the one discussed in more general terms earlier – the question of whether it is a comedy. It is even more acute here than in the earlier plays. Chekhov was from the very first markedly more insistent than before that the play was funny, and even after the material had changed out of all recognition in the writing he remained firm on this point. He designates it a comedy on the title-page, as he had *The Seagull*. He wrote to Stanislavsky's wife: 'What has emerged in my play is not a drama but a comedy, in places even a farce . . .' (He used the French term, not the designation 'joke' or 'vaudeville' which he applied to his one-act plays.) To Knipper: 'The last act will be cheerful – in fact the whole play will be cheerful and frivolous . . .'

It does in fact seem to me to be a comedy in some sense that

the other plays are not, and I think it is possible to grasp this
aspect of it without losing sight of its painfulness; indeed, to
see the suffering of the characters as being expressed through
the comic inappropriateness of their reactions. The slothful
reluctance of the Gayevs to face what is happening to them,
their inability to save the ship by jettisoning the cargo, is
undoubtedly comic. And Chekhov is right about the last act;
it is predominantly cheerful. The crisis has occurred at the
end of Act Three, as it does in *Uncle Vanya*. What it calls
forth in the characters, however, is not a spirit of endurance,
as it does in the earlier play, but the absurd lightening of the
spirits that occurs, as Chekhov has observed with the most
wonderful ironic shrewdness, after a decision has been taken,
however terrible, and the worst has actually happened. It is
notable that in this last play, with his own death only months
away, Chekhov is struck not so much by the inexorable
nature of terrible events as by their survivability, by their way
of slipping out of the mind, once they have occurred, and of
disappearing in the endless wash of further events.

But the cheerfulness is deeply poignant. The worst *has*
happened, and it is a bad worst. The Gayevs' happiness has
been irretrievably lost, as both brother and sister for one
moment realise before they leave the house; and their future
will be even bleaker than Nina's on her tours of second-rate
provincial theatres, or Vanya's and Sonya's at the account-
books of their provincial estate, or the Prozorov sisters' in
their grim northern exile. A few months work at the bank for
Gayev; a few months with her hopeless lover in Paris for
Ranyevskaya. Then resolution and love and the last of the
money will all run out. They will have neither home nor
occupation; nothing. There is something absurd about their
prospects, though, because the Gayevs remain too feckless to
understand them; they lack the tragic dignity that Sonya and
her uncle and the Prozorov sisters all muster in the end. This
is why, finally, the play is a comedy. It is the comedy of
inertia and helplessness in the face of truly desolating loss.

There is no simple formula for playing it, or for responding to it; the problem it sets us is the problem of life itself.

Michael Frayn, 1988

# The Evils of Tobacco

# Characters

NYUKHIN, *his wife's husband; she being the proprietress of a conservatory of music and a boarding-school for young ladies.*

The scene is the platform of an assembly hall in a provincial town.

NYUKHIN, *wearing long sideboards but no moustache, and dressed in a worn and ancient tailcoat, makes a majestic entrance, bows, and adjusts his waistcoat.*

NYUKHIN. Ladies and, if I may say so, gentlemen. (*Combs his fingers through his sideboards.*) It has been suggested to my wife that at this point I should give a talk on some improving theme. So . . . A talk? All right – a talk. It's all the same to me. I'm not a professor of anything, of course, I'm not someone with academic qualifications, but I have none the less worked for the past thirty years – and worked without cease, worked, I might add, to the detriment of my health – on various questions of pure science – turning them over in my mind, and even on occasion writing learned articles, or rather not exactly learned articles, but something of the sort, in the local paper. I recently composed a very substantial article, I might say, under the title 'Certain insects and the damage they do'. My daughters thought very highly of it, particularly the section on bedbugs, but then I reread it and tore it up. Because whatever you write it makes no difference – it all just comes back to insect powder. We've even got bedbugs in the piano . . . I have chosen, as the subject of today's talk, tobacco and the harm it does. (*Takes a snuffbox out of his pocket and opens it.*) I've no personal feelings in the matter, but my wife felt it would be a suitable choice, and . . . (*He takes a pinch.*) . . . it makes no odds to me. (*Sneezes.*) But I do suggest, ladies and gentlemen, that you treat what I have to say with all due seriousness . . . (*Sneezes.*) . . . otherwise I might as well save my breath. If anyone here finds lectures on scientific subjects as dry as dust, then, please, let him . . . (*Sneezes, and then looks at the contents of the snuffbox suspiciously.*) I believe my daughters have been putting something in here again . . . Yes, if anyone does, I say, let him stand up now and . . . (*Blows his nose.*) . . . depart forthwith. I would ask any doctors present to pay particular attention. They may pick up a few useful tips, because tobacco, beside its harmful effects, has medical applications as well. Thus, for example, if we place a fly inside a snuffbox, we discover it dies, most probably from nervous disorder. Tobacco, I think I may safely say, is of vegetable origins . . . When I speak in public I tend to wink my right eye, but please attach no significance to this – it's merely a result of nervous tension. I am in fact a martyr to nervous tension, and I started winking my right eye in 1889, on the thirteenth of September of that year, the very day my wife presented me with my fourth daughter. All my daughters have been born on the thirteenth of the month . . . However . . . (*Glances at his watch.*) . . . time is running out and we mustn't let ourselves be distracted from the matter in hand. Let me merely remark that my wife runs a conservatoire of music and a private boarding-academy for young ladies, or not exactly an academy, perhaps, but something of that sort. Strictly between ourselves, my wife is fond of complaining about the world's shortcomings, but she has a little money put by, some forty or fifty thousand rubles, I believe, while I have not a kopeck to my name. Well, there you are. I look after all the housekeeping in the school. I buy the provisions, manage the servants, keep account of the outgoings, stitch the copybooks, get rid of the bedbugs, walk my wife's dog, and catch the mice. I make sure there are no more than five girls to a toothbrush, and no more than ten to a towel . . . Last night I had the task of issuing the cook with flour and fat, because we were going to have pancakes. Well, now, today, to cut a long story short, when the pancakes were already made, my wife arrived in the kitchen to say that three girls were having their pancakes stopped for bad conduct. So we were three pancakes over. What were we going to do with them? First my wife said to put them away in the cellar, but then she thought for a moment and with great kindness she said: 'You can eat them yourself, dummy.' That's what she calls me when she's not in a good mood – 'dummy'. Or 'snake-in-the-grass'. Or 'Satan'. I don't know why Satan. She's usually not in a good mood. Take yesterday, for instance. She wouldn't give me any dinner. 'What's the point of feeding you?' she says. 'You dummy.' Anyway, the result of all this was that I just gulped the pancakes down without chewing them, which may account for some of the winking now. However . . . (*Looks at his watch.*) . . . we've let ourselves get somewhat carried away. To return to our subject, then . . . Though I'm sure you'd prefer to be listening to some symphony concert, or something out of an opera. (*Sings.*) I've forgotten where that comes from. Speaking of forgetting, I also forgot to mention that apart from all the housekeeping in my wife's school I'm responsible for the teaching of mathematics, physics, chemistry, geography, history, tonic sol-fa, and literature, et cetera. For dancing, singing, and drawing my wife charges extra, though in fact I'm the one who teaches them as well. Our conservatoire is located in Five Dogs Lane, number thirteen. That's probably why I haven't had much success in life, because we live at number thirteen. Also my daughters were all born on the thirteenth, and the house has thirteen windows . . . Anyway . . . My wife is available for consultation at home, no appointment necessary, and the school prospectus can be obtained from the janitor for thirty kopecks. (*Gets some leaflets out of his pocket.*) I could pass these round, for that matter, if anyone's interested. Thirty kopecks! Anyone? (*Pause.*) No one? Twenty kopecks? (*Pause.*) Well, never mind. Yes, number thirteen. Nothing's gone right for me; I've just got older and stupider . . . Here I am giving this talk, and to look at me you'd think I was as merry as a cricket. But inside I feel like screaming at the top of my voice, or taking wing and flying to the other end of the earth. And I've no one to tell my troubles to. You'll say, 'What about your daughters?' What about my daughters? I talk to them and they laugh at me . . . Seven daughters, my wife's got . . . No, just a moment – six . . . No, seven! Twenty-eight, the eldest; seventeen, the youngest. There's only one man in the entire establishment, and that's me. But parents entrusting their daughters to us need have no fears on that score. My wife handles the situation so delicately that the girls don't think of me as a member of the opposite sex at all . . . (*Absently takes out his snuffbox as he talks.*) Yes, my life hasn't been all it might have been, but as a father, as a family man . . . (*Is about to take a pinch of snuff when he stops, looks at it suspiciously, and smells it cautiously.*) Pepper, the little she-devils . . . I hope no one will think my daughters' pranks are any reflection on school discipline. In matters of discipline the school can only work hand in hand with the family. It's the families that I blame in these cases . . . No, thirty-three years I've been married, and I can honestly say that they have been the best years of my life. By and large. (*Looks round.*) I don't think she's arrived yet, so I can speak quite frankly on this score . . . They're taking a long time to get themselves married, my daughters, but I suppose this is because they're shy. Also because they never see any men. My wife doesn't like entertaining, and she finds inviting people to dinner a quite needless expense, but I can tell you in confidence . . . (*He comes down to the footlights.*) . . . my daughters can usually be found on all the major holidays at their aunt's. That's Natalya Semyonovna, the one who's got rheumatism and a yellow dress with black spots that looks as if it had cockroaches crawling over it. They'll give you something to eat there, too. And so long as my wife's not there you can, you know . . . (*Demonstrates drinking.*) I should warn you – one glass and I'm away. And then I feel so good inside myself – and so sad, all at the same time – I can't tell you what I feel like! I remember what it was like being young, and I just long to run away – oh, if you knew how much I longed to! (*Animatedly.*) Just to throw up everything and run away with never a glance behind . . . Run where? What would it matter where? Just to get away from this mean shabby life that's turned me into the pitiful old fool I am, away from that stupid, petty, evil, evil, evil miser who's spent the last thirty-three years tormenting me, away from music and school meals and my wife's money and all this rubbish, all this vileness . . . Just to stop somewhere far, far away in the middle of the fields, just to stand there like a tree or a telegraph-pole or a scarecrow under the wide open sky and gaze all night at the shining silent moon above, just to forget, forget . . . Oh, how I should love not to remember anything! Oh, how I should love to tear off this shabby old coat I got married in thirty years ago . . . (*Tears it off.*) . . . this coat I give all these endless talks on some improving theme in . . . There, take that! (*Stamps on the coat.*) Take that! I'm old and poor and pitiful. I'm like this waistcoat – look, it's all worn out round the back. (*He demonstrates.*) I don't want anything! I scorn it all! I was young once, I had brains, I went to university, I dreamed dreams, I thought I was a proper person . . . I don't want anything now! Just to be left in peace, that's all, just to be left in peace! (*Looks off, then quickly puts his coat back on.*) However, my wife's out there in the wings . . . She's arrived and she's waiting for me out there . . . (*Looks at his watch.*) We've come to the end of our time . . . If she asks you please tell her I did give the talk . . . Tell her the old dummy behaved himself properly. (*Looks off and clears his throat.*) She's looking this way . . . (*Raising his voice.*) And since, therefore, as we have just seen, tobacco contains a deadly poison, you should on no account smoke, and I hope that my little talk on 'The Evils of Tobacco' will prove to have been of some, if I may say so, use. That is all I have to say, and I am very pleased to have had the opportunity to get it off my chest.

*He bows and makes a majestic exit.*

*Curtain.*

# Swan Song

# Characters

SVETLOVIDOV, *an elderly comic actor (68)*
NIKITA IVANICH, *an elderly prompter*

The action takes place on the empty stage of a second-rate provincial theatre, at night, after the performance is over. Right – a row of roughly-carpentered, unpainted dressing-room doors. Left and upstage – piles of junk. In the middle of the stage – an overturned stool. Night. Darkness.

SVETLOVIDOV, *in the costume of* CALCHAS, *the High Priest of Jupiter in Offenbach's 'La Belle Hélène', and holding a candle, enters from one of the dressing-rooms and laughs.*

SVETLOVIDOV. Well, here's a fine how-do-you-do! Here's a fine state of affairs! Fell asleep in my dressing-room! The show finished hours ago – everyone's gone home – and what am I doing? – I'm quietly taking forty winks! Oh, you stupid old so-and-so! You silly old devil! Must have got so tight I dropped off as I sat there. There's a bright thing to do. (*Calls.*) Yegorka! Yegorka, damn you! Petrushka! They've gone to bed, the devils. Damn them, the pair of them. Yegorka! (*Picks up the stool, sits down on it, and puts the candle on the floor.*) Silence. No answer but the echoes. I tipped them three rubles apiece today – you won't find them now for love nor money. Off they went, the swine, and I presume locked up after them. (*Twists his head back and forth.*) Drunk! Ugh! And all because it was my benefit night . . . My God, how much of that vodka and beer did I get down me? My whole body feels like the bottom of a parrot's cage. I've got twelve tongues sleeping rough inside my mouth . . . Horrible . . . (*Pause.*) How stupid . . . The old fool's got drunk and he doesn't even know himself what it was all in aid of . . . Oh, heavens above! My back's breaking, my head's splitting, I've got the shivers, and I feel as cold and dark inside me as the grave. Even if you don't care about your health you might at least take a little pity on your old age, you stupid clown. (*Pause.*) Old age. Oh yes, you can get up to your tricks, you can put a brave face on it and play the fool, but your life's over. Sixty-eight years you've kissed goodbye to now, for heaven's sake! You won't see them again. The whole bottle drunk – only the last drop left at the bottom . . . Only the dregs . . . So there we are. That's the way it is. Like it or not, it's time to rehearse the part of the corpse. Old father death is waiting in

the wings . . . (*Gazes out front.*) I've been on the stage for forty-
five years, though, and I do believe this is the first time I've ever
seen a theatre in the middle of the night. I do believe it is . . .
Curious . . . (*Comes down to the footlights.*) Can't see a thing . . .
Just make out the prompt-booth . . . and the box there . . . the
conductor's stand . . . Everything else – blackness! A black,
bottomless pit, like the tomb, with death hiding in it . . . Brr!
Cold! There's a draught from out there like the draught from an
empty fireplace . . . Just the place to raise a few ghosts! God,
but you can feel the fear strike into you . . . My spine's crawling
. . . (*Calls.*) Yegorka! Petrushka! Where are you, damn you?
My God, though, what am I doing swearing like this? Give up
swearing, for God's sake! Give up drinking! You're an old man!
It's time to die! People get up in the morning and go to church
when they're sixty-eight, they get ready for death. And what are
*you* doing? Swearing, drunk as a pig, tricked out in this clown's
costume . . . I'm not fit to be seen! Better go and get dressed
. . . Oh, it's eerie! If I stay here all night like this I might die of
fright . . .

*He goes towards his dressing-room. As he does so,* NIKITA
IVANICH *appears from the furthest dressing-room at the back of
the stage, wearing a white dressing-grown.*

*At the sight of him* SVETLOVIDOV *cries out in terror and cowers
back.*

SVETLOVIDOV. Who's that? What is it? Who do you want?
(*Stamps his feet.*) Who is it?

NIKITA. It's me, sir!

SVETLOVIDOV. Who?

NIKITA (*slowly coming towards him*). Me, sir. Nikita Ivanich. The
prompter. Me, sir!

SVETLOVIDOV (*sinks helplessly on to the stool, breathing heavily
and shaking all over.*) Good God! It's who? It's you? Is it?
Nikitushka? What on earth are you doing here?

NIKITA. I sleep in the dressing-rooms, sir. You won't tell anyone, sir, will you. I haven't got anywhere else to go, so help me God.

SVETLOVIDOV. You, is it, Nikitushka . . . Good God, good God! We took sixteen curtains, we got three bouquets and a lot else besides, everyone was in ecstasies – and no one could wake up a poor drunken old man and take him home . . . I'm an old man, Nikitushka! I'm sixty-eight. I'm ill. My poor sick heart's fading away . . .

*Seizes* NIKITA IVANICH's *hand and weeps.*

Don't leave me, Nikitushka! I'm old, I've no strength left, I've got to die . . . I'm frightened, I'm frightened!

NIKITA (*gently and respectfully*). Time you were going home, Vasily Vasilich.

SVETLOVIDOV. I'm not going! I've no home to go to! No home! No home!

NIKITA. God save us, forgotten where you live now, have you?

SVETLOVIDOV. I don't want to go home! I'm all on my own there. I haven't got anyone in the world, Nikitushka. No family, no wife, no children. I'm as lonely as the wind in the fields. I've no one to remember me when I'm gone. I get frightened on my own. No one to warm me when I'm cold, no one to be nice to me, no one to put me to bed when I'm drunk. Who do I belong to? Who needs me? Who loves me? No one loves me, Nikitushka!

NIKITA (*on the verge of tears*). The audience loves you, Vasily Vasilich!

SVETLOVIDOV. The audience has gone home and gone to bed and forgotten all about its clown! No, no one needs me, no one loves me . . . No wife, no children . . .

NIKITA. Nonsense, now, what are you grieving about?

SVETLOVIDOV. I'm human, aren't I? I'm alive? I've got blood flowing in my veins, not water? I'm a gentleman, Nikitushka, I come from a good family. Before I fell into this pit I served in the army – I was in the artillery. And what a fine young fellow I was! What a handsome young, upright young, dashing young, fiery young fellow I was! My God, though where's it all gone?

But what an actor I became then! Didn't I, Nikitushka, didn't I?

*He gets up, leaning on* NIKITA IVANICH's *arm.*

Where's it all gone, that time, where is it now? Lord, Lord . . . I looked out into that pit tonight, and it all came back to me, it all came back! That pit out there has swallowed up forty-five years of my life. And what a life it's been, Nikitushka! I look out into that pit now and I see it all down to the last little thing, I see it like your face in front of me. The delights of youth – the faith, the fire – the love of women! Ah, the women, Nikitushka!

NIKITA. Time you were in bed, Vasily Vasilich.

SVETLOVIDOV. When I was a young actor, when I was just starting to get my teeth into it, I remember there was a woman who loved me for my art. An elegant creature she was, as graceful as a poplar, as young and innocent, as pure and passionate, as a summer dawn! One glance from her blue eyes, one flash of her amazing smile, and no darkness could resist. The waves of the sea break against the rocks, but the waves of her hair would have broken cliffs and melted icebergs. I remember one day standing in front of her as I'm standing in front of you now . . . She was lovelier than ever that day, and she gave me a look I shall remember in my grave . . . All the sweetness, softness, profundity and brilliance of youth! Intoxicated with happiness, I fell on my knees before her and asked her to marry me. (*Lowering his voice.*) And what did she say? She said, 'Give up the stage!' Give – up – the stage! Do you see? She didn't mind being in love with an actor, but *marry* one? Not on your life! I was appearing that day, I remember. A low comic part. And as I performed I felt as if my eyes had been opened. I saw that there was no sacred art about it – that it was all delirium and delusion – that I was other people's creature, the plaything of their idle fancy, their jester, their buffoon! And I saw the audience for what it was! From then on I didn't trust their applause or their bouquets or their ecstasies. Oh yes, Nikitushka! They applaud me, they pay a ruble for my photograph, but they don't see me as someone like themselves. They see me as trash, as something not much better than a courtesan. They scrape acquaintance with me so they can boast about it, but they wouldn't demean themselves by marrying their sisters or daughters to me. I don't trust them an inch!

NIKITA. You don't look yourself, Vasily Vasilich! You've got me frightened now. Let's go home, for the love of God.

SVETLOVIDOV. I grew up that day. And dear it cost me, Nikitushka! After that little incident . . . after *her* . . . I lost all sense of aim and direction, I stumbled on without looking where I was going. I played fools and scoffers, I clowned, I sowed corruption – yet what an artist I was, what a talent I had! I buried that talent, I cheapened myself. I coarsened my language, I lost the divine image and likeness. That black pit opened its jaws and swallowed me up! I've never felt it before, but tonight . . . I woke up and looked back, and there were sixty-eight years behind me. Old age! I saw it tonight for the first time. My song is sung! (*Sobs.*) My race is run!

NIKITA. There now, Vasily Vasilich! There now! Don't take on so. Oh, Lord in heaven! (*Calls.*) Petrushka! Yegorka!

SVETLOVIDOV. But what a talent I had! What power! You can't imagine! What diction, how much feeling and grace, what a range of emotion inside this breast! (*He strikes his chest.*) I was overpowering! Listen, listen . . . Wait, let me get my breath . . . *King Lear*, say . . . . The sky black, rain, thunder – boom, boom! – lightning striping the blackness – zzzz! – then:

> Blow, winds, and crack your cheeks! rage! blow!
> You cataracts and hurricanoes, spout
> Till you have drench'd our steeples, drown'd the cocks!
> You sulphurous and thought-executing fires,
> Vaunt-couriers to oak-cleaving thunderbolts,
> Singe my white head! And thou, all-shaking thunder,
> Smite flat the thick rotundity o'the world!
> Crack nature's moulds, all germens spill at once
> That make ingrateful man!

(*Impatiently.*) Quick, the Fool! (*Stamps his feet.*) Come on, come on, the Fool's lines! Quick, quick!

NIKITA (*as the* FOOL). O nuncle, court holy-water in a dry house is better than this rain-water out o'door. Good nuncle, in, and ask thy daughters' blessing: here's a night pities neither wise man nor fool.

SVETLOVIDOV.

> Rumble thy bellyful! Spit, fire! spout, rain!
> Nor rain, wind, thunder, fire are my daughters:
> I tax not you, you elements, with unkindness;
> I never gave you kingdom, call'd you children . . .

The power there! The talent! The artistry! Another bit . . . something else that goes back to the old days. Let's have . . . (*Goes off into a peal of happy laughter.*) . . . a bit of *Hamlet*! All right, then . . . How does it go . . .? Oh, yes . . . (*As Hamlet:*) O, the recorders! – let me see one. To withdraw with you: – why do you go about to recover the wind of me, as if you would drive me into a toil?

NIKITA. O, my lord, if my duty be too bold, my love is too unmannerly.

SVETLOVIDOV. I do not well understand that. Will you play upon this pipe?

NIKITA. My lord, I cannot.

SVETLOVIDOV. I pray you.

NIKITA. Believe me, I cannot.

SVETLOVIDOV. I do beseech you.

NIKITA. I know no touch of it, my lord.

SVETLOVIDOV. 'Tis as easy as lying: govern these ventages with your fingers and thumb, give it breath with your mouth, and it will discourse most eloquent music. Look you, these are the stops.

NIKITA. But these cannot I command to any utterance of harmony: I have not the skill.

SVETLOVIDOV. Why, look you now, how unworthy a thing you make of me! You would play upon me; you would seem to know

my stops; you would pluck out the heart of my mystery; you
would sound me from my lowest note to the top of my compass:
and there is much music, excellent voice, in this little organ; yet
cannot you make it speak. 'Sblood, do you think I am easier to
be play'd on than a pipe? Call me what instrument you will,
though you can fret me, yet you cannot play upon me. (*Laughs
and claps.*) Bravo! Encore! Bravo! Where's all this damned old
age, then? Not a sign of it! Old age? Nonsense! Old age?
Rubbish! Power, pumping like a fountain out of every vein!
Youth, Nikitushka! Freshness! Life! Where you've got talent
there's no room for old age! Have I gone mad, Nikitushka? Are
these mere ravings?

*The sound of doors being opened, off.*

What was that?

NIKITA. Petrushka and Yegorka must have come back . . . No,
you've got the talent, Vasily Vasilich! You've got the talent!

SVETLOVIDOV (*calls, in the direction of the banging doors*). In here,
you drunkards! (*To* NIKITA IVANICH:) We'll go and get
dressed . . . Old age? No such thing! Stuff and nonsense . . .
(*Laughs cheerfully.*) What are you crying about? My dear old
idiot, what's all this snivelling for? Come on, now, that's
enough of that. What's that face for? Come on, come on.

*He puts his arm around* NIKITA IVANICH, *on the verge of tears
himself.*

You mustn't cry. Where you've got art, where you've got talent,
there's no room for old age, there's no room for loneliness or
being ill. Even death's only half itself. (*Weeps.*) No, you're
right, Nikitushka, our song is sung, our race is run. What talent
do I have? I'm a squeezed lemon, a melting icicle, a rusty nail.
And what are you? A prompter, an old theatre rat . . . Off we
go, then.

*They begin to move off.*

What talent do I have? All I'm good for in serious plays is an
attendant lord . . . and I'm getting old for that . . . Yes . . .
You remember that speech in *Othello*, Nikitushka?

> O, now for ever
> Farewell the tranquil mind! farewell content!
> Farewell the plumed troop and the big wars
> That make ambition virtue! O, farewell,
> Farewell the neighing steed, and the shrill trump,
> The spirit-stirring drum, the ear-piercing fife,
> The royal banner and all quality,
> Pride, pomp and circumstance of glorious war!

NIKITA. You've got the talent, Vasily Vasilich! You've got the
talent!

SVETLOVIDOV.

> And, O you mortal engines, whose rude throats
> Th'immortal Jove's dread clamours counterfeit,
> Farewell! Othello's occupation's gone!

*Exit, with* NIKITA IVANICH. *The curtain slowly falls.*

# The Bear

# Characters

POPOVA, *a charming widow with an estate and dimples*
SMIRNOV, *a landowner in the prime of life*
LUKA, POPOVA's *elderly footman*

The drawing-room in POPOVA's country residence.

POPOVA *and* LUKA. POPOVA *is in deep mourning, with a photograph from which she never lifts her eyes.*

LUKA. It's not right, madam . . . You'll only go and do yourself a mischief so . . . Cook and parlourmaid are out picking berries – every breath you draw out there today is a joy from heaven. Why, even the cat knows how to take her pleasure in life – her, too, she's out-of-doors, catching the little birds. And here you are, sitting inside the live day long like a nun in a nunnery, and no pleasure in life at all. Just you think, now, a whole year's gone by since you set foot outside the house!

POPOVA. Nor shall I set foot outside it ever. Why should I? My life is over. *He* is lying in his grave, and I have entombed myself within these four walls. We've both died.

LUKA. Hark at you! That I should hear such things! Your husband's dead, and there it is – it was God's will, and may his soul rest in peace. You've grieved your grief, and that's enough, it's time to put an end to it. You can't weep and wear your weeds forever. I had a wife, too, in my day, and she died, and what did I do? I grieved and wept a month, and that was enough of her. Wail my whole life away? Even my old lady wasn't worth that. ( *Sighs.* ) You've forgotten all your neighbours. You won't go to them, and you won't let them come to you. Forgive me, but we live like spiders – we never see the white light of day. The mice have eaten our livery . . . It would be one thing if there was no folk of the right sort hereabouts, but the district's full of gentlemen . . . There's a regiment over in town, and the officers – a sugar-plum, every one, a delight to the eye! Every Friday in their camps a regimental ball, every day a brass band playing . . . Oh, madam! Oh, my dear, dear madam! All young and lovely, as blooming as strawberries and cream – if only you could take your pleasure in life . . . Looks don't last for ever! Ten years from now you'll be the one wanting to show off your

fine feathers to the officers, you'll be the one wanting to throw
dust in their eyes, and then it'll be too late.

POPOVA (*decisively*). Please – never mention the subject again!
Since my husband died, as you know, life has lost all meaning
for me. You look at me and I seem to be alive, but seem to be is
all it is! I swore on his grave never to come out of mourning and
never to look upon the light of day. You understand? Let his
shade see how I love him . . . All right, I know it was no secret
from you that he treated me badly, that he was cruel to me and
even . . . yes, unfaithful to me. But *I* shall be faithful unto the
grave – I shall prove to him that *I* am capable of love. And he'll
see at last from beyond the tomb exactly what sort of woman I
was.

LUKA. Better to take a walk in the garden than say such things,
better to have Toby and Giant harnessed up and call on your
neighbours.

POPOVA. Oh . . .! (*Weeps.*)

LUKA. Madam! Sweet madam! What's this, now? Lord have
mercy!

POPOVA. He loved Toby so much! He always rode Toby when he
was going over to the Korchagins or the Vlasovs. He was such a
wonderful horseman! Such a graceful bearing as he hauled with
all his might on the reins! Do you remember? Oh, Toby, Toby!
See that he's given an extra handful of oats today.

LUKA. Ma'am.

An urgent peal on the doorbell.

POPOVA (*starts*). Who's that? Tell them I'm not at home.

LUKA. Very good, ma'am.

Exit LUKA.

POPOVA (*looking at the photograph*). You watch, Nikolai – you'll
see I'm capable of love and forgiveness. While I have breath in
my body, while this poor heart of mine still beats, my love will
never die. (*Laughs, on the verge of tears.*) Aren't you ashamed of
yourself? Here am I, locking myself away like a nice good little

wife and being faithful to you unto the grave, and there are you
. . . Well, you should be ashamed of yourself! Deceiving me,
making scenes, leaving me on my own for weeks at a time . . .

*Enter* LUKA.

LUKA (*in alarm*). Madam, it's someone asking for you. He wants
to see you . . .

POPOVA. You told him, I presume, that I have been at home to no
one since the day my husband died?

LUKA. I did so, but he wouldn't pay no heed. He says it's a very
pressing matter.

POPOVA. I – am – not – at home!

LUKA. I told him! But all he does is swear, the great hobgoblin,
and comes barging in! He's got into the dining-room!

POPOVA (*in irritation*). Very well. Show him in, then. Such
boorishness!

*Exit* LUKA.

How tedious these people are! What do they want with me?
Why must they intrude upon me? (*Sighs.*) No, I see I shall have
to retire to a nunnery in good earnest . . . (*Reflects.*) A nunnery,
yes, why not?

*Enter* SMIRNOV *and* LUKA.

SMIRNOV (*to* LUKA). Blockhead! Talk too much, that's your
trouble! Jackass! (*Sees* POPOVA. *With dignity*:) Allow me to
introduce myself – Smirnov. Grigory Stepanovich Smirnov,
landowner and lieutenant of artillery, retired. I am obliged to
trouble you on a matter of extreme urgency.

POPOVA (*without offering her hand*). What do you want?

SMIRNOV. Your late husband, with whom I had the honour to be
acquainted, left debts outstanding, on two notes of hand in my
favour, amounting to twelve hundred rubles. Since the interest
on my mortgage falls due tomorrow I should be grateful if you
would pay me the money today.

POPOVA. Twelve hundred rubles . . . And how had my husband

incurred these debts?

SMIRNOV. He used to buy oats off me.

POPOVA (*to* LUKA, *sighing*). Yes, Luka, don't forget to tell them to give Toby an extra handful of oats today.

    *Exit* LUKA.

If my husband left debts to you then of course I shall pay them. Forgive me, though – I've no money in hand today. My steward will be back from town the day after tomorrow, and I will tell him to pay you what you're owed, but until then I cannot oblige . . . In addition to which it's exactly seven months today since my husband died, and I am in no mood to concern myself with money matters.

SMIRNOV. If I don't pay the interest tomorrow, however, I'm in a mood to go head over heels into the bankruptcy court! They're going to seize my estate!

POPOVA. You will get your money the day after tomorrow.

SMIRNOV. I don't need it the day after tomorrow – I need it today.

POPOVA. Forgive me, but I can't pay it today.

SMIRNOV. And I can't wait until the day after tomorrow.

POPOVA. But what can I do, if I haven't got it?

SMIRNOV. So you can't pay it, then?

POPOVA. I can't pay it.

SMIRNOV. Ah. And that's your final word?

POPOVA. That's my final word.

SMIRNOV. Positively your final word?

POPOVA. Positively my final word.

SMIRNOV. My most humble thanks. I shan't forget this. (*Shrugs.*) And still they expect me to keep calm about it! I've just met the tax-collector on the way here. 'Grigory Stepanovich,' he says, 'why are you always in such a temper?' Well, for pity's sake, how could I not be in a temper? I'm desperate for money. Started out yesterday at the crack of dawn – went round everyone who owes me. Not one of them paid up! Got dog-tired, spent the night next to the vodka barrel in some god-

forsaken tavern. Wind up here, forty miles from home, think
I'll get my hands on something at last, and I'm greeted with 'not
in the mood'! Temper? Of course I'm in a temper!

POPOVA. I made myself quite clear, I think. My steward will be
back from town, and then you'll get your money.

SMIRNOV. I haven't come to see your steward; I've come to see
you! Why, by all the flaming devils of hell – pardon my
language – why should I want to see your steward?

POPOVA. My dear sir, forgive me. I am not accustomed to these
curious turns of phrase, nor to being spoken to in that tone of
voice. That is as much as I am prepared to listen to.

*She makes a swift exit.*

SMIRNOV. How about that? Not in the mood . . . Seven months
ago her husband died! What about *me*, though? Have I got to
pay my interest or haven't I? I'm asking you – have I or haven't
I? All right, your husband's dead, you're not in the mood, and
all the rest of it, your steward's gone off somewhere, damn him
– and what am *I* supposed to do? Wave my creditors goodbye
from an air-balloon? Take a running jump and bash my head
against the wall? I go to see Gruzdyov – he's not in. Yaroshevich
– he's gone into hiding. I curse Kuritzin halfway to hell and
practically throw him out of the window. Matuzov's got
cholera, and this one's *not in the mood*. None of them who'll pay
up, the swine! And all because I've mollycoddled them! All
because I'm a babe-in-arms, a weak woman, a spineless toe-rag!
I've been too soft with them! Just you wait, though! You'll find
out who you're dealing with! They're not going to make a fool
of me, damn them! I'm going to stay here until she pays up!
Grr . . .! I'm in such a rage today, such a rage! My knees are
shaking – I can't breathe . . .! Phew, Lord – I'm feeling
positively *faint* with rage! (*Calls.*) Fellow!

*Enter* LUKA.

LUKA. Yes, sir?
SMIRNOV. Water!

*Exit* LUKA.

No, but the logic of it! A man's desperate for money, ready to
hang himself – and she won't pay up because, oh dear me, she's
not inclined to concern herself with money matters! A real piece
of feminine logic! That's precisely why I never have liked and
never will like talking to women. I'd rather sit on a barrel of
gunpowder. Grr . . .! Her and her fancy dresses – they've made
me so cross I can feel the shivers going up and down my spine! I
just have to see one of the fair sex in the distance and I get
cramps in my legs. Intolerable tribe!

*Enter* LUKA. *He serves the water.*

LUKA. Madam is indisposed. She's not receiving.
SMIRNOV. Get out!

*Exit* LUKA.

Indisposed! Not receiving! All right, my precious – don't receive!
I'm going to stay right here until you hand over the money. Be
indisposed for a week, if you like – I'll stay here for a week.
Indisposed for a year – I'll stay here for a year. I'm going to have
what's mine! You won't soften my heart by being all in black, or
having dimples in your cheeks . . . We know all about dimples!
(*Calls out of the window.*) Semyon, unharness! We shan't be
leaving for some time! I'm staying here! Go to the stables – tell
them to give the horses oats! You've got the left trace-horse all
tangled up in the reins again, you scumbag! (*Mimics him.*) 'Never
worry, sir!' I'll give you never worry! (*Moves away from the
window.*) Feel terrible. Intolerable heat, no one paying up, rotten
night's sleep, and now this woman in fancy dress who's *not in the
mood* . . . My head's aching . . . Perhaps I should have a glass of
vodka? Perhaps I should. (*Calls.*) Fellow!

*Enter* LUKA.

LUKA. Yes, sir?
SMIRNOV. A glass of vodka!

*Exit* LUKA.

Agh! (*Sits down and takes a look at himself.*) Must admit I'm a bit of a sight. Covered in dust, mud all over my boots; haven't had a wash or a comb through my hair; straw on my waistcoat . . . Maybe she took me for a bandit. (*Yawns.*) Not very polite, appearing in someone's drawing-room in this state . . . Never mind, though – I'm not here as a guest, I'm here as a creditor, and no one's laid down the correct wear for creditors . . .

*Enter* LUKA. *He serves the vodka.*

LUKA. Very much at home you're making yourself, sir.

SMIRNOV (*angrily*). What?

LUKA. I never meant . . . I only meant . . .

SMIRNOV. Who do you think you're talking to? Hold your tongue!

LUKA (*aside*). Come down on our heads like a plague, he has, the great hobgoblin. Sent by the devil himself, this one . . .

*Exit* LUKA.

SMIRNOV. Oh, what a rage I'm in! Such a rage I could grind the entire world to powder! Downright *faint* with rage . . . (*Calls.*) Fellow!

*Enter* POPOVA, *her eyes downcast.*

POPOVA. My dear sir, I have long since grown unaccustomed, in my isolation, to the sound of the human voice, and I cannot bear shouting. I earnestly beseech you to end this intrusion!

SMIRNOV. Pay me the money and I'll go.

POPOVA. I've told you quite plainly: I have no money to hand at present – you must wait until the day after tomorrow.

SMIRNOV. I also had the honour to tell you quite plainly: I don't need the money the day after tomorrow – I need it today. If you don't pay me the money today, then tomorrow there will be nothing for it but to hang myself.

POPOVA. But what can I do if I haven't *got* the money? Such an extraordinary way to behave!

SMIRNOV. So you're not going to pay me now? No?

POPOVA. I can't.

SMIRNOV. In that case I shall stay here until I get it. (*Sits down.*) You're going to pay me the day after tomorrow? Fine! Then I shall sit here like this until the day after tomorrow. Stay sat here precisely so . . .(*Jumps up.*) Listen – have I got to pay the interest tomorrow or haven't I? Or do you think this is all some kind of joke?

POPOVA. My dear sir, I must ask you not to shout! We're not in the stables!

SMIRNOV. I'm not talking about stables. I'm simply asking you – Have I got to pay the interest tomorrow or haven't I?

POPOVA. You don't know how to behave in female company!

SMIRNOV. I most certainly do know how to behave in female company!

POPOVA. No, you don't! You're a coarse, ill-brought-up fellow! Decent people don't speak to women so!

SMIRNOV. Oh, but this is amazing! How do you want me to talk to you? In French, perhaps? (*Lisps angrily.*) *Madame, je vous prie* . . . How utterly enchanting that you won't pay the money . . . *Ah, pardon* for troubling you! What utterly enchanting weather today! And black is absolutely your colour! (*Bows and scrapes.*)

POPOVA. That's coarse and not very clever.

SMIRNOV (*mimics her*). 'Coarse and not very clever.' And I don't know how to behave in female company! Madam, I have seen more women in my time than you've seen sparrows! Three duels I have fought over women! Twelve women I have thrown over – and been thrown over by nine more. Oh, yes! There was a time when I behaved like an idiot, when I was all sweet words and soft music, all scattered pearls and clicking heels . . . I loved, I suffered, I sighed to the moon, I felt weak at the knees, I melted, I went hot and cold . . . I loved passionately, I loved desperately, I loved all the ways there are to love, God help me, I chattered like a magpie about the emancipation of women, I spent half my substance on the tender passion, but now – no, thank you! You won't catch me like that now! I've had enough! Dark, mysterious eyes, scarlet lips, dimples, moonlight, whispers, panting breath – madam, I wouldn't give you a brass kopeck for the lot of it! Women? From the highest to the lowest – present company excepted – they're all hypocrites, fakers, gossipmongers, grudgebearers, and liars down to their fingertips; all vain and petty-minded and merciless; their logical powers are a disgrace; and as for what's in here . . . (*He strikes his forehead.*) . . . then forgive me if I'm frank – but a chaffinch could knock spots off any philosopher in a skirt! Look at one of the so-called gentle sex and what do you see? Fine muslins and ethereal essences, a goddess walking the earth, a million delights. But you look into her heart and what is she then? A common or garden crocodile! (*He seizes the back of a chair, which splinters and breaks.*) But the most outrageous thing of all – this crocodile for some reason thinks its crowning achievement, its privilege and monopoly, is the tender passion! Because you can hang me up by my heels, damn it, if a woman knows how to love anything but a lapdog! All a woman can do in love is whimper and snivel! Where a man suffers and sacrifices, all a woman's love consists in is swirling her skirt around and leading him ever more firmly by the nose. You have the misfortune to be a woman, so you know what women are like. Tell me, in all honesty – have you ever in your life seen a woman who could be sincere and constant and true? You haven't! The only ones who are constant and true are old crones and freaks! You'll find a horned cat or a white woodcock before you'll find a constant woman!

POPOVA. So who, in your opinion, if I may ask, is constant and true in love? Not a man, by any chance?

SMIRNOV. A man, certainly, a man!

POPOVA. A man! (*Gives an angry laugh.*) A man – constant and true in love! News to me, I must say! (*Heatedly.*) What right do you have to say such a thing? Constant and true – men? If that's what you're telling me then let me inform you that of all the

men I have ever known the best was my late husband. I loved
him passionately. I loved him with my whole being, as only a
young and intelligent woman can love. I gave him my youth and
happiness, my life and fortune; I breathed him; I worshipped him
like a heathen. And what happened? This best of men deceived
me most shamelessly at every step! After his death I found a
whole drawer of his desk full of love letters. And while he was
alive – I can scarcely bear to recall it – he left me on my own for
weeks at a time – he pursued other women in front of my eyes,
he betrayed me, he squandered my money right and left, he
mocked my feelings . . . And in spite of it all I loved him and I
was true to him . . . And dead as he is, I remain true and
constant. I have entombed myself forever within these four
walls and I shall wear this mourning unto my grave . . .

SMIRNOV (*with a scornful laugh*). Mourning! What do you take
me for? As if I didn't know why you were wearing this fancy
dress, or why you'd shut yourself up inside these four walls! Oh
yes! Because it's so mysterious and poetic! Some young
mooncalf in cadet-school goes past the estate, some half-pint
poet, and he looks up at the windows and he thinks: 'That's
where she lives, the mysterious lady who has shut herself up
within four walls for love of her husband.' We know all these
tricks!

POPOVA (*flaring up*). What? How dare you say such things to me!

SMIRNOV. You've buried yourself alive, but you haven't forgotten to powder your nose!

POPOVA. How dare you talk to me like this!

SMIRNOV. Don't shout at me, thank you – I'm not your steward!
I'll call a spade a spade, if you please. I'm not a woman and I'm
accustomed to speaking my mind! So kindly stop your
shouting!

POPOVA. I'm not shouting – you're shouting! Kindly go away and
leave me alone!

SMIRNOV. Give me the money and I'll go.

POPOVA. I won't give you the money!

SMIRNOV. Oh yes you will!

POPOVA. Not a kopeck, so there! You can just go away and leave me alone!

SMIRNOV. I don't have the pleasure of being your husband or your fiancé, so don't make scenes at me, if you please. (*Sits down.*) I don't like it.

POPOVA (*choking with anger*). You've sat yourself down?

SMIRNOV. I have.

POPOVA. Please go!

SMIRNOV. Give me the money! (*Aside.*) Oh, I'm in such a rage, I'm in such a rage!

POPOVA. I've no desire to converse with impertinent hobbledehoys! Kindly get out of here! (*Pause.*) You won't go?

SMIRNOV. No.

POPOVA. No?

SMIRNOV. No!

POPOVA. Very well, then! (*Rings.*)

*Enter* LUKA.

POPOVA. Luka, show this gentleman out!

LUKA (*goes up to* SMIRNOV). Sir, will you go away when you're told? There's nothing here for you . . .

SMIRNOV (*jumping up*). Hold your tongue! Who do you think you're talking to? I'll chop you up for salad!

LUKA (*clutching his heart*). Oh, Lord above! Oh, by all the saints! (*Falls into a chair.*) Oh, I'm going to pass right out! I can't breathe!

POPOVA. Where's Dasha, then? Dasha! (*Calls.*) Dasha! Pelageya! Dasha! (*Rings.*)

LUKA. Oh! They're all out picking berries! There's no one in the house! I'm going to pass clean out! Water!

POPOVA. Kindly get out of here!

SMIRNOV. Would you mend your manners a little?

POPOVA (*bunching her fists and stamping her feet*). You peasant! You coarse bear! You lout! You monster!

SMIRNOV. I beg your pardon? What did you say?

POPOVA. I said you're a bear, you're a monster!

SMIRNOV (*advancing on her*). What right do you have, may I ask, to insult me?

POPOVA. Yes, I'm insulting you! What of it? You think I'm frightened of you?

SMIRNOV. And you think you can go round insulting people with impunity, do you, just because you're a woman? I demand satisfaction!

LUKA. Oh, Lord above! Oh, by all the saints! Water!

SMIRNOV. With pistols!

POPOVA. You think I'm frightened of you, just because you've got ham fists and a throat like a bull? Do you? You utter lout!

SMIRNOV. I'm going to have satisfaction! I don't permit anyone to insult me, and I don't give a straw if you're a member of the weaker sex!

POPOVA (*trying to shout him down*). You bear! You bear! You bear!

SMIRNOV. High time we gave up our narrow-minded view that only men should pay for their insults! You want equality? – Then let's have equality, and to hell with it! Just give me satisfaction!

POPOVA. You want to fight a duel? By all means!

SMIRNOV. Here and now!

POPOVA. Here and now! My husband left a pair of pistols. I'll go and get them. (*Hurries towards the door and then returns.*) It will give me the greatest pleasure to put a bullet in your thick wooden head! To hell with you!

*Exit* POPOVA.

SMIRNOV. I'll wing her like a chicken! I'm not some sentimental young puppy! There's no weaker sex as far as I'm concerned!

LUKA. Sweet kind sir . . .! (*Goes down on his knees.*) Have pity on an old man, and go away from here! You've frightened me to death, and now you're going to start fighting duels!

SMIRNOV (*paying him no attention*). Fighting duels! Now that really is equality, that really is the emancipation of women! Both sexes level! I'll shoot her on principle! But what sort of woman is she? (*Mimics her.*) 'To hell with you . . . I'll put a bullet in your thick wooden head . . .' What sort of woman is that? She went quite red – her eyes flashed . . . She took up the challenge! Upon my soul, I've never seen such a thing in my life . . .

LUKA. Go away, sir! For the love of God, now!

SMIRNOV. This is something *like* a woman! This is something that makes sense to me! A real woman! Not some whingeing, whining, wishy-washy creature, but fire, gunpowder, skyrockets! Shame to kill her, even!

LUKA (*weeps*). Dear good sir, go away, go away!

SMIRNOV. I've taken a liking to her! A positive liking! Dimples and all! I'm even ready to forget the debt. I'm not in a rage any more. What an astonishing woman!

POPOVA *enters with the pistols.*

POPOVA. Here are the pistols. But before we fight, kindly show me how to use them. I've never held a pistol in my life.

LUKA. God save us! I'll go and fetch the gardener and the coachman. What brought this plague down on our heads?

*Exit* LUKA.

SMIRNOV (*examining the pistols*). Now, there are various different types of gun in use. There are special Mortimer percussion-lock duelling pistols. But these are revolvers. Smith and Wesson system – triple action with extractor, centre fire. Fine guns! Worth at least ninety rubles a pair. Now, you hold a revolver like this . . . (*Aside.*) Her eyes, though, her eyes! She'd start a forest fire with them!

POPOVA. Like that?

SMIRNOV. That's the way . . . Then you cock it . . . Take aim like this . . . Head back a little! Extend the arm properly . . . That's right . . . Then you press your finger on this little thing – and that's all there is to it. Rule number one: don't get excited, and don't rush taking aim. Try to keep your arm steady.

POPOVA. All right . . . Awkward, having a duel indoors. We'll go into the garden.

SMIRNOV. Right. I must warn you, though – I shall fire into the air.

POPOVA. This really is the limit! Why?

SMIRNOV. Because . . . because . . . That's my business!

POPOVA. What, lost your nerve? Have you? Aha! No, sir, you won't get out of it like that! Kindly follow me! I shan't rest until I've put a bullet into your head! Into this head here, this loathsome head! So, you've lost your nerve, have you?

SMIRNOV. Yes – lost my nerve.

POPOVA. You're lying! Why don't you want to fight?

SMIRNOV. Because . . . because . . . I've taken a liking to you.

POPOVA (*with an angry laugh*). He's taken a liking to me! He has the gall to say he's taken a liking to me! (*Pointing to the door.*) Please.

> SMIRNOV *silently lays down his revolver, takes his cap, and goes. He stops at the door, and for a while they look at each other in silence. Then he goes uncertainly across to her.*

SMIRNOV. Listen . . . Are you still angry with me? I'm as cross as two sticks myself, but the thing is . . . How can I put it . . .? Listen, the fact is, not to mince words, this is rather a how-do-you-do . . . (*Shouts.*) I mean, is it my fault if I like you? (*Seizes the back of a chair, which splinters and breaks.*) Very fragile furniture you've got, damn it! I like you! You see? I'm . . . I'm rather in love with you!

POPOVA. Get away from me! I hate you!

SMIRNOV. My God, but what a woman! I've never seen anything like it in my life! I'm finished! I'm done for! Caught like a mouse in a mousetrap.

POPOVA. Get back, or I'll fire!

SMIRNOV. Fire away! You don't know what happiness it would be to die in the sight of these miraculous eyes – to be shot by a revolver held by this tiny soft hand . . . I've gone mad! Decide now, because if I leave we shall never see each other again! I'm a landowner – decent sort – ten thousand a year – fine stable – hit a kopeck in the air . . . Will you be my wife?

POPOVA (*brandishing the revolver, outraged*). I demand satisfaction!

SMIRNOV. I've gone completely mad! Don't know what I'm doing . . . (*Shouts.*) Fellow! Water!

POPOVA (*shouts*). Give me satisfaction!

SMIRNOV. Mad as a hatter! Fallen in love like a schoolboy!

*He seizes her hand. She cries out in pain.*

I love you! (*Kneels.*) I love you as I've never loved before! Twelve women I've thrown over – been thrown over by nine more – but not one of them I loved the way I love you . . . Turned into a heap of jelly . . . Here I am, kneeling like an idiot, offering you my hand . . . Should be ashamed of myself! Haven't fallen in love for five years – swore to high heaven – and now all of a sudden – head over heels like a hunter off a horse! I'm proposing to you. Yes or no? Don't want to? Then don't! (*Gets up and goes quickly across to the door.*)

POPOVA. Wait . . .

SMIRNOV (*stops*). Well?

POPOVA. Nothing. Go . . . Or rather, wait . . . No – go, go! I hate the sight of you! Or no . . . Don't go! Oh, if you only knew what a rage I'm in, what a tearing rage! (*Throws the revolver down on the table.*) My fingers are all swollen from that horrible thing . . . (*Tears at her handkerchief in her fury.*) What are you standing there for? Get out!

SMIRNOV. Farewell.

POPOVA. Yes, yes – off you go, then! (*Shouts.*) Where are you going? Wait a moment . . . Oh, be off with you! Heavens, I'm in such a rage! Don't come near me, don't come near me!

SMIRNOV (*going to her*). I'm in a great rage with myself! Fallen in love like a schoolboy, got down on my knees . . . Gone hot and cold all over . . . (*Rudely.*) I love you! That's the last thing I need, to go falling in love with you! I've got the interest to pay, I've got the hay to get in, and now you on top of it all . . .

*Puts his arm round her waist.*

Never forgive myself for this . . .

POPOVA. Get away from me! Take your hands off me! I hate you!
I demand satisfaction!

*A prolonged kiss.*

*Enter* LUKA *holding an axe, the* GARDENER *with a rake, the*
COACHMAN *with a pitchfork, and* VARIOUS WORKMEN *with*
*staves.*

LUKA (*at the sight of the kissing couple*). Oh, Lord preserve us!

*Pause.*

POPOVA (*with downcast eyes*). Luka, tell them in the stables – no
oats for Toby at all today.

*Curtain.*

# The Proposal

# Characters

CHUBUKOV, *a landowner*
NATALYA STEPANOVNA, *his daughter,* (25)
LOMOV, *a neighbour of* CHUBUKOV's; *a plump, healthy, but very hypochondriacal landowner*

The action takes place on CHUBUKOV's estate, in the drawing-room of his house.

CHUBUKOV. *Enter* LOMOV, *in tails and white gloves.* CHUBUKOV *goes to meet him.*

CHUBUKOV. My dear fellow! Of all the people in the world! Ivan Vasilyevich! What a pleasure!

*Shakes his hand.*

What a surprise! My dear, dear fellow! How have you been keeping?

LOMOV. Oh . . . Thank you. And you, if I may ask?

CHUBUKOV. Oh, we keep quietly toddling along. Sustained by your prayers, and all the rest of it. Have a seat, I do most humbly beseech you . . . So good of you to remember your neighbours. But my dear good chap, why so formal? Tails, gloves, and all the rest of it? Not on your way somewhere, are you?

LOMOV. Only here, my dear Stepan Stepanich.

CHUBUKOV. Then why the tails, my dear old chap? It looks like New Year's Eve!

LOMOV. The thing is this. (*Takes him by the arm.*) I have a certain request to make. My dear Stepan Stepanich, this is not the first time I have had the honour of asking for your help, and you have always been – how shall I put it . . .? I'm sorry, I'm getting myself all worked up. My dear Stepan Stepanich . . . I'll just have a drink of water. (*Drinks water.*)

CHUBUKOV (*aside*). He's after money! He's not getting any! (*To* LOMOV:) So what's the trouble, then, my dear old fellow?

LOMOV. The thing is this, my dear my dear Stepanich . . . ah, Stepan Stepan Mydearich . . . I'm getting myself into a terrible state, as you can see . . . To put it in a nutshell, you're the only person who can help me, although of course I've done nothing to deserve it and . . . and I've not the slightest right to expect it . . .

CHUBUKOV. My dear good chap, don't prolong the agony! Get it off your chest! What is it?

LOMOV. Here we are, then. Without more ado. The thing is that I have come to ask for the hand of your daughter in marriage.

CHUBUKOV (*joyfully*). My dear dear dear dear fellow! Ivan Vasilyevich! Say it again – I'm not sure I heard aright . . .

LOMOV. I have the honour to ask for the . . .

CHUBUKOV (*interrupts him*). My dear dear dear dear dear dear fellow! I'm so delighted, and all the rest of it! Tickled to death, et cetera et cetera! (*Embraces and kisses him.*) Long been my dearest wish. (*Sheds a tear.*) My dear good dear old fellow! Always loved you like a son. God send you both love and harmony and all the rest of it. So looked forward to this day . . .! But why am I standing here like a complete imbecile? I'm stunned with joy, absolutely stunned! Oh, my heartfelt, heartfelt . . . I'll go and call her, et cetera et cetera.

LOMOV (*touched*). What do you think, my dear Stepan Stepanich – can I count on her acceptance?

CHUBUKOV. A handsome young fellow like yourself – look at you! – and she's going to up and say no? I should think she's as mad as a kitten about you, and so on . . . Stay there!

*Exit* CHUBUKOV.

LOMOV. Freezing . . . I'm shivering all over. Examination fever. Take the plunge – that's the main thing. Never get married if you keep thinking about it, keep hesitating, keep talking about it, keep waiting for some ideal love, some real love . . . Brrr . . . So cold! Natalya Stepanovna knows how to run a house, she's not bad-looking, she's educated . . . what more do I want? It's just that I'm in such a state I've got my buzzing in the ears coming on. (*Drinks water.*) I can't not get married, after all . . . In the first place I'm 35 – what people call the critical age. On top of which I need a regular, well-ordered life . . . I've got a weak heart – I keep having palpitations. I fly up easily – I'm always getting into a state about things . . . Here I am now – I've got a tremble in my lip and a twitch in my right eyelid . . .

But the worst thing is trying to sleep. I get into bed, and I'm just starting to drop off when I get this sudden thing in my left side – woomph! – and it goes straight up into my shoulder and head . . . I jump out of bed like a lunatic, I walk up and down for a bit, I lie down again, I'm just starting to drop off, when suddenly, in my left side again – woomph! If it happens once it happens a dozen times . . .

*Enter* NATALYA STEPANOVNA.

NATALYA. Oh, good Lord, it's you! Papa said, 'There's a man come to collect some goods.' Ivan Vasilyevich . . .

LOMOV. My dear Natalya Stepanovna!

NATALYA. Oh, and in my pinny, look – all any old how . . . We're podding the peas for drying. Why haven't we seen you for so long? Have a seat . . .

*They sit.*

Do you want some lunch?

LOMOV. I have eaten, thank you.

NATALYA. Do smoke if you want to . . . Matches, look . . . Wonderful weather. Such rain yesterday, though! The men didn't do a stroke all day. How much have you got in? Can you imagine, I just went guzzle guzzle – mowed the entire meadow. Now I'm regretting it. Frightened all my hay's going to rot. Should have waited. What's all this, though? Tails? Never thought I'd live to see you in tails! Off to a ball, are you? You're looking very handsome today, I must say . . . Why are you all dressed up like this?

LOMOV (*growing agitated*). Now, my dear Natalya Stepanovna . . . The thing is this. I have decided to ask you to . . . to listen to what I have to say. Now, this will of course come as something of a surprise – you may even be rather cross about it – but the point is this . . . (*Aside.*) So hideously cold!

NATALYA. What is it, then? (*Pause.*) Go on.

LOMOV. I shall be as brief as I can. You know, of course, my dear Natalya Stepanovna, that I have had the honour of being

acquainted with your family for a long time – since I was a child.
My dear departed aunt and her husband, from whom, as I
believe you know, I inherited my estate, always had the greatest
respect for your father and your dear departed mother. We
Lomovs and you Chubukovs have always been on very friendly
– one might almost say family – terms. My land, moreover, as
you know, marches with yours. My Ox Lea Meadows abut your
birchwoods.

NATALYA. Sorry, but I'm going to interrupt you. You say '*My*
Ox Lea Meadows.' Not yours, surely?

LOMOV. Mine, I think, yes.

NATALYA. Goodness gracious! Ox Lea Meadows are ours, not
yours!

LOMOV. I think not, my dear Natalya Stepanovna. I think mine.

NATALYA. This is news to me. How do they come to be yours?

LOMOV. How do you mean, how? I'm talking about the Ox Lea
Meadows that make a wedge between your birchwoods and
Burnt Swamp.

NATALYA. Exactly. They're ours.

LOMOV. No, you're wrong, my dear Natalya Stepanovna –
they're mine.

NATALYA. Oh, come, now, Ivan Vasilyevich. Since when have
they been yours?

LOMOV. Since when? They've always been ours, to the best of my
recollection.

NATALYA. I'm sorry, but really!

LOMOV. My dear Natalya Stepanovna, it's all there in the
documents. The ownership was at one time in dispute, that's
true. But now everyone knows they're mine. There's no dispute
about it. I think you'll find that my aunt's grandmother granted
the use of the meadows, rent-free for an unspecified period of
time, to your father's grandfather's peasants in consideration of
their making bricks for her. Your father's grandfather's
peasants enjoyed this rent-free use of the meadows for some
forty years and became accustomed to regard them as their own.
But then, when the land register was published . . .

NATALYA. It's not like that at all! My father and my great-grandfather both regarded their land as extending right up to Burnt Swamp – so Ox Lea Meadows were ours. What possible dispute can there be? I don't understand. I find all this rather vexing!

LOMOV. I'll show you the documents!

NATALYA. No, it's just your little joke, isn't it. Or else you're having me on. It's rather a shock, that's all. We own a piece of land for nearly three hundred years, and suddenly we're informed it's not ours! I'm sorry, but I can scarcely believe my ears . . . It's not the meadows I mind about. A dozen acres all told – they're not worth more than three hundred rubles or so. It's the unfairness of it that outrages me. Say what you like, but I cannot abide unfairness.

LOMOV. Listen to what I'm saying, I implore you! Your father's grandfather's peasants, as I have, I believe, already said, made bricks for my aunt's grandmother. My aunt's grandmother, wishing to do them a favour in return . . .

NATALYA. Aunts – grandmothers – grandfathers – I don't know what you're talking about! All I know is that the meadows are ours!

LOMOV. Excuse me, but they're mine!

NATALYA. Ours! You can stand there arguing all day – you can put on fifteen lots of tails – but they're ours, ours, ours! I've no wish to take what's yours and no great desire to lose what's mine, thank you very much!

LOMOV. It's not that I *want* the meadows – it's the principle of the thing. If *you* want them – please – I'll give you them.

NATALYA. *I* can perfectly well give them to *you*, for that matter, since they're mine! This is all very strange, to say the least. We've always thought of you as a good neighbour, as a friend. Last year we lent you our threshing-machine, which meant that we had to finish threshing our corn in November. And here you are treating us as if we were Gypsies! Giving me my own land! I'm sorry, but that's not very neighbourly! I think it's downright impertinence, if you want to know, . . .

LOMOV. So you're telling me I'm some kind of landgrabber, are you? Madam, never in my life have I laid a finger upon another man's land, and no one is going to make such an accusation with impunity. (*Moves rapidly across to the carafe and drinks water.*) Ox Lea Meadows are mine!

NATALYA. You're a liar! They're ours!

LOMOV. Mine!

NATALYA. Liar! I'm going to prove it to you! I'm going to send my men straight down there today to mow them!

LOMOV. You're what?

NATALYA. My men, today – they'll be down there mowing them!

LOMOV. I'll throw them out on their necks!

NATALYA. You wouldn't dare!

LOMOV (*clutching at his heart*). Ox Lea Meadows are mine! You understand? Mine!

NATALYA. Don't shout at me, thank you! You can shout and wheeze with rage at home, but while you're here I must ask you to keep yourself under control!

LOMOV. If I were not in terrible agony with these palpitations, madam, if the blood were not pounding in my temples, I should take a very different tone with you! (*Shouts.*) Ox Lea Meadows are mine!

NATALYA. They're ours!

LOMOV. They're mine!

NATALYA. They're ours!

LOMOV. They're mine!

*Enter* CHUBUKOV.

CHUBUKOV. What? What? What? What's all this shouting?

NATALYA. Papa, explain to this gentleman, will you, who Ox Lea Meadows belong to – us or him?

CHUBUKOV (*to* LOMOV). My dear fellow, they're ours!

LOMOV. Excuse me, Stepan Stepanich, but how do they come to be yours? Don't *you* start being unreasonable as well! My aunt's grandmother granted temporary rent-free use of the meadows to your grandfather's peasants. The peasants enjoyed this use of the land for forty years and became accustomed to regard it as their own. But when the register was published . . .

CHUBUKOV. My dear sweet man, forgive me. You're forgetting that the peasants didn't pay your aunt's grandmother, and all the rest of it, precisely because at that time the ownership of the meadows was in dispute, et cetera et cetera. But the point is that now, as any fool knows, they're ours. You obviously haven't seen the land register!

LOMOV. But I can prove to you they're mine!

CHUBUKOV. My dear darling man, you can't!

LOMOV. I can!

CHUBUKOV. Dearest heart, why are you shouting like this? You won't prove anything by shouting. I've no wish to take what's yours, and absolutely no intention at all of giving up what's mine. Why should I? If it came right down to it, and you were absolutely determined to lay claim to the meadows, then, my dear sweet dear dear darling fellow, I should sooner give it to the peasants than you. So there!

LOMOV. I don't understand! What right do you have to give away other people's property?

CHUBUKOV. I'll be the judge of what right I have, thank you very much. And by the by, young man, I'm not used to having that tone taken with me, and all the rest of it. I'm twice as old as you are, young man, and I'll thank you to keep a civil tongue in your head, et cetera et cetera.

LOMOV. No, but you just take me for a fool, don't you – you think you can laugh at me. You call my land yours – and then you expect me to keep calm and talk to you politely! That's not the way good neighbours should behave! You're not a neighbour – you're a landgrabber!

CHUBUKOV. What was that? What did you say?

NATALYA. Papa, go straight out and send the men down to mow the meadows!

CHUBUKOV (to LOMOV). What was that you said, my dear sir?

NATALYA. Ox Lea Meadows are ours, and I won't ever give them up, I won't, I won't!

LOMOV. We'll see about that! I'm going to prove to you in court that they're mine.

CHUBUKOV. In court? Well might you go to court, my dear sir! Well might you! I know you! This is precisely what you've been waiting for, a chance to go to court, and all the rest of it. You're a born troublemaker! All your family were! Troublemakers, the lot of them!

LOMOV. I'll thank you not to insult my family! The Lomovs have all been honest citizens. None of them who've ever been taken to court for embezzlement, like your uncle!

CHUBUKOV. No, but the Lomovs have all been mad!

NATALYA. All of them! All of them! All of them!

CHUBUKOV. Your grandfather drank like a fish, and all the rest of it, and this famous aunt of yours – her younger sister ran off with an architect!

LOMOV. And your mother was deformed! (*Clutches at his heart.*) Woomph! – in my side! Feel the blood rushing to my head! Oh, my heavens! Water, water!

CHUBUKOV. And your father did nothing but gorge and gamble!

NATALYA. And your aunt was the biggest gossip in the neighbourhood!

LOMOV. My left leg's paralysed . . . And as for you, you underhand schemer . . . Oh, my heart . . .! Everyone knows what you were up to at the elections . . . I've got spots before the eyes . . . Where's my hat?

NATALYA. How low! How dishonourable! How vile!

CHUBUKOV. What about you, then, you two-faced conniving snake-in-the-grass! Yes, sir – you, sir!

LOMOV. Hat . . . Heart . . . Which way am I going? Where's the door? Oh, I think I'm dying . . . Can't pick my foot up . . . (*Goes to the door.*)

CHUBUKOV (*following him*). Then drag it out after you and don't ever bring it back!

NATALYA. Take us to court! We'll see what happens!

LOMOV *stumbles out.*

CHUBUKOV. So much for him! (*Walks up and down in agitation.*)

NATALYA. So much for good neighbours!

CHUBUKOV. The scoundrel! The scarecrow!

NATALYA. The monster! Takes your land – then turns round and curses you!

CHUBUKOV. And you know what? This hobgoblin, this walking blight, has the cheek to come here and propose! How about that?

NATALYA. Propose? How do you mean, propose?

CHUBUKOV. How do I mean, propose? I mean he came here to propose to you!

NATALYA. To propose? To me? Why on earth didn't you say so before?

CHUBUKOV. Got himself up in his tails to do it! The stupid little sausage!

NATALYA. He was going to propose to me? Ah! (*Falls into the armchair and moans.*) Get him back! Ah! Get him back! Get him back!

CHUBUKOV. Get him back?

NATALYA. Quick, quick! I'm going to faint! Get him back! (*Has hysterics.*)

CHUBUKOV. What is it? What's the matter? (*Clutches his head.*) Oh, what a wretched fate is mine! I'll shoot myself! I'll hang myself! They're all driving me mad!

NATALYA. I'm dying! Get him back!

CHUBUKOV. All right! I'll get him! Don't howl! (*Runs out.*)

NATALYA (*alone, moaning*). What have we done? What have we done? Get him back!

CHUBUKOV (*runs back in*). He's coming, he's coming! You'll have to talk to him yourself – I'm damned if I'm going to.

NATALYA (*moaning*). Get him back!

CHUBUKOV (*shouting*). I've told you – he's coming! Oh, Lord in heaven, what a profession, being the father of a grown-up daughter! I'll cut my throat! I will – I'll cut my throat! We've cursed the fellow uphill and down, we've shamed him, we've thrown him out – and you're the one who did it! Yes, you!

NATALYA. Me? It was you!

CHUBUKOV. Oh, of course, it was all my fault!

     LOMOV *appears in the doorway.*

Well, you talk to him yourself!

     *Exit* CHUBUKOV.

LOMOV (*enters, in an exhausted state*). Terrible palpitations . . . My leg's gone numb . . . Pain in my side . . .

NATALYA. Forgive me, we became a little heated . . . I remember now – Ox Lea Meadows *are* yours.

LOMOV. My heart's beating like a drum . . . Mine, the Meadows, yes . . . I've got a twitch in both eyelids . . .

NATALYA. Yours, the Meadows, yours, yours. Have a seat, do . . .

     *They sit.*

Yes, we were wrong.

LOMOV. It was just the principle of the thing. I don't care about the land, but I do care about the principle of the thing . . .

NATALYA. The principle – exactly . . . But let's talk about something else.

LOMOV. Particularly since I have *proof.* My aunt's grandmother granted your father's grandfather's peasants . . .

NATALYA. Yes, yes, yes . . . (*Aside.*) I don't know where to start . . . (*To* LOMOV:) Shall you be going hunting again soon?

LOMOV. For blackcock, yes – I'm hoping to start after the harvest. Oh, but have you heard? Such bad luck. You remember Finder? He's gone lame.

NATALYA. Oh, no! How did that happen?

LOMOV. No idea . . . He must have dislocated something or got bitten by the other dogs. (*Sighs.*) My best dog, not to mention the money! You know I paid 125 rubles for him?

NATALYA. Oh, too much, Ivan Vasilyevich, too much!

LOMOV. I thought it was a bargain. He's a wonderful dog.

NATALYA. Papa got Flyer for 85 rubles, and after all, Flyer's a vastly better dog than Finder.

LOMOV. Flyer? Better than Finder? What do you mean? (*Laughs.*) Flyer is better than Finder?

NATALYA. Well, of course he is! Flyer's young, certainly, he's not out of his puppy coat yet, but in his line, in his action, you won't find a better dog in the country.

LOMOV. Forgive me, but you're forgetting his jaw, surely. He's undershot, and undershot dogs always have a poor bite!

NATALYA. Undershot? First I've heard of it!

LOMOV. I assure you – his bottom jaw's shorter than his top jaw.

NATALYA. You've measured them, have you?

LOMOV. Yes – I've measured them! He's all right for coursing, certainly, but when it comes to holding, well . . .

NATALYA. In the first place, Flyer is a pure-bred borzoi, by Harness out of Chiseller, whereas heaven alone knows where your spotty mongrel sprang from. In the second place, your dog is as old as the hills and as ugly as sin.

LOMOV. Old he may be, but I shouldn't swap him for five of your Flyers. What? – Finder's a dog – Flyer's a – well, it's ridiculous! Dogs like that – they're as common as dirt – every little whipper-in's got one. 25 rubles at the outside.

NATALYA. There's some demon of contradiction got into you today, Ivan Vasilyevich. First you claim the meadows are yours, then you claim Finder's better than Flyer. I can't bear people who won't say that they really think. You know perfectly well that Flyer's a hundred times better than that stupid Finder of yours, so why say the opposite?

LOMOV. You obviously think I'm blind or stupid. Can't you understand that Flyer is undershot?

NATALYA. He's not.

LOMOV. He's undershot!

NATALYA (*shouts*). He's not!

LOMOV. Then why are you shouting, madam?

NATALYA. Why are you talking nonsense? It's absolutely outrageous! Your Finder is ready to be put down, and here you are comparing him with Flyer!

LOMOV. I'm sorry, but I can pursue this debate no further. I am
suffering from palpitations of the heart.

NATALYA. I've noticed with sportsmen that the ones who talk
most are the ones who have least idea what they're talking
about.

LOMOV. Be quiet, madam, I beg of you. I'm about to have a heart
attack . . . (*Shouts.*) Be quiet!

NATALYA. I shan't be quiet until you admit that Flyer is a
hundred times better than your Finder!

LOMOV. He isn't – he's a hundred times worse! I hope he drops
dead! Oh, my head . . . my eyes . . . my shoulder . . .

NATALYA. Yes, well, there's no need for your Finder to drop
dead, because he's dead already!

LOMOV (*weeps*). Be quiet, will you! I'm having a heart attack!

NATALYA. I won't be quiet!

*Enter* CHUBUKOV.

CHUBUKOV. *Now* what's happening?

NATALYA. Papa, just tell us frankly, in all honesty. Which is the
better dog – our Flyer or his Finder?

LOMOV. Stepan Stepanich, I implore you, just tell us one thing.
Is Flyer undershot or is he not? Yes or no?

CHUBUKOV. What if he is? What does it matter? There still isn't
a better dog in the whole district, and all the rest of it.

LOMOV. But in fact my Finder's better, isn't he. In all honesty!

CHUBUKOV. Don't get excited, my dear fellow. Listen. Your
Finder has his points, by all means. He's pure-bred, he's strong
on his feet, and he's got a good fallaway. But, my dear dear
fellow, if you want to know the truth, that dog has two bad
faults. He's old, and he has a short muzzle.

LOMOV. I'm sorry, I'm having palpitations of the heart . . . Let's
just look at the facts . . . In Maruskin's cornfield, if you recall,
my Finder ran neck and neck with the count's Tormentor,
while your Flyer was half a mile behind.

CHUBUKOV. He was behind because the count's man had taken
the whip to him.

LOMOV. Yes, and for good reason! All the other dogs were after a fox – your Flyer was after a sheep!

CHUBUKOV. That's not true! My dear good man, I have a very short fuse, so let's bring this discussion to an end. The count's man took the whip to him because everyone's jealous of their neighbour's dog. They all hate everyone else! You're not beyond reproach yourself, sir! As soon as you notice that someone's dog is better than your Finder you immediately start all this kind of thing . . . I haven't forgotten, you know!

LOMOV. I haven't forgotten, either!

NATALYA (*mimics him*). I haven't forgotten, either . . . And what is it *you* haven't forgotten?

LOMOV. Palpitations . . . Leg's gone again . . . Can't move . . .

NATALYA (*mimics him*). Palpitations . . . Fine one you are to go hunting! You should be in bed over the kitchen stove, like someone's grandfather! You should be squashing cockroaches, not hunting foxes! Palpitations . . .

CHUBUKOV. Yes! Hunting, indeed! You should be sitting at home with these palpitations of yours, not running round on top of a horse. It's not as if you actually hunted – all you go for is to pick quarrels and get in the way of other people's dogs, et cetera et cetera. I have a very short fuse, so let's leave it at that. A hunter! You're not a hunter!

LOMOV. And you think you're a hunter, do you? All you go for is to suck up to the count and get on with your scheming! Oh, my heart! You . . . schemer!

CHUBUKOV. What? A schemer, sir? Me, sir? (*Shouts.*) Hold your tongue, sir!

LOMOV. Schemer!

CHUBUKOV. You young puppy!

LOMOV. You old rat! You Jesuit!

CHUBUKOV. Hold your tongue, or I'll shoot you like a partridge! You blatherskite!

LOMOV. Everyone knows – oh, my heart! – your poor wife used to beat you . . . My leg . . . my head . . . my vision's gone . . . I can't stand up!

CHUBUKOV. Your housekeeper's got you on a piece of string!

LOMOV. Go on, go on, go on . . . I'm having a heart attack! My shoulder's missing! Where's my shoulder . . .? I'm dying! (*Falls into an armchair.*) Doctor! Get a doctor! (*Faints.*)

CHUBUKOV. Little whippersnapper! Little milksop! Little blatherskite! I feel faint. (*Drinks water.*) I'm going to faint!

NATALYA. A hunter! Don't make me laugh! You can't even sit on a horse! (*To her father:*) Papa! What's wrong with him? Papa – look at him! (*Screams.*) He's dead!

CHUBUKOV. I'm going to faint! I can't breathe! Air, give me some air!

NATALYA. He's dead! (*Pulls at* LOMOV's *sleeve.*) Ivan Vasily-evich! Ivan Vasilyevich! What have we done? He's dead! (*Falls into an armchair.*) A doctor! Fetch a doctor! (*Has hysterics.*)

CHUBUKOV. What? What? What's the matter with you?

NATALYA (*moans*). He's dead . . . dead . . .!

CHUBUKOV. Who's dead? (*Looks at* LOMOV.) So he is! Heavens above! Water! Fetch a doctor!

*Lifts a glass to* LOMOV's *lips.*

Come on, have a drink . . . He's not drinking . . . He's dead, then, and all the rest of it . . . Oh, did any man have such wretched luck as me? Why don't I put a bullet through my head? How have I come all this way in life without cutting my throat? What am I waiting for? Give me a knife! Give me a pistol!

*LOMOV stirs.*

He's coming round! Here, have some water! That's more like it . . .

LOMOV. Spots . . . Mist . . . Where am I?

CHUBUKOV. For heaven's sake, just marry her, and get it over with! She says yes!

*Joins* LOMOV *and his daughter's hands.*

The answer's yes, and all the rest of it! I give you my blessing, et cetera et cetera. Just leave me in peace, that's all I ask!

LOMOV. Um? What? (*Gets up.*) Who?

CHUBUKOV. She said yes! All right? Give her a kiss and . . . and to hell with it!

NATALYA (*moans*). He's alive . . . Yes, yes, I'm saying yes.

CHUBUKOV. Give her a kiss, then!

LOMOV. Who – her?

*Kisses* NATALYA STEPANOVNA.

Oh, very nice . . . I'm sorry – what's all this about? Oh, yes, I know . . . My heart . . . All these spots . . . No, I'm very happy . . .

*Kisses her hand.*

Leg's gone . . .

NATALYA. I'm . . . yes, very happy, too.

CHUBUKOV. That's a load off my mind . . . Phew!

NATALYA. Anyway, you can admit it now. Flyer's a better dog than Finder.

LOMOV. No, he's not!

NATALYA. Yes, he is!

CHUBUKOV. The start of another happy marriage! Champagne!

LOMOV. He's not a better dog!

NATALYA. He is! He is! He is!

CHUBUKOV (*struggling to shout them down*). Champagne! Champagne! Champagne!

*Curtain*

# The Seagull

This translation of *The Seagull* was first performed at the Palace Theatre, Watford on 7 November 1986, with the following cast:

| | |
|---|---|
| ARKADINA, *an actress* | Prunella Scales |
| KONSTANTIN, *her son* | Lorcan Cranitch |
| SORIN, *her brother* | Antony Brown |
| NINA, *the young daughter of a wealthy landowner* | Irina Brook |
| SHAMRAYEV, *a retired lieutenant, Sorin's steward* | Donald Morley |
| POLINA, *his wife* | Jan Carey |
| MASHA, *his daughter* | Ingrid Craigie |
| TRIGORIN, *a novelist* | Paul Shelley |
| DORN, *a doctor* | Denys Hawthorne |
| MEDVEDENKO, *a teacher* | Tim Preece |
| YAKOV, *a workman* | Stephen Gray |
| SERVANTS | Ian Connaghan |
| | Ewan MacKinnon |
| A MAID | Emma Bingham |

| | |
|---|---|
| *Directed by* | Patrick Mason |
| *Designed by* | Joe Vanek |
| *Lighting by* | Mark Pritchard |

The action takes place on Sorin's country estate.
Between Acts Three and Four two years have elapsed.

It was subsequently produced by the Royal Shakespeare Company at the Swan Theatre, Stratford-on-Avon, on 31 October 1990, and is due to be produced in July 1991 in London at the Barbican, with the following cast:

| | |
|---|---|
| ARKADINA, *an actress* | Susan Fleetwood |
| KONSTANTIN, *her son* | Simon Russell Beale |
| SORIN, *her brother* | Alfred Burke |
| NINA, *the young daughter of a wealthy landowner* | Amanda Root |
| SHAMRAYEV, *a retired lieutenant,*<br>Sorin's steward | Trevor Martin |
| POLINA, *his wife* | Cherry Morris |
| MASHA, *his daughter* | Katy Behean |
| TRIGORIN, *a novelist* | Roger Allan |
| DORN, *a doctor* | John Carlisle |
| MEDVEDENKO, *a teacher* | Graham Turner |
| YAKOV, *a workman* | Arnold Yarrow |
| A MAN COOK | David Summer |
| A MAID | Mary Chater |

| | |
|---|---|
| *Directed by* | Terry Hands |
| *Designed by* | Johan Engels |
| *Lighting by* | Terry Hands and<br>Wayne Dowdeswell |

# Act One

*A section of the park on* SORIN's *estate. A broad avenue leads away from the audience into the depths of the park towards the lake. The avenue is closed off by a stage which has been hurriedly run up for some home entertainment, so that the lake is completely invisible. Right and left of the stage is a shrubbery. A few chairs and a garden table.*

*The sun has just set. On the improvised stage, behind the lowered curtain, are* YAKOV *and other* WORKMEN; *coughing and banging can be heard.* MASHA *and* MEDVEDENKO *enter left, on their way back from a walk.*

MEDVEDENKO. Why do you always wear black?

MASHA. I'm in mourning for my life. I'm unhappy.

MEDVEDENKO. Why? (*Reflectively.*) I don't understand. You've got your health. Your father may not be rich, but he's not badly off. I have a much harder time than you. I get 23 rubles a month all told – less deductions for the pension – and I don't go round in mourning.

*They sit.*

MASHA. It's not a question of money. Even a beggar can be happy.

MEDVEDENKO. Theoretically. In practice it comes down to this: my mother and I, plus my two sisters and my little brother – and only 23 rubles a month coming in. You mean we don't have to eat and drink? There's no need for tea and sugar? No need for tobacco? I don't know how to manage.

MASHA (*looking round at the improvised stage*). The show will be starting soon.

MEDVEDENKO. Yes. A play written by Konstantin, and his

Nina will be acting in it. Two people in love, and today their souls will merge as they strive to create a single artistic impression. Whereas my soul and yours have no point of contact. I love you – I can't stay at home I long to see you so much – I walk three miles here and three miles back every day – and all I get from you is indifference. Well, it's understandable. I've no money – I've a large family . . . Who wants to marry a man who can't even support himself?

MASHA. Oh, fiddle. (*Takes a pinch of snuff.*) I'm very touched that you love me, but I can't say the same in return, and that's all there is to it. (*Offers him the snuffbox.*) Have a pinch.

MEDVEDENKO. Not for me.

*Pause.*

MASHA. So close. We'll probably have a storm during the night. If you're not philosophising you're going on about money. You seem to think the worst thing that can happen to anyone is poverty, but I think it's a thousand times easier to go round in rags and beg your bread than it is to . . . Well, you wouldn't understand . . .

*Enter, right,* SORIN *and* KONSTANTIN.

SORIN (*leaning on a stick*). The thing with me, though, is that I somehow never feel quite up to the mark when I'm in the country. No question about it – I'll never get used to being here. Went to bed at ten last night and woke up at nine this morning feeling I'd slept for so long that my brain had stuck to my skull, etcetera, etcetera. (*Laughs.*) Then after dinner I dropped off again, and now I feel as if a horse and cart had gone over me. It's like being in a bad dream, when all's said and done . . .

KONSTANTIN. You're right – you ought to be living in town. (*Sees* MASHA *and* MEDVEDENKO.) Listen, you'll be called when it starts – you're not supposed to be here now. Go away, will you.

SORIN (*to* MASHA). And would you mind asking your father to have the dog let loose? It howls otherwise. My sister was awake all night again.

MASHA. You can talk to my father yourself – I'm not going to. Spare me that, at any rate. (*To* MEDVEDENKO.) Come on, then.

MEDVEDENKO (*to* KONSTANTIN). You'll let us know before it starts, then.

*Exeunt* MASHA *and* MEDVEDENKO.

SORIN. So the dog will be howling all night again. It's a funny thing – I've never been able to live as I please when I've been in the country. In the old days I used to take a month's leave and come here to relax, simple as that, but then they'd so pester you with all kinds of nonsense that from the moment you arrived you'd want to be away again . . . Now I'm retired, though, there's nowhere else to go, when all's said and done. Like it or lump it . . .

YAKOV (*to* KONSTANTIN). We're off for a swim, then.

KONSTANTIN. All right, but I want you standing by in ten minutes time. (*Looks at his watch.*) Not long before it starts.

YAKOV. Sir.

*Exit* YAKOV.

KONSTANTIN (*glancing over the improvised stage*). Now how about this for a theatre. Curtain at the front, wings at the side – then nothing beyond but empty space. No scenery. The back of the stage opening straight on to the lake and the horizon. The curtain goes up at half-past eight precisely, as the moon rises.

SORIN. Splendid.

KONSTANTIN. If Nina's late then of course the whole effect will be ruined. She ought to be here by now. Her father and stepmother keep guard over her – getting out of the house is like escaping from prison. (*Adjusts his uncle's tie.*) Your hair needs a comb through it – so does your beard. You could do with a trim, couldn't you?

SORIN (*combing his beard*). It's the tragedy of my life. Even as a young man I always looked as though I'd been at the bottle, simple as that. Women never liked me. (*Sitting down.*) Why is my sister out of sorts?

KONSTANTIN. Why? Because she's bored. (*Sitting down beside him.*) Because she's jealous. She's already set her mind against me, and against having theatricals, and against my play, in case her novelist takes a fancy to Nina. She doesn't know anything about my play, but she already hates it.

SORIN (*laughs*). Oh, come, come . . .

KONSTANTIN. She's already vexed that in this one little theatre it's Nina who will have the success, and not her. (*Looks at his watch.*) A comic tale of human psychology, my mother. Talented, unquestionably; intelligent, quite capable of being moved by a book. Recite you the whole of Nekrasov by heart. Ministers to the sick like an angel. But you try saying something nice about Duse in her hearing! Oh dear me no! She's the one who has to have the nice things said about her and no one else, she's the one who has to be written about, shouted about, admired for her extraordinary performance in *La Dame aux Camélias*, or whatever; and because this drug isn't available here in the country she gets bored and ill-tempered, and all of us become her enemies – it's all our fault. Then again she's superstitious – she's afraid of three candles and the thirteenth of the month. She's mean with her money. She's got seventy thousand rubles sitting in a bank in Odessa – I know that for a fact. But ask her if you can borrow some and she'll burst into tears.

SORIN. You've got it into your head that your mother doesn't like your play, and you're working yourself up about it in advance, simple as that. Calm down, now – your mother worships you.

KONSTANTIN (*pulling the petals off a flower*). She loves me – she loves me not . . . She loves me – loves me not . . . Loves me – loves me not. (*Laughs.*) There you are – she doesn't love me. Well, of course she doesn't. She wants to live and love and dress in light colours, and there am I, twenty-five years old, perpetually reminding her that she's stopped being young. When I'm not there she's thirty-two – when I am she's forty-three; and that's why she hates me. Then again I don't acknowledge the theatre. She loves the theatre – she thinks she's serving humanity and the sacred cause of art, whereas in my view the modern theatre is an anthology of stereotypes and received ideas. When the curtain goes up, and there, in a room with three walls lit by artificial lighting because it's always evening, these great artists, these high priests in the temple of art, demonstrate how people eat and drink, how they love and walk about and wear their suits; when out of these banal scenes and trite words they attempt to extract a moral – some small and simple moral with a hundred household uses; when under a thousand different disguises they keep serving me up the same old thing, the same old thing, the same old thing – then I run and don't stop running, just as Maupassant ran from the sight of the Eiffel Tower, that weighed on his brain with its sheer vulgarity.

SORIN. We couldn't do without the theatre.

KONSTANTIN. What we need are new artistic forms. And if we don't get new forms it would be better if we had nothing at all. (*Looks at his watch.*) I love my mother, I love her deeply. But then she smokes, she drinks, she quite openly lives with that novelist, they're always bandying her name about in the papers – and I'm sick of it. Though sometimes what prompts me is just ordinary mortal egotism; I start to regret that my mother is a well-known actress, and I feel I should be happier if she were an ordinary woman. Uncle, what could be sillier or more hopeless than the position I've found myself in often enough: solid rows of celebrities sitting in her drawing-room, artists and writers, and me the only one among them who's a nobody, being put up with purely because I'm her son. Who am I? What am I? I left university half-way through owing to circumstances beyond the editor's control, as the phrase goes; I've no talents; I've no money; while according to my passport I'm a shopkeeper, a Kiev shopkeeper. My father *did* come from Kiev, of course – he *was* from the shopkeeping classes – although he was also a well-known actor. So that when all those artists and writers in her drawing-room would turn their gracious attention upon me I had the impression that with every glance they were measuring the depth of my nonentity. I could guess what they were thinking, and the humiliation of it hurt . . .

SORIN. Speaking of writers, tell me, what sort of fellow is this novelist of hers? Difficult to make him out. He never says anything.

KONSTANTIN. He's intelligent, straightforward, a person of somewhat – shall we say? – melancholy disposition. A very decent sort of man. He's still well short of forty, but he's already famous and thoroughly jaded . . . These days he drinks nothing but beer and has no time for young people. If we're talking about his work then it's – how can I put it? – well, it's charming, it's clever . . but . . if you've read Tolstoy or Zola then you won't want to read Trigorin.

SORIN. Yes, but take me, now – I've a soft spot for literary men. Once upon a time there were two things I passionately wanted in life: I wanted to marry and I wanted to become a literary man, and I never managed either. So there we are. Nice to be even a minor literary man, when all's said and done.

KONSTANTIN (*listens*). I can hear footsteps . . . (*Embraces his uncle.*) I can't live without her . . . Even the sound of her footsteps is wonderful . . . I'm so happy I don't know what I'm doing!

*Goes quickly across to meet* NINA *as she enters.*

My enchantress, my dream . . .

NINA (*anxiously*). I'm not late . . . Tell me I'm not late . . .

KONSTANTIN (*kissing her hands*). No, no, no . . .

NINA. I've been worrying about it all day. I was so terrified! I was afraid my father wouldn't let me go . . . But he's just gone out with my stepmother. The sky red – the moon already starting to rise – and I kept whipping and whipping the horse. (*Laughs.*) I'm glad, though. (*Firmly presses* SORIN's *hand.*)

SORIN (*laughs*). We've been crying, haven't we . . . We can't have that, now.

NINA. It's nothing . . . Look how out of breath I am. I'm going in half-an-hour, we must hurry. You mustn't, mustn't, for heaven's sake, make me late. My father doesn't know I'm here.

KONSTANTIN. It's time to start, in any case. We must go and call everyone.

SORIN. I'll do it. Right away, simple as that. (*Goes off right, singing Schumann's 'Two Grenadiers', then looks round.*) I started singing like that once, and one of the deputy prosecutors looked at me and said: 'You know, sir, you have a very powerful voice.' Then he thought for a moment and he added: 'Very powerful, but very disagreeable.' (*Laughs and goes off.*)

NINA. My father and his wife won't let me come here. They say you're all Bohemians . . . They're afraid I might run off to be an actress . . . But it's the lake that draws me here, like a seagull . . . My heart's full of you. (*Looks round.*)

KONSTANTIN. We're alone.

NINA. I think there's someone there . . .

*They kiss.*

NINA. What sort of tree is that?

KONSTANTIN. Elm.

NINA. Why does it have such a dark colour?

KONSTANTIN. It's evening – everything looks dark. Don't go early, please don't.

NINA. I can't stay.

KONSTANTIN. Supposing I came to your house, Nina? I'll stand in the garden all night and look up at your window.

NINA. You can't – the watchman will see you. Treasure's not used to you yet – he'll bark.

KONSTANTIN. I love you.

NINA. Shh . . .

KONSTANTIN (*hearing footsteps*). Who's that? Is that you, Yakov?

YAKOV (*behind the improvised stage*). Sir.

KONSTANTIN. Stand by. Time to start. Is the moon rising?

YAKOV. Sir.

KONSTANTIN. Have you got the spirits? And the sulphur? When the red eyes appear there must be a smell of sulphur. (*To* NINA.) Go on, then, it's all ready. Are you nervous?

NINA. Yes, very. I don't mind your mother, I'm not afraid of her, but you've got Trigorin here . . . When I think of acting in front of him I'm terrified, I'm ashamed . . . He's a famous writer . . . Is he young?

KONSTANTIN. Yes, he is.

NINA. Such wonderful stories he writes!

KONSTANTIN (*coldly*). I wouldn't know. I haven't read them.

NINA. Your play's so difficult to do. It doesn't have any living characters.

KONSTANTIN. Living characters! The point is not to show life the way it is, or the way it ought to be, but the way it comes to you in dreams.

NINA. It doesn't have much action, your play – it's just a kind of recitation. And I think a play absolutely has to have love in it . . .

*They both go behind the improvised stage. Enter* POLINA *and* DORN.

POLINA. It's getting damp. Go back and put your galoshes on.

DORN. I'm hot.

POLINA. You won't look after yourself. It's just pig-headedness. You're a doctor – you know perfectly well that dampness in the air is bad for you, but no, you want to make me suffer. Last night you sat out on the verandah all evening just to spite me . . .

*DORN hums.*

You were so wrapped up in your conversation with *her* – you never noticed the cold. Admit it, now – you're fond of her.

DORN. I'm fifty-five.

POLINA. Oh, fiddle, that's not old for a man. You're perfectly well preserved and you're still attractive to women.

DORN. So what do you want me to do?

POLINA. You'll all bow down in front of an actress. Not one of you who won't!

DORN (*hums*). If artists are popular people, if they get treated differently from – what shall we say? – from businessmen, then that's the way the world's made. That's our yearning for higher things.

POLINA. You've always had women falling in love with you and hanging round your neck. Is that supposed to be a yearning for higher things?

DORN (*shrugs*). If you like. There's been much that was good in the relationships women have had with me. What they liked most about me was the fact I was a first-class doctor. Ten years or so back, you may recall, I was the only one in the whole province who could deliver a baby decently. Added to which I was always a man of honour.

POLINA (*seizes his hand*). Oh, my dear!

DORN. Hush, now. They're coming.

*Enter* ARKADINA *on* SORIN's *arm,* TRIGORIN, SHAMRAYEV, MEDVEDENKO, *and* MASHA.

SHAMRAYEV. In 1873, at Poltava during the Fair, she gave an amazing performance. Sheer delight! A wonderful performance! And do you know where Chadin is these days, the comic actor? In *Krechinsky's Wedding* there was no one to touch him – he was better than Sadovsky, I promise you, dear lady. Where is he these days?

ARKADINA. You keep asking me about people who came out of the Ark! How should I know? (*Sits.*)

SHAMRAYEV (*sighs*). Pashka Chadin! They don't make them like that any more. The theatre's not what it was. Once there were mighty oaks – now we see mere stumps.

DORN. There's not much in the way of brilliant talent these days, it's true, but your average actor is of a much higher standard.

SHAMRAYEV. I can't agree. Though it's all a question of taste. *De gustibus aut bene aut nihil.*

KONSTANTIN *comes out from behind the improvised stage.*

ARKADINA (*to* KONSTANTIN). 'Come hither, my dear Hamlet, sit by me . . .' My precious, when's it going to begin?

KONSTANTIN. In a minute. If you would just be patient.

ARKADINA. 'O Hamlet, speak no more:
Thou turn'st mine eyes into my very soul;
And there I see such black and grained spots
As will not leave their tinct.'

KONSTANTIN. 'Nay, but to live
In the rank sweat of an enseamed bed
Stew'd in corruption, honeying and making love
Over the nasty sty . . .'

*A horn sounds behind the improvised stage.*

Ladies and gentlemen, the performance is about to begin. Your attention, if you please. (*Pause.*) I'm going to start. (*Knocks with a stick and speaks in a loud voice.*) You honoured ancient shades that hover in the hours of night above this lake, make our eyes grow heavy, and let us dream of what will be in two hundred thousand years from now!

SORIN. In two hundred thousand years from now there won't be anything.

KONSTANTIN. Then let them show us this not-anything.

ARKADINA. Let them. We're fast asleep.

*The curtain rises. The view over the lake is revealed, with the moon above the horizon and its reflection in the water. On a large stone sits NINA, all in white.*

NINA. Men and lions, partridges and eagles, spiders, geese, and antlered stags, the unforthcoming fish that dwelt beneath the waters, starfish and creatures invisible to the naked eye; in short – all life, all life, all life, its dismal round concluded, has guttered out . . . Thousands of centuries have passed since any living creature walked the earth, and this poor moon in vain lights up her lantern. In the meadows the dawn cry of the crane is heard no more, and the May bugs are silent in the lime groves. Cold, cold, cold. Empty, empty, empty. Fearful, fearful, fearful. (*Pause.*) The bodies of all living creatures have fallen into dust, and Everlasting Matter has turned them into stones, into water, into clouds; while all their souls have merged into one. And this one universal world soul is me . . . me . . . In me are the souls of Alexander the Great, of Caesar, of Shakespeare, of Napoleon, and of the least of leeches. In me the consciousness of human beings has merged with the instincts of animals. All, all, all do I remember, and every life I live again in my own self.

*Marsh-lights appear.*

ARKADINA (*quietly*). A touch of the Decadent School here, I think.

KONSTANTIN (*pleading and reproachful*). Mama!

NINA. I am quite alone. Once in every hundred years I open my lips to speak, and my voice echoes cheerlessly through this emptiness where no one listens . . . Even you, pale fires, are not listening to me . . . In the late watches of the night you are born from the rotting swamp, and wander the world till dawn, yet without the power of thought or will, without a flicker of life. For fear that life might appear to you, the Father of Eternal Matter, who is the Devil, effects in you, as he does in stones and water, a constant replacement of the atoms, and you are in a state of continual flux. One thing alone in the universe stays unchanging and constant – spirit itself. (*Pause.*) Like a prisoner flung into some deep dry well I have no knowledge of where I am or of what awaits me. All I am allowed to know is that in this stubborn, bitter struggle with the Devil, marshal of all material forces, I am fated to be victor; and that matter and spirit will thereafter merge in wondrous harmony to usher in the reign of Universal Will. But that will come about only after long tens of thousands of years, when moon and bright Sirius and earth alike will gradually turn to dust . . . And until that time, horror, horror . . .

*Pause. Two red spots appear against the background of the lake.*

Here comes my mighty adversary, the Devil, now. I see his fearful crimson eyes . . .

ARKADINA. There's a smell of sulphur. Is there supposed to be?

KONSTANTIN. Yes.

ARKADINA (*laughs*). I see – it's an effect.

KONSTANTIN. Mama!

NINA. He pines for human company . . .

POLINA (*to* DORN). You've taken your hat off. Put it on – you'll catch cold.

ARKADINA. He's taken it off to the Devil, the Father of Eternal Matter.

KONSTANTIN (*out loud, losing his temper*). Right, the play's over! That's it! Curtain!

ARKADINA. What are you getting cross about?

KONSTANTIN. That's it! Curtain! Can we have the curtain,
  please? (*Stamps his foot.*) Curtain!

> *The curtain is lowered.*

I'm sorry! I was forgetting that playwriting and acting are
reserved for the chosen few. I've infringed their monopoly!
It . . . I . . .

> *He tries to say something else, but then flaps his hand and goes
> off left.*

ARKADINA. What's got into him?

SORIN. Irina, my dear girl, that really is no way to deal with
  youthful pride.

ARKADINA. Why, what did I say?

SORIN. You offended him.

ARKADINA. He told us himself beforehand – it was an
  amusing skit. That's how I took it – as a skit.

SORIN. All the same . . .

ARKADINA. Now it turns out to be some great work of art! Oh,
  for heaven's sake! So he got up all this performance and
  perfumed the air with sulphur not to amuse us but to give us
  all an object-lesson in the art of writing and acting. Really,
  it's becoming a bore. These perpetual attacks on me, this
  campaign of pinpricks – it would tax the patience of a saint!
  He's a wilful, difficult boy.

SORIN. He wanted to give you pleasure.

ARKADINA. Oh, really? But he didn't pick some normal kind
  of play to do it with, did he? – He made us sit through these
  weary poetic ravings. For the sake of amusement I'm
  prepared to sit through even the ravings of delirium, but what
  we had here, I take it, were pretensions to new theatrical
  forms, to a new artistic era. So far as I could see, though, we
  didn't get new forms, we simply got bad manners.

TRIGORIN. Each of us writes as his fancy takes him and his talent allows.

ARKADINA. Let him write as his fancy takes him and his talent allows, just so long as he leaves me alone.

DORN. Jupiter wroth means Jupiter wrong.

ARKADINA. I'm not Jupiter – I'm a woman. (*Lights a cigarette.*) I'm not angry – I merely find it a bore that a young man should spend his time in such a tedious way. I didn't mean to offend him.

MEDVEDENKO. No one has any basis for separating spirit from matter, because for all we know spirit is nothing but the totality of material atoms. (*To* TRIGORIN, *with animation.*) But, you know, what someone ought to put in a play is how we teachers live. A hard, hard time we have of it!

ARKADINA. I'm sure you do, but let's not talk about either plays or atoms. Such a glorious evening! Listen, everyone – is that singing? (*Listens.*) How lovely!

POLINA. It's on the other side of the lake.

*Pause.*

ARKADINA (*to* TRIGORIN). Sit beside me. Ten years or so back on the lake here you could hear constant music and singing almost every night. There were six estates on this side. I remember laughter and noise and guns going off and everyone falling in love, falling in love . . . And the leading actor in all of this, the idol of all six estates, was . . . here he is – (*She nods at* DORN.) – the doctor. He's enchanting even now, but in those days he was irresistible. My conscience is beginning to prick, however. Why did I offend that poor boy of mine? I feel uneasy. (*Calls.*) Kostya! My son! Kostya!

MASHA. I'll go and look for him.

ARKADINA. Would you, my dear?

MASHA (*moving off left*). Halloo-oo! Halloo-oo!

*She goes off.* NINA *comes out from behind the improvised stage.*

NINA. We're obviously not going to do any more of it – I might as well come out. Hello.

*She exchanges kisses with* ARKADINA *and* POLINA.

SORIN. Bravo! Bravo!

ARKADINA. Bravo! Bravo! We all thought you were wonderful. With those looks, with that marvellous voice, you simply cannot stay lost in the depths of the countryside – it would be a sin. I'm sure you must have a talent. You hear? You absolutely must go on the stage!

NINA. Oh, that's my dream! (*Sighs.*) It will never come true, though.

ARKADINA. Who knows? Now, may I introduce: Trigorin – Boris Alekseyevich.

NINA. Oh, I'm so pleased to meet you . . . (*Overcome with embarrassment.*) I read everything you write . . .

ARKADINA (*sitting* NINA *down beside her*). Don't be embarrassed, my dear. He's a famous man, but he has a simple heart. You see – he's as embarrassed as you are.

DORN. I suggest they take the curtain up now. It's eerie like that.

SHAMRAYEV (*calls*). Yakov, take the curtain up, there's a good fellow!

*The curtain goes up.*

NINA (*to* TRIGORIN). It's a strange play, didn't you think?

TRIGORIN. I couldn't understand a word of it. I enjoyed watching it, though. You did it with such sincerity. And the scenery was lovely. (*Pause.*) There must be a lot of fish in that lake.

NINA. Yes, there are.

TRIGORIN. I love fishing. There's no greater pleasure I know than sitting on the bank at the end of the day and watching the float.

NINA. But I think that for anyone who has experienced the

pleasure of creating something all other pleasures must pale into insignificance.

ARKADINA (*laughing*). You mustn't talk like that. When people say nice things to him he just wishes the earth would swallow him up.

SHAMRAYEV. I remember an occasion at the Opera in Moscow when Silva, the famous bass, sang bottom C. Now that night, with malice aforethought, the bass from our church choir was sitting up in the gallery. Imagine our utter astonishment when suddenly we hear from the gallery, 'Bravo, Silva!' – a whole octave lower . . . Like this. (*In a deep but insubstantial bass.*) 'Bravo, Silva!' The whole theatre simply froze.

*Pause.*

DORN. A quiet angel flew past.

NINA. I must go. Goodbye.

ARKADINA. Go where? So early? We shan't let you.

NINA. Papa's waiting for me.

ARKADINA. Cruel man! Really . . .

*They kiss.*

Well, if you must you must. Such a shame to let you go.

NINA. If you knew how hard it is for me to leave!

ARKADINA. Someone ought to see you home, my pet.

NINA (*in alarm*). Oh, no, no!

SORIN (*pleading with her*). Do stay!

NINA. I really can't.

SORIN. Stay for one hour, simple as that. No harm, surely.

NINA (*on the verge of tears, after she has thought for a moment*). I mustn't! (*Presses his hand and quickly goes off.*)

ARKADINA. An unlucky girl, if truth be told. Apparently her late mother made all her huge wealth over to her husband – every last kopeck. Now the girl is left with nothing because her father in his turn has already made the whole lot over to his second wife. It's quite scandalous.

DORN. A real swine, though, her father, to give him his due.

SORIN (*rubbing his chilled hands*). We'd better be going, too, or it will get damp. My legs are aching.

ARKADINA. You look as if you've got a pair of wooden legs – you can scarcely walk on them. Come, then, away, ill-starred old man.

*She takes his arm.*

SHAMRAYEV (*offering* POLINA *his arm*). Madame?

SORIN. I can hear that dog howling again. (*To* SHAMRAYEV.) Be a good fellow, would you, and tell them to let it loose?

SHAMRAYEV. Can't be let loose, I regret to say. I'm afraid of thieves getting into the granary. I've got the millet in there. (*To* MEDVEDENKO, *who is walking beside him.*) Yes, a whole octave lower – 'Bravo, Silva!' And he wasn't an opera singer – just a simple member of the church choir.

MEDVEDENKO. What would someone in a church choir be paid?

*Everyone except* DORN *goes off.*

DORN (*alone*). Well, I don't know, I may be stupid, I may be mad, but I liked the play. There's something in it. When that little girl was talking about being on her own – and then when the Devil's red eyes appeared – I could feel my hands shaking with excitement. Something fresh and untutored about it . . . Here he comes, I think. I'd like to be a little nicer to him.

*Enter* KONSTANTIN.

KONSTANTIN. They've all gone.

DORN. I'm here.

KONSTANTIN. Masha's been looking all over the park for me. Intolerable creature.

DORN. Listen, I liked your play very much indeed. It was a strange kind of thing, and I didn't see the end of it, but it made a powerful impression none the less. You have talent; you must go on.

> KONSTANTIN *squeezes his hand hard and embraces him impetuously*.

So over-sensitive! Tears in your eyes . . . What was I going to say? Yes, you took a subject from the realm of abstract ideas. That was right, because a work of art must always express some substantial thought. Nothing can be excellent unless it be serious. You look quite pale!

KONSTANTIN. So you're saying – 'Go on'!

DORN. I am . . . But write about nothing that isn't important and eternal. I've lived my life with variety and taste, I'm a contented man, but I can tell you, if it had been granted to me to experience the lift of the heart that artists know in the moment of creation, then I think I should have scorned this material envelope of mine, and everything to do with it, and I should have left the ground and soared up into the heights.

KONSTANTIN. I'm sorry – where's Nina?

DORN. And another thing. In anything you write there must be a clear and definite thought. You must know why you're writing. If you don't, if you go down the picturesque path that has no definite goal at the end of it, then you'll lose your way, and your talent will destroy you.

KONSTANTIN (*impatiently*). Where's Nina?

DORN. She went home.

KONSTANTIN (*in despair*). What am I going to do? I want to see her . . . I have to see her . . . I'm going to go there . . .

> *Enter* MASHA.

DORN (*to* KONSTANTIN). Now, calm down, my friend.

KONSTANTIN. I'm going to go, all the same. I must go.

MASHA (*to* KONSTANTIN). Will you go into the house? Your mother's waiting. She's feeling uneasy about you.

KONSTANTIN. Tell her I've gone. And please, all of you, leave me alone! Just leave me alone! Don't follow me around!

DORN. Now, now, now, come on . . . Not the way . . . Not right.

KONSTANTIN (*on the verge of tears*). Goodbye, doctor. Thank you . . .

*He goes off.*

DORN (*sighs*). Youth, youth!

MASHA. Whenever there's nothing more to be said then people say: 'Youth, youth . . .' (*Takes a pinch of snuff.*)

DORN (*takes the snuffbox away from her and flings it into the bushes*). That's a filthy habit! (*Pause.*) I think they've started playing cards inside. I must go.

MASHA. Wait a moment.

DORN. What is it?

MASHA. Yet another thing I want to tell you. I'd like to talk for a moment . . . (*Becoming agitated.*) I don't like my father . . . but you have a special place in my heart. I don't know why, but all my life I've felt you were close to me . . . Help me. Please help me, or I shall do something silly – I shall make a mockery of my life, I shall ruin it . . . I can't go on . . .

DORN. What do you mean? Help you with what?

MASHA. I'm in such torment. No one knows, no one knows the torment I'm in! (*Lays her head on his breast; quietly.*) I'm in love with Konstantin.

DORN. You're all so over-sensitive! So over-sensitive! And so much love around . . . Oh, the spells woven by this lake! (*Tenderly.*) But what can I do, my child? What can I do?

CURTAIN

# Act Two

*The croquet lawn. In the distance to the right is the house, with a wide verandah, while to the left can be seen the lake, with the sun sparkling on it. Flower-beds and midday heat. At the side of the lawn, on a garden seat in the shade of an old lime-tree, are sitting* ARKADINA, DORN, *and* MASHA. DORN *has a book open in his lap.*

ARKADINA (*to* MASHA). Both of us stand up.

*They both stand.*

Side by side. Now, you're twenty-two and I'm nearly twice that. Doctor, which of us is the younger-looking?

DORN. You are, of course.

ARKADINA. You see? And why? Because I work, I'm alive to the world around me, I'm always busy; whereas you're such a stick-in-the-mud, you don't know how to live . . . Also I make it a rule not to look into the future. I never think about old age, I never think about death. What will be, will be.

MASHA. Yes, but I feel as though I'd been born a long, long time ago; I'm dragging my life behind me like a dress with an endless train . . . And often I've no desire to go on living. (*Sits.*) Well, that's all nonsense, of course. You just have to shake yourself out of it.

DORN *quietly sings Siebel's aria, 'Faites-lui mes aveux,' from Act III of Gounod's* Faust.

ARKADINA. Then again, my dear, I'm as careful about my appearance as an Englishman. I always keep myself firmly in hand. My dress, my hair – always *comme il faut*. Should I ever allow myself to go out of the house – even into the garden here – in a housecoat, or with my hair not done? Never. If I've kept my looks it's because I've never stopped caring about my appearance, I've never let myself go in the way that some women do . . . (*Walks about the lawn, hands on her hips.*) There you are, you see – spry as a kitten. I could play a girl of fifteen still.

DORN. Nonetheless and notwithstanding, I'm still reading, am I? (*Picks up the book.*) We stopped at the corn-chandler and the rats . . .

ARKADINA. And the rats, yes. Go on, then. (*Sits.*) Or rather, give it to me and I'll read. It's my turn. (*Takes the book and runs her eyes over it to find the place.*) The rats . . . Here we are . . . (*Reads.*) 'And, to be sure, it is as dangerous for people in society to make much of writers and to entice them into their homes as it would be for a corn-chandler to keep rats in his shop. And yet there is a vogue for them. So, when a woman has designs upon a writer whom she wishes to take up, she lays siege to him with compliments and attentions and little marks of favour . . . .' Well, that may be how it is with the French, but with us there's nothing like that – we don't work to a programme. Before a woman takes a writer up in this country she's usually head over heels in love with him, thank you very much. You don't have to look far – take me and Trigorin, for instance . . .

*Enter* SORIN, *leaning on his stick, with* NINA *beside him, and* MEDVEDENKO *pushing an empty wheelchair behind them.*

SORIN (*in the tone of voice used for being nice to a child*). So – we're all smiles, are we? We're all bright and cheerful today? (*To* ARKADINA.) We're all sunshine and smiles! Our father and stepmother have gone into town, and now we're as free as the air for three whole days.

NINA (*sits beside* ARKADINA *and embraces her*). I'm happy! I'm all yours now.

SORIN (*sits in his wheelchair*). As pretty as a picture she is today.

ARKADINA. Attractive, well turned out . . . What a sensible

girl. (*Kisses her.*) Still, we mustn't praise her too much or it will bring bad luck. Where's Trigorin?

NINA. He's at the bathing-place, fishing.

ARKADINA. You'd think he'd get bored with it. (*Resumes her book.*)

NINA. What are you reading?

ARKADINA. Maupassant, my sweet – *On the Water.* (*Reads a few lines to herself.*) Anyway, the next bit is neither amusing nor true. (*Shuts the book.*) I am troubled in my soul. Can anyone tell me what the matter is with my son? Why is he being so stern and boring? He spends whole days together on the lake – I scarcely see him.

MASHA. He's sick at heart. (*To* NINA, *shyly.*) Please – read a bit of his play!

NINA (*shrugs*). Do you really want me to? It's so dull!

MASHA (*restraining her enthusiasm*). When he reads something himself his eyes blaze and his face grows pale. He's got a wonderful sad voice; yes, and the manner of a poet.

SORIN *snores.*

DORN. Sleep well!

ARKADINA. Petrusha!

SORIN. Um?

ARKADINA. Are you asleep?

SORIN. Certainly not.

*Pause.*

ARKADINA. You're not having any medical attention, are you. It's not right.

SORIN. I'd be delighted to have some medical attention. It's the doctor here who won't give me any.

DORN. Medical attention? When you're sixty?

SORIN. Even when you're sixty you still want to live.

DORN (*irritably*). Tch! Well, take some valerian drops, then.

ARKADINA. I have a feeling it would be good for him to go to a spa somewhere.

DORN. All right. He could go to a spa. Or not go to a spa.

ARKADINA. Make sense of that, if you can!

DORN. There's nothing to make sense of. It's all perfectly plain.

*Pause.*

MEDVEDENKO. Your brother ought to give up smoking.

SORIN. Oh, fiddle.

DORN. No, not fiddle. Alcohol and tobacco make you lose the sense of yourself. Smoke a cigar or drink a glass of vodka and you're no longer you – you're you plus someone else. The self grows blurred, and you start to see yourself as a third person – not as 'I' but as 'he'.

SORIN (*laughs*). It's all very well for you to talk. You've lived in your time. But how about me? I spent twenty-eight years working in the Department of Justice, but I still haven't lived, when all's said and done, I still haven't experienced anything, and I long to live, no question about it. You've had your fill in life and you don't care any more, so you tend to be philosophical, but I want to live, and so I drink sherry at dinner and smoke cigars, it's as simple as that. As simple as that.

DORN. Life has to be taken seriously. Swallowing medicine when you're sixty and feeling sorry you didn't have much fun when you were young – forgive me if I'm blunt – but that's fatuous.

MASHA (*stands up*). It must be lunchtime. (*Walks limply and lethargically.*) My leg's gone to sleep . . . .

*Exit* MASHA.

DORN. Lunch . . . She's going to go and have a couple of drinks first.

SORIN. The poor child hasn't found happiness in life.

DORN. Oh, pish, you old civil servant.

SORIN. You speak as someone's who's eaten his fill.

ARKADINA. Oh, what could be more boring than this sweet country boredom! Heat, quiet, nothing anyone wants to do, everyone philosophising away . . . It's nice being with you, my friends, it's a pleasure to listen to you, and yet . . . to be sitting in a hotel room somewhere learning your lines – could anything be better than that?

NINA (*enthusiastically*). Oh, yes! I know what you mean.

SORIN. It's better in town, no doubt about it. You sit in your office, no one gets past the attendant without being announced, there's the telephone, there are cabs in the street – it's as simple as that . . .

DORN *sings* '*Faites-lui mes aveux* . . .'

*Enter* SHAMRAYEV, *followed by* POLINA.

SHAMRAYEV. So this is where they are! A very good day to you all! (*Kisses* ARKADINA'*s hand, then* NINA'*s.*) Delighted to find you in good health. (*To* ARKADINA.) My wife tells me you're proposing to go into town together. Is this true?

ARKADINA. Yes, we are.

SHAMRAYEV. Hm . . . Well, splendid, splendid, but what are you going *in*, dear lady? We're carting the rye today – all the men are busy. And which horses were you thinking of using, may I ask?

ARKADINA. Which horses? How should *I* know?

SORIN. We've got carriage horses, haven't we?

SHAMRAYEV (*becoming agitated*). The carriage horses? But where am I going to get harness for them? Where am I going to get harness? Amazing, isn't it? Past comprehension! Dear lady! I revere your talent, I'll gladly give you ten years of my life, but horses I cannot give you!

ARKADINA. But supposing I *have* to go? What an extraordinary state of affairs!

SHAMRAYEV. Dear lady! You don't realise what farming involves!

ARKADINA (*flares up*). Oh, the same old story! In that case, I'm leaving for Moscow today. Have horses rented for me in the village – otherwise I shall *walk* to the station!

SHAMRAYEV (*flares up*). In that case I resign! Find yourself another steward!

*Exit* SHAMRAYEV.

ARKADINA. Every summer here it's the same, every summer I'm insulted! I'm not going to set foot in this place again!

*Exit* ARKADINA *left, where the bathing-place is assumed to be. A minute later she can be seen crossing towards the house, followed by* TRIGORIN *with his fishing-rods and bucket.*

SORIN (*flares up*). This is downright impertinence! This is downright heaven knows what! I'm sick of it, when all's said and done. Fetch all the horses directly!

NINA (*to* POLINA). But saying no to someone like that, a famous actress! Surely her slightest wish – her slightest whim, even – is more important than your farming? It's simply unbelievable!

POLINA (*in despair*). What can I do? Put yourself in my position. What can I do?

SORIN (*to* NINA). Come on, we'll go to my sister. We'll all plead with her not to leave. Isn't that right? (*Looks in the direction that* SHAMRAYEV *went off.*) The intolerable man! The tyrant!

NINA (*stops him getting up*). Sit down, sit down . . . We'll push you there . . .

*She and* MEDVEDENKO *push the wheelchair.*

How terrible, though!

SORIN. Yes, yes, it *is* terrible . . . But he won't go – I'll have a talk with him by and by.

*They go off. Only* DORN *and* POLINA *remain.*

DORN. How boring people are. Really your husband ought to

be thrown out on his neck, but in fact the whole thing will
end with that old woman and his sister apologising to him.
You'll see!

POLINA. He's sent the carriage horses out to the fields with all
the others. Every day we have this sort of trouble. If you knew
how it upsets me! It's making me ill – look, I'm shaking . . .
He's so coarse – I can't bear it. (*Pleading.*) Yevgeni, my dear,
my precious, take me to live with you . . . Time's running
out for us, we're not young any more, and oh, to stop
hiding, even at the end of our lives, to stop lying . . .

*Pause.*

DORN. I'm fifty-five. It's a little late in the day to change my
way of life.

POLINA. I know why you reject me – I know there are other
women besides me. You can't take them all to live with you.
I understand that. Forgive me, I'm being tiresome.

NINA *appears near the house, picking flowers.*

DORN. No, no.

POLINA. I'm tormented by jealousy. Of course – you're a
doctor – you can't avoid women. I understand that . . .

NINA *approaches.*

DORN. What's going on in there?

NINA. She's crying, and her brother's got his asthma.

DORN (*gets up*). I'd better go and give them both some
drops . . .

NINA (*gives him the flowers*). Here, have these!

DORN. *Merci bien.* (*Goes towards the house.*)

POLINA (*going to him*). What lovely flowers! (*Near the house, in
muffled tones.*) Give me those flowers! Give me those flowers!

*As soon as she gets the flowers she tears them up and throws
them on the ground. They both go into the house.*

NINA (*alone*). How curious to see a famous actress crying, especially over such a tiny thing! And isn't this curious, too? – a famous writer, the darling of the public, someone they write about in all the papers, someone they sell pictures of, someone who's translated into foreign languages – and he spends the whole day fishing – he's delighted to have caught a couple of chub. I thought famous people were proud and unapproachable. I thought they despised the common herd – I thought their renown, the brilliance of their name, gave them a kind of revenge for the way the herd set birth and wealth above all else. But here they are crying, fishing, playing cards, laughing, and losing their tempers like everybody else . . .

*Enter* KONSTANTIN, *hatless, with a gun and a seagull he has killed.*

KONSTANTIN. You're alone?
NINA. Yes, I'm alone.

KONSTANTIN *lays the seagull at her feet.*

What does that signify?
KONSTANTIN. I had the dishonour to kill this seagull today. I'm laying it at your feet.
NINA. What's the matter with you? (*Picks the seagull up and looks at it.*)
KONSTANTIN (*after a pause*). Soon I shall kill myself in the same way.
NINA. You're not the person I used to know.
KONSTANTIN. No, I'm not. Not since you stopped being the person I used to know. You've changed towards me. You look at me coldly, you're embarrassed by my being here.
NINA. You've got so irritable recently. You put things obliquely all the time, in some kind of symbols. This seagull, too – this is obviously a symbol of something, but I'm sorry, I don't know what it means . . . (*Lays the seagull on the bench.*) I'm

too simple to understand you.

KONSTANTIN. It all started that evening when my play was such an idiotic failure. Women never forgive failure. I burnt it, every last torn-up shred of it. If you knew how unhappy I am! It's terrifying the way you've grown cold towards me – it's unbelievable – it's as if I'd woken up and found that this lake had dried up, or drained away into the earth. You just said that you were too simple to understand me. Oh, what is there to understand? The play wasn't liked, you despise my inspiration, you've begun to think of me as an ordinary person – a nonentity – someone like everybody else . . . (*Stamps his foot.*) I know just what you mean, just exactly what you mean! It's like having a nail in my brain, curse it – and curse this pride of mine, too, that sucks my blood, sucks it like a serpent . . .

*Sees* TRIGORIN, *who is reading a book as he walks.*

Here comes the man with the real talent, entering like Hamlet, even down to the book. (*Mimics him.*) 'Words, words, words . . .' The sun hasn't reached you yet, and already you're smiling, your expression has melted in its rays. I won't stand in your way.

*He quickly goes off.*

TRIGORIN (*noting something down in the book*). Takes snuff and drinks vodka . . . Always in black. Loved by teacher . . .
NINA. Hello.
TRIGORIN. Hello to you. An unexpected turn of events, I gather, means that we are leaving today. It's hardly probable that you and I will see each other again. A pity. I don't often get the chance to meet girls of your age, not ones who are also interesting and attractive, and I can't remember now – can't clearly picture to myself – what it feels like to be eighteen or nineteen. So the girls who appear in my stories usually strike a false note. I should have liked to put myself in your place

for a while, just for an hour or so, to find out how your mind
worked and what sort of creature you were.

NINA. I should have liked to put myself in your place for a
while.

TRIGORIN. Why?

NINA. To know what it felt like to be a famous and talented
writer. What *does* fame feel like? What is the sensation of
being famous?

TRIGORIN. What does it feel like? It doesn't feel like anything,
so far as I know. I've never thought about it. (*After a moment's
reflection.*) Either you have an exaggerated idea of how famous
I am, or else it has no sensation at all.

NINA. But when you read about yourself in the papers?

TRIGORIN. If they're praising me it's nice. If they're abusing
me then I feel put out for a couple of days.

NINA. Strange and marvellous world! If you knew how I envied
you! People have such different lots in life. Some of them can
scarcely drag out their dull, obscure existence – all of them
alike, all of them unhappy; while others – you, for example
– you're one in a million – you're granted an absorbing, sunlit
life that's full of meaning . . . You're happy . . .

TRIGORIN. Me? (*Shrugs.*) Hm . . . You talk about fame and
happiness and some kind of absorbing, sunlit life, but to me
– forgive me – all these fine words are like those soft, sticky
sweets – the sort I never eat. You're very young and you're
very kind.

NINA. You have a wonderful life!

TRIGORIN. What's so specially good about it, though? (*Looks
at his watch.*) I have to go and write. I'm sorry, I'm rather
pressed for time . . . (*Laughs.*) You've trodden on my pet
corn, as they say, and I'm starting to get worked up and
slightly irritated. All right, then – let's talk about it. Let's talk
about my wonderful sunlit life . . . Now, where shall we
begin? (*After a moment's thought.*) There are such things
as mental fixations when day and night a man can think

of nothing else except the moon, let's say. I have such a moon of my own. Day and night I am in the grip of a single obsession: I have to write, I have to write, I have to write . . . Scarcely have I finished one story than for some reason I have to write another, and then a third, and after the third a fourth . . . I write without cease, like a traveller with a fresh relay of horses waiting at every post, and I can't do otherwise. I ask you – what's sunlit or wonderful about that? It's a cruel life! Here I am talking to you, getting myself quite worked up, but at the same time I don't forget for a single moment that I have an unfinished story waiting for me. I see that cloud up there, looking like a grand piano, and I think, I shall have to put in a story somewhere that there was a cloud in the sky looking like a grand piano. I smell the scent of the heliotropes. I make a rapid mental note: cloying perfume, widow's purple, put in when describing summer evening. I catch us both up at every phrase, at every word, and I hasten to lock all these words and phrases away in my literary larder – you never know, they may come in handy! When I finish work I rush off to the theatre, or I go fishing; there at least I might relax and forget myself – but no, because inside my head a heavy iron ball is already beginning to shift – a new idea, and already I can feel the pull of my desk, and I have to rush off to write, write, write again. And that's how it always is, always and always, and I have no peace from myself, and I feel that I'm eating up my own life – that to make the honey I give to some remote reader I'm gathering the sweetness from my own best flowers – that I'm picking the flowers themselves and trampling their roots. I surely must be mad! My friends and relations surely can't be treating me like a sane man! 'What are you writing? What are you going to give us next?' Always the same thing, over and over again, and I get the feeling that this constant attention from my friends, this praise, this admiration, is all nothing but a trick, that I'm being lied to like an invalid, and sometimes I'm afraid they're just about to creep up on me from behind, that they're going to seize me like the wretched clerk in that story of Gogol's and cart me off to the madhouse. And in the years when I was a beginner still, the years when I was young, the best years, my trade was one long torment to me. The young writer – particularly when he's not successful – feels clumsy, inept, and useless; his nerves are on edge; he can't stop himself hanging round people connected with literature and art; an unacknowledged and unnoticed figure who's afraid to look people in the eye, like a compulsive gambler with no money. I couldn't see my reader, but in my imagination, for some reason, he was always someone unfriendly and mistrustful. I was afraid of the public, I found it terrifying, and whenever I had a new play produced I saw everyone with dark hair as antagonistic, and everyone with fair hair as coldly indifferent. It was terrible! It was a torment!

NINA. But surely inspiration, and the actual process of creation, give you moments of elevation, moments of happiness?

TRIGORIN. Yes, they do. When I'm writing it's rather agreeable. And reading the proofs – that's agreeable. But . . . scarcely has something come off the press than I can't bear it – I can see it's all wrong, it's a mistake, it should never have been written at all – and I feel disappointed, I feel deeply worthless . . . (*Laughs.*) But the public reads it and says: 'Yes, it's charming, it's clever . . . Charming, but nowhere near Tolstoy.' Or: 'It's a fine piece of writing, but Turgenev's *Fathers and Children* is better.' To my dying day it will go on being merely charming and clever, charming and clever, and nothing more, and when I'm dead my friends will say as they pass my grave: 'There lies Trigorin. He was a good writer, but he wasn't as good as Turgenev.'

NINA. Forgive me, but I refuse to understand what you're saying. You've simply been spoiled by success.

TRIGORIN. What success? I've never given any pleasure to myself. I don't like myself as a writer. The worst thing is that

I go round in some kind of daze, and often I don't understand what it is I'm writing . . . I love this water here, the trees, the sky; I have a feeling for nature – it arouses this passion I have, the irresistible desire to write. But then of course I'm not just a landscape-painter; I'm a citizen as well – I love my country, I love the common people. I feel that if I'm a writer then I have some obligation to deal with the people, with their sufferings and their future, to deal with science and the rights of man and so on and so forth; and deal with it all I do, in haste, urged on and snapped at on all sides. I rush back and forth like a fox bayed by hounds. I can see that life and science are getting further and further ahead of me all the time, while I fall further and further behind, like a peasant missing a train. And in the end I feel that all I can write is landscapes, and that in everything else I'm false – false to the marrow of my bones.

NINA. You've been overworking, and you haven't the time or the taste to become aware of your own importance. You may be dissatisfied with yourself, but in other people's eyes you're a great and wonderful man! If I were a writer like you I should sacrifice my whole life to the crowd – but I should know all the time that their happiness lay purely in reaching up to me, and they'd drag my chariot in triumph through the streets.

TRIGORIN. Dragging people in chariots, well . . . Agamemnon now, am I?

*They both smile.*

NINA. For the happiness of being a writer or an actress I'd put up with hunger and disappointment, and my family turning their backs on me. I'd live in a garret and eat black bread, I'd endure my dissatisfaction with myself and my consciousness of my own shortcomings; but then to make up for it I should demand glory . . . real resounding glory . . . (*Covers her face with her hands.*) My head's spinning . . . Oh . . . !

ARKADINA (*calls, off, from the house*). Boris! Boris?

TRIGORIN. I'm being summoned . . . Time to pack, I suppose. I don't feel like leaving, though. (*Looks around at the lake.*) Just look at the bounteousness of it . . . ! How fine!

NINA. You see the house and garden on the other side?

TRIGORIN. Yes.

NINA. My mother's dead now, but that was her estate. I was born there. I've spent my whole life around this lake – I know every little island in it.

TRIGORIN. A fine place you live in! (*Sees the seagull.*) What's that?

NINA. A seagull. Konstantin shot it.

TRIGORIN. Beautiful bird. I really don't feel like leaving. Why don't you try to persuade her to stay? (*Makes a note in his book.*)

NINA. What's that you're writing?

TRIGORIN. Nothing. Just jotting something down . . . An idea came into my head . . . (*Hides the book.*) An idea for a short story. A girl like you, living beside a lake since she was a child. She loves the lake the way a seagull might – she's as happy and free as a seagull. But one day by chance a man comes along and sees her. And quite idly he destroys her, like this seagull.

*Pause.*
ARKADINA *appears at the window.*

ARKADINA. Boris! Where are you?

TRIGORIN. Coming! (*Crosses to her, turning round to look at* NINA. *At the window, to* ARKADINA.) What is it?

ARKADINA. We're staying.

*Exit* ARKADINA *into the house.*

NINA (*comes downstage and reflects for a moment*). A dream!

CURTAIN

# Act Three

*The dining-room in* SORIN's *house. Doors left and right. Sideboard. Medicine cabinet. Dining-table in the middle of the room. Suitcase and cardboard boxes; signs of preparations for departure.* TRIGORIN *is eating lunch.* MASHA *is standing at the table.*

MASHA. I'm telling you all this because you're a writer. You can use it in something. Quite seriously, if he had wounded himself badly I couldn't have gone on living for another moment. I've got courage, though. I thought, 'Right!' – and I made up my mind to tear this love out of my heart, to tear it out by the roots.

TRIGORIN. How?

MASHA. I'm going to get married. To Medvedenko.

TRIGORIN. The schoolteacher?

MASHA. Yes.

TRIGORIN. I don't see the need for that.

MASHA. Loving without hope, waiting year after year for something to happen . . . I'm certainly not marrying for love, but I'll have new troubles to drown out the old. Be a change, anyway. Have another one, shall we?

TRIGORIN. Won't that be rather a lot?

MASHA. Oh, come on! (*Pours a glass each.*) There's no need to look at me like that. Women are more often drinkers than you realise. A few of them drink openly, like me, but most of them do it in secret. Oh yes. And always vodka or brandy. (*Clinks glasses.*) Here's to you! There's no nonsense about you – I'll be sorry to see you go.

*They drink.*

TRIGORIN. I don't much want to go myself.

MASHA. Ask her to stay, then.

TRIGORIN. No, she won't stay now. Her son's being extremely awkward. First he was trying to shoot himself; now, so I gather, he's going to challenge me to a duel. I don't know what for. He huffs and puffs, he preaches his 'new forms' . . . But there's room for all, surely, new and old alike – there's no need to elbow each other aside.

MASHA. How about jealousy? Not that it's any business of mine.

*Pause.* YAKOV *crosses left to right with a suitcase.* NINA *enters and stops by the window.*

My schoolteacher isn't very clever, but he's a kind man, and he's poor, and he's very much in love with me. I feel sorry for him. I even feel sorry for his old mother. Anyway, let me wish you all the best. Remember me kindly. (*Shakes his hand warmly.*) I'm very grateful to you for taking an interest. Send me your books, though – and you must sign them! Don't put what you put for everybody else. Put 'To Masha, of dubious descent, and resident in this world for reasons unknown.' Goodbye!

*Exit* MASHA.

NINA (*holding out a hand closed into a fist towards* TRIGORIN). Odds or evens?

TRIGORIN. Evens.

NINA (*sighs*). No. I've only got one bean in my hand. The question was, 'Should I become an actress or not?' If only someone could tell me!

TRIGORIN. It's not something that anyone *can* tell you.

NINA. We're saying goodbye to each other and . . . we may never see each other again. I should like to give you this little medallion to remember me by. I've had your initials engraved on it . . . and on this side the title of your book, *Days and Nights.*

TRIGORIN. What a very gracious gesture! (*Kisses the medallion.*)

It's a delightful present!

NINA. Remember me sometimes.

TRIGORIN. I shall remember you. I shall remember you as you were on that bright and sunny day – do you recall? – a week ago, when you were wearing a summer dress . . . and we had a talk . . . and there on the garden seat lay a white seagull.

NINA (*reflectively*). The seagull, yes . . . (*Pause.*) We can't say anything else – there are people coming . . . Give me two minutes before you leave, I beg of you.

> *She goes off left. As she does so* ARKADINA *enters right with* SORIN, *who is wearing a tailcoat with a decoration pinned to it, then* YAKOV, *who is preoccupied with collecting things up for the departure.*

ARKADINA. Now, why don't you stay at home, you poor old man? What do you want to go traipsing round calling on people for, with your rheumatism? (*To* TRIGORIN.) Who was that went out just now? Was that Nina?

TRIGORIN. Yes.

ARKADINA. *Pardon*, we're intruding . . . (*Sits.*) I think I've packed everything. What a torment it is.

TRIGORIN (*reads from the medallion*). *Days and Nights*, page 121, lines 11 and 12.

YAKOV (*clearing things from the table*). Am I to pack the fishing-rods, too?

TRIGORIN. Yes, I shall need them again. The books you can give away, though.

YAKOV. Sir.

TRIGORIN (*to himself*). Page 121, lines 11 and 12. What do they say? (*To* ARKADINA.) Have you got my books in the house?

ARKADINA. My brother's study – the corner cupboard.

TRIGORIN. Page 121 . . .

> *Exit* TRIGORIN.

ARKADINA. Really, Petrusha, I should stay at home if I

were you . . . .

SORIN. You're leaving. I shall get depressed sitting at home without you.

ARKADINA. What's happening in town, then?

SORIN. Nothing much, but all the same. (*Laughs*.) They're laying the foundation-stone for the new government building, etcetera, etcetera . . . I'd like to get out and about for an hour or two, anyway – I've been lying here like an old boot, stuck here like a gudgeon in the mud. I've ordered the horses for one o'clock, we can go together.

ARKADINA (*after a pause*). Well, you go on living here, then – don't get too bored, don't catch any colds. Keep an eye on my son. Look after him. Admonish him. (*Pause*.) I'm leaving, so I'll never know why Konstantin tried to shoot himself. The main reason, I think, was jealousy, and the sooner I take Trigorin away from here the better.

SORIN. I don't know quite how to put this, but there were other reasons, too. There he is, no question about it – young man, intelligent, he lives in the country, miles from anywhere, and he's no money, no position, no future. Nothing to do. He's ashamed of his idleness – he's frightened of it. I'm devoted to him and he's quite attached to me, but when all's said and done he feels there's no place for him in the house – he feels like a poor relation here, a parasite. Pride, no question about it . . .

ARKADINA. Oh, he's a trial to me! (*Lost in thought*.) Maybe he should get a job . . .

SORIN (*whistles for a moment, then, irresolutely*). I wonder if the best thing wouldn't be for you to . . . give him a little money. The first thing he needs to do is to dress like a normal human being, it's as simple as that. Look, he's been wearing that one same jacket for the past three years. He hasn't got an overcoat to his back . . . . (*Laughs*.) Then again it wouldn't hurt the boy to see a bit of the world . . . Go abroad, perhaps . . . It really wouldn't cost all that much.

ARKADINA. All the same . . . I suppose I might arrange a little more for clothes, but as for going abroad . . . No, at the moment I can't even manage the clothes. (*Decisively.*) I've no money!

SORIN *laughs.*

I haven't!

SORIN (*whistles for a moment*). Well, there we are. Forgive me. Don't be angry, my dear. I believe you . . . You're a good and generous woman.

ARKADINA (*on the verge of tears*). I've no money!

SORIN. If I had any money, no question, I'd give him some myself, but I've nothing, not a kopeck. (*Laughs.*) My entire pension is taken by that steward of mine to spend on planting crops and raising cattle and keeping bees, and I might as well pour it straight down the drain. The bees drop dead, the cows drop dead, and they never let me have any horses . . .

ARKADINA. All right, I have money, but I happen to be in the theatrical profession – my outfits alone have nearly ruined me.

SORIN. You're a dear kind girl . . . I respect your feelings . . . Yes . . . But I think I'm having another of my . . . you know . . . (*Staggers.*) Head's going round. (*Holds on to the table.*) Not feeling too good, simple as that.

ARKADINA (*frightened*). Petrusha! (*Trying to support him.*) Petrusha, my dear . . . (*Calls.*) Help me! Help . . . !

*Enter* KONSTANTIN, *his head bandaged, and* MEDVEDENKO.

ARKADINA. He's ill!

SORIN. I'm all right, I'm all right . . . (*Smiles and drinks some water.*) It's passed off . . . simple as that . . .

KONSTANTIN (*to his mother*). There's no need to be frightened, Mama, it's not dangerous. Uncle often has these turns now. Uncle, you must have a lie-down.

SORIN. For a moment, yes . . . I'm still going into town. I'll
have a little lie-down, then I'll go . . . no question about
it . . .

*He begins to go off, leaning on his stick.*

MEDVEDENKO (*taking his arm*). There's a riddle: in the
morning on four, at midday on two, in the evening on
three . . .
SORIN (*laughs*). Quite. And at night on your back. Thank you
– I can manage on my own . . .
MEDVEDENKO. Well, there's politeness . . .

*Exeunt* MEDVEDENKO *and* SORIN.

ARKADINA. He gave me such a fright!
KONSTANTIN. It's bad for his health, living in the country.
He's pining away. Now, Mama, if you had a sudden attack
of generosity and lent him a couple of thousand rubles he
could live in town all year.
ARKADINA. I haven't any money. I'm an actress, not a bank-
manager.

*Pause.*

KONSTANTIN. Will you change my dressing, Mama. You do
it so nicely.
ARKADINA (*gets iodoform and dressings out of the medicine
cabinet*). The doctor's late, though.
KONSTANTIN. He promised to be here at ten, and it's twelve
already.
ARKADINA. Sit down. (*Takes the bandage off his head.*) You
look as if you're wearing a turban. Someone who came to the
kitchen door yesterday was asking what nationality you were.
It's nearly healed, though. Only the merest trifle left to go.
(*Kisses him on the head.*) You're not going to start playing with
guns again while I'm away, are you.
KONSTANTIN. No, Mama. That was just a moment of crazy

despair when I lost control of myself. It won't happen again. (*Kisses her hand.*) You have magic in your hands. I remember a long time ago, when you were still working in the State theatre – when I was little – there was a fight in the courtyard of our block, and a washerwoman living in one of the apartments got badly knocked about. Do you remember? When they picked her up she was unconscious . . . You kept going to see her, you took her medicine, you bathed the children in her washtub. Surely you remember?

ARKADINA. No. (*Puts a new bandage on.*)

KONSTANTIN. There were two ballet-dancers living in the same block . . . They used to come and have coffee with you . . .

ARKADINA. I remember that.

KONSTANTIN. They were terribly religious. (*Pause.*) These last few days I've loved you as tenderly and whole-heartedly as I did when I was a child. I've no one left apart from you. But why, why has that man come between us?

ARKADINA. Konstantin, you don't understand him. He's someone of the highest integrity . . .

KONSTANTIN. However, when they told him I was going to challenge him to a duel his integrity didn't hinder his cowardice. He's leaving. Ignominiously fleeing!

ARKADINA. Oh, nonsense! I'm taking him away. You can't be pleased by our relationship, of course, but you're perfectly intelligent, and I must insist that you respect my freedom.

KONSTANTIN. I do respect your freedom, but you must allow me to be free, too, you must let me have my own opinion of that man. Someone of the highest integrity! Here we are on the point of quarrelling over him while he sits in the drawing-room or the garden somewhere laughing at us . . . Educating Nina, trying to convince her once and for all that he's a genius.

ARKADINA. You take pleasure in being disagreeable to me. That man is someone I have great respect for, and I must ask you not to speak ill of him in my presence.

KONSTANTIN. I don't have great respect for him, however. You want me to think he's a genius as well, but I'm sorry, I can't tell a lie – his work nauseates me.

ARKADINA. That's jealousy. People with no talent themselves, only pretensions, are always reduced to running down people who do have real talent. It must be a great comfort!

KONSTANTIN (*ironically*). Real talent! (*Furiously.*) I've more talent than the lot of you, if it comes to that! (*Tears the bandage off his head.*) You and your dull, plodding friends have got a stranglehold on art, and the only things you consider legitimate and real are the ones you do yourselves – everything else you crush and smother! I don't acknowledge any of you! I don't acknowledge you, I don't acknowledge him!

ARKADINA. And what are you? A Decadent!

KONSTANTIN. Go off to your nice little theatre and act in your miserable mediocre plays!

ARKADINA. I've never acted in plays like that in my life! Leave me alone! You couldn't write so much as a miserable farce! You shopkeeper! Yes – Kiev shopkeeper! Parasite!

KONSTANTIN. Miser!

ARKADINA. Ragbag!

> KONSTANTIN *sits down and weeps quietly.*

Nonentity! (*Passing to agitation.*) Don't cry. There's no need to cry . . . (*Weeps.*) You mustn't cry . . . (*Kisses him on his brow, his cheeks, his head.*) My own dear child, forgive me . . . Forgive your wicked mother. Forgive your unhappy mother.

KONSTANTIN (*embraces her*). If only you knew! I've lost everything. She doesn't love me, I can't write any more . . . All my hopes have foundered . . .

ARKADINA. Don't despair . . . Everything will be all right. I'm taking him away now – she'll go back to loving you. (*Wipes his tears.*) Enough, enough. We're friends again.

KONSTANTIN (*kisses her hands*). Yes, Mama.

ARKADINA (*gently*). Be friends with him, too. No duels . . .
You won't, will you?

KONSTANTIN. Very well . . . But please, Mama, I don't want
to meet him. It's hard for me . . . more than I can bear . . .

*Enter* TRIGORIN.

So . . . I'm going . . . (*Quickly puts the medical supplies back
in the cabinet.*) The doctor can do the dressing later . . .

TRIGORIN (*searches in a book*). Page 121 . . . Lines 11 and 12
. . . Here we are . . . (*Reads.*) 'If ever you have need of my
life, then come and take it.'

KONSTANTIN *picks up the bandage from the floor and goes
out.*

ARKADINA (*glancing at the clock*). They'll be bringing the
horses very shortly.

TRIGORIN (*to himself*). If ever you have need of my life, then
come and take it.

ARKADINA. You're packed, I hope?

TRIGORIN (*impatiently*). Yes, yes . . . (*Lost in thought.*) Why do
I hear a note of sadness in that cry from a pure heart, and why
has my own heart so painfully contracted . . . ? If ever you
have need of my life, then come and take it. (*To* ARKADINA.)
Let's stop another day!

ARKADINA *shakes her head.*

Just one more day!

ARKADINA. My dear, I know what keeps you here. But do take
a hold of yourself. You're a little intoxicated – you must be
sober again.

TRIGORIN. You must be sober, too – be understanding and
sensible, I implore you – see all this like the true friend you
are . . . (*Presses her hand.*) You're capable of sacrifice . . . Be
my friend – let me go . . .

ARKADINA (*in great agitation*). You're as captivated as that?

TRIGORIN. I feel as if a voice were calling me to her! Perhaps this is the very thing I need.

ARKADINA. Some provincial girl's love? How little you understand yourself!

TRIGORIN. Sometimes people fall asleep on their feet – and that's how I am now, talking to you but feeling all the time as if I were asleep and dreaming of her . . . Sweet and marvellous dreams have taken hold of me . . . Let me go . . .

ARKADINA (*trembling*). No, no . . . I'm a woman like any other – you can't speak to me so . . . Don't torment me, Boris . . . It frightens me . . .

TRIGORIN. If you choose you can be a woman unlike any other. A young love – a love full of charm and poetry – bearing me off into the land of dreams . . . in all this wide world no one but her can give me happiness! The sort of love I've never known yet . . . I'd no time for it when I was young, when I was beating on editors' doors, when I was struggling with poverty . . . Now here it is, that love I never knew – it's come, it's calling to me . . . What sense in running away from it?

ARKADINA (*with fury*). You've gone mad!

TRIGORIN. If you like.

ARKADINA. You've all conspired to torment me today! (*Weeps.*)

TRIGORIN (*clutches his head*). She doesn't understand! She won't understand!

ARKADINA. Am I really so old and ugly that you can talk to me about other women without so much as batting an eyelid? (*Embraces and kisses him.*) Oh, you're out of your senses! My wonderful man, my marvellous man . . . The last page of my life! (*Kneels.*) My joy, my pride, my delight . . . (*Embraces his knees.*) Leave me for a single hour and I'll never survive it, I'll go mad, my amazing man, my magnificent man, my sovereign lord . . .

TRIGORIN. Someone may come in. (*Helps her to her feet.*)

ARKADINA. Let them – I'm not ashamed of my love for you. (*Kisses his hands.*) My treasure, my wild and desperate man, you want to behave like a lunatic, but I don't want you to, I won't let you . . . (*Laughs.*) You're mine . . . you're mine . . . This brow of yours is mine, these eyes are mine, this lovely silken hair is mine . . . You're all mine. You're such a talented man, such an intelligent man, you're the finest writer alive today, you're the sole hope of Russia . . . You have so much sincerity, so much simplicity and freshness and wholesome humour . . . With one stroke you're able to convey the essence of a person or a landscape, your characters live and breathe. Impossible to read you without delight! You think this is mere incense at your altar? That I'm flattering you? Look into my eyes . . . look into them . . . Do I look like a liar? See for yourself – I'm the only one who can appreciate you, the only one who tells you the truth, my sweet, my marvel . . . You'll come away? Yes? You won't abandon me . . . ?

TRIGORIN. I've no will of my own . . . I've never had a will of my own . . . Flabby, crumbling, endlessly submissive – is that really what pleases a woman? Pick me up, carry me off – just don't let me out of your sight for an instant.

ARKADINA (*to herself*). Now he's mine. (*Easily, as if nothing had happened*). Anyway, you can stay if you like. I'll go, and you can come on later, in a week's time. There's really no reason for you to hurry, is there?

TRIGORIN. No, no, we'll go together.

ARKADINA. Whichever you like. Together – all right, together . . .

  *Pause.* TRIGORIN *notes something down in his book.*

What's that?

TRIGORIN. I heard a rather nice turn of phrase this morning – 'Virgins' forest . . .' Might come in handy. (*Stretches.*) So, we're going to be travelling? Stations and carriages again, station restaurants and station cutlets, conversations on trains . . .

*Enter* SHAMRAYEV.

SHAMRAYEV. I have to inform you, with the utmost regret, that the horses are ready. It's time, dear lady, to go to the station; the train arrives at five minutes after two. Now you won't forget, if you will be so kind, to inquire into the whereabouts of that actor, Suzdaltzev? Is he alive and well? We used to go drinking together once upon a time . . . His performance in *The Great Mail Robbery* was beyond compare . . . At that time, as I recall, he was working with the tragedian Izmailov – another remarkable character . . . Don't hurry yourself, dear lady, another five minutes yet. Once, in some melodrama, they were playing conspirators, and when they were suddenly discovered he was supposed to say: 'Caught, like rats in a trap!' Izmailov – 'Caught, like trats in a rap!' (*Laughs.*) Trats in a rap!

> *While he has been speaking,* YAKOV *has been busy with the suitcases, the* MAID *has been bringing* ARKADINA *her hat, coat, umbrella, and gloves, and everyone has been helping her to put her things on. The* MAN COOK *has looked in from the lefthand door, and then a few moments later come uncertainly all the way in. Enter* POLINA, *followed later by* SORIN *and* MEDVEDENKO.

POLINA (*offering a punnet*). Some plums for the journey . . . They're very sweet. You might feel like something nice . . .

ARKADINA. That's very kind of you.

POLINA. Goodbye, my dear. If anything was not as it should have been then please forgive me. (*Weeps.*)

ARKADINA (*embraces her*). Everything was fine, everything was fine. Only you mustn't start crying.

POLINA. Our lives are running out!

ARKADINA. But what can we do?

> SORIN, *wearing hat and Inverness, and carrying a stick, comes out of the lefthand door and crosses the room.*

SORIN. Time to go. You don't want to be late, when all's said and done. I'm going to get in.

> *Exit* SORIN.

MEDVEDENKO. Yes, and I'm going to walk to the station . . . See you off. I'll have to look sharp . . .

> *Exit* MEDVEDENKO.

ARKADINA. Goodbye, then, my dears . . . We'll see each other again next summer, if we're spared . . .

> *The* MAID, YAKOV, *and the* COOK *kiss her hand.*

Don't forget me.

> *Gives the* COOK *a ruble.*

Here, a ruble. That's for all three of you.

COOK. Thank you kindly, ma'am. Have a good journey, now! Very grateful to you!

YAKOV. God send you good fortune!

SHAMRAYEV. Give us the pleasure of hearing from you! (*To* TRIGORIN.) Goodbye, then.

ARKADINA. Where's Konstantin? Will you tell him I'm going? I must say goodbye to him. Well, then, remember me kindly. (*To* YAKOV.) I gave cook a ruble. That's for all three of you.

> *They all go off right. The stage is empty. Noises off, of the sort that occur when people are being said goodbye to. The* MAID *comes back and takes the basket of plums off the table, then goes out again.* TRIGORIN *comes back in.*

TRIGORIN. I've forgotten my stick. I think it's out on the verandah.

*Crosses towards the lefthand door and meets* NINA *as she enters.*

There you are. We're leaving.

NINA. I had a feeling we'd see each other again. (*Excitedly.*) I've made up my mind, once and for all – I'm going on the stage. By tomorrow I shan't be here – I'm getting away from my father, I'm abandoning everything, I'm starting a new life . . . I'm leaving, just like you . . . for Moscow. We shall see each other there.

TRIGORIN (*looking round*). Stay at the Slavyansky Bazar . . . Let me know as soon as you arrive . . . Grokholsky's house, on Molchanovka . . . I must hurry . . .

   *Pause*

NINA. Another minute . . .

TRIGORIN (*keeping his voice down*). You're so lovely . . . Oh, what joy it is to think we shall be seeing each other again before long!

   *She lays her head against his chest.*

I shall see those marvellous eyes again, this inexpressibly lovely, tender smile . . . these gentle features, this look of angelic innocence . . . My dear . . .

   *A prolonged kiss.*

CURTAIN

# Act Four

*Two years have elapsed.*
*One of the reception-rooms in* SORIN's *house which* KONSTANTIN *has turned into a working study. Doors left and right leading to inner rooms. A glass door, centre, opening on to the verandah. Apart from the usual living-room furniture there is a writing table in the righthand corner, a Turkish divan beside the lefthand door, a cupboard full of books, and more books on the window-ledges and chairs. – Evening. A single shaded lamp is alight. Twilight. The sighing of the trees can be heard, and the howling of the wind in the chimneys. The sound of the watchman's rattle as he passes. Enter* MEDVEDENKO *and* MASHA.

MASHA (*calls*). Hello? Are you there? (*Looks round.*) No one.
   The old man keeps asking every minute, 'Where's Kostya?
   Where's Konstantin?' He can't live without him . . .
MEDVEDENKO. He's frightened of being alone. (*Listens.*)
   What terrible weather! All yesterday, too, all last night.
MASHA (*turns up the lamp*). There are waves on the lake. Huge
   waves.
MEDVEDENKO. The garden's quite dark. They should tell
   someone to knock down that theatre. It's as hideous as bare
   bones, and the curtain slaps in the wind. When I was going
   past yesterday evening I could have sworn there was someone
   crying in there.
MASHA. Well, then . . .

   *Pause.*

MEDVEDENKO. Let's go home, Masha!
MASHA (*shakes her head*). I'm staying the night.
MEDVEDENKO (*pleading*). Masha, let's go! The baby could be

hungry, who knows?

MASHA. Oh, fiddle. Matryona will feed him.

*Pause.*

MEDVEDENKO. It's a shame, though. This will be his third night without his mother.

MASHA. What a bore you've become. At least it was philosophical vapourings before – now it's the baby and let's go home all the time, the baby and let's go home – I never hear anything else out of you.

MEDVEDENKO. Let's go, Masha!

MASHA. You go.

MEDVEDENKO. Your father won't give me any horses.

MASHA. Yes, he will. Just ask him – he'll give you some.

MEDVEDENKO. Well, perhaps I'll ask him. So you'll be coming tomorrow?

MASHA (*takes a pinch of snuff*). Yes, yes, tomorrow. You keep badgering away . . .

*Enter* KONSTANTIN *and* POLINA. KONSTANTIN *has brought pillows and a blanket, and* POLINA *bed-linen. They put all this on the Turkish divan, then* KONSTANTIN *crosses to his desk and sits down.*

What's that for, Mama?

POLINA. He's asked to have a bed made up for him in here with Konstantin.

MASHA. I'll do it . . . (*She makes up the bed.*)

POLINA (*sighs*). Second childhood . . . (*Crosses to the writing table, rests her elbows on it, and looks at a manuscript. Pause.*)

MEDVEDENKO. I'll be off, then. Goodbye, Masha. (*Kisses his wife's hand.*) Goodbye, Mother. (*Tries to kiss his mother-in-law's hand.*)

POLINA (*with annoyance*). Oh, come on, now! Off you go.

MEDVEDENKO (*to* KONSTANTIN). Goodbye, then.

KONSTANTIN *proffers his hand in silence. Exit*
MEDVEDENKO.

POLINA (*looking at the manuscript*). No one ever dreamed you'd
turn out to be a real writer, Kostya. But now, thanks be to
God, you've even started to get money from those literary
magazines. (*Runs her hand through his hair.*) You've turned
into a handsome man, too . . . Dear Kostya, be a good boy,
now, and be a bit kinder to my poor Masha . . . !

MASHA (*making the bed*). Leave him, Mama.

POLINA (*to* KONSTANTIN). She's a sweet, good girl. (*Pause.*)
All a woman needs, Kostya, is the odd kind glance. I know
from my own experience.

KONSTANTIN *gets up from his desk and silently leaves the
room.*

MASHA. Now you've put his back up. What did you have to go
badgering him for?

POLINA. I feel sorry for you, Masha.

MASHA. A lot of help that is.

POLINA. My heart aches for you. Do you think I can't see
what's happening? Do you think I don't understand?

MASHA. It's all nonsense. Love without hope – that's just in
novels. Fiddle! You mustn't lose your grip on yourself, that's
all, you mustn't keep waiting for something to happen, like
a sailor waiting for the weather . . . Once love has dug itself
into your heart you have to get it out again. They've promised
to transfer my husband to another district. As soon as we've
got there I shall forget it all . . . I shall tear it out of my heart
by the roots.

*A melancholy waltz can be heard from the next room but one.*

POLINA. That's Kostya playing. He's down in the dumps,
then.

MASHA (*noiselessly performs one or two turns of the waltz*). The

main thing, Mama, is not to have him in front of my eyes all
the time. Just let them give Semyon his transfer and, believe
me, in a month I shall have forgotten him. So fiddle-de-dee.

*The lefthand door opens.* SORIN, *in his wheelchair, is pushed
in by* DORN *and* MEDVEDENKO.

MEDVEDENKO. I've got six of us at home now. With flour at
two kopecks a pound.

DORN. You'll just have to manage.

MEDVEDENKO. Yes, you can laugh. You've got plenty of
money.

DORN. Money? In thirty years of practice, my friend, thirty
years of unrelenting practice, when night and day I couldn't
call my soul my own, I managed to save a miserable two
thousand rubles – and even that I went through while I was
abroad just now. I've nothing.

MASHA (*to her husband*). Haven't you gone?

MEDVEDENKO (*guiltily*). How can I? When they won't give me
any horses!

MASHA (*with bitter irritation, lowering her voice*). I just want you
out of my sight!

*The wheelchair comes to a halt in the lefthand half of the room.*
POLINA, MASHA, *and* DORN *sit down beside it.*
MEDVEDENKO *moves sadly aside.*

DORN. So many changes here, though! You've turned this
drawing-room into a study.

MASHA. It's more convenient for Konstantin, working in here.
He can go out into the garden to think whenever he feels like
it.

*The knocking of the watchman's mallet, off.*

SORIN. Where's my sister?

DORN. Gone to the station to meet Trigorin. Back in a moment.

SORIN. If you thought it necessary to get my sister here then

I must be dangerously ill. (*Falls silent for a moment.*) A fine business, I must say – here I am, dangerously ill, and they won't give me any medicine.

DORN. What would you like, then? Valerian drops? Bicarbonate of soda? Quinine?

SORIN. Yes, and now we get the moralising. Oh, what a penance it is! (*Nodding at the divan.*) Is that made up for me?

POLINA. For you, yes.

SORIN. Thank you.

DORN *hums to himself*.

Now, I should like to give Kostya an idea for a story. It would be entitled: *The Man who wanted to.* Once, when I was young, I wanted to become a man of letters – and I never became one. I wanted to speak well – and I've always spoken appallingly. (*Mimics himself.*) 'Simple as that, etcetera etcetera . . . I mean . . . you know . . .' – I used to drag out a summing-up to such lengths I'd break into a sweat. I wanted to get married – and I never got married. I wanted always to live in town – and here I am ending my days in the country, simple as that.

DORN. You wanted to get to the fourth grade of the civil service – and you did.

SORIN (*laughs*). I wasn't trying for that. That came of its own accord.

DORN. Come now, giving vent to your dissatisfaction with life at the age of sixty-two is not very handsome.

SORIN. It's like talking to the gatepost. Can't you get it into your head that I want to live?

DORN. That's fatuous. According to the laws of nature every life must have an end.

SORIN. You speak as someone who's eaten his fill. You've had your fill so you're indifferent to life – it's all one to you. But even you will dread to die.

DORN. The dread of death is an animal dread . . . It has to be suppressed. The only people who can rationally fear death are the ones who believe in eternal life, and who dread for their sins. But firstly, you're an unbeliever, and secondly – what are your sins? You served twenty-five years in the Department of Justice, that's all!

SORIN (*laughs*). Twenty-eight . . .

*Enter* KONSTANTIN. *He sits down on a stool at* SORIN's *feet.* MASHA *does not take her eyes off him all the time he is there.*

DORN. We're stopping Konstantin from working.

KONSTANTIN. No, it's all right.

*Pause.*

MEDVEDENKO. May I ask you, Doctor, which foreign city you liked best?

DORN. Genoa.

KONSTANTIN. Why Genoa?

DORN. There's a splendid street life there. When you come out of your hotel in the evening the whole street is jammed with people. You wander aimlessly about in the crowd, hither and thither, this way that way, and you share its life, you spiritually merge with it. You begin to believe that it would in fact be possible to have a single world soul of the sort that your friend Nina once acted in your play. Where is she now, by the way? Where is she and how is she?

KONSTANTIN. She's well, as far as I know.

DORN. I heard she was leading some strange sort of life. What's it all about?

KONSTANTIN. It's a long story, Doctor.

DORN. In a nutshell.

*Pause.*

KONSTANTIN. She ran away from home and took up with Trigorin. You know that much?

DORN. I know that much.

KONSTANTIN. She had a child. The child died. Trigorin decided he was no longer in love with her and reverted to his former attachment, as was only to be expected. Not that he'd ever given it up. Being the spineless creature that he is he'd somehow contrived to keep a foothold in both camps. So far as I can make out, Nina's private life has not been a total success.

DORN. How about the stage?

KONSTANTIN. Even worse, I think. She made her debut at a summer theatre outside Moscow, and then went to the provinces. I wasn't letting her out of my sight at that point, and for some time wherever she went I went, too. She kept taking on big parts, but she played them crudely and vulgarly, with a lot of howling and sawing of the air. There were moments when she showed some talent in shouting, or dying, but they were only moments.

DORN. So there is talent there, at any rate?

KONSTANTIN. It was difficult to tell. There probably is. I could see her, but she wouldn't see me, and her maid would never let me into her room. I undertood her feelings, and I didn't insist. (*Pause.*) What else can I tell you? When I was home again I started getting letters from her. Intelligent, warm, interesting letters. She never complained, but I could sense that she was deeply unhappy, that there was a sick nervous strain in every line. Even her imagination was a little distraught. She'd sign herself 'The Seagull'. It was like that play of Pushkin's where the old miller goes mad with grief and says he's a raven. She kept saying in the letters that she was a seagull. Now she's here.

DORN. How do you mean, here?

KONSTANTIN. In town, at the inn. She's been living in a room there for the best part of a week. I'd have gone to call on her – in fact Masha here did go – but she won't see anyone. Semyon says he saw her yesterday evening, in the fields a mile or so from here.

MEDVEDENKO. Yes, I did. She was going away from here, towards town. I said hello to her and asked why she didn't come to see us. She said she would.

KONSTANTIN. She won't, though. (*Pause.*) Her father and stepmother have disowned her. They've put watchmen everywhere to stop her even getting near the estate.

*Crosses to his writing-table with the doctor.*

How easy it is, Doctor, to be a philosopher on paper, and how difficult to be one in real life!

SORIN. She was a delightful girl.

DORN. I beg your pardon?

SORIN. I said she was a delightful girl. One former civil servant of the fourth grade was even in love with her for a while.

DORN. You old rake.

SHAMRAYEV *laughs, off.*

POLINA. It sounds as if they've arrived from the station.

KONSTANTIN. Yes, I can hear Mama.

*Enter* ARKADINA *and* TRIGORIN, *followed by* SHAMRAYEV.

SHAMRAYEV (*as he enters*). We're all getting older, we're all getting a little weather-beaten – but you, dear lady, go on being young . . . Dressed in light colours, full of life and grace . . .

ARKADINA. You're tempting fortune again, you tiresome man!

TRIGORIN (*to* SORIN). Hello! Still not better, then? We can't have that! (*Joyfully, at the sight of* MASHA.) And you're here!

MASHA. You recognised me, then? (*Shakes hands.*)

TRIGORIN. Married?

MASHA. Long since.

TRIGORIN. Happy?

*He exchanges bows with* DORN *and* MEDVEDENKO, *then goes uncertainly up to* KONSTANTIN.

I'm told you're ready to let bygones be bygones.

KONSTANTIN *holds out his hand.*

ARKADINA (*to her son*). He's brought the magazine with your new story.

KONSTANTIN (*to* TRIGORIN, *taking the volume*). Thank you. Most kind.

*They sit.*

TRIGORIN. I bring greetings from all your admirers. You're the talk of Petersburg and Moscow alike, and people keep asking me about you. They want to know what sort of person you are – how old – are you fair or are you dark? They all think you're middle-aged, I don't know why. And no one knows your real name, since you always publish under a pen-name. You're as mysterious as the Man in the Iron Mask.

KONSTANTIN. Are you here for long?

TRIGORIN. No, I'm leaving for Moscow tomorrow. I have to. I'm rushing to finish a story, and then I've promised something for a collection. Life as ever, in a word.

*While they are talking,* ARKADINA *and* POLINA *are setting up a card-table in the middle of the room and putting a cloth on it.* SHAMRAYEV *is lighting the candles and setting chairs. They get a lotto set out of the cupboard.*

Not a very warm welcome from the weather. A cruel wind. In the morning, if it drops, I'm going down to the lake for some fishing. I must take a look at the garden as I go, and the spot where your play was performed – do you remember? I've been developing an idea for a story. I just need to refresh my memory of the setting.

MASHA (*to her father*). Let my husband take a horse! He's got to get home.

SHAMRAYEV (*mimics her*). Horse . . . home . . . (*Sternly.*) You know as well as I do – they've just been out to the station.

They can't go running all over the countryside again.

MASHA. There *are* other horses . . . (*Sees that her father is not responding and flaps her hand.*) Oh, what's the use . . .?

MEDVEDENKO. Masha, I'll walk. Really . . .

POLINA (*sighs*). Walk, in weather like this . . . (*Sits down at the card-table.*) Come on, then, everyone.

MEDVEDENKO. I mean, it's only three miles or so . . . Goodbye . . . (*Kisses his wife's hand.*) Goodbye, Mother. (*His mother-in-law reluctantly gives him her hand to be kissed.*) I wouldn't disturb anyone, only it's the baby . . . (*Bows to everyone.*) Goodbye . . .

*Exit* MEDVEDENKO, *with apologetic gait.*

SHAMRAYEV. I dare say he'll manage it. He's not a general.

POLINA (*raps on the table*). Come on, then. Let's not waste time – they'll be calling us for supper in a minute.

SHAMRAYEV, MASHA, *and* DORN *sit down at the table.*

ARKADINA (*to* TRIGORIN). When the long autumn evenings come they play lotto here. Look – an antique set that we used when our poor mother played with us as children. Won't you try a round with us before supper?

*Sits down with* TRIGORIN *at the table.*

It's a boring game, but it's all right when you get used to it.

*She gives everyone three cards each.*

KONSTANTIN (*leafing through the magazine*). He's read his own story, and he hasn't even cut the pages of mine.

*He puts the magazine down on his writing-table, then goes to the lefthand door. As he passes his mother he kisses her head.*

ARKADINA. How about you, Kostya?

KONSTANTIN. Will you excuse me? I don't really feel like it . . . I'm going to walk up and down for a bit.

*Exit* KONSTANTIN.

ARKADINA. The stake is ten kopecks. Put in for me, will you, Doctor.

DORN. Ma'am.

MASHA. Has everyone put in? I'm starting . . . Twenty-two!

ARKADINA. Yes.

MASHA. Three!

DORN. Right.

MASHA. Have you put it on? Eighty-one! Ten!

SHAMRAYEV. Not so fast.

ARKADINA. Oh, but my dears, the reception I got in Kharkov! My head is still spinning!

MASHA. Thirty-four!

*A melancholy waltz is played, off.*

ARKADINA. The students gave me an ovation . . . Three baskets of flowers, two garlands, and this . . . (*Takes a brooch off her breast and throws it on to the table.*)

SHAMRAYEV. Oh, yes! Yes, indeed!

MASHA. Fifty . . . !

DORN. Fifty-what? Just fifty?

ARKADINA. I was wearing an amazing outfit . . . Whatever else, I do know how to dress.

POLINA. That's Kostya playing. The poor boy's pining.

SHAMRAYEV. They're being very rude about him in the papers.

MASHA. Seventy-seven!

ARKADINA. Why does he pay any attention?

TRIGORIN. He's not having much success. He still just can't find his own voice. There's something odd and formless about his work – something verging at times on the nightmarish. Never a single living character.

MASHA. Eleven!

ARKADINA (*glances at* SORIN). Petrusha, is this boring for you?

(*Pause.*) He's asleep.

DORN. One former civil servant of the fourth grade is fast asleep.

MASHA. Seven! Ninety!

TRIGORIN. If I'd lived on an estate like this, beside a lake, do you think I should ever have taken up writing? I should have wrestled the passion down, and done nothing but fish.

MASHA. Twenty-eight!

TRIGORIN. To catch a ruff or a perch – that is perfect happiness!

DORN. I believe in the boy, though. There's something there! There's something there! He thinks in images, his stories are bright and colourful, and they speak to me strongly. The only sad thing is that he doesn't have any clear aims. He produces an impression but nothing more, and you can't get all that far on impressions alone. (*To* ARKADINA.) Are you pleased to have a son who's a writer?

ARKADINA. Can you imagine, I still haven't read anything by him. I never have time.

MASHA. Twenty-six!

KONSTANTIN *comes quietly in and goes to his desk.*

SHAMRAYEV (*to* TRIGORIN). And we still have one of your things here.

TRIGORIN. What's that?

SHAMRAYEV. Konstantin somehow managed to shoot a seagull, and you told me to have it stuffed.

TRIGORIN. I don't remember that. (*Reflecting.*) No recollection!

MASHA. Sixty-six! One!

KONSTANTIN (*flings open the window and listens*). Pitch dark. I can't think why I feel so uneasy.

ARKADINA. Kostya, shut the window, there's a draft.

KONSTANTIN *shuts the window.*

MASHA. Eighty-eight!

TRIGORIN. Ladies and gentlemen, I have a full house.

ARKADINA (*merrily*). Bravo! Bravo!

SHAMRAYEV. Bravo!

ARKADINA. Always, wherever he goes, that man has all the luck. (*Gets up.*) Now let's go and have something to eat, though. Our visiting celebrity hasn't had a proper meal today. We'll go on again after supper. (*To her son.*) Kostya, leave your writing — let's go and eat.

KONSTANTIN. I won't, Mama. I'm not hungry.

ARKADINA. As you wish.

*Wakes* SORIN.

Petrusha — supper!

*Takes* SHAMRAYEV's *arm.*

I'll tell you all about the reception I got in Kharkov . . .

POLINA *extinguishes the candles on the table, then she and* DORN *push the wheelchair. They all go out through the lefthand door.* KONSTANTIN *remains alone on stage at his writing table.*

KONSTANTIN (*about to write, runs through what he has written already*). I've talked so much about new forms, and now I feel I'm gradually slipping into the same old pattern myself. (*Reads*) 'The poster on the fence was announcing to the world . . . Her pale face, framed by her dark hair . . .' 'Announcing to the world . . .' 'framed . . .' It's undistinguished. (*Deletes.*) I'll start with the man being woken by the sound of the rain, and all the rest can go. The description of the moonlit night — that's long and laboured. Trigorin has developed his special little tricks — it's easy for him . . . He has the neck of a broken bottle glittering on the bank of the millpool and the shadow of the water-wheel black beside it — and there's his moonlit night set up; while I have the shimmering light, plus the silent twinkling of the stars, plus the distant sound of a piano fading in the silent scented air . . . It's excruciating. (*Pause.*) Yes, I'm coming more and more to the conclusion that it's not a question of forms, old or new, but of writing without thought to any forms at all — writing because it flows freely out of your heart.

*Someone taps on the window nearest to the desk.*

What was that? (*Looks out of the window.*) I can't see anything . . . (*Opens the glass door and looks into the garden.*) Someone running down the steps. (*Calls*) Who's there?

*He goes out. He can be heard walking rapidly across the verandah. A moment later he comes back in with* NINA.

Nina! Nina!

NINA *lays her head on his chest and sobs, trying to control herself.*

(*Moved*). Nina! Nina! It's you . . . it's you . . . I had a kind of premonition — my mind's been in a torment all day. (*Takes her hat and shawl.*) Oh, my dear girl, my love — she's come! We mustn't cry, we mustn't.

NINA. There's someone here.

KONSTANTIN. There's no one.

NINA. Lock the doors — someone may come in.

KONSTANTIN. No one's going to come in.

NINA. Your mother's here, I know. Lock the doors . . .

KONSTANTIN (*locks the righthand door with its key, then crosses to the lefthand door*). There's no lock on this one. I'll barricade it with the chair. (*Puts an armchair against the door.*) Don't worry, no one's going to come in now.

NINA (*gazes intently into his face*). Let me look at you. (*Looks round.*) It's warm in here, it's nice . . . This was the drawing-room then. Have I changed a lot?

KONSTANTIN. Yes, you have . . . You've lost weight, and

your eyes have got bigger. Nina, it's strange somehow to be seeing you. Why didn't you ever let me in? Why didn't you come sooner? I know you've been living here for almost a week . . . I've been coming every day, several times a day, and standing under your window like a beggar.

NINA. I was afraid you'd hate me. Every night I dream that you're looking at me and not recognising me. If only you knew what things had been like! I've been coming here from the moment I arrived . . . walking by the lake. I've been by your house many times, but I couldn't make up my mind to come in. Let's sit down.

*They sit.*

We'll sit and talk. Talk and talk. It's nice in here – it's warm, it's cosy . . . You hear the wind? It says in Turgenev somewhere: 'Lucky the man who on nights like these has a roof over his head and a warm corner.' I'm the seagull. No, that's not right. (*Rubs her forehead.*) What was I talking about? Oh, yes . . . Turgenev . . . 'And Lord help all homeless wanderers . . .' It's all right. (*Sobs.*)

KONSTANTIN. Nina, you're crying again . . . Nina!

NINA. It's all right – it's a relief . . . I haven't cried these two whole years. Then last night I went to look at the garden to see if our theatre was still there. And it is – it's been standing there all this while. I cried for the first time in two years, and I felt a weight lifting, I felt my heart clearing. You see? – I've stopped crying. (*Takes him by the hand.*) So, you've become a writer now . . . You're a writer – I'm an actress . . . We're launched upon the world, even us . . . I used to be full of joy in life, like a little child – I'd wake up in the morning and start singing – I loved you – I had dreams of glory . . . And now? First thing tomorrow morning I'm off to Yeletz – third class, with the peasants – and in Yeletz I shall have the more educated local businessmen pressing their attentions upon me. It's a rough trade, life!

KONSTANTIN. Why Yeletz?

NINA. I'm contracted for the entire winter season. It's time to be getting there.

KONSTANTIN. Nina, I've cursed you, I've hated you, I've torn up your letters and your photographs – but not a moment when I didn't know that I was bound to you, heart and soul, for all eternity. It's not within my power to cease loving you, Nina. From the moment I lost you and began to be published I've found my life unliveable – nothing but pain . . . It's as if my youth had suddenly been stripped from me – I feel I've been living in this world for ninety years. I say your name – I kiss the ground you've walked upon. Wherever I look I see your face – I see the tender smile that shone on me in the summer of my life . . .

NINA (dismayed). Why is he talking like this?

KONSTANTIN. I'm all alone. I've no one's affection to warm me – I'm as cold as the grave – and whatever I write, it's dry and stale and joyless. Stay here, Nina, I beg you, or else let me come with you!

NINA quickly puts on her hat and shawl.

KONSTANTIN. Nina, why? Nina, for the love of God . . .

He watches her put her things on. Pause.

NINA. My horses are at the gate. Don't come out – I'll find my own way . . . (On the verge of tears.) Give me some water.

KONSTANTIN (gives her a drink of water). Where are you going now?

NINA. Into town. (Pause.) Is your mother here?

KONSTANTIN. Yes, she is . . . Uncle was taken ill last Thursday and we wired her to come.

NINA. Why do you say you kissed the ground I walked upon? I ought to be put to death. (Leans on the table.) I'm so tired! If only I could rest . . . just rest! (Raises her head.) I'm the seagull . . . That's not right. I'm the actress. Yes!

*Hears* ARKADINA *and* TRIGORIN *laughing. Listens, then runs to the lefthand door and looks through the keyhole.*

*He's* here, too . . . (*Crosses back to* KONSTANTIN.) Yes, of course . . . Not that it matters . . . Of course, though . . . He didn't believe in the theatre – he did nothing but laugh at my ambitions – and gradually I stopped believing, too – I began to lose heart . . . Then there were the burdens of love – the jealousy, the perpetual anxiety for my little boy . . . I became a paltry thing, a nonentity – my acting lost all meaning . . . I didn't know what to do with my hands, I didn't know how to stand, I couldn't control my voice. You don't understand what it's like when you feel you're acting badly. I'm the seagull. No, that's not right . . . Do you remember – you shot a seagull? One day by chance a man comes along and sees her. And quite idly he destroys her . . . An idea for a short story . . . That's not right . . . (*Rubs her forehead.*) What was I talking about . . .? Acting, yes . . . I'm not like that now . . . I've become a real actress. I take pleasure in my performance – I delight in it. I'm in a state of intoxication up there – I feel I'm beautiful. And now, while I've been staying here, I've kept walking round – walking and walking, thinking and thinking – and I've had the feeling that with every day my spiritual strength has grown . . . I know now, Kostya, I understand now, that in our work – and it makes no difference whether we're acting or whether we're writing – the main thing is not the fame, not the glory, not all the things I used to dream of; it's the ability to endure. Learn to bear your cross; have faith. I have faith, and for me the pain is less. And when I think about my vocation, I'm not afraid of life.

KONSTANTIN (*sadly*). You've found your way – you know where you're going. While I'm still floundering in a chaos of dreams and images without knowing who or what it's all for. I've no faith, nor any idea where my vocation lies.

NINA (*listens*). Sh . . . I'm going. Goodbye. When I've become a great actress come and see me perform. You promise? But now . . . (*Presses his hand.*) It's late. I can scarcely stand . . . I'm so tired, I'm so hungry . . .

KONSTANTIN. Stay here – I'll give you some supper . . .

NINA. No, no . . . Don't come out – I'll find my own way . . . The horses are close by . . . So she's brought him with her? Well, there we are – it makes no difference. Don't tell Trigorin anything when you see him . . . I love him. I love him even more than before . . . An idea for a short story . . . I love him; I love him passionately; I love him to the point of desperation. It was good before, Kostya! Do you remember? Such a bright, warm, joyous, innocent life. Such feelings. Feelings like graceful, delicate flowers . . . Do you remember? (*Recites.*) 'Men and lions, partridges and eagles, spiders, geese, and antlered stags, the unforthcoming fish that dwelt beneath the waters, starfish and creatures invisible to the naked eye; in short – all life, all life, all life, its dismal round concluded, has guttered out. Thousands of centuries have passed since any living creature walked the earth, and this poor moon in vain lights up her lantern. In the meadows the dawn cry of the crane is heard no more, and the May bugs are silent in the lime groves . . .'

> Embraces KONSTANTIN *impulsively, and runs out through the glass door.*

KONSTANTIN (*after a pause*). Just so long as no one meets her in the garden and then tells Mama. It might distress Mama . . .

> Over the next two minutes he silently tears up all his manuscripts and throws them under the desk, then opens the righthand door and goes out.

DORN (*off, trying to open the lefthand door*). Odd. The door seems to be locked . . .

*He enters, and puts the armchair back in its place.*

Obstacle race.

*Enter* ARKADINA *and* POLINA, *followed by* YAKOV, *bearing bottles and* MASHA, *then* SHAMRAYEV *and* TRIGORIN.

ARKADINA. Put the wine, and the beer for Boris Alekseyevich, on the table here. We're going to drink as we play. Do sit down, everyone.

POLINA (*to* YAKOV). Look sharp, now, and bring some tea as well. (*Lights the candles and sits down at the card-table.*)

*SHAMRAYEV takes TRIGORIN across to the cupboard.*

SHAMRAYEV. This is the thing I was telling you about earlier . . . (*Gets the stuffed seagull out of the cupboard.*) You asked me to have it done.

TRIGORIN (*looks at the seagull*). No recollection! (*After a moment's thought.*) No recollection!

*A shot, off right. Everyone jumps.*

ARKADINA (*alarmed*). What was that?

DORN. Nothing to worry about. Something in my medicine chest bursting, I expect. No cause for alarm.

*He goes off through the righthand door, and a few moments later comes back in again.*

Yes, that's what it was. A bottle of ether bursting. (*He hums to himself.*)

ARKADINA (*sitting down at the table*). Oh, it frightened me! It reminded me of the time when . . . (*Puts her hands over her face.*) I thought for a moment I was going to faint . . .

DORN (*leafing through a magazine; to* TRIGORIN). There was an article in here a couple of months back . . . From a correspondent in America, and I wanted to ask you, quite offhand . . . (*Puts an arm behind* TRIGORIN's *back and leads him away downstage.*) . . . this being a question that very much interests me . . . (*Lowers his voice.*) Get her out of here, will you. The fact is, he's shot himself . . .

CURTAIN

# Uncle Vanya

This translation of *Uncle Vanya* was first produced by
Michael Codron at the Vaudeville Theatre, London, on 24
May 1988, with the following cast:

| | |
|---|---|
| SEREBRYAKOV, *Professor emeritus* | Benjamin Whitrow |
| YELENA, *his wife, 27* | Greta Scacchi |
| SONYA, *his daughter by his first marriage* | Imelda Staunton |
| MARIA VASILYEVNA, *the widowed mother of the Professor's first wife* | Rachel Kempson |
| VANYA, *her son* | Michael Gambon |
| ASTROV, *a doctor* | Jonathan Pryce |
| TELEGIN, *an impoverished landowner* | Jonathan Cecil |
| MARINA, *the old nurse* | Elizabeth Bradley |
| WORKMAN | Tom Hardy |
| WATCHMAN | Peter Honri |

*Directed by* Michael Blakemore
*Designed by* Tanya McCallin
*Lighting by* Mick Hughes
*Associate Producer* David Sutton

The action takes place on Professor Serebryakov's estate.

# Act One

*The garden, with part of the house, and the verandah. On the path, beneath an ancient poplar, stands a table set with tea-things. Garden seats and chairs; on one of the seats lies a guitar. Near the table is a swing. Early afternoon. Overcast.*

*MARINA, a dumpy old woman who moves only with difficulty, is sitting by the samovar and knitting a stocking. ASTROV is walking up and down nearby.*

MARINA (*pours a glass of tea*). Here you are, then, my dear.

ASTROV (*takes the glass reluctantly*). I don't really want it.

MARINA. A drop of vodka, perhaps?

ASTROV. No. I don't drink vodka every day. It's too close, for that matter. (*Pause.*) Nanna, how long have we known each other?

MARINA (*thinking about it*). How long? Oh my Lord, I wish I could remember . . . You arrived in these parts . . . when . . . ? Sonya's mother was still alive. Her last two winters you were coming to us . . . So that's, what, eleven years. (*After a moment's thought.*) Or maybe even longer . . .

ASTROV. I've changed a lot in that time?

MARINA. Oh, a lot. You were a young man then, you were good-looking. You've aged, my love. Your looks aren't what they were. And then you like your drop to drink.

ASTROV. Yes . . . In the last ten years I've become a different man. You know why, Nanna? Because I've had to work too hard. On my feet from morning to night – never a moment to myself – go to bed and lie there just waiting to be dragged out again to a patient. In all the time we've known each other I've had not a single day off. Of course I've aged. Anyway, life is a dull, stupid, dirty business at the best of times. It drags its feet, this life of ours. You're

surrounded by cranks and crackbrains – there's something
odd about the lot of them. Live with them for a few years
and gradually, without noticing it, you start getting a bit
odd yourself. It's inevitable. (*Twirling his long moustache.*)
Look, I've grown this great moustache. Stupid thing. I've
got a bit odd, Nanna . . . I haven't gone soft in the head
yet, thank God, my brains are all there, only my feelings
have got somehow blunted. Nothing I want. Nothing I
need. No one I love . . . Just you, maybe. (*Kisses her head.*)
I had a nanny like you when I was a child.

MARINA. You want something to eat, perhaps?

ASTROV. No. In the third week of Lent I went over to
Malitzkoye – they had an epidemic there . . . Typhus . . .
Peasants lying packed together in their huts . . . Mud,
stench, calves on the floor alongside the patients . . . Baby
pigs, even . . . I was on the go all day, not a moment to sit
down, nothing to eat or drink . . . Got home, and still no
chance to rest because they'd carted a shunter in from the
railway. I put him on the table to operate, and he goes and
dies on me under the chloroform. And just when I didn't
need them my feelings came to life, and I got a stab of
conscience as if I'd killed him deliberately . . . I sat down
and I closed my eyes, so, and I thought: the people who
come after us, a hundred, two hundred years from now,
the people we're beating a path for – will they ever spare a
thought for us? They won't, Nanna, will they!

MARINA. People won't, but God will.

ASTROV. Yes! Thank you. Well said.

> *Enter* VANYA *from the house. He has had a sleep after lunch
> and has a somewhat rumpled appearance. He sits on a garden
> seat and straightens his stylish tie.*

VANYA. Yes . . . (*Pause.*) Yes . . .

ASTROV. Had a good sleep?

VANYA. Yes . . . Very good. (*Yawns.*) Ever since the professor
and his wife arrived life's been all out of joint . . . I've been

sleeping at the wrong time, eating fancy lunches and fancy dinners, drinking wine . . . It's bad for the system, all that! There was never a spare moment before – Sonya and I used to work like beavers. Now Sonya does it all on her own, while I just sleep, eat, and drink . . . It's not right!

MARINA (*shaking her head*). I don't know! The professor doesn't get up till noon, and the samovar's been on the boil all morning waiting for him. When they weren't here we had dinner at one, same as everyone else. With them here it's at seven. The professor sits up at night reading and writing, and suddenly at two o'clock in the morning there's the bell . . . What do they want? Tea! Wake up the servants for him, get the samovar out . . . I don't know!

ASTROV. And they're going to be here for some time yet, are they?

VANYA (*whistles*). A hundred years. The professor has decided he's going to live here.

MARINA. Now here we go again! The samovar's been on the table for two hours, and they've gone off for a walk.

VANYA. They're coming, they're coming . . . Don't fret yourself.

*Voices can be heard. From the depths of the garden, returning from their walk, come* SEREBRYAKOV, YELENA, SONYA, *and* TELEGIN.

SEREBRYAKOV. Splendid, splendid . . . Wonderful views.

TELEGIN. Quite remarkable, Professor.

SONYA. Tomorrow we'll make an expedition to the local forest. Would you like that, Papa?

VANYA. Tea, then, everyone!

SEREBRYAKOV. My friends, send my tea into the study, be so kind. I have one or two things still to do this afternoon.

SONYA. You're sure to enjoy the forest . . .

*YELENA, SEREBRYAKOV, and* SONYA *go off into the house.* TELEGIN *goes to the table and sits down beside* MARINA.

VANYA. An oppressively hot day, and our great scholar goes out with an umbrella, in his overcoat, gloves, and galoshes.

ASTROV. He plainly takes good care of himself.

VANYA. But what a beauty she is! What a beauty! In all my life I've never seen a woman more lovely.

TELEGIN (*to* MARINA). Whatever I do today – ride through the open fields, stroll in the shade of the garden, look at this table here – I feel pure indescribable happiness! It's enchanting weather, the birds are singing, we're all of us living in peace and harmony together. What more could we want? (*Accepting a glass of tea.*) Thank you most kindly!

VANYA (*dreamily*). Her eyes . . . A marvellous woman!

ASTROV (*to* VANYA). So, tell us something.

VANYA (*inertly*). Tell you what?

ASTROV. Nothing new?

VANYA. Not a thing. It's all old. I'm the same as I always was, or possibly worse, because I've grown idle. I don't do anything. Just grumble away like some cantankerous old codger. Mama goes babbling on like an old jackdaw about the emancipation of women, one eye on the grave, the other scanning those clever books of hers for the dawn of a new life.

ASTROV. What about the professor?

VANYA. The professor, as always, sits writing in his study from morning until far into the night. The poor paper! He'd do better to write his autobiography. What a wonderful subject he'd make! A retired professor, a dried haddock with a doctorate . . . Gout and rheumatism and migraine, and a liver swollen with envy . . . This old dried haddock lives on his first wife's estate – much against his will – because he can't afford to live in town. He complains endlessly about his misfortune, although in actual fact he's quite unusually fortunate. (*Irritably.*) Just consider for a moment exactly how fortunate. The son of a lowly sacristan – but he went to a seminary, he took various degrees, he got a chair, he joined the upper ranks of society, he became the son-in-law of a senator, and so on and so forth. Leave all that aside, though.

Just consider this. A man spends precisely twenty-five years reading and writing about Art when he understands precisely nothing about it. For twenty-five years he chews over other men's thoughts about realism and naturalism and every other kind of rubbish. For twenty-five years he reads and writes about things that clever people have known for years already, and that stupid people don't care about anyway. For twenty-five years, in other words, he's been shovelling a lot of nothing from here to nowhere. And yet what an opinion he has of himself! What pretensions! He's reached retiring age, and not a soul has ever heard of him. He's completely unknown. So for twenty-five years he's been usurping another's rightful place. Yet lo and behold – he paces the earth like a demi-god!

ASTROV. I do believe you're jealous.

VANYA. Yes, I'm jealous! And his success with women! Far greater than any Don Juan has ever known! His first wife, my sister – a lovely tender creature, as pure as the blue sky up there, with a noble heart and a generous soul, and more admirers than he's had pupils – she loved him the way only the angels can, when they love beings as fine and pure as themselves. Our mother still worships him, still walks in holy terror of him. His second wife, a beautiful, intelligent woman – you saw her just now – she married him when he was an old man already, and gave him her youth and beauty, her freedom, her radiance. Why? For what in return?

ASTROV. Is she faithful to the professor?

VANYA. Regrettably she is.

ASTROV. Why regrettably?

VANYA. Because this faithfulness of hers is false through and through. Much rhetoric in it but little logic. Deceiving an aged husband you can't bear the sight of – that's immoral; attempting to stifle your own hapless youth and living feelings – that's not immoral.

TELEGIN (*plaintively*). Vanya, I don't like it when you say that kind of thing. Really, now . . . A man who deceives his wife

or a woman who betrays her husband – that's someone who
can't be trusted – someone who might betray his country!

VANYA (*irritated*). Oh, do dry up, Ilyusha!

TELEGIN. Let me have my say, Vanya. My wife ran off with
her fancy man the day after our wedding because of my
pockmarked appearance. From that day forth I've never
broken my bond. I still love her, I'm still faithful to her, I help
her in so far as I'm able, I've spent all I possessed on bringing
up the children she had by her fancy man. I've been deprived
of happiness, but I do have my pride left. What can she say?
Her youth is gone, her beauty has faded in accordance with
the laws of nature, her fancy man is dead . . . What does she
have left?

> *Enter* SONYA *and* YELENA. *A moment later* MARIA
> VASILYEVNA *enters with a book. She sits down and reads,
> is served with tea and drinks it without looking.*

SONYA (*to* MARINA, *hurriedly*). Nanna, the peasants have
come. Go and have a word with them – I'll do the tea . . .
(*Pours tea.*)

> MARINA *goes off.* YELENA *takes her cup and drinks it sitting
> on the swing.*

ASTROV (*to* YELENA). I'm here to see your husband, you
realize. You wrote to say he was very ill, that he had
rheumatism and so on. But he turns out to be perfectly well.

YELENA. Yesterday evening he was in very low spirits – he was
complaining of pains in his legs. But today he's all right . . .

ASTROV. Meanwhile I've come galloping eighteen miles. Well,
no matter – it's not the first time. Anyway, I'll stay the night,
so at least I'll get a proper dose of sleep.

SONYA. Wonderful. It's such a rare thing for you to spend the
night here. I don't suppose you've had dinner?

ASTROV. No, ma'am, I haven't.

SONYA. Then you can very conveniently have dinner here. We
dine at seven these days. (*Drinks.*) Cold tea!

TELEGIN. The samovar has lost a lot of its heat by this time.

YELENA. Never mind, Ivan Ivanych. We can drink it cold just as well.

TELEGIN. Excuse me, but not Ivan Ivanych. Sorry, but it's Ilya Ilich . . . Ilya Ilich Telegin. I'm Sonya's godfather, and the Professor, your husband, knows me very well. Sorry, but I live here now, you see, on this estate . . . You may have been kind enough to notice me having dinner with you every day.

SONYA. He's our great tower of strength, our right-hand man. (*Tenderly.*) Come on, Godfather, I'll give you some more tea.

MARIA VAS. Oh!

SONYA. What's the matter, Grandmama?

MARIA VASILYEVNA. I forgot to tell Alexandre . . . I'm quite losing my memory . . . I had a letter today from Pavel Alekseyevich in Kharkov . . . He sent his new pamphlet . . .

ASTROV. Anything interesting?

MARIA VASILYEVNA. Interesting, yes, but somehow rather curious. He's attacking the very things that he was defending seven years ago. It's quite appalling!

VANYA. Nothing's appalling. Drink your tea, *maman*.

MARIA VASILYEVNA. But I want to talk!

VANYA. But we've been talking and talking and reading pamphlets for fifty years. It's time we stopped.

MARIA VASILYEVNA. You've taken a dislike to the sound of my voice for some reason. Forgive me, Jean, but this last year you have changed out of all recognition . . . You used to be someone with clear convictions, an example of enlightenment . . .

VANYA. Oh, yes! I was an example of enlightenment that no one ever got any light from . . . (*Pause.*) An example of enlightenment . . . You couldn't have made a crueller joke! I'm forty-seven now. Until last year I was just like you – deliberately trying to blind myself with all this theory of yours, so as not to see the reality of life – and I thought I was doing the right thing. Now, though – oh, if only you knew! I can't sleep at night for spleen and anger that I've so stupidly wasted my time, when I could have had everything I now can't because of my age!

SONYA. Uncle Vanya, you're being boring!

MARIA VASILYEVNA (*to her son*). You seem to be making some kind of accusation against your former convictions . . . But it's not the convictions which are to blame – it's you. You failed to keep in mind that convictions are nothing in themselves, mere words . . . You should have got down to business.

VANYA. We can't all be perpetual writing machines, like your Herr Professor.

MARIA VASILYEVNA. What do you mean by that, pray?

SONYA (*imploringly*). Grandmama! Uncle Vanya! I implore you!

VANYA. Not another word. Wordless apologies.

*Pause.*

YELENA. Nice weather today, though . . . Not too hot . . .

*Pause.*

VANYA. Nice weather for hanging yourself . . .

TELEGIN *strums on the guitar.* MARINA *goes by the house calling the chickens.*

MARINA. Cheep, cheep, cheep . . .

SONYA. Nanna, what were the peasants here for?

MARINA. Same old thing – about that piece of waste ground. Cheep, cheep, cheep . . .

SONYA. Which one are you after?

MARINA. Speckles. She's gone off with her chicks . . . I don't want the crows getting them . . .

*Exit* MARINA. TELEGIN *plays a polka; they all listen in silence. Enter a* WORKMAN.

WORKMAN. The doctor – is he here? (*to* ASTROV.) Begging your pardon, sir, but they've sent over for you.

ASTROV. Where from?

WORKMAN. The factory.

ASTROV (*with annoyance*). Oh, thank you very much indeed. I suppose I'll have to go . . . (*Looks round for his cap.*) What a bore, damn it . . .

SONYA. It's a shame, isn't it . . . Come back for dinner afterwards.

ASTROV. No, it'll be too late by that time. (*To the* WORKMAN.) Listen, be a good chap and fetch me a glass of vodka.

*Exit* WORKMAN.

(*Finds his cap.*) In some play by Ostrovsky there's a man with large moustaches and small abilities. That's me. Well, goodbye to everyone . . . (*To* YELENA.) If you felt like looking in on me at any time – you could come with Sonya here – it would give me real pleasure. I have a small estate – eighty acres or so, but if you're interested there's a nursery and a model orchard, the like of which you won't find for many hundred miles around. I have the state forest next door to me . . . The Warden there is old and ailing, so in fact I run it all.

YELENA. Yes, people have told me you've got a great passion for forests. Very valuable work, of course, but it must surely interfere with your real vocation. After all, you are a doctor.

ASTROV. God alone knows what our real vocation is.

YELENA. It's interesting, though, is it?

ASTROV. Yes, it's an interesting business.

VANYA (*ironically*). Oh, highly!

YELENA (*to* ASTROV). You're still a young man – what, thirty-six, thirty-seven, by the look of you – and it can't be as interesting as you say. Just trees and more trees. Monotonous, I should think.

SONYA. No, it's extremely interesting. The doctor plants new woodlands every year – they've sent him a bronze medal and a diploma for it. He makes great efforts to stop people destroying the existing forests. Just listen to him and you'll agree with every word. He says that forests adorn the earth, that they teach man to appreciate beauty and give him a intimation of majesty. Forests moderate the harshness of the climate. And in countries with a gentle climate human beings spend less of their strength on the struggle with nature; they become gentler in their turn. In places like that people are lithe and beautiful, with quick responses, and well-turned speech, and graceful movements. Their arts and sciences flourish, their philosophy is never sombre, they treat women with grace and honour . . .

VANYA (*laughing*). Bravo, bravo . . . ! This is all very fine, but it fails to convince. (*To* ASTROV.) So with your permission, my friend, I shall continue to build my outhouses of wood and burn wood in my stoves.

ASTROV. You can burn peat in your stoves, and build your outhouses of brick. I've no objection, anyway, to cutting the forests to meet our needs, but why destroy them? The Russian forests are ringing beneath the axe; thousands of millions of trees are perishing; the habitats of animals and birds are being laid waste; rivers are dwindling and drying up; marvellous landscapes are vanishing beyond recall; and all because man in his idleness hasn't sense enough to bend down and pick up his fuel from the earth. (*To* YELENA.) Isn't that the truth? Only a reckless barbarian would burn that beauty in his stove, and destroy what we cannot replace. Man is endowed with reason and creative powers to increase and multiply his inheritance, yet up to now he has created nothing, only destroyed. The forests grow ever fewer; the rivers parch; the wild life is gone; the climate is ruined; and with every passing day the earth becomes uglier and poorer. (*To* VANYA.) You sit there looking at me ironically, you don't take me seriously, and . . . and yes, perhaps it is indeed just another of my odd ideas, but when I go past trees on the peasants' land, trees that I have saved from being cut down, or when I hear the sigh and rustle of my young woodlands, planted with my own hands, then I know that I have some slight share in controlling the climate, and that if a thousand years from now human beings are happy then it will be just a tiny bit my fault. When I plant a birch tree and then see it green and swaying in the wind my heart fills with pride, and I . . .

*Sees the* WORKMAN, *who has brought a glass of vodka on a tray.*

However . . . (*Drinks.*) I must go. It's probably all some crackbrained notion, anyway. Goodbye!

*He goes towards the house.* SONYA *takes his arm and goes with him.*

SONYA. When will you come and see us again?
ASTROV. I don't know . . .
SONYA. Another month from now . . . ?

ASTROV *and* SONYA *go off into the house.* MARIA VASILYEVNA *and* TELEGIN *remain by the table.* YELENA *and* VANYA *go towards the verandah.*

YELENA. You were being impossible again. Did you have to annoy your mother, did you have to talk about perpetual writing machines? And at lunch today you quarrelled with my husband again. So petty!

VANYA. But if I hate him?

YELENA. There's no call to hate him – he's the same as everyone else. He's no worse than you.

VANYA. If you could see the way you look, the way you move . . . The indolence of your life! The sheer indolence of it!

YELENA. The indolence, yes, and the tedium! Everyone's rude about my husband, everyone looks at me with pity – oh, the poor thing, she's got an elderly husband! All this sympathy for me – oh, I know exactly what it's about! It's the same as Astrov was saying just now: you recklessly destroy forests, all of you, and soon there won't be anything left standing on the face of the earth. You do exactly the same with human beings – you recklessly destroy them, and soon, thanks to you, there will be neither faithfulness nor innocence left in the world, nor any capacity for self-sacrifice. Why do you have to lose your head at the sight of any woman who doesn't belong to you? Because – the doctor was right – in all of you there lurks a demon of destruction. You've no pity for forests, nor for birds, nor for women, nor for one another . . .

VANYA. I don't care for all this philosophising!

*Pause.*

YELENA. You could see the tension and the fatigue in that doctor's face. An interesting face. Sonya likes him, obviously – she's in love with him and I can see why. He's been here three times already since I arrived, but I'm too timid – I haven't once talked to him properly or been nice to him. He's got it into his head I'm an evil woman. The reason you and I are friends, probably, is because we're both such dull and tedious people! Tedious, the pair of us! Don't look at me that way – I don't like it.

VANYA. How can I look at you any other way if I'm in love with you? You're my happiness, you're life, you're my youth! I know the chance that you might feel the same is negligible – nil, in fact. But there's nothing I want from you – just let me look at you, let me listen to your voice . . .

YELENA. Sh, people might hear!

*They go into the house.*

VANYA (*following her*). Let me talk about my love – don't drive me away – and that alone will be the summit of happiness for me . . .

YELENA. It's such a torment . . .

*They both go off into the house.* TELEGIN *strikes the strings and plays a polka.* MARIA VASILYEVNA *makes a note of something in the margins of the pamphlet.*

CURTAIN

# Act Two

*The dining-room in* SEREBRYAKOV'S *house. Night. The* WATCHMAN *can be heard knocking in the garden.*

SEREBRYAKOV *sits dozing in an armchair by the open window.* YELENA *sits beside him, also dozing.*

SEREBRYAKOV (*waking*). Who is it? You, Sonya?

YELENA. Me.

SEREBRYAKOV. Oh, you . . . Unbearable pain!

YELENA. Your rug's fallen on the floor. (*Tucks his legs up.*) I'll shut the window.

SEREBRYAKOV. No, I'm stifling . . . I dozed off just then and dreamed I had someone else's left leg. I woke up with this agonising pain. And no, it's not gout – it's more like rheumatism. What time is it?

YELENA. Twenty past twelve.

*Pause.*

SEREBRYAKOV. Look in the library tomorrow morning, will you, and see if you can find a Batyushkov. I think we've got one.

YELENA. Um?

SEREBRYAKOV. I want you to find me a complete Batyushkov in the morning. I remember we used to have one. But why is it so difficult to get my breath?

YELENA. You're tired. You didn't sleep last night, either.

SEREBRYAKOV. They say Turgenev had gout and it turned into angina. I'm afraid I might get it. Oh, this damned, disgusting business of being old! Curse it, curse it! When I got old I became offensive to myself. And all of you must find it offensive to look at me.

YELENA. You talk about being old as if it's all our fault.

SEREBRYAKOV. You're the one who finds me most offensive of all.

     YELENA *moves and sits herself some way off.*

And of course you're right. I'm not a fool – I understand. You're young, you're healthy, you're beautiful, you want to live your life; while I'm an old man, practically a corpse. Do you think I don't understand? And of course it's idiotic that I'm still alive. Just wait, though – I shall release you all soon enough. I shan't have to drag on much longer.

YELENA. I'm exhausted . . . For the love of God be quiet.

SEREBRYAKOV. Everyone's exhausted, apparently, everyone's bored, everyone's wasting his youth, and all because of me, while I'm the only one who's having a good time. Oh, of course! Naturally!

YELENA. Stop it! You're tormenting me to death!

SEREBRYAKOV. I'm tormenting everyone to death. Of course.

YELENA (*on the verge of tears*). It's unbearable! Just tell me what you want of me!

SEREBRYAKOV. Nothing.

YELENA. Then stop it. I beg you.

SEREBRYAKOV. It's curious, though, isn't it – if my brother-in-law opens his mouth, or that old idiot of a mother of his, that's fine, everyone listens. But if I so much as breathe a word everyone starts to feel miserable. Even my voice is offensive. All right, so I'm offensive, I'm an egotist, I'm a tyrant – but don't I have some right in my old age to a little egotism? Haven't I earned it? Don't I have a right, I ask you, to some peace in my declining years, to some attention from people?

YELENA. No one's disputing your rights.

     *The window bangs in the wind.*

The wind's got up. I'm going to close the window. (*She closes it.*) It's going to start raining any moment. No one is disputing your rights.

*Pause. In the garden the* WATCHMAN *knocks and sings a song.*

SEREBRYAKOV. You spend your life in the pursuit of learning, you grow accustomed to the study and the lecture-hall and distinguished colleagues – and then suddenly, without rhyme or reason, you wake up in this crypt, seeing stupid people every day and listening to banal conversation . . . I want to live, I like success, I like being well-known and making a stir. I might as well be in Siberia. Yearning for the past all the time, following other people's successes, being frightened of dying . . . I can't do it! It's not in me! And then on top of it all to find that people won't forgive me for being old!

YELENA. Just wait, just be patient; in five or six years I shall be old as well.

*Enter* SONYA.

SONYA. Papa, you were the one who had Dr Astrov sent for, and now he's come you won't see him. It's very thoughtless. You've disturbed someone quite needlessly.

SEREBRYAKOV. What use is he to me, this Astrov of yours? He knows as much about medicine as I do about astronomy.

SONYA. We can't fetch the entire medical profession here for your gout.

SEREBRYAKOV. Well, I'm not going to talk to some kind of holy fool.

SONYA. Please yourself. (*Sits.*) It makes no difference to me.

SEREBRYAKOV. What time is it?

YELENA. Getting on for one.

SEREBRYAKOV. Stifling . . . Sonya, give me the drops on the table.

SONYA. Here. (*Gives him the drops.*)

SEREBRYAKOV (*irritably*). Oh, not those! No good asking anyone to do anything!

SONYA. Now, please, don't start playing up. Some people may enjoy it, but don't inflict it on me, thank you very much. I don't like it. I haven't time anyway. I've got to be up early

– I've got the haymaking.

*Enter* VANYA, *wearing a dressing-gown and carrying a candle*.

VANYA. We're going to have a storm.

*Lightning*.

There! Yelena, Sonya – go to bed. I've come to take over.

SEREBRYAKOV (*alarmed*). No, no! Don't leave me with him! No! He'll just keep talking to me!

VANYA. But they must have a break! This is the second night they've been up!

SEREBRYAKOV. Let them go to bed, then, but you go away, too. Please. I implore you. We used to be friends, remember – no arguments. We'll talk another time.

VANYA (*smiling*). We used to be friends . . . Used to be . . .

SONYA. Be quiet, Uncle Vanya.

SEREBRYAKOV (*to his wife*). My dear, don't leave me with him! He'll go on and on at me.

VANYA. This is becoming slightly ludicrous.

*Enter* MARINA, *carrying a candle*.

SONYA. You should be in bed, Nanna. It's the middle of the night.

MARINA. Fine chance of that. The samovar's still on the table.

SEREBRYAKOV. No one getting any sleep, everyone worn to a shadow – just me having the time of my life.

MARINA (*going up to* SEREBRYAKOV, *gently*). What's the matter, then, my dear? Hurts, does it? I've got an ache in my legs myself, such an ache. (*Puts his rug straight.*) You've had this trouble a long time. The old mistress, Sonya's mother, couldn't sleep at night for grieving . . . She loved you with all her heart . . . (*Pause.*) Old people, they're like children – they want someone to feel sorry for them, but no one's sorry for you when you're old.

*Kisses* SEREBRYAKOV's *shoulder.*

Off we go to bed, my dear . . . Off we go, my love . . · I'll make you some lime tea – I'll warm up those feet of yours . . . I'll pray to God for you . . .

SEREBRYAKOV (*touched*). Off we go, then, Marina.

MARINA. I've got an ache in my legs, too, such an ache.

*Takes him off, accompanied by* SONYA.

Yes, she did nothing but grieve, the old mistress, she did nothing but weep . . . You were still little then, Sonya, you didn't understand . . . Come on, my dear, come on . . .

*Exeunt* SEREBRYAKOV, SONYA, *and* MARINA.

YELENA. I'm at my wits' end with him. I can scarcely stay on my feet.

VANYA. You're at your wits' end with him – I'm at my wits' end with myself. This is the third night in a row I haven't slept.

YELENA. Things have come to a fine pass in this house. Your mother hates everything and everyone except her pamphlets and the professor; the professor's on edge because he doesn't trust me and he's afraid of you; Sonya's angry with her father and angry with me – she hasn't spoken to me for the last fortnight; you hate my husband and you openly despise your own mother; *I'm* on edge – I must have burst into tears about twenty times today . . . A fine state this house is in.

VANYA. Let's leave the philosophising!

YELENA. You're an intelligent, educated man. I should have thought you must realize that the end of the world won't be in fire and slaughter – it will be in enmity and hatred, in all these petty quarrels . . . Your task should be not recrimination but reconciliation.

VANYA. Reconcile me first with myself! My dear . . . .

*He presses his lips to her hand.*

YELENA. Let go! (*Takes her hand away.*) Go away!

VANYA. Soon the rain will be over, and everything in nature will revive and breathe a sigh of relief. The only thing the storm won't revive is me. Day and night the same thought chokes me like a demon sitting on my chest – that my life is lost beyond recall. There's no past – that was squandered on things of no importance – and the present is horrible in its absurdity. That's my life for you, and my love; where can I put them, what can I do with them? My feelings are running to waste as pointlessly as a ray of sunlight in a bottomless pit. I'm running to waste myself.

YELENA. When you tell me about your love I feel a kind of dullness settle over me, and no words come. I'm sorry, there's nothing I can say to you. (*Makes to go.*) Good night.

VANYA (*blocking her way*). And then if only you knew how painful it is to think that beside me in this very house another life is running to waste – yours! What are you waiting for? What cursed philosophy is stopping you? Listen, just listen . . .

YELENA (*staring at him*). You're drunk!

VANYA. Possibly, possibly . . .

YELENA. Where's the doctor?

VANYA. In there . . . He's staying the night in my room. Possibly, possibly . . . All things are possible!

YELENA. You were drinking again today? Why do you do it?

VANYA. At least it gives a semblance of life . . . Don't try to stop me, Yelena!

YELENA. You never drank before and you never talked so much . . . Go to bed! I'm tired of you.

VANYA (*pressing his lips to her hand*). My dear . . . you wonderful woman!

YELENA (*with annoyance*). Leave me alone. It really is becoming offensive.

*Exit* YELENA.

VANYA (*alone*). She's gone . . . (*Pause.*) Ten years ago I used to meet her at my sister's. She was seventeen then, and I was thirty-seven. Why didn't I fall in love with her then and propose to her? It would have been so easy! And now she would have been my wife . . . Yes . . . We should both have been woken by the storm tonight; she would have been frightened of the thunder, and I should have put my arms round her and whispered: 'Don't be afraid, I'm here.' Oh, wonderful thoughts! So sweet I can't help laughing . . . but such a muddle they're making inside my head . . . Why am I old? Why can't she understand what I'm trying to tell her? Those rhetorical tricks of hers, the indolent moralizing, her silly indolent thoughts about the end of the world – I find all that deeply repellent. (*Pause.*) Oh, I've been so duped! I worshipped that man, that miserable gout-ridden professor, I worked like an ox for him! Sonya and I squeezed every last drop out of this estate; we haggled over peas and curds and sunflower oil like a couple of bargaining peasants; we went short ourselves so as to make kopecks into rubles and send them to him. I was proud of him and his learning – I lived and breathed him! Every word he wrote or uttered seemed to me touched with genius . . . But, oh God – now? Here he is, retired, and the sum total of his life is revealed: when he is gone not one solitary page of all his labour will remain – he's utterly unknown – he's nothing! A soap bubble! And I have been duped . . . I see that – duped like an idiot . . .

*Enter* ASTROV *in a frock-coat, but without wasitcoat or tie, and slightly drunk. He is followed by* TELEGIN *with his guitar.*

ASTROV. Play!
TELEGIN. They're all asleep!
ASTROV. Play!

TELEGIN *strums quietly.*

(*to* VANYA). All on your own in here? No ladies? (*Puts his hands on his hips and sings quietly.*) It was the storm that woke me up. Fair drop of rain. What's the time?

VANYA. God knows.

ASTROV. I thought I heard the professor's wife.

VANYA. She was in here just now.

ASTROV. Magnificent woman. (*Examines the medicine bottles on the table.*) Medicines. Every prescription under the sun! Labels from Kharkov and Moscow and Tula . . . He's inflicted his gout on every city in the land. Is he ill or is he putting it on?

VANYA. He's ill.

*Pause.*

ASTROV. Why are you so miserable today? Feeling sorry for the professor, are you?

VANYA. Leave me alone.

ASTROV. Or are you in love with Mrs Professor?

VANYA. I regard her as a friend.

ASTROV. Got to that, has it?

VANYA. What do you mean, 'got to that'?

ASTROV. A woman can become a man's friend only through the following progression: first – acquaintance; then – mistress; thereafter, certainly – friend.

VANYA. A vile piece of wisdom.

ASTROV. Is it? I suppose it is . . . I must admit, I'm becoming a rather vile sort of man. Look, I'm even drunk. I usually get drunk like this once a month. I've got the cheek of the devil when I'm in this state. I can do anything! I take on the trickiest operations and bring them off marvellously; I draw up the most far-reaching plans for the future; at times like this I don't even think there's anything odd about me – I believe I'm doing mankind some colossal service . . . Colossal! And at times like this I have my own philosophical system, and all the rest of you, my friends, are just insect-life as far as I'm concerned . . . just microbes. (*To* TELEGIN.) Play up, Ilyusha!

TELEGIN. With all my heart, old friend, but honestly – the

whole house is fast asleep!

ASTROV. Play!

> TELEGIN *strums quietly.*

We could do with another drink. Come on, I think there's still some cognac left in our room. As soon as it's light we'll drive over to my place. All right?

> *Sees* SONYA *entering.*

Excuse me – I'm not wearing a tie.

> *He goes out quickly;* TELEGIN *follows him.*

SONYA. So, Uncle Vanya, you've got drunk with the doctor again. You've become drinking companions. Well, he's always been like that, but why do you have to be? It's most unfitting at your age.

VANYA. Age doesn't come into it. Where there's no real life people live on illusions. It's better than nothing.

SONYA. The hay lying mown in the fields, rain every day, everything rotting – and all you can think of is illusions. You've given up the estate work entirely . . . I do it all on my own – I'm absolutely worn out . . . (*In alarm.*) Uncle, you've tears in your eyes!

VANYA. Tears? What tears? Nonsense . . . You looked at me just then like your poor dead mother. My sweet . . . (*Greedily kisses her hands and face.*) My sister . . . my sweet sister . . . Where is she now? If she had known! Oh, if she had known!

SONYA. What, Uncle? Known what?

VANYA. It's so hard to bear . . . Well, never mind . . . Later . . . Don't worry . . . I'll go away . . .

> *Exit* VANYA.

SONYA (*knocks on the door*). Doctor! You're not asleep, are you? In here a moment!

ASTROV (*from the other side of the door*). Just coming!

*A short pause, and then* ASTROV *enters, now wearing waistcoat and tie.*

What is it?

SONYA. Drink yourself, if that's not something you find offensive, but don't make Uncle drink. It's bad for him.

ASTROV. Very well. We'll drink no more. (*Pause.*) I'm just going home. So that's settled. By the time they've harnessed the horses it will be dawn.

SONYA. It's raining. Wait until morning.

ASTROV. The storm's passing – I'll only catch the edge of it. I'm going. And, please, no more calls to see your father. I tell him it's gout – he tells me it's rheumatism; I tell him to stay in bed – he sits in a chair. And today he wouldn't so much as speak to me.

SONYA. He's been spoilt. (*Hunts in the sideboard.*) Would you like a bite of something?

ASTROV. Yes. Thank you.

SONYA. I love little midnight feasts. I think there's something in the sideboard. They say he had great success with women all his life, and it was the ladies who spoilt him. Here, take the cheese.

*They both stand at the sideboard and eat.*

ASTROV. I didn't eat today, just drank. He's a difficult man, your father. (*Gets a bottle out of the sideboard.*) May I? (*Pours a glass.*) There's no one around, so I can speak my mind. You know, I don't think I should last a month in your house – I'd suffocate in this atmosphere . . . Your father, entirely taken up with his gout and his books; Uncle Vanya and his gloom; your grandmother; and then there's your stepmother . . .

SONYA. What's the matter with my stepmother?

ASTROV. Everything about a person should be beautiful: their face and clothes – and their heart and mind. Would the mirror on her wall say she was fairest of them all? She just eats and sleeps and goes for little walks, and captivates us all with her looks – that's all she does. She's no responsibilities, other people do all the work for her . . . Isn't that right? And a life of idleness can't be an innocent one. (*Pause.*) Well, perhaps I'm being too severe. I'm dissatisfied with life, like your Uncle Vanya, and we're turning into a pair of old grousers.

SONYA. You're not contented with life, then?

ASTROV. Life in general I love, but our life, our narrow Russian provincial life, I cannot endure – I despise it from the bottom of my soul. And as far as my own personal life goes, then God knows there's certainly nothing good about *that*. Look, if you're going through the forest on a dark night and there's a gleam of light in the distance then you don't notice how tired you are or how dark it is or how the briars keep hitting you in the face . . . I work – you know this – harder than anyone in the district, it's never been easy for me. I find life intolerably painful at times; but I've no gleam of light in the distance. I don't hope for anything for myself, I don't have much love for others . . . For a long time now there's been no one I've loved.

SONYA. No one?

ASTROV. No one at all. The only person I feel a certain tenderness towards is your Nanna, for old times' sake. The peasants are all alike – backward, living in filth – and there's not much common ground between them and the educated classes. Who are themselves a weariness to the soul. All of them, all our good kind friends, have petty thoughts and petty feelings. They can't see further than the end of their nose – they're just plain stupid. And those of them who are a little more intelligent, a little less paltry, are hysterical instead, and preoccupied with analysis and introspection . . . They whine, they pursue little vendettas and sick-minded slanders. They come sidling up to you and look at you out of the corner of their eye and decide: 'Oh, he's raving mad!' Or: 'Bit high-falutin, this one.' And when they don't know quite what label to stick on me they say: 'He's a strange one, he's a strange fellow!' I love the forest – that's strange:

I don't eat meat – that's another strange thing. A direct, innocent, open approach to nature or people is a thing of the past . . . It doesn't exist! (*Goes to take another drink.*)

SONYA (*stops him*). No, I beg you, I implore you – don't drink any more.

ASTROV. Why not?

SONYA. It's so unworthy of you! You're a man of refinement, you're so gently-spoken . . . And not just that – you're handsome in a way that no one else I know is. So why do you want to be like ordinary people who drink and play cards? Don't do it, I implore you! You always say that people don't create, they just destroy what heaven has given them. So why, why are you destroying yourself? You mustn't, you mustn't, I implore you, I entreat you.

ASTROV (*holds out his hand to her*). I'll drink no more.

SONYA. Give me your word.

ASTROV. My word of honour.

SONYA (*presses his hand tightly*). Thank you!

ASTROV. *Basta!* I've sobered up. Look, I'm completely sober, and will so remain for as long as I live. (*Looks at his watch.*) Let's go on with our conversation, then. What I'm saying is this: I've had my day, my time is past . . . I've grown old, I've worked myself too hard, I've got coarsened, my feelings are all blunted, and I don't think now I could attach myself to another human being. There's no one I love . . . and no one now I ever shall love. The thing that does still have a hold on me is beauty. I can't be indifferent to it. Your stepmother, for instance. I think if she wanted to she could turn my head in a day . . . But then that's nothing to do with love, nothing to do with attachment . . . (*Puts his hand over his eyes and shudders.*)

SONYA. What's the matter?

ASTROV. Oh . . . In Lent one of my patients died under the chloroform.

SONYA. It's time you put that out of your mind. (*Pause.*) Tell me something . . . If I had a friend, or a younger sister, and if you found out that she was . . . well, in love with you, say, how would you respond to that?

ASTROV (*shrugs*). I don't know. Not at all, I suppose. I'd make it clear to her that I couldn't love her . . . and that I'd got other things to think about. Anyway, I must go if I'm going. Goodbye, then, my dear, or we'll be here all night.

*Shakes her hand.*

I'll go through the drawing-room if I may – I'm afraid I may get held up by your uncle otherwise.

*Exit* ASTROV.

SONYA (*alone*). He didn't say anything . . . His heart and mind are still hidden from me, so why do I feel so happy? (*Laughs with happiness.*) 'You're refined,' I told him, 'you're noble, you're gently-spoken . . .' It wasn't the wrong thing to say, was it? His voice is so vibrant and caressing – I can hear it lingering in the air. But when I said that about my younger sister he didn't understand . . . (*Wringing her hands.*) Oh, what a terrible thing it is that I'm not beautiful! What a terrible thing! Because I know I'm not beautiful – I know, I know . . . Last Sunday, as everyone was coming out of church, I heard people talking about me, and one woman said: 'She's good-hearted and kind, but it's a pity she's so plain . . .' Plain . . .

*Enter* YELENA.

YELENA (*opens the windows*). The storm's over. What wonderful air! (*Pause.*) Where's the doctor?

SONYA. Gone.

*Pause.*

YELENA. Sonya!
SONYA. What?
YELENA. How long are you going to go on pouting at me? We

154

UNCLE VANYA

haven't done each other any harm. Why should we be enemies? Enough, now . . .

SONYA. I've been wanting to say it, too . . .

*Embraces* YELENA.

No more crossness.

YELENA. That's better.

*They are both moved.*

SONYA. Has Papa gone to bed?

YELENA. No, he's sitting in the drawing-room . . . We don't speak to each other for weeks at a time – heaven knows why . . . (*Sees the sideboard open.*) What's this?

SONYA. The doctor was having a bite of supper.

YELENA. There's some wine . . . Let's drink to being friends.

SONYA. Yes, why not?

YELENA. Out of the same glass . . . (*Pours.*) That will be nicer. So – friends?

SONYA. Friends.

*They drink and kiss each other.*

I've been wanting to make up for a long time, but I kept feeling somehow ashamed of it . . . (*Weeps.*)

YELENA. Why are you crying?

SONYA. It's nothing. Just crying.

YELENA. There now, there now . . . (*Weeps.*) You funny girl – now I've started to cry as well . . . (*Pause.*) You're cross with me because you thought I married your father for his money . . . If oaths mean anything to you then I'll give you my oath I married him for love. I was fascinated by him because he was a learned and famous man. It wasn't real love, it was artificial, but I certainly thought it was real then. I'm not to blame. But from the very day of our wedding you've never ceased to punish me with those clever suspicious eyes of yours.

SONYA. Anyway, pax, pax! Let bygones be bygones, yes?

YELENA. You mustn't look at people like that, you know – it's not your style. You must trust everyone – life's impossible if you don't.

*Pause.*

SONYA. Tell me truly, now we're friends . . . Are you happy?

YELENA. No.

SONYA. I knew you weren't. One more question. Be frank – would you like to have a husband who was young?

YELENA. What a child you are still. Of course I should. (*Laughs.*) Go on, then, ask me something else. Go on . . .

SONYA. Do you like the doctor?

YELENA. Yes, very much.

SONYA (*laughs*). I've got a silly face on, haven't I . . . He's gone, and here I am still hearing his voice, hearing his step, looking at the dark glass in the window and thinking I can see his face there. Let me finish . . . I can't say it out loud, though – I can feel my cheeks burning. Let's go to my room – we can talk there. Do you think I'm silly? Admit it, now . . . Say something to me about him.

YELENA. Say what?

SONYA. He's a clever man . . . He can do anything . . . He's a doctor, he plants trees . . .

YELENA. It's not just a question of trees and medicine . . . Listen, my love, he's someone with real talent. You know what that means, having talent? It means being a free spirit, it means having boldness and wide horizons . . . He plants a sapling, and he has some notion what will become of it in a thousand years time; he already has some glimpse of the millennium. Such people are rare; they must be loved . . . He drinks, he can be a little coarse at times – but what of it? A man of talent in Russia can't be a simple innocent. Just think what this doctor's life is like! Impassable mud on the roads, freezing weather, snowstorms, huge distances, crude and uncivilized peasants, disease and poverty on every hand; and in conditions like those it's hard for anyone working and

struggling day after day to preserve himself to the age of forty
in simple innocence and sobriety . . .

*Kisses* SONYA.

I wish you happiness with all my heart; you deserve it . . .
(*Gets up.*) I'm a tedious person, though, a minor character
. . . In music, in my husband's house, in all my romances –
everwhere, in fact, that's all I've been – a minor character.
In all conscience, Sonya, if you think about it, I'm very, very
unhappy! (*Walks up and down in agitation.*) There's no
happiness for me in this world! None! Why are you laughing?

SONYA (*laughs, covering her face*). I'm so happy . . . so happy!

YELENA. I feel like playing the piano . . . I wouldn't mind
playing something now.

SONYA. Yes, do.

*Embraces* YELENA.

I can't sleep . . . Do play!

YELENA. In a moment. Your father isn't asleep. Music irritates
him when he's ill. Go and ask him. If he doesn't mind, then
yes, I'll play. Go on.

SONYA. I'm going!

*Exit* SONYA. *The sound of the* WATCHMAN *and his dogs in
the garden.*

YELENA. I haven't played for a long time. I'll play, and I'll
cry and cry like a child. (*Out of the window.*) Is that you
Yefim?

WATCHMAN (*off*). Ma'am!

YELENA. Keep the dogs quiet, the master's not well.

WATCHMAN (*off*). I'll take myself off, then! (*Whistles to his
dogs.*) Hey, boy! Here, boy!

*Pause.* SONYA *returns.*

SONYA. No!

CURTAIN

# Act Three

*The drawing-room in* SEREBRYAKOV'S *house. Three doors, left, right, and centre. Day.*

VANYA *and* SONYA, *sitting.* YELENA, *walking round the room thinking about something.*

VANYA. Herr Professor is graciously pleased to desire us all to assemble here in the drawing-room today at one o'clock. (*Looks at his watch.*) Quarter to one. He has something to announce to the world.

YELENA. Oh, some bit of business, I expect.

VANYA. He hasn't got any business. Writing rubbish, complaining, and being jealous – that's all the business he's got.

SONYA (*reproachfully*). Uncle!

VANYA. I'm sorry, I'm sorry. (*Indicates* YELENA.) Look at her! Reeling as she walks from sheer indolence. How charming! How very charming!

YELENA. Droning, droning on the whole day long! I wonder you don't get sick of it. (*Leadenly.*) I'm bored to death. I can't think what I can do.

SONYA (*shrugs*). There are plenty of things. If only you wanted to.

YELENA. For instance?

SONYA. Do some of the estate work – teach – treat the sick. Isn't that plenty enough? When you and Papa weren't here Uncle Vanya and I used to go to market and sell the flour.

YELENA. I don't know how to. It wouldn't be interesting, anyway. It's only in uplifting novels that people go out and teach and doctor the peasants. How can I just suddenly turn round and start teaching and doctoring?

SONYA. What I don't understand is how anyone could fail to. Give it a little while and you'll get used to it. (*Embraces her.*) Don't be bored, my dear. (*Laughs.*) You're bored – you can't find a job to do – and boredom and idleness are catching. Look: Uncle Vanya does nothing but follow you round like a shadow – and I've dropped what I was doing to come running here to talk to you. I've grown idle, and I can't afford to be! The doctor used to come and visit us only very occasionally – once a month – it was hard to persuade him; and now he comes every day – he's quite given up his trees and his practice. You must have bewitched us.

VANYA (*to* YELENA). Why are you languishing? (*Briskly.*) Use your intelligence, my dear! You have mermaid's blood in your veins – so be a mermaid! Run wild for once in your life – rush off and fall madly in love with some fellow-sprite – then splash you go, head first into a hole at the bottom of the river – while Herr Professor and all the rest of us stand helplessly looking on.

YELENA (*angrily*). Leave me alone, will you! It's so unkind!

*She tries to go. He prevents her.*

VANYA. Come on, now, my sweet, forgive me . . . I apologize.

*Kisses her hand.*

Pax.

YELENA. It would test the patience of a saint, you must admit.

VANYA. As a peace token I'll bring you a bouquet of roses – I picked them for you this morning . . . Autumn roses – lovely, mournful roses . . .

*Exit* VANYA.

SONYA. Autumn roses – lovely, mournful roses . . .

*They both look out of the window.*

YELENA. September already. We shall have to get through the winter here somehow! (*Pause.*) Where's the doctor?

SONYA. In Uncle Vanya's room. He's painting something. I'm glad Uncle Vanya's gone – I must have a word with you.

YELENA. What about?

SONYA. What about?

*She lays her head on* YELENA's *breast.*

YELENA. There, now, there.

*She strokes* SONYA's *hair.*

There, now.

SONYA. I'm not beautiful.

YELENA. You have beautiful hair.

SONYA. Don't say that! (*Looks round to glance at herself in the mirror.*) When a woman isn't beautiful people say to her: 'You have beautiful eyes, you have beautiful hair . . .' I've loved him for six years now – loved him more than my own mother. I hear his voice all the time, I feel the pressure of his hand on mine; and I look at the door and wait – I keep thinking he's going to come in any moment. And I keep running to you like this to talk about him. He comes every day now, but he doesn't look at me, he doesn't see me . . . It's such torture! I've no hope – none, none at all! (*In despair.*) I've no strength left . . . I prayed all night . . . Often I go up to him and start the conversation myself. I look him straight in the face . . . I haven't the pride, I haven't the strength to control myself . . . Yesterday I couldn't stop myself confessing to Uncle Vanya . . . And all the servants know I'm in love with him. Everyone knows.

YELENA. What about him?

SONYA. No. He never notices me.

YELENA (*thoughtfully*). He's a funny man . . . I've an idea. Let me have a talk to him . . . I'll be very discreet and I won't say anything directly . . . (*Pause.*) It's quite true – to be kept in suspense all this time . . . Let me try!

SONYA *nods.*

All right, then. Either he loves you or he doesn't – it's easy enough to find out. Now, don't worry, my pet – I'll do it very discreetly – he'll never even notice. We just want to know which it is: yes or no. (*Pause.*) If it's no, then he should stop coming here. Right?

SONYA *nods.*

It's easier when you don't see people. We won't delay, then – we'll cross-examine him forthwith. He was going to show me something he's drawing . . . Go and tell him I want to see him.

SONYA (*in great agitation*). You will tell me the whole truth?

YELENA. Of course. Whatever the truth, I think, at any rate it can't be as terrible as being in suspense. You can rely on me, my sweet.

SONYA. All right, all right . . . I'll say you want to see his drawings . . .

*Starts to go, and then stops at the door.*

No, better to stay in suspense . . . At least there's still hope . . .

YELENA. What's this, now?

SONYA. Nothing.

*Exit* SONYA.

YELENA (*alone*). Is there anything worse than knowing the secrets of another's heart and not being able to help? (*Reflects.*) He's not in love with her, that's plain enough, but why shouldn't he marry her? She's not beautiful, but for a country doctor, at his age, she'd make a fine wife. She's intelligent, she's kind and good . . . That's all beside the point, though, that's all beside the point . . . (*Pause.*) I know how it is for that poor child. In the midst of all this desperate boredom, where all the people around her are just perambulating grey blobs, where every word spoken is vile, where there's nothing going on but eating, drinking, and sleeping, *he* makes one of his occasional appearances; and he's not like the others – he's handsome, he's interesting, he's fascinating – and it's like the bright moon rising in the midst of darkness . . . To fall under the spell of a man like that, to forget oneself . . . I think I've become slightly fascinated, too. When he's not here, yes, I'm bored – and now here I am smiling at the thought of him . . . Uncle Vanya tells me I have mermaid's blood in my veins. 'Run wild for once in your life . . .' So – perhaps that's what I should do . . . Fly off as free as a bird away from all of you, away from your half-asleep faces, away from all this talk – forget your very existence . . . But I'm a coward, I'm too timid . . . I should be tormented by conscience . . . I feel guilty as it is, with his coming here every day – because I can guess why he comes – I'm already almost down on my knees in front of Sonya, weeping and begging her to forgive me . . .

*Enter* ASTROV *with a map.*

ASTROV. Good afternoon.

*He shakes hands with her.*

You wanted to see what I've been painting?

YELENA. You promised yesterday you'd show me your work . . . Can you spare the time?

ASTROV. Of course.

*He spreads the map out on the card-table and fixes it with drawing-pins.*

Where were you born?

YELENA (*helps him*). St. Petersburg.

ASTROV. And where did you study?

YELENA. At the Conservatoire.

ASTROV. You may not find this very interesting.

YELENA. Why not? I don't know the country, it's true, but I've read a lot.

ASTROV. I've got my own work-table in the house here. In Vanya's room. When I get completely exhausted, and I can't think properly any more, I drop everything and come running over here to distract myself with this thing for an hour or two . . . Vanya and Sonya click away on the abacus, and I sit beside them at my table, busy with my colouring, and it's warm and peaceful, and the cricket chirps. I don't allow myself this pleasure very often, though – once a month . . . (*Indicates the map.*) Now, look at this. It represents this part of the country as it was fifty years ago. The light and dark green colouring indicates forest; half of the entire surface-area is forest. Where the green is hatched with red there were elk and wild goats . . . I've indicated the fauna as well as the flora. On this lake there were swans and geese and ducks, and what the old people call a power of birds of every sort – the place was swarming with them. Apart from villages, look, you can see a scattering of various settlements and smallholdings, little monasteries, watermills . . . Cattle and horses were abundant. They're marked in blue. This district, for example, was thick with blue; there were complete herds, and two or three horses per farm. (*Pause.*) Now let's look down here. As it was twenty-five years ago. By this time only a third of the surface-area is under forest. The goats have gone, but there are still elk. The green and blue are paler now. And so on, and so on. Let us move on to the third section – the district as it is today. There's green here and there, but it's not solid, it's only in patches; the elk, the swans, and the capercailzies have all vanished . . . Of the former settlements, smallholdings, monasteries, and mills – not a trace. Overall it's the picture of a gradual but incontrovertible decline, which by the look of it will be complete in another ten or fifteen years. You'll tell me that civilizing factors are at work here, that the old life must naturally give way to the new. And, yes, I see that if these ruined forests had been replaced by roads and railways, if there were factories and schools here, then the peasants would be healthier and wealthier and wiser – but nothing of the kind! The district still has the same swamps and mosquitoes, the same lack of

roads, the same poverty and typhus and diptheria and fires
. . . What we are faced with here is a decline resulting from
the unequal struggle for existence, a decline brought about
by stagnation, by ignorance, by a total lack of awareness, by
frozen, sick, and hungry men who, to preseve the last flickers
of life, to save their children, instinctively, blindly, grasp at
anything they can use to relieve their hunger and warm
themselves, and who destroy it all without thought for the
morrow . . . Almost everything has been destroyed now; and
nothing yet has been created in its place. (*Coldly.*) I see from
your expression that you're not interested.

YELENA. I understand so little about it.

ASTROV. There's nothing to understand – you're simply not
interested.

YELENA. I was thinking about something else, to tell you the
truth. Forgive me. I have to subject you to a little cross-
examination, and I feel somewhat awkward about it – I don't
know how to begin.

ASTROV. A cross-examination?

YELENA. Yes, but . . . a rather innocent one. Let's sit down,
shall we?

*They sit.*

YELENA. It's to do with a certain young lady. We'll be quite
straightforward about this, shall we – a friendly conversation,
no talking in riddles. All right?

ASTROV. All right.

YELENA. It's to do with my stepdaughter, Sonya. Do you like
her?

ASTROV. Yes, I have a high regard for her.

YELENA. Do you like her as a woman?

ASTROV (*after a moment*). No.

YELENA. Just a few words more and we'll be finished. You
haven't noticed anything?

ASTROV. Noticed anything?

YELENA (*takes his hand*). You don't love her, I can see it in your

eyes . . . It's very painful for her. You must understand that
– and stop coming here.

ASTROV (*rises*). I've had my day . . . Anyway, I've no time for
all this . . . (*Shrugs.*) I haven't the time. (*He is embarrassed.*)

YELENA. Oh dear, what a disagreeable conversation! I'm so
flustered – I feel as if I'd been dragging a ten-ton weight
around. Anyway, we've finished, thank heavens. We'll forget
this ever took place and . . . and you must leave. You're an
intelligent man, you'll understand . . . (*Pause.*) I've gone
quite red.

ASTROV. If you had told me this a month or two ago I might
have given it some thought, but now . . . (*Shrugs.*) Still, if she
finds it painful, then naturally . . . There's only one thing I
don't understand, and that is why you needed this cross-
examination.

*He looks her in the eye and wags his finger.*

You're a sly one!

YELENA. What do you mean?

ASTROV. You're being sly! All right, so Sonya finds the
situation painful. I accept that – but what's the point of
this cross-examination? (*Briskly, preventing her from
speaking.*) Come on, now, don't put on your surprised face –
you know perfectly well why I come here every day . . .
Why I come, and who I come to see – you know that
perfectly well. My sweet sparrowhawk, I've been swooped
upon before!

YELENA. Sparrowhawk? I don't understand.

ASTROV. A beautiful, silky-smooth ferret, then . . . You must
have victims! For a whole month now I've done nothing – I've
let it all go and come thirsting after you – and you find that
terribly pleasing . . . So there we are. I'm sure you knew that
even without any cross-examination. (*Folds his arms and bends
his head.*) I submit. Take, eat!

YELENA. You've gone mad!

ASTROV (*laughs through his teeth*). You've gone bashful . . .

YELENA. I'm not the sort of person you think! I swear I'm
not!

*She tries to go. He bars her way.*

ASTROV. I'm leaving today, and I shan't come here any more,
but . . .

*He takes her hand and looks round.*

. . . Where are we going to meet? Tell me quickly – where?
Someone may come in – quick now . . . (*Passionately.*) You
wonderful, magnificent woman . . . One kiss . . . Let me just
kiss your sweet-scented hair . . .

YELENA. I swear to you . . .

ASTROV (*prevents her from speaking*). Why do you need to
swear to me? Oh, so beautiful! Such hands!

*Kisses her hands.*

YELENA. Now that's enough . . . Go away. (*Pulls her hands
back.*) You've forgotten yourself.

ASTROV. Tell me, though, tell me – where shall we meet
tomorrow?

*Takes her by the waist.*

You can see, it's inevitable, we must go on meeting.

*Kisses her; and as he does so* VANYA *enters with a bouquet of
roses, and stops in the doorway.*

YELENA (*not seeing* VANYA). Have pity on me . . . Leave me
be . . .

*Lays her head on* ASTROV's *chest.*

No!

*She tries to go.* ASTROV *restrains her by the waist.*

ASTROV. Come to the forestry office tomorrow . . . About
two . . . All right? All right? Will you?

YELENA (*sees* VANYA). Let me go! (*Moves away towards the
window in great confusion.*) This is appalling.

VANYA (*puts the bouquet down on a chair, and in his agitation mops*

*his face and under his collar with his handkerchief*). It's all right
. . . Never mind . . . It's all right . . .

ASTROV (*with ill-grace*). Very passable weather today, my dear
sir. Overcast this morning – looked like rain – sun's out now,
though. We're having a beautiful autumn, it must in all
honesty be said . . . And the winter crops are coming along.
(*Rolls the map into a tube.*) The only thing is, the days are
drawing in . . .

> *Exit* ASTROV. YELENA *goes quickly across to* VANYA.

YELENA. You'll do your best, you'll use all the influence you
have, to see that my husband and I get away from here today.
You understand? Today!

VANYA (*wipes his face*). What? Oh, yes . . . Right . . . I saw it
all, Yelena, I saw the whole thing . . .

YELENA (*tensely*). You understand? I must be away from here
today!

> *Enter* SEREBRYAKOV, SONYA, TELEGIN, *and* MARINA.

TELEGIN. I'm a little off-colour myself, Professor. Haven't
been right for the last couple of days. Something a bit, you
know, in my head . . .

SEREBRYAKOV. Where are the others, though? I hate this
house. It's like a maze. Twenty-six enormous rooms –
everyone goes wandering off – you can never find anyone.
(*Rings.*) Ask Maria Vasilyevna and my wife to come in, will
you.

YELENA. I'm here.

SEREBRYAKOV. Be seated, if you please, ladies and gentlemen.

> SONYA *goes across to* YELENA.

SONYA (*impatiently*). What did he say?

YELENA. I'll tell you afterwards.

SONYA. You're trembling? You're upset?

> *Searches* YELENA's *face.*

I see . . . He said he wouldn't come here any more . . . Am I right? (*Pause.*) Tell me – am I right?

YELENA *nods.*

SEREBRYAKOV (*to* TELEGIN). A man can put up with ill-health, hard as that may be. What I cannot bear is the whole tenor of rural life. I feel as if I'd fallen off the earth on to some alien planet. Be seated, ladies and gentlemen, I beg of you. Sonya! (*Pause.*) She's deaf. (*To* MARINA.) You, too, Nanna – sit down.

MARINA *sits down and knits a stocking.*

Ladies and gentlemen. Lend me your ears, if I may so express myself, and they shall be with interest returned unto you. (*Laughs.*)

VANYA (*agitatedly*). You don't need me, perhaps? May I go?

SEREBRYAKOV. On the contrary, I need you most of all.

VANYA. Why? What for?

SEREBRYAKOV. A little unfriendly, your manner . . . Why are you angry? (*Pause.*) If I have in some way offended against you, please – forgive me.

VANYA. Oh, not that tone of voice! Let's get down to it. What do you want?

*Enter* MARIA VASILYEVNA.

SEREBRYAKOV. And here is *maman*. I will begin, then. (*Pause.*) I have asked you to come here today, ladies and gentlemen, to tell you that the Inspector-General is on his way. Joking aside, however. The matter is a serious one. I have assembled you all, ladies and gentlemen, to seek your help and counsel. And knowing as I do your unfailing kindness, I believe I shall not be disappointed. The world I inhabit is the world of learning, the world of books, and I have ever been a stranger to the practical life. I cannot manage without the guidance of people who know their way around in these matters, and I am looking to you, Vanya, and

(*to* TELEGIN) to you, my friend, and to you, *maman* . . . The
point is that *manet omnes una nox*, the same night awaits us
all, which is to say that we are all in the hands of God. I
am old and ailing, and I therefore think it fit to set my
affairs in order insofar as they affect my family. My own
life is over – it is not myself I am thinking of; but I have a
young wife and an unmarried daughter. (*Pause*.) It is
impossible for me to go on living in the country. We were
not created for the country. It is equally impossible,
though, to live in town on the kind of revenues that we
receive from this estate. If we were to sell our forest, let us
say, that would be an extraordinary measure which we
could not adopt every year. Ways must be sought of
guaranteeing us a permanent and more or less fixed
amount of income. I have thought of one such way, and
beg leave to present it for your consideration. I shall set it
forth in outline; the details later. Our estate yields an
average return of no more than two per cent. I propose to
sell it. If we invest the money which this produces in stocks
and shares then we shall earn between four and five per
cent, and there will, I believe, be even a surplus of some
few thousand rubles which will enable us to purchase a
modest villa within reasonable distance of St. Petersburg.

VANYA. Wait a moment . . . I think my hearing must be going.
Repeat what you just said.

SEREBRYAKOV. Invest the money in stocks and shares and use
the surplus that remains to buy a villa near St. Petersburg.

VANYA. Not about St. Petersburg . . . You said something else.

SEREBRYAKOV. I propose to sell the estate.

VANYA. That was it. You're going to sell the estate – wonderful
– brilliant idea . . . But what do you want *us* to do with
ourselves – me and my aged mother and Sonya here?

SEREBRYAKOV. All this we shall go into at the proper time.
Not now.

VANYA. Wait a moment. I've evidently been walking round up
to now in a state of complete idiocy. Up to now I was stupid
enough to believe that this estate belonged to Sonya. My late

father purchased it as a dowry for my sister. Up to now I supposed in my naïvety that we were not living under Turkish law, and that from my sister the estate had passed to Sonya.

SEREBRYAKOV. Yes, the estate belongs to Sonya. No one is disputing that. Without Sonya's consent I shall take no decision about selling it. I am, in any case, proposing to do this for Sonya's benefit.

VANYA. This is past all comprehending! Either I've gone mad, or . . . or . . .

MARIA VASILYEVNA. Jean, *il ne faut pas le contredire.* Believe me, Alexandre knows what's right and what's wrong better than we do.

VANYA. No, give me some water. (*Drinks water.*) Go ahead – say anything you like!

SEREBRYAKOV. I don't understand why you're getting excited. I'm not saying my plan is ideal. If everyone finds it inappropriate I shan't insist.

*Pause.*

TELEGIN (*in embarrassment*). I have a profound reverence for learning, Professor, but I have something more – I have family feeling. My brother's wife's brother, you may perhaps know him, held a master's degree . . .

VANYA. Wait a moment, Ilyusha, we've got business to deal with. Later, afterwards . . . (*To* SEREBRYAKOV.) Ask *him*. The estate was purchased from his uncle.
his uncle.

SEREBRYAKOV. What would be the point of my asking? What would it tell us?

VANYA. This estate was purchased at the going rate then for ninety-five thousand rubles. My father paid only seventy thousand down, and the other twenty-five were carried as a debt. Now, listen to me . . . This estate would never have been bought at all if I had not renounced my inheritance in favour of my sister, whom I loved most passionately. On top of which I worked like an ox for ten years and paid off the entire debt . . .

SEREBRYAKOV. I'm sorry I ever started this conversation.

VANYA. The estate is clear of debt and in working order thanks purely to my own personal efforts. And now I've got old I'm to be thrown out on my neck!

SEREBRYAKOV. I don't understand what you're driving at!

VANYA. For twenty-five years I have run this estate, I have worked, and I have sent you the money, like the most conscientious of bailiffs, and not once in all that time have you offered me a word of thanks. From start to finish – from when I was young until the present day – you have paid me the princely salary of five hundred rubles a year – and not once has it entered your head to give me a single ruble more!

SEREBRYAKOV. How was I to know? I'm not a practical man – I don't understand these things. You could have given yourself more – as much as you liked.

VANYA. Why didn't I steal? Why don't you all despise me for not stealing? It would have been no more than simple justice, and I shouldn't be a beggar now!

MARIA VASILYEVNA (*sternly*). Jean!

TELEGIN. Don't, Vanya, don't! My dear old friend . . . ! I'm shaking . . . Why spoil good relations?

*Kisses him.*

Don't do it.

VANYA. For twenty-five years I have been shut up between four walls with this mother of mine like a mole in the dark . . . All our thoughts and feelings were centred on you. The days we spent talking about you and your works, being proud of you, uttering your name in reverential tones; the nights we blighted reading books and journals for which I now feel nothing but profound contempt!

TELEGIN. Don't, Vanya, don't . . . I can't bear it . . .

SEREBRYAKOV (*with rage*). I don't understand what it is you want.

VANYA. We thought you were some kind of superior being – we knew your articles by heart . . . But now my eyes have been opened! I see it all! You write about art, but you've not the slightest understanding of art! All those works of yours that I used to love – they're not worth a brass button! You've made fools of us!

SEREBRYAKOV. Everyone – please! Make him see reason! I'm going!

YELENA (*to* VANYA). I insist you be silent! Do you hear?

VANYA. I won't be silent!

*Bars* SEREBRYAKOV's *way.*

Wait, I haven't finished! You've blighted my life! I haven't lived, I haven't lived! Through your kind efforts I have destroyed the best years of my life! You're my worst enemy!

TELEGIN. I can't bear this . . . I can't . . . I'm going . . .

*Exit* TELEGIN *in great agitation.*

SEREBRYAKOV. What do you want of me? And what right do you have to take that tone with me? A little nobody like you! If the estate belong to you then take it – I don't need it!

YELENA. I'm not staying another moment in this hell! (*Shouts.*) I can't endure it any longer!

VANYA. My life has vanished! I have the talent, I have the brains, I have the nerve . . . If I had led a normal life I could have been a Schopenhauer, I could have been a Dostoyevsky . . . I don't know what I'm saying! I'm going mad . . . Mother, I'm in despair! Mother!

MARIA VASILYEVNA (*sternly*). Do as Alexandre tells you!

SONYA *kneels in front of* MARINA *and clings to her.*

SONYA. Nanna! Nanna!

VANYA. Mother! What am I going to do? No, don't say anything, there's no need! I know what I'm going to do! (*To* SEREBRYAKOV.) I'll give you something to remember me by!

*Exit* VANYA *through the centre door.* MARIA VASILYEVNA *goes after him.*

SEREBRYAKOV. In heaven's name, what is all this? Get this madman away from me! I can't stay under the same roof! He lives in there . . . (*Indicates the centre door.*) . . . almost on top of me . . . Let him move into the village, or into the lodge, or *I'll* move out, but remain in the same house as him I cannot . . .

YELENA (*to her husband.*) We're leaving today! You must give orders at once.

SEREBRYAKOV. An absolute little nobody!

SONYA, *on her knees, turns to her father.*

SONYA (*agitatedly, on the verge of tears*). You must be merciful, Papa! Uncle Vanya and I are so unhappy! (*Restraining her despair.*) You must be merciful! Remember when you were younger how Uncle Vanya and Grandmother used to work at night translating books for you, copying your papers . . . Whole nights they spent, whole nights together! Uncle Vanya and I have worked without rest – we were afraid to spend a kopeck on ourselves – we sent everything to you . . . We stinted our bread! I'm not saying the right things, it's coming out all wrong, but you should understand our feelings, Papa. You must be merciful!

YELENA (*to her husband, disturbed*). For the love of God, make it up with him . . . I implore you.

SEREBRYAKOV. Very well, I'll make it up with him . . . I'm not blaming him, I'm not angry, but you must agree that his behaviour is a little odd, to say the least. If you'll excuse me, then, I'll go and have a word with him.

*Exit* SEREBRYAKOV *through the centre door.*

YELENA. Be a little gentler with him – soothe him down . . .

*Exit* YELENA *after him.*

SONYA (*clinging to* MARINA). Nanna! Nanna!

MARINA. Never you mind, now, child. The geese will have their cackle, then they'll quieten . . . Cackle and quieten, cackle and quieten . . .

SONYA. Nanna!

MARINA (*strokes her hair*). You're shivering as though you'd been out in the freezing cold! There, now, you poor orphan child, God will have mercy. A drop of lime tea, or raspberry, now, and you'll feel better . . . Don't grieve, child . . . (*Looking at the centre door, feelingly.*) You see? They've quietened down, those old geese, drat them!

*A shot, off.* YELENA *is heard to scream.* SONYA *shudders.*

Oh, heaven preserve us!

SEREBRYAKOV *runs in, reeling in alarm.*

SEREBRYAKOV. Stop him! Restrain him! He's gone mad!

YELENA *and* VANYA *struggle in the doorway.*

YELENA (*trying to take the revolver away from him*). Give it me! Give it me, I tell you!

VANYA. Let go! Let go of me!

*He breaks free, runs into the room, and looks around for* SEREBRYAKOV.

Where is he? Ah, there he is!

*Fires at him.*

Bang! (*Pause.*) Didn't I hit him? Another botch-up? (*With rage.*) Oh, hell, hell . . . hell and damnation . . .

*Hammers on the floor with the revolver, and sinks exhausted into a chair.* SEREBRYAKOV *is stunned.* YELENA *leans against the wall, about to faint.*

YELENA. Take me away from this place! Take me away, kill me, anything, but . . . I can't stay in this place – I can't!

VANYA (*in despair*). Oh, what am I doing? What am I doing?
SONYA (*quietly*). Nanna! Nanna!

**CURTAIN**

# Act Four

VANYA's room. It serves both as his bedroom and as the estate office. By the window is a large table with account books and papers of various sorts; a high counting-house desk; cupboards and scales. There is a somewhat smaller table for ASTROV with paints and drawing materials on it, and a portfolio beside it. A starling in a cage. On the wall hangs a map of Africa, of no discernible use to anyone here. A huge sofa upholstered in oilcloth. On the left, a door leading to the interior of the house; on the right, a door to the porch. In front of this righthand door a mat has been laid to prevent the peasants dirtying the floor. Autumn evening. Silence.

TELEGIN and MARINA sit facing each other, winding stocking wool.

TELEGIN. Quick, now, or they'll be calling us to say goodbye. They've ordered the horses already.

MARINA (*trying to wind faster*). Only a little bit left.

TELEGIN. They're off to Kharkov. That's where they're going to live.

MARINA. Better so.

TELEGIN. They've taken fright . . . 'Not another hour will I stop in this place,' she says. 'We're leaving, and that's flat . . . We'll put up in Kharkov, and we'll send for our things once we've settled in . . .' They're going with what they stand up in. So there it is – they weren't fated to live here. They just weren't fated to . . . Predestined not to.

MARINA. Better so. All the noise they raised just now, all that shooting – they ought to be ashamed of themselves!

TELEGIN. Yes, it was a regular field of battle.

MARINA. That my eyes should see such things. (*Pause.*) We'll go back to living in the old way, like we did before. Eight

o'clock in the morning – tea; one o'clock – dinner; and sit
down to supper in the evening; everything in its proper place,
the same as in other people's houses . . . like Christians.
(*With a sigh.*) Sinner that I am, it's a long time since I had
noodles.

TELEGIN. Yes, it's a long time since they made us noodles.
(*Pause.*) A good long time . . . I was going through the village
this morning and the storekeeper called after me. 'Look at
you!' he says. 'Living on their charity!' It left such a bitter
taste in my mouth.

MARINA. You pay no heed, my dear. We're all living on the
charity of God. You, Sonya, her uncle – we're all the same,
we're none of us sitting idle, we're all of us working! Every
one of us . . . Where is Sonya?

TELEGIN. In the garden. Still going round with the doctor
looking for her uncle. They're afraid he might lay hands on
himself.

MARINA. Where's his pistol?

TELEGIN (*in a whisper*). I've hidden it in the cellar!

MARINA (*grinning*). Oh, this world of sin!

*Enter* VANYA *and* ASTROV *from outside.*

VANYA. Leave me alone. (*To* MARINA *and* TELEGIN.) Go
away, will you. Let me have a moment to myself! I can't bear
being watched over.

TELEGIN. We're going, Vanya, we're going.

TELEGIN *tiptoes out.*

MARINA. You old goose, you!

*She makes a cackling noise at* VANYA, *then gathers up her
wool and goes out.*

VANYA. Leave me alone!

ASTROV. With the greatest of pleasure – I should have been on
my way a long time ago. But let me say it again – I am not
leaving until you give me back what you've taken from me.

VANYA. I haven't taken anything from you.

ASTROV. I'm serious, now. Don't waste my time. I'm late enough as it is.

VANYA. I haven't taken anything.

*They both sit down.*

ASTROV. No? All right, I'll give you a little longer, and then I'm sorry, but I shall have to use force. We'll tie you up and search you. Seriously.

VANYA. If you like. (*Pause.*) To be such a fool, though – to shoot twice and miss both times! That's something I shall never forgive myself!

ASTROV. If you wanted to put a bullet in something you might have done better to try your own head.

VANYA (*shrugs*). It's a funny thing. I'm guilty of attempted murder, but no one's arresting me, no one's charging me. So they must think I'm insane. (*Gives a bitter laugh.*) *I'm* insane, but not people who adopt the mask of a professor, of some learned sage, to conceal their total lack of talent, and their dullness, and their utter callousness. They're not insane. Nor are people who marry old men and then publicly deceive them. I saw you, I saw you with your arms round her!

ASTROV. Yes, sir, I had my arms round her, sir, and pooh to you. (*He thumbs his nose.*)

VANYA (*looking at the door*). No, but it's an insane world, if you people are still part of it.

ASTROV. And that's another stupid remark.

VANYA. So what? I'm insane, I'm not responsible for my actions – I have the right to make stupid remarks.

ASTROV. The joke's worn thin. You're not insane, you're just someone who's got a bit odd. You're a buffoon. There was a time when I had the same idea – that being odd must be sick, must be abnormal. But I've come round to the view now that oddity is the normal condition of mankind. You're entirely normal.

VANYA (*covers his face with his hands*). I'm so ashamed! If you

knew how ashamed I felt! There's no pain in the world to
compare with these pangs of shame. (*In anguish.*)
Unendurable! (*Bends his head low over the table.*) What can I
do? What can I do?

ASTROV. Nothing.

VANYA. Give me something to take! Oh, God in heaven . . . I'm
forty-seven years old; suppose I live to be sixty, then I've still
got another thirteen years to go. It's a long time! How am I
to get through these thirteen years? What am I going to be
doing, what am I going to occupy them with? Oh, imagine,
though . . .

> *Convulsively squeezes* ASTROV's *hand.*

Just imagine, if one could somehow live the rest of one's life
differently. If one could wake up some clear, quiet morning
and feel that one had begun life afresh, that the past was all
forgotten, had dissolved like smoke. (*Weeps.*) If one could
begin a new life . . . Give me some idea how to do it . . .
where to begin . . .

ASTROV (*with irritation*). Oh, come on, now! What's all this
about a new life? Our situation, yours and mine, is hopeless.

VANYA. Is it?

ASTROV. I'm sure it is.

VANYA. Give me something . . . (*Indicating his heart.*) I've got
a burning pain here.

ASTROV (*cries out angrily*). Oh, stop it! (*Relenting.*) People living
a century or two after we're gone, who'll despise us for
leading such stupid and tasteless lives – they may find a way
to be happy, but as for us . . . There's only one hope left for
you and me – that when we're lying in our graves we might
have pleasant dreams. (*Sighs.*) Yes, my friend. In the whole
district there were only two people of any substance and
any culture – you and me. But in ten years or so this narrow
provincial life, this despicable life, has dragged us under.
Its rotten exhalations have poisoned our blood, and we
have become as vile as all the others. (*Sharply.*) But you

won't talk me out of it, though. You give me back what
you've taken from me.

VANYA. I haven't taken anything from you.

ASTROV. You've taken a bottle of morphine out of my medicine
chest. (*Pause*.) Listen, if you absolutely insist upon putting
an end to it all then go into the forest and shoot yourself. Give
me back the morphine, though, or else people will talk –
they'll jump to conclusions and think I gave it to you . . . It's
going to be quite bad enough having to do the post mortem.
You think that'll be fun?

*Enter* SONYA.

VANYA. Leave me alone.

ASTROV (*to* SONYA). Your uncle has purloined a bottle of
morphine out of my medicine chest and he won't give it back.
Tell him, will you, that it's . . . well, not very clever. Also
I'm pressed for time. I should be on my way.

SONYA. Uncle Vanya, did you take the morphine?

*Pause.*

ASTROV. He did. I know he did.

SONYA. Give it back. Why are you trying to frighten us?
(*Gently*.) Give it back, Uncle Vanya! I may be just as unhappy
as you, but I'm not giving way to despair. I'm enduring it,
and I shall go on enduring until my life comes to its natural
end . . . You endure as well. (*Pause*.) Give it back!

*Kisses his hands.*

Dear uncle, dear sweet kind uncle, give it back! (*Weeps*.)
You're a good man, you must have pity on us and give it back.
Endure, uncle! Endure!

VANYA *gets the bottle out of the table and gives it to* ASTROV.

VANYA. Here, take it. (*To* SONYA.) But quickly now, work,
something to do, otherwise I can't go on . . · I just can't go
on . . .

SONYA. Yes, yes, work. Just as soon as we've seen everyone off we'll sit down to work . . . (*Sorts agitatedly through the papers on the table.*) We're so behind with everything . . .

ASTROV (*puts the bottle in his medicine chest, which he then straps up*). Now I can be off, then.

*Enter* YELENA.

YELENA. Vanya? We'll be leaving in a moment . . . Go and see my husband – he's got something to say to you.

SONYA. Do go, Uncle Vanya. (*Takes* VANYA *by the arm.*) We'll both go. You and Papa must make it up. You absolutely must.

*Exeunt* SONYA *and* VANYA.

YELENA. I'm leaving.

*Gives* ASTROV *her hand.*

Goodbye.

ASTROV. So soon?

YELENA. They've brought the horses.

ASTROV. Goodbye, then.

YELENA. A little while ago you promised me you'd leave.

ASTROV. I haven't forgotten. I am just leaving. (*Pause.*) You've taken fright? (*Takes her hand.*) Is this really so dreadful?

YELENA. Yes.

ASTROV. You could stay, though! Yes? Tomorrow, in the forest . . .

YELENA. No . . . It's been decided . . . That's precisely why I'm facing you so bravely – because it's been decided that we're leaving . . . I'm going to ask one thing of you – to think better of me. I should like you to have some respect for me.

ASTROV. Oh . . . (*He makes a gesture of impatience.*) Please stay. Admit it, now – you've nothing in the world to do, no aim in life, nothing to occupy your attention, and you're going to give way to your feelings sooner or later – it's inevitable. Better, surely, if it's not in Kharkov or Kursk, but here in the bosom of nature . . . Poetic, at least – it's beautiful even in autumn . . . You've got the forest, you've got decayed estates *à la* Turgenev.

YELENA. What an absurd man you are . . . I'm angry with you, but all the same . . . I shall remember you with pleasure. You're an interesting and unusual person. We shall never see each other again, so why try to hide it? I was, yes, a little carried away by you. So, let's shake hands and part friends. Remember me kindly.

ASTROV (*shaking hands*). Yes, off you go, then . . . (*Reflectively.*) You seem in fact to be a good and sincere person; but there also seems to be something curious about your whole way of being. Here was everyone working away, going about their business, creating something – and as soon as you and your husband arrived they had to drop it all and spend the whole summer worrying about nothing but his gout and you. The pair of you infected us all with your idleness. I got carried away – I've done nothing for a whole month, while people have been falling sick and peasants have been pasturing their cattle in my woods and plantations . . . So, you see, you and your husband sow destruction wherever you go . . . I'm joking, of course, but all the same it is . . . odd, and I'm sure that had you stayed there would have been devastation on the most colossal scale. I should have been done for, and the outlook for you would have been . . . less than bright. So, off you go, then. *Finita la commedia!*

YELENA (*takes a pencil off his table and quickly hides it away*). I'll take this pencil to remember you by.

ASTROV. It is curious, though, isn't it . . . To have known each other and now suddenly for some reason never to see each other again. It's the same with everything in this world . . . Before anyone comes, until Uncle Vanya walks in with a bouquet, will you allow me to . . . kiss you . . . Kiss you goodbye . . . Yes?

*Kisses her cheek.*

So . . . There we are, then.

YELENA. I should like to wish you all the best. (*Looks round.*) Oh, hang it all – just for once in my life!

*She embraces him abruptly, and then they both at once move quickly apart.*

I must go.

ASTROV. Go quickly. If the horses are here you can start.

YELENA. I think people are coming.

*They both listen.*

ASTROV. *Finita!*

*Enter* SEREBRYAKOV, VANYA, MARIA VASILYEVNA *with a book*, TELEGIN, *and* SONYA.

SEREBRYAKOV (*to* VANYA). Dead and buried, then, the whole thing, and let it so remain. Since it happened, in these few short hours, I have gone over so much and so much in my mind that I believe I could write a complete treatise for future generations on how to live one's life. I gladly accept your apologies and ask you to accept mine. Goodbye, then.

*He and* VANYA *kiss three times.*

VANYA. You'll get precisely what you got before. Everything will be as it was.

*YELENA embraces* SONYA. SEREBRYAKOV *kisses* MARIA VASILYEVNA's *hand.*

SEREBRYAKOV. *Maman* . . .

MARIA VASILYEVNA *kisses him.*

MARIA VASILYEVNA. Alexandre, have your photograph taken again and send me a copy. You know how dear you are to me.

TELEGIN. Goodbye, professor! Don't forget us, now!

*SEREBRYAKOV kisses his daughter.*

SEREBRYAKOV. Goodbye, my dear . . . Goodbye to everyone.

*Gives his hand to* ASTROV.

Thank you for the pleasure of your company . . . I respect your way of thinking, I respect your impulsiveness and your enthusiasm, but permit an old man to make one parting observation: get down to the practicalities, ladies and gentlemen! Get down to practicalities!

*General farewells.*

My best wishes to you all!

*Exit* SEREBRYAKOV, *followed by* MARIA VASILYEVNA *and* SONYA. VANYA *firmly kisses* YELENA's *hand.*

VANYA. Goodbye . . . Forgive me . . . We shall never see each other again.

YELENA (*moved*). Goodbye, my dear.

*Kisses him on the head, and goes out.*

ASTROV (*to* TELEGIN). Ilyusha, tell them they might as well bring my horses at the same time.

TELEGIN. I'll tell them.

*Exit* TELEGIN. ASTROV *and* VANYA *are left on their own.* ASTROV *clears his paints off the table and puts them away in his suitcase.*

ASTROV. Why don't you go and see them off?

VANYA. Let them go – I just . . . haven't the heart. I'm so wretched. Quickly, I must get myself occupied with something. Work, work! (*Rummages among the papers on the table.*)

*Pause. There is the sound of harness-bells.*

ASTROV. They've gone. The professor's pleased, I should imagine. You wouldn't get him back now for all the tea in China.

*Enter* MARINA.

MARINA. They've gone. (*Sits down in the armchair and winds wool.*)

*Enter* SONYA.

SONYA. They've gone. (*Wipes her eyes.*) Please God everything's all right. (*To her uncle.*) So, let's do something, Uncle Vanya.

VANYA. Work, work . . .

SONYA. A long, long time since we last sat together at this table. (*Lights the lamp on the table.*) No ink, by the look of it . . . (*Takes the inkwell across to the cupboard and refills it.*) I'm sad they've gone.

MARIA VASILYEVNA *comes slowly in.*

MARIA VASILYEVNA. They've gone! (*Sits down and immerses herself in her reading.*)

SONYA (*sits at the table and leafs through an account-book*). Uncle Vanya, let's start by writing out the accounts. We're terribly behind. There were people sending round a second time for their accounts today. Go on, then. You do one, I'll do the next . . .

VANYA (*writes*). 'Invoice . . .'

*They both write in silence.*

MARINA (*yawns*). I could just drop off now . . .

ASTROV. Silence. The scratching of pens, the chirp of the cricket. All warm and snug . . . I don't feel much like leaving.

*The sound of harness-bells.*

They're bringing the horses . . . I suppose it only remains to say goodbye to you, my friends, and goodbye to my table, and then – off I go! (*Puts the maps away in the portfolio.*)

MARINA. Why all the hustle and bustle? Stay here, why not?

ASTROV. I mustn't.

VANYA (*writes*). 'Balance outstanding – two hundred and seventy-five rubles . . .

*Enter the* WORKMAN.

WORKMAN (*to* ASTROV). The horses are here.
ASTROV. Right.

> *Gives him the medicine-chest, the suitcase, and the portfolio.*

Here, take these. Mind you don't buckle the portfolio.
WORKMAN. Sir.

> *Exit the* WORKMAN.

ASTROV. Well, then . . . (*Goes to make his farewells.*)
SONYA. When shall we see you again?
ASTROV. Not before next summer, I suppose. Scarcely in the winter . . . Of course, in an emergency just let me know and I'll come over.

> *Shakes people's hands.*

Thank you for having me here, and for all your kindness . . . well, for everything.

> *Goes across to* MARINA *and kisses her on the head.*

Goodbye, Nanna.
MARINA. You won't have a glass of tea before you go?
ASTROV. I won't, Nanna.
MARINA. A drop of vodka, perhaps?
ASTROV (*irresolutely*). Well . . .

> *Exit* MARINA. *Pause.*

One of my horses is running a little lame. I noticed it yesterday, when he was taken to be watered.
VANYA. He'll need to be re-shod.
ASTROV. I'll have to look in at the blacksmith's. No help for it. (*Goes over to the map of Africa and looks at it.*) While out in Africa here the heat must be terrible now!
VANYA. Yes, probably.

> MARINA *returns carrying a tray with a glass of vodka and a*

*piece of bread on it.*

MARINA. Here you are.

ASTROV *drinks the vodka.*

Good health to you, my dear. (*Bows low.*) You should have a morsel of bread with it, though.

ASTROV. No, just like that . . . So, all the best! (*To* MARINA.) No need to see me out, Nanna.

*Exit* ASTROV. SONYA *goes after him with a candle to show him out.* MARINA *sits down in her armchair.*

VANYA (*writes*). 'Second of February – twenty pounds of sunflower oil . . . Sixteenth of February – another twenty pounds of sunflower oil . . . Buckwheat . . .'

*Pause. The sound of harness-bells.*

MARINA. He's gone.

*Pause.* SONYA *returns, and puts the candle on the table.*

SONYA. He's gone . . .

VANYA (*calculates on the abacus and writes*). In total . . . fifteen . . . twenty-five . . .

SONYA *sits down and writes.*

MARINA (*yawns*). Oh, sinners that we are . . .

*Enter* TELEGIN *on tiptoe. He sits down by the door and quietly strums his guitar.* VANYA *strokes* SONYA's *hair.*

VANYA. Oh, my child, I'm so wretched! If you only knew how wretched I was!

SONYA. What can we do, though? We must live our lives! (*Pause.*) We shall live our lives, Uncle Vanya. We shall live out the long, long succession of days and endless evenings; we shall patiently bear the trials we're sent; we shall labour for others from now into our old age without respite; and when our time comes we shall die with resignation; and there, beyond the grave, we shall say that we have suffered and wept, that it went hard with us; and God will be moved to pity; and you and I, Uncle, dear Uncle, shall see a life of light and beauty and grace; and we shall rejoice; and we shall look back on the unhappiness of this present time with tenderness, with a smile – and we shall rest. I have faith, Uncle, I have a burning and passionate faith . . .

*Kneels before him and lays her head upon his hands.*

(*wearily.*) We shall rest!

TELEGIN *quietly plays his guitar.*

We shall rest! We shall hear the angels; we shall see the sky all dressed in diamonds; we shall see all this world's evil and all our sufferings drown in the mercy that will fill the earth; and our life will become as quiet and gentle and sweet as a caress. I have faith, I have faith . . .

*Wipes away his tears with her handkerchief.*

Poor Uncle Vanya, poor Uncle Vanya, you're crying . . . (*On the verge of tears herself.*) You've never known joy in all your life, but you wait, Uncle Vanya, you wait . . . We shall rest . . .

*Embraces him.*

We shall rest!

*The sound of the* WATCHMAN *knocking.* TELEGIN *quietly strums his guitar;* MARIA VASILYEVNA *writes in the margins of her pamphlet;* MARINA *winds her wool.*

We shall rest!

*The curtain slowly falls.*

# Three Sisters

This version of *Three Sisters* was first performed at the Royal Exchange Theatre, Manchester, on 11 April 1985, with the following cast:

| | |
|---|---|
| ANDREY PROZOROV | Nicholas Blane |
| NATASHA, *his fiancée, later his wife* | Cheryl Prime |
| OLGA ⎫ | Emma Piper |
| MASHA ⎬ *his sisters* | Janet McTeer |
| IRINA ⎭ | Niamh Cusack |
| KULYGIN (*Fyodor*), *a teacher in the local high school, and Masha's husband* | David Ashton |
| LIEUTENANT-COLONEL VERSHININ, *the battery commander* | Sven Bertil Taube |
| LIEUTENANT THE BARON TUSENBACH | Christopher Bramwell |
| JUNIOR CAPTAIN SOLYONY | Rory Edwards |
| DR. CHEBUTYKIN, *the medical officer* | Espen Skjonberg |
| SECOND-LIEUTENANT FEDOTIK | Adrian Palmer |
| SECOND-LIEUTENANT RODE | Mark Addy |
| FERAPONT, *an elderly watchman from the local Executive Board* | Roy Heather |
| ANFISA, *the family's nanny, now eighty* | Helena McCarthy |

*Directed by* Casper Wrede
*Designed by* Di Seymour
*Lighting by* Geoffrey Beacroft
*Sound by* Ian Gibson
*Music by* Mick Wilson

The action takes place in the chief town of one of the provinces.

The first performance in London was at the Greenwich Theatre on 23 March 1987, with the following cast:

| | |
|---|---|
| ANDREY | Martyn Stanbridge |
| NATASHA | Cathryn Harrison |
| OLGA | Sara Kestelman |
| MASHA | Joanne Whalley |
| IRINA | Katharine Schlesinger |
| KULYGIN | David Allister |
| VERSHININ | Ian Ogilvy |
| TUSENBACH | Paul Jesson |
| SOLYONY | Ron Cook |
| CHEBUTYKIN | Peter Sallis |
| FEDOTIK | Trevor Brohier |
| RODE | Bill French |
| FERAPONT | Jeremy Swift |
| ANFISA | Elizabeth Bradley |

Directed by Elijah Moshinsky
Design and lighting by John Bury
Dance Supervision by Eleanor Fazan
Music Supervision by Stephen Oliver

The same production opened at the Albery Theatre on 3 June 1987, presented by Bill Kenwright, with the following cast changes:

| | |
|---|---|
| ANDREY | Hywel Bennett |
| NATASHA | Susan Penhaligon |
| MASHA | Francesca Annis |
| TUSENBACH | Rob Heyland |
| CHEBUTYKIN | Geoffrey Chater |
| FERAPONT | Walter Brown |

# Act One

*The interior of the Prozorovs' house. The drawing-room, with a colonnade beyond which the main reception room can be seen. It is noon, and the day is bright and cheerful. The table in the big room beyond is being laid for lunch.* OLGA, *who is wearing the dark blue dress laid down for a teacher in a girls' high school, stands correcting exercise-books the whole time – walks up and down correcting them.* MASHA, *in a black dress, her hat in her lap, sits reading a book.* IRINA, *in white, stands lost in her own thoughts.*

OLGA. It's exactly a year since Father died. A year ago today – May the fifth – it was on your name-day, Irina. It was very cold, we had snow. I thought I should never survive it, and there you were lying in a dead faint. But now here's a year gone by, and we can think about it again quite calmly. You're back in white, your face is shining . . .

*The clock strikes twelve.*

The clock kept striking then, too.

*Pause.*

I remember the band playing as they carried Father's body on the bier, I remember them firing the volley over the grave. He was a general, he had a brigade, but not many people came. Though it was raining at the time. Sleeting – sleeting hard.

IRINA. Why keep harking back?

BARON TUSENBACH, CHEBUTYKIN, *and* SOLYONY *appear on the other side of the colonnade, around the table in the main room.*

OLGA. It's warm today. We can have the windows wide. The birch trees aren't out yet, though. Father got his brigade and left Moscow with us eleven years ago, and I well remember what Moscow was like at this time of year, at the beginning of May. Everything would be in blossom already, everything would be warm, everything would be awash with sunshine. Eleven years have gone by, but I remember it all as if it were yesterday. Oh God, I woke up this morning, I saw the light flooding in, I saw the spring, and I felt such a great surge of joy, such a passionate longing for home.

CHEBUTYKIN. Stuff and nonsense, sir!

TUSENBACH. Utter rubbish, of course.

> MASHA, *lost in thought over her book, quietly whistles a tune.*

OLGA. Don't whistle, Masha. How could you?

> *Pause.*

I'm at school each day, then I give lessons for the rest of the afternoon, and I end up with a perpetual headache, I end up thinking the kind of thoughts I'd have if I were an old woman already. And in fact these last four years since I've been teaching I have felt as if day by day, drop by drop, my youth and strength were going out of me. And the only thing that grows, the only thing that gets stronger, is one single dream . . .

IRINA. To go to Moscow. To sell up the house, to finish with everything here, and off to Moscow . . .

OLGA. Yes! To Moscow, as soon as ever we can!

> CHEBUTYKIN *and* TUSENBACH *laugh.*

IRINA. Our brother will most likely be a professor. All the same, he won't want to live here. The only one who's stuck here is poor Masha.

OLGA. Masha will come to Moscow for the whole summer, every year.

MASHA *quietly whistles a tune.*

*[handwritten margin note: looking optimistic]*

IRINA. God willing, it'll all work itself out. (*Looking out of window.*) Beautiful weather. I don't know why my heart is so full of light! This morning I remembered I was the name-day girl, and I felt a sudden rush of joy. I remembered when I was little, and Mama was still alive. And I can't tell you what thoughts I felt stirring, what wonderful thoughts!

OLGA. Today you're all shining, you look lovelier than ever. Masha's lovely, too. That brother of ours would be a good-looking man, only he's put on a lot of weight – it doesn't suit him. I've aged, though, I've got terribly thin, I suppose from all my irritation with the girls at school. But today I'm free, I'm home, my headache's gone, and I feel I've got younger overnight. I'm twenty-eight, that's all . . . Everything is for the best, everything is from God, but I can't help feeling it would be better if I were married and stayed at home all day.

*Pause.*

*I* should have loved my husband.

TUSENBACH (*to* SOLYONY). What nonsense you do talk! I'm sick of listening to you. (*Coming into the drawing-room.*) I forgot to say. You'll be getting a visit today from our new battery commander, Vershinin. (*Sits down at the upright piano.*)

OLGA. Good. I shall be delighted.

IRINA. Is he old?

TUSENBACH. Not particularly. Forty, forty-five, at most. (*Quietly strums on the piano.*) Splendid fellow, by all accounts. Certainly no fool. Talks a lot, that's the only thing.

IRINA. Is he an interesting man?

TUSENBACH. He's all right, apart from having a wife and mother-in-law and two little girls. Been married before, too. He makes his calls, and everywhere he goes he tells everyone he's got a wife and two little girls. He'll be telling you next. His wife's a bit touched. Long plait like a schoolgirl – all high-flown talk and philosophising. And she makes frequent attempts at suicide, evidently to spite her husband. I'd have left a woman like that long ago, but he puts up with it, and all he does is complain.

SOLYONY (*coming out of the main room into the drawing-room with* CHEBUTYKIN). With one hand I can lift only fifty pounds, whereas with two I can lift 180 – 200 even. From which I conclude that two men are not twice as strong as one, but three times as strong, or even more . . .

CHEBUTYKIN (*reading a newspaper as he walks*). For falling hair . . . dissolve quarter of an ounce of mothballs in half a bottle of spirit . . . apply daily . . . (*Writes it down in a notebook.*) Must make a note of that! (*To* SOLYONY:) So there we are, you put the cork in the bottle, with a glass tube running through it . . . Then you take a pinch of common or garden alum . . .

IRINA. Ivan Romanich! Dear Ivan Romanich!

CHEBUTYKIN. My little girl! What is it, my precious?

IRINA. Tell me, why am I so happy today? As if I were sailing, with the wide blue sky above me, and great white birds soaring in the wind. Why is it? Why?

CHEBUTYKIN (*kissing both her hands, tenderly*). My own white bird . . .

IRINA. I woke up this morning, I got up, I washed – and suddenly I felt everything in this world was clear to me – I felt I knew how life had to be lived. Dear Ivan Romanich, I can see it all. A human being has to labour, whoever he happens to be, he has to toil in the sweat of his face; that's the only way he can find the sense and purpose of his life, his happiness, his delight. How fine to be a working man who rises at first light and breaks stones on the road, or a shepherd, or a teacher, or an engine driver on the railway ... Lord, never mind being human even – better to be an ox, better to be a simple horse, just so long as you work – anything rather than a young lady who rises at noon, then drinks her coffee in bed, then takes two hours to dress ... that's terrible! In hot weather sometimes you long to drink the way I began longing to work. And if I don't start getting up early and working, then shut your heart against me, Ivan Romanich.

CHEBUTYKIN (*tenderly*). I'll shut it, I'll shut it tight.

OLGA. Father trained us to rise at seven. Now Irina wakes at seven and lies there till nine o'clock at least, just thinking. She looks so serious, though! (*Laughs.*)

IRINA. You're used to seeing me as a child, so then you find it odd when I look serious. I'm twenty!

TUSENBACH. A longing to work – oh, heavens, how well I know that feeling! I've never done a stroke of work in my life. I was born in Petersburg, that cold and idle city, and none of my family had ever known what it was to work, they'd never known care. When I used to come home from cadet school a servant would pull my boots off for me, while I played the fool. My mother regarded me with an indulgent eye, though, and she was astonished when other people took a different view. I was protected from work. But I only just managed it by the skin of my teeth! Because the time has come when the piled thunderclouds are advancing upon us all. A great healthy storm is brewing, and it's going to blow our society clean of idleness and indifference, clean of prejudice against work and rotting boredom. I'm going to work, but then in twenty years time, in thirty years time, everyone will be working. Every single one of us!

CHEBUTYKIN. I shan't be working.

TUSENBACH. You don't count.

SOLYONY. In twenty years time you won't be alive, thank God. A couple of years from now and you'll have had a stroke, or I shall have lost my temper and put a bullet through your lovely face. (*Takes a bottle of scent out of his pocket and sprinkles his chest and arms.*)

CHEBUTYKIN (*laughs*). But I really never have done anything at all. From the time I left university I haven't lifted a finger. Not a solitary book have I read even, nothing but newspapers ... (*Takes another newspaper out of his pocket.*) You see ...? I know from reading newspapers who Dobrolyubov was, let's say, I know he was a famous critic, but what the devil he wrote – heaven knows, not the slightest idea ...

*The sound of knocking from the floor below.*

Ah ... They want me downstairs, I've got a visitor. Back in a moment ... Wait here ... (*Goes out hurriedly, combing his beard.*)

IRINA. He's up to something.

TUSENBACH. Yes. He's got his special face on. He's obviously going to come back in a moment with a present for you.

IRINA. Oh, for heaven's sake!

OLGA. Yes, it's awful. He's always doing stupid things.

MASHA. On a far sea shore an oak tree grows,
      And from it hangs a golden chain;
      A talking cat forever goes
      Around that chain and round again.

*She gets up and hums quietly.*

OLGA. You're not very cheerful today, Masha.

MASHA, *still humming, puts on her hat.*

Where are you off to?

MASHA. Home.

IRINA. What a funny way to behave . . .

TUSENBACH. Walking out on your sister's party!

MASHA. What does it matter? I'll come this evening. Goodbye, my sweet . . . (*Kisses* IRINA.) Best wishes, once again – health and happiness . . . In the old days, when Father was alive, we'd have thirty or forty officers coming every time it was someone's name-day, and there was a lot of noise. Whereas today we've scarcely got two people to rub together, and it's as silent as the tomb . . . I'm off . . . I'm down in the dumps today – don't take any notice of me. (*Laughing through her tears.*) We'll have a little talk later. Goodbye for now, my dear – I'll walk myself somewhere.

IRINA (*displeased*). What an odd creature you are . . .

OLGA (*with tears in her eyes*). I understand you, Masha.

SOLYONY. If a man philosophises, then what comes out is philosophy, though it may be full o' sophistry. But if a woman philosophises, or let's say two women, then it's bound to be not so much philosophy as full o' gossipy.

MASHA. What do you mean by that, you horribly frightening man?

SOLYONY. Never mind. The peasant had no time to gasp. Before he felt the bear's hard clasp. As the poet says.

*Pause.*

MASHA (*to* OLGA, *angrily*). Don't howl!

*Enter* ANFISA *and* FERAPONT *with a cake.*

ANFISA. In here, my dear. Come on, you've got clean feet.

(*To* IRINA:) From the Council, from Protopopov ... It's a cake.

IRINA. Thank you. Will you say thank you to him? (*Takes the cake.*)

FERAPONT. What?

IRINA (*louder*). Say thank you to him!

OLGA. Nanny, give him a piece of cake. Off you go, then, Ferapont – they'll give you some cake outside.

FERAPONT. What?

ANFISA. Come on, my dear. Off we go ... (*Goes out with* FERAPONT.)

MASHA. I don't like that Protopopov man. There's something about him that reminds me of a bear. He shouldn't have been invited.

IRINA. I didn't invite him.

MASHA. That's all right, then.

*Enter* CHEBUTYKIN, *followed by a* SOLDIER *carrying a silver samovar. There is a murmur of surprise and displeasure.*

OLGA (*hides her face in her hands*). A silver samovar! This is awful! Does he think it's a wedding anniversary? (*Goes out to the table in the main room.*)

IRINA. Ivan Romanich, my sweet, what are you doing?

TUSENBACH (*laughs*). I told you!

MASHA. Ivan Romanich, you're simply shameless!

CHEBUTYKIN. My dears, my loves, you're all I have, you're all that's most precious to me in the world. I'm nearly sixty – I'm an old man, a lonely, useless old man ... There's no good in me at all except this love I have for you. If it weren't for you I should have departed this world a long time ago ... (*To* IRINA:) My dear, my little girl, I've known you since the day you were born ... I used to carry you in my arms ... I loved your poor dead mother ...

IRINA. But why such expensive presents?

CHEBUTYKIN (*on the verge of tears, angrily*). Expensive presents . . . Get along with you! (*To the* ORDERLY:) Take the samovar in there . . . (*Mockingly.*) Expensive presents . . .

*The* ORDERLY *takes the samovar into the main room.*

ANFISA (*crossing the drawing-room*). Some strange colonel, my dears! He's taken his coat off, my pets – he's on his way up. Now, Irinushka, you be nice and polite to him . . . (*Going out.*) It's past lunchtime already, too . . . Oh my lord . . .

TUSENBACH. Vershinin, presumably.

*Enter* VERSHININ.

Lieutenant-Colonel Vershinin!

VERSHININ (*to* MASHA *and* IRINA): Allow me to introduce myself – Vershinin. So very glad to be with you at last. But how you've changed! Dear me!

IRINA. Do sit down. This is a great pleasure for us.

VERSHININ (*gaily*). I'm so glad! I'm so glad! But there are three of you, aren't there – three sisters? I remember there being three girls. Your faces I don't recall, but the fact that your father, Colonel Prozorov, had three little girls – that I recall perfectly – indeed I saw it for myself. How time flies! Ah me, how time flies!

TUSENBACH. The colonel is from Moscow.

IRINA. From Moscow? You're from Moscow?

VERSHININ. I am indeed. Your late father was a battery commander there; I was in the same brigade. (*To* MASHA:) Now your face I believe I do just remember.

MASHA. I don't remember you, though!

IRINA. Olya! Olya! (*Calls into the main room.*) Olya, come here!

*OLGA comes out of the main room into the drawing-room.*

Colonel Vershinin turns out to be from Moscow.

VERSHININ. So you're Olga, you're the eldest ... You're Maria ... And you're Irina, you're the youngest ...

OLGA. You're from Moscow?

VERSHININ. I am. I was at university in Moscow and I began my service career in Moscow. I served there for a long time, until finally I was given a battery here, and transferred, as you see. I don't really remember you – all I remember is that you were three sisters. Your father has stayed in my memory very clearly. I sit here and close my eyes and I see him as if he were standing in front of me: I used to come to your house in Moscow ...

OLGA. I thought I remembered them all, and now suddenly ...

IRINA. You're from Moscow ... It's like a bolt from the blue!

OLGA. We're moving there, you see.

IRINA. We think we shall actually be there by the autumn. It's our home town – we were born there ... In Old Basmannaya Street ...

*She and* OLGA *both laugh with delight.*

MASHA. Out of the blue we've met someone from home. (*Animatedly.*) Now it's come back to me! You remember, Olya, we used to talk about 'the lovelorn major'. You were a lieutenant then and you were in love with somebody, and why it was I don't know, but everyone used to tease you by calling you the major ...

VERSHININ (*laughs*). That's me. The lovelorn major – that's right ...

MASHA. You only had a moustache in those days ... Oh, how you've aged! (*Through her tears.*) How you've aged!

VERSHININ. Yes, when they used to call me the lovelorn

major I was young still, and they were right – I was in love. That's not the case now.

OLGA. But you still don't have a single grey hair. You've aged, yes, but you're not old yet.

VERSHININ. I shall be forty-three next birthday, nonetheless. Have you been away from Moscow for long?

IRINA. Eleven years. What are you doing, Masha, you're crying, you funny thing . . . (*Through her tears.*) I'm going to cry, too . . .

MASHA. I'm all right. So which street did you live in?

VERSHININ. Old Basmannaya.

OLGA. So did we . . .

VERSHININ. At one time I lived in Nemetzkaya Street. I used to walk from there to the Krasny Barracks. There's a rather depressing bridge on the way – you can hear the noise of the water underneath it. If you're on your own it strikes a chill into your heart.

*Pause.*

But here you have such a broad and brimming river! A magnificent river!

OLGA. Yes, only there's the cold here. The cold and the mosquitoes . . .

VERSHININ. Oh, come now! This is a good healthy Russian climate. The forest, the river . . . it's birch country here, too. The good old humble birch – I love it above all trees. It's a fine place to live. The only odd thing is that the railway station is thirteen miles out of town . . . And nobody knows why.

SOLYONY. I know why.

*Everyone looks at him.*

Because if the station were near then it wouldn't be far, and if it's far then naturally it can't be near.

*An awkward silence.*

TUSENBACH. Something of a humorist, the captain.

OLGA. Now I've placed you, too. I remember you.

VERSHININ. I knew your mother.

CHEBUTYKIN. A good woman she was, God rest her soul.

IRINA. Mama's buried in Moscow.

OLGA. In the Novo-Devichi . . .

MASHA. Can you imagine, I'm already beginning to forget her face. It will be the same with us – we shan't be remembered, either. We shall be forgotten.

VERSHININ. Yes. We shall be forgotten. Such is indeed our fate – there's nothing we can do about it. What we find serious, significant, highly important – the time will come when it's all forgotten, or when it all seems quite unimportant after all.

*Pause.*

And this is interesting: we can't possibly know now what's eventually going to be considered elevated and important, and what people are going to think pathetic and ridiculous. The discoveries made by Copernicus – or Columbus, let's say – didn't they seem uncalled-for and absurd at first? While some empty nonsense written by a crank looked like the truth? And it may be that our present way of life, with which we feel so much at home, will in time seem odd, uncomfortable, foolish, not as clean as it should be – perhaps even wicked.

TUSENBACH. Who knows? Perhaps, on the other hand, our way of life will be thought elevated and remembered with respect. There's no torture now, no executions or invasions; and yet, at the same time, there's so much suffering.

SOLYONY (*in a little voice*). Cheep, cheep, cheep . . . If there's one thing the baron loves it's a nice bit of philosophising.

TUSENBACH. Will you please leave me alone . . .? (*Sits elsewhere.*) It's becoming tedious.

SOLYONY (*in his little voice*). Cheep, cheep, cheep . . .

TUSENBACH (*to* VERSHININ). The suffering to be observed nowadays – and there is so much of it – does nevertheless testify to a certain moral elevation that society has achieved . . .

VERSHININ. Yes, yes, of course . . .

CHEBUTYKIN. You said just now, baron, that our way of life may one day be thought elevated. But people are still as low as ever . . . (*Stands up.*) Look how low I am. You have to tell me my way of life is elevated just to console me, obviously.

*A violin is played, off.*

MASHA. That's Andrey playing – our brother.

IRINA. He's the scholar of the family. He's probably going to be a professor. Papa was a soldier, but his son plumped for an academic career.

MASHA. At Papa's wish.

OLGA. We've been teasing him today. It appears that he is a tiny bit in love.

IRINA. With a certain young lady who lives hereabouts. She'll be coming today, most probably.

MASHA. Oh, but the way she dresses! It's not just dowdy, it's not just unfashionable – it's downright pitiful. Some outlandish skirt in a shade of bright yellow, with an appalling little fringe – and a red blouse. And those wishy-washy white cheeks of hers! Andrey isn't in love – that I won't concede – he has some taste, after all. He's just teasing us, just playing the fool. I heard yesterday she's to marry Protopopov, the chairman of the local Executive Council. Very suitable . . . (*Through the side door.*) Andrey! Come here a minute, dear!

*Enter* ANDREY.

OLGA. This is my brother Andrey.

VERSHININ. Vershinin.

ANDREY. Prozorov. (*Wipes his face, which is covered in per-spiration.*) You're our new battery commander?

OLGA. Can you imagine, the colonel comes from Moscow.

ANDREY. Really? Well, the best of luck to you, because now my sisters will never give you any peace.

VERSHININ. I've already managed to weary them.

IRINA. Look at the picture-frame that Andrey gave me today! (*Shows the frame.*) He made it himself.

VERSHININ (*looking at the frame and not knowing what to say*) Indeed . . . a thing of . . .

IRINA. And that frame there – the one over the piano – he made that as well.

ANDREY *flaps his hand and moves away.*

OLGA. He's not only the scholar of the family – he also plays the violin and he makes all kinds of little woodwork things. Well, he's the complete all-rounder. Andrey, don't go away! He's got this trick of disappearing all the time. Come back!

MASHA *and* IRINA *take him by the arms and laughingly bring him back.*

MASHA. Come on, come on!

ANDREY. Leave me alone, will you, please?

MASHA. You are absurd! They used to call the colonel here the lovelorn major, and he wasn't the slightest bit cross about it.

VERSHININ. Not at all!

MASHA. And I'm going to call you the lovelorn fiddler.

IRINA. Or else the lovelorn professor!

OLGA. He's in love! Our dear Andrey is in love!

IRINA (*clapping*). Bravo, bravo! Encore! Our dear little
Andrey is in love!

CHEBUTYKIN (*goes up behind* ANDREY *and seizes him with
both arms around his waist*).

> For love and love alone
> was man put in his earthly home!

(*Roars with laughter, still holding the newspaper.*)

ANDREY. That will do now, that will do . . . (*Wipes his face.*)
I didn't sleep all night, and now I feel a bit the worse
for wear. I was reading until four o'clock, then I went
to bed, but it was quite fruitless. My thoughts kept going
round, and it gets light early here – the sun simply comes
stealing into the bedroom. There's a book I want to translate from the English during the course of the summer,
while I'm still here.

VERSHININ. You read English?

ANDREY. Yes. Poor Father – he piled education on to us.
It's ridiculous, but I have to confess that after he died I
began to put on weight. A year and I'm out to here. It's
as if my body had shaken off some load. Thanks to Father
my sisters and I know French, German, and English. Irina
knows Italian as well. But what it cost us!

MASHA. Knowing three languages in this town is a pointless
embellishment. It's not even an embellishment – it's some
kind of useless appendage like a sixth finger. We know
much more than we need to.

VERSHININ. Listen to them! (*Laughs.*) You know much
more than you need to, do you? I think the town so dull
and dreary that it has no place for someone of intelligence
and education truly doesn't exist – couldn't exist. All right,
let us concede that among the hundred thousand inhabitants
of this town – of this, certainly, rude and backward town
– there are no more than three people like you. Obviously
you're not going to prevail over the sea of darkness around

you. In your own lifetime you'll gradually be forced to give ground to that crowd of a hundred thousand – you'll be swallowed up in it; life will choke you. All the same, you won't disappear, you won't be without influence. After you will come maybe six people of your sort, then twelve, and so on, until in the end people like you are in the majority. In two or three hundred years life on earth will be astonishingly, unimaginably beautiful. This is the life that man must have, and if it eludes him in the mean-time then he must have a premonition of it, he must wait and dream and make himself ready for it, and this means he must understand more and know more than his father and grandfather did. (*Laughs.*) And you're complaining that you know much more than you need to.

MASHA (*takes off her hat*). I'll stay for lunch.

IRINA (*with a sigh*). Really, we should have been taking a note of all that . . .

ANDREY *is missing. He has gone out unnoticed.*

TUSENBACH. Many years from now, you tell us, life on earth will be astonishingly beautiful. True. But to have a hand in that life now, albeit a remote hand, we must pre-pare ourselves for it, we must work . . .

VERSHININ (*gets up*). Yes. But what a lot of flowers you've got! (*Looking round.*) And magnificent quarters. I envy you! I've spent all my life knocking about in lodgings with two chairs and a sofa, and a stove that always smokes. Flowers like these are the very thing my life has lacked . . . (*Rubs his hands.*) Ah, well, there we are!

TUSENBACH. Yes, but we have to work. You're probably thinking, that's what touches a German heart. But I'm Russian, I promise you. I can't even speak German. My father's Russian Orthodox . . .

*Pause.*

VERSHININ (*walks about the stage*). I often think, supposing we could start our life afresh – and this time with our eyes open? Supposing the first life, the one we've already lived, was a kind of rough draft, and the second one was the fair copy! Then what we'd all mostly try to do, I think, would be not to repeat ourselves. Or at any rate we'd create new surroundings for ourselves, we'd set up quarters like these with flowers, with a sea of light ... I have a wife and two little girls, on top of which my wife is a sick woman, and so it goes on, and anyway, if I were starting life over again I shouldn't get married ... Not for any money!

*Enter* KULYGIN *in a uniform tailcoat.*

KULYGIN (*goes up to* IRINA). My dear sister-in-law, may I offer you all suitable compliments on this happy day? And my most sincere and heartfelt best wishes for your good health, and for everything else a girl of your age might properly be wished. And may I make you a present of this little book? (*Gives it to her.*) The history of our school over the last fifty years, written by me. It's just a little thing I wrote because I had nothing better to do, but read it anyway. Good day, ladies and gentlemen! (*To* VERSHININ:) Kulygin – teacher in the local high school. Seventh grade of the civil service – a lieutenant-colonel of the civilian world! (*To* IRINA:) In that little book you'll find a list of all those who passed through our school in the last fifty years. *Feci quod potui, faciant meliora potentes.* I have done what I could; let those who can do better. (*Kisses* MASHA.)

IRINA. You gave me some sort of book like this at Easter, surely?

KULYGIN (*laughs*). No! Did I? In that case give it back, or better still give it to the colonel here. Take it, colonel. Read it some time when you're bored.

VERSHININ. Thank you. (*On the point of leaving.*) I'm so very pleased to have made your acquaintance . . .

OLGA. You're not going? No, no, no!

IRINA. You'll stay and have lunch with us. Please.

OLGA. Do stay!

VERSHININ (*bows*). I seem to have chanced upon a name-day. Forgive me – I had no idea – I didn't offer you my compliments . . . (*Goes out with* OLGA *into the main room.*)

KULYGIN. Today, ladies and gentlemen, is the Sabbath day, the day of rest, and rest we will, rejoice we will, each according to his age and station. The carpets need to be taken up for the summer and put away till winter . . . With insect-powder or mothballs . . . The Romans were healthy because they knew how to work – and they knew how to rest as well. They had *mens sana in corpore sano*. Their mind and body were uniform in their development. Our headmaster says that the most important thing in any life is its attainment to the uniform . . . (*Takes* MASHA *by the waist, laughing.*) Masha loves me. My wife loves me. The curtains as well as the carpets . . . I'm in merry mood today – I'm in excellent spirits. Masha, we're due at the headmaster's at four o'clock. A little outing is being got up for the teaching staff and their families.

MASHA. I'm not going.

KULYGIN (*pained*). My dear Masha, why ever not?

MASHA. We'll talk about it later . . . (*Angrily.*) All right, I'll go, only please leave me alone . . . (*Moves away.*)

KULYGIN. After which we shall be spending the evening at the headmaster's. In spite of his ill health, that man makes a supreme effort to be sociable. A wonderful person. A splendid man. After the staff meeting yesterday he said to me: 'I'm tired, you know! I'm tired!'

(*Looks at the clock on the wall, then at his watch.*)

Your clock is seven minutes fast. 'Yes,' he says, 'I'm tired.'

*The violin plays, off.*

OLGA. Ladies and gentlemen, this way, please. Lunch is served. We're having a pie!

KULYGIN. Ah, my dear Olga! My dear, dear Olga! Yesterday I worked from first thing in the morning until eleven at night, went tired to bed, and am today a happy man. (*Goes out to the table in the main room.*) My dear Olga . . .

CHEBUTYKIN (*puts the newspaper in his pocket and combs his beard.*) Pie? Splendid!

MASHA (*to* CHEBUTYKIN, *sternly*). Just watch you don't drink anything today. Do you hear? It's bad for you to drink.

CHEBUTYKIN. Oh, pish and tush! That's all past history. It's two years since I last went on the spree. (*Impatiently.*) Goodness, woman, what does it matter?

MASHA. Don't you dare start drinking, all the same. Don't you dare, now. (*Angrily, but so that her husband shall not hear.*) Damnation, another whole evening of boredom at the headmaster's!

TUSENBACH. I shouldn't go, if I were you . . . Very simple answer.

CHEBUTYKIN. Don't go, my precious.

MASHA. 'Don't go,' that's right . . . This damned life, this intolerable life . . . (*Goes into the main room.*)

CHEBUTYKIN (*follows her*). Now, now, now!

SOLYONY (*going through into the main room*). Cheep, cheep, cheep . . .

TUSENBACH. Stop it, will you? That's enough!

SOLYONY. Cheep, cheep, cheep . . .

KULYGIN (*cheerfully*). Your health, Colonel! A teacher's what I am, and very much at ease in this house is how I feel. Masha's husband . . . And a dear kind woman she is . . .

VERSHININ. I'm going to drink a toast in this dark vodka . . . (*Drinks*.) Your health! (*To* OLGA:) I feel so much at home here . . .!

*Only* IRINA *and* TUSENBACH *are left in the drawing-room.*

IRINA. Masha's out of sorts today. She got married at eighteen, when she thought he was the cleverest man in the world. That's not how it seems now. The kindest, yes, but not the cleverest.

OLGA (*impatiently*). Andrey, will you come!

ANDREY (*off*). Coming. (*Enters and goes to the table.*)

TUSENBACH. What are you thinking about?

IRINA. Nothing. I don't like that Solyony of yours. He frightens me. He just talks nonsense . . .

TUSENBACH. He's a queer fish. I feel sorry for him and irritated by him at the same time. Mostly sorry, though. I think he's shy . . . When we're alone together he's usually very intelligent and friendly, whereas in company he's rude, he's forever picking quarrels. Let me just be near you for a little. What are you thinking about?

*Pause.*

You're twenty years old – I'm not yet thirty. So many years left in front of us – a long, long corridor of days, full of my love for you . . .

IRINA. Please don't talk to me about love.

TUSENBACH (*not listening*). I thirst most desperately to live and strive and labour, and this thirst in my heart has merged into my love for you, Irina. And you're beautiful – it's as if you were taunting me – and life seems beautiful in that same way. What are you thinking about?

IRINA. You say that life is beautiful. But supposing it only

seems to be? For the three of us, for me and my sisters,
life hasn't been beautiful up to now – it's choked us like
choking weeds ... Now the tears have started. Can't have
that ... (*Quickly wipes her face and smiles.*) Work, that's
what we must do – work. That's why we feel so gloomy,
why we see life in such dark colours – it's because we
don't know what it is to work. We were born of people
who despised it ...

*Enter* NATASHA. *She is wearing a pink dress with a green
belt.*

NATASHA. They're sitting down to lunch already ... I'm
late ... (*Glances in the mirror in passing and sets herself to
rights.*) I think my hair's all right, isn't it ...? (*Seeing*
IRINA.) Irina, dear – best wishes! (*Kisses her firmly and at
length.*) You've got a lot of people here – honestly, I'm
ashamed to be seen ... Hello, baron!

OLGA (*coming into the drawing-room*). And here's Natasha.
How are you, my dear?

*They exchange kisses.*

NATASHA. I'm just saying best wishes to Irina. You've got
such a lot of company – I feel terribly embarrassed ...

OLGA. Oh, come now – it's just family and friends. (*Lowering
her voice, startled.*) You're wearing a green belt! My dear,
it's wrong!

NATASHA. Green means something bad, does it?

OLGA. No, it just doesn't go ... And it looks peculiar,
somehow ...

NATASHA (*plaintively*). Does it? It's not really green,
though, you see, it's more sort of neutral. (*Follows* OLGA
*into the main room.*)

*In the main room people are sitting down to lunch. The
drawing-room is deserted.*

KULYGIN. Irina, here's to a handsome husband. High time you were getting married.

CHEBUTYKIN. Natasha, here's to a little someone for you, too.

KULYGIN. Natasha already has a little someone.

MASHA (*taps her plate with a fork*). A toast! A short life and a merry one, God help us!

KULYGIN. Beta minus for conduct.

VERSHININ. Delicious liqueur. What's it made with?

SOLYONY. Black beetles.

IRINA (*plaintively*). Ugh! How disgusting . . .!

OLGA. For supper we're having roast turkey and apple pie. Isn't it wonderful – I've got the whole day at home. I'm home all evening . . . Do come this evening, everyone . . .

VERSHININ. May I come, too?

IRINA. Please.

NATASHA. They're very informal here.

CHEBUTYKIN. For love and love alone
　　　　　　　Was man put in his earthly home. (*Laughs.*)

ANDREY (*angrily*). Will you stop it, all of you? Aren't you tired of it?

*Enter* FEDOTIK *and* RODE *with a large basket of flowers.*

FEDOTIK. They've gone in to lunch already, though.

RODE (*loudly, with a guttural accent*). Gone in to lunch? Oh, yes, so they have . . .

FEDOTIK. Hold on a moment! (*Takes a photograph.*) One! Just half a moment more . . . (*Takes another photograph.*) Two! Now we're all set!

*They take the basket and go into the main room, where they are given a noisy reception.*

RODE (*loudly, to* IRINA): The best of wishes to you, all the very best! Enchanting weather today, simply magnificent.

I've been out walking all morning with some of the boys from the school. I take them for gymnastics. If I have my way, the entire high school will be for the high jump!

FEDOTIK (*to* IRINA): You can move, it's all right! (*Taking a photograph.*) You're looking very pretty today. (*Takes a top out of his pocket.*) Oh, and I've got a top for you . . . It makes the most amazing sound . . .

IRINA. Oh, how lovely!

MASHA. On a far seashore an oak tree grows,

And from it hangs a golden chain . . .

And from it hangs a golden chain . . . (*Pathetically.*) What am I saying that for? I've had those lines on my brain all day . . .

KULYGIN. Thirteen at table!

RODE (*loudly*). No one here, surely, is superstitious?

*Laughter.*

KULYGIN. Thirteen at table means that we have those amongst us who are in love. Not you by any chance, doctor . . .?

*Laughter.*

CHEBUTYKIN. I'm an old reprobate, but why Natasha here should be blushing I can't understand for the life of me.

*Loud laughter.* NATASHA *runs out of the main room into the drawing-room.* ANDREY *follows her.*

ANDREY. Come on, now, don't take any notice of them! Wait . . . stop a moment, I beg you . . .

NATASHA. I'm ashamed of myself . . . I don't know what's wrong with me, but they were making me a laughing-stock. Leaving the table like that was very ill-mannered, but I can't cope with it . . . I simply can't . . . (*Buries her face in her hands.*)

ANDREY. My dear, I beg you, I implore you – don't upset yourself. They're only joking, I assure you – they mean it kindly. My dear, my sweet, they're all kind, good-hearted people who love me and who love you. Come over here by the window – they can't see us here . . . (*Looks round.*)

NATASHA. I'm so unused to being in company . . .!

ANDREY. Oh, you're so young, you're so miraculously and beautifully young! My dear, my sweet, don't upset yourself so . . .! Trust me, just trust me . . . I feel so wonderful – my heart is full of love, full of joy . . . They can't see us! They can't, they can't! *Why* I first began to love you – *when* I first began to love you – it's all a mystery to me. My dear, my sweet, my pure in heart, be my wife! I love you, love you . . . as I've never loved before . . .

*They kiss.*

*Enter* TWO OFFICERS. *Seeing the couple kissing, they stop in amazement.*

**CURTAIN**

# Act Two

*The same*

*Eight o'clock in the evening. An accordion can just be heard, off, playing in the street outside. Darkness. Enter* NATASHA *in a housecoat, carrying a candle. She goes across and stops outside the door leading to* ANDREY'*s room.*

NATASHA. Andryusha? What are you doing in there? Reading, are you? It's all right, I was just wondering ... (*Goes across and opens another door, looks inside, and closes it again.*) Make sure there isn't a candle burning ...

ANDREY (*enters with a book in his hand*). What do you want, Natasha?

NATASHA. Just making sure there are no candles alight ... It's Shrovetide – the servants are all excited. You've got to keep a sharp lookout to stop anything happening. Twelve o'clock last night I'm on my way through the dining-room and what do I see? – there's a candle burning. Who lit it? – I still haven't got to the bottom of that. (*Puts her candle down.*) What time is it?

ANDREY (*glancing at the clock*). Quarter past eight.

NATASHA. Olga and Irina aren't back yet, either. They're still slaving, poor pets. Olga at her staff meeting, Irina at her telegraph office ... (*Sighs.*) I was saying to your sister only this morning. 'Irina,' I said, 'you must look after yourself, my pet.' But she won't listen. Quarter past eight, did you say? I'm worried about Bobik. I think he's not at all well, the poor little sweet. Why is he so cold? Yesterday he had a temperature, and today he's like ice ... I'm so worried!

ANDREY. It's all right, Natasha. The child's perfectly well.

NATASHA. He'd better go on to invalid food, all the same.

I'm worried about him. And at ten o'clock tonight, so I'm told, we're going to have the mummers here. I know it's Shrovetide, but I'd sooner they didn't come, Andryusha.

ANDREY. Well, I don't know. They were invited, of course.

NATASHA. He woke up this morning, my little baby boy, and he looked at me, and all of a sudden he smiled. He knew it was me! 'Hello, Bobik!' I said. 'Hello, love!' And he laughed. They understand, you see – they understand perfectly well. So, anyway, I'll tell them not to let the mummers in.

ANDREY (*irresolutely*). It's really up to my sisters. They're in charge of the house.

NATASHA. They're in charge, too. I'll tell them. They're so kind . . . (*Moves to go.*) I've ordered sour milk for supper. The doctor says you're to eat nothing but sour milk, otherwise you'll never lose weight. (*Stops.*) Bobik's so cold. I'm worried it may be too cold for him in his room. We must put him in another room, at any rate until the weather's warmer. Irina's room, for example – that would be perfect for a baby. It's dry, it gets the sun all day. You'll have to tell her – she can share with Olga for the time being . . . It won't matter – she's not home during the day, she's only here at night . . .

*Pause.*

Andrey, my pet, why aren't you saying anything?

ANDREY. Just thinking. Anyway, there's nothing to say . . .

NATASHA. No . . . Something I meant to tell you . . . Oh, yes, Ferapont – he's come round from the Council, he wants to see you.

ANDREY (*yawns*). Send him in.

NATASHA *goes.* ANDREY, *bending close to the candle that she has forgotten, reads his book. Enter* FERAPONT. *He is wearing an old tattered overcoat, with the collar up and his ears muffled.*

Hello, my old friend. What do you want?

FERAPONT. The Chairman's sent a book and a paper of some sort. Here you are ... (*Hands over a book and a packet.*)

ANDREY. Thank you. Right. Why are you so late? It's gone eight now, you know.

FERAPONT. What?

ANDREY (*louder*). I said, you're late. It's past eight o'clock.

FERAPONT. That's right. It was still light when I got here, but they wouldn't let me in. The master's busy, they said. So, all right, he's busy – I'm not in a hurry to get anywhere. (*Thinking that* ANDREY *is asking him something.*) What?

ANDREY. Nothing. (*Examining the book.*) Friday tomorrow, no one at the office. No matter – I'll go in all the same ... do some work. Boring at home ...

*Pause.*

Oh, my dear old friend, how strangely things do change, how life mocks us! Just out of boredom today, just out of idleness, I picked up this book – my old university lectures, and I had to laugh ... Dear God, I'm secretary to the local Executive Council – a body that Protopopov is *chairman* of. I'm the secretary, and the most I can hope for is to become a member of it. Me – a member of a local Executive Council! Me – a man who dreams every night that he's a professor of Moscow University, a distinguished scholar, the pride of Russia!

FERAPONT. No idea ... I don't hear too well ...

ANDREY. If you could hear properly I don't suppose I'd be talking to you. I've got to talk to someone, but my wife doesn't understand me, and I'm afraid of my sisters, I don't know why – I'm afraid they'll jeer at me, I'm afraid they'll shame me ... I don't drink, I've no fondness for taverns, but oh, my friend, what I'd give to be in Moscow now, sitting in Testov's in Theatre Square, or the Grand Hotel in Resurrection.

FERAPONT. In Moscow – so one of the contractors was saying at the Council the other day – there were these merchants eating pancakes. One of them ate forty pancakes, and apparently he dropped dead. Either forty or fifty. I don't remember.

ANDREY. You can sit in some enormous restaurant in Moscow – you don't know a soul – not a soul knows you – and yet you don't feel a stranger. While here you know everyone, and everyone knows you, and you're a stranger all the same, a total stranger . . . A lonely stranger.

FERAPONT. What?

*Pause.*

And this contractor was saying – may have been a lie, of course – he was saying how they were going to stretch a rope, apparently, right the way across Moscow.

ANDREY. What for?

FERAPONT. No idea. This contractor was saying.

ANDREY. Nonsense. (*Reads his book.*) Have you ever been to Moscow?

FERAPONT (*after a pause*). Never. It wasn't God's will.

*Pause.*

Am I to go?

ANDREY. You may. Take care of yourself.

FERAPONT *goes*

Take care, now. (*Reading.*) You can come back tomorrow and collect these papers . . . Off you go, then . . .

*Pause.*

He's gone.

*Doorbell.*

What a business it all is ... (*Stretches and goes off into his room with no great haste.*)

> The NURSE *sings, off, as she rocks the baby. Enter* MASHA *and* VERSHININ. *While they talk the* MAID *is lighting the lamp and the candles.*

MASHA. I don't know.

*Pause.*

I don't know. Being used to something accounts for a lot, of course. For example, it took us a long time after Father died to get used to having no orderlies all of a sudden. But leaving familiarity aside, I think what I'm saying is no more than simple truth. It may not be so in other places, but in our town the most worthwhile people – the most honourable, the most educated – are the military.

VERSHININ. I'm thirsty. I shouldn't mind some tea.

MASHA (*glancing at the clock*). They'll be bringing it in a moment. I was married off at eighteen, and I was afraid of my husband because he was a teacher and I was only just out of school. I thought then that he was terribly learned and clever and important. That's no longer the case, though, I regret to say.

VERSHININ. Quite ... indeed ...

MASHA. I'm not talking about my husband – I've got used to him – but among the civilians there are so many people who are vulgar and rude and uneducated. I'm upset by vulgarity – it offends me. I feel pain when I see that someone is lacking in refinement, lacking in gentleness and manners. When I find myself among my husband's teaching colleagues I do quite simply feel pain.

VERSHININ. Indeed ... But so far as I can see it doesn't matter whether they're military or civilians – they're equally uninteresting, in this town at least. It doesn't matter at all! Talk to your local intellectual – be he soldier or be he civilian – and he's fed up with his wife, he's fed up with his home, he's fed up with his estate, he's fed up with his horses ... What characterises the Russian is above all the loftiness of his thinking, but, tell me, why are his aspirations in life so low? Why?

MASHA. Why indeed?

VERSHININ. Why is he fed up with his children, why is he fed up with his wife? And then again why are his wife and children fed up with him?

MASHA. You're a little out of sorts today.

VERSHININ. Possibly. I haven't eaten this evening – I've had nothing to eat all day. My daughter's not very well, and when my girls are ill I'm seized with alarm, I'm racked by guilt for their having such a mother. You should have seen her today! What a squalid creature she is! We started squabbling at seven o'clock in the morning, and at nine I walked out and slammed the door.

*Pause.*

I never talk about it normally. It's curious – you're the only one I ever complain to. (*Kisses her hand.*) Don't be angry with me. You're the only one. I've no one apart from you, no one at all ...

*Pause.*

MASHA. What a noise the stove's making. The wind was moaning in the chimney just before Father died. That same sound exactly.

VERSHININ. Are you superstitious?

MASHA. Yes.

VERSHININ. Strange. (*Kisses her hand.*) You magnificent, magical woman. Magnificent, magical! It's dark in here, but I can see the shining of your eyes.

MASHA (*sits on another chair*). There's more light here . . .

VERSHININ. I'm in love, I'm in love, I'm in love . . . In love with your eyes, with the way you move. I dream about it . . . Magnificent, magical woman!

MASHA (*laughing quietly*). When you talk to me like that, I don't know why, but I just find myself laughing, even though it frightens me. Please don't do it again . . . (*Her voice drops.*) Or rather do – what does it matter . . .? (*Covers her face with her hands.*) What does it matter? There's someone coming, talk about something else . . .

*Enter* IRINA *and* TUSENBACH *through the main room.*

TUSENBACH. My surname is triple-barrelled. The Baron Tusenbach-Krone-Altschauer. But I'm Russian and I'm Orthodox, just like you. I have little of the German left in me – only the patience and obstinacy with which I weary you. I escort you home every evening.

IRINA. I'm so tired!

TUSENBACH. Every day I'm going to come to the telegraph office, and every day I'm going to escort you home. I'll go on doing it for ten years, for twenty years, until you dismiss me . . . (*Joyfully, at the sight of* MASHA *and* VERSHININ.) Oh, hello, it's you!

IRINA. Here I am, home at last. (*To* MASHA.) Some woman came in just now sending a telegram to her brother in Saratov, to tell him her son had died today, and she absolutely could not remember the address. So she sent it without one, just to Saratov. She was standing there in tears. And suddenly, for no reason at all, I turned on her. 'Oh,' I said, 'I've no time for all this.' It was such a stupid thing to happen. Is it today the mummers are coming?

MASHA. Yes.

IRINA (*sits down in an armchair*). Rest. Tired.

TUSENBACH (*with a smile*). When you come home from work you look such a young little, unhappy little thing . . .

*Pause.*

IRINA. Tired. No, I don't like my work, I don't like it at all.

MASHA. You've lost weight . . . (*Whistles a tune.*) You've got younger-looking, and your face has become boyish.

TUSENBACH. That's because of the way she does her hair.

IRINA. I shall have to look for another job – this one's not for me. What I so longed for, what I dreamed of, are the very things it doesn't have. It's work with no poetry in it, mindless labour . . .

*Knocking on the floor.*

The doctor's knocking. (*To* TUSENBACH:) Be a dear and knock back . . . I really can't . . . So tired . . .

TUSENBACH *knocks on the floor.*

He'll be here in a moment. We ought to be formulating some plan of action. The doctor and that brother of ours were playing cards in the Mess yesterday, and they lost again. I gather Andrey lost two hundred rubles.

MASHA (*indifferently*). Spilt milk.

IRINA. A fortnight ago he lost, in December he lost. If only he'd hurry up and lose the lot maybe we'd get out of this town. Dear Lord, I dream of Moscow every night – I'm like a woman possessed. (*Laughs.*) We're moving there in June, and before we get to June we've got to get through . . . February, March, April, May . . . nearly half a year!

MASHA. Just so long as Natasha doesn't somehow find out about him losing the money.

IRINA. Natasha? I don't think it matters much to her.

CHEBUTYKIN, *who has only just got out of bed – he has been taking a rest after dinner – comes into the ballroom and combs his beard, then sits down at the table and takes a newspaper out of his pocket.*

MASHA. Here he is . . . Has he paid his rent?

IRINA (*laughs*). No. Not a kopek for the last eight months. It's gone out of his head, evidently.

MASHA (*laughs*). Sitting there so full of himself!

*They all laugh. Pause.*

IRINA (*to* VERSHININ). Why are you so quiet?

VERSHININ. I don't know. I'm longing for some tea. Half my life for a glass of tea! I haven't eaten all day . . .

CHEBUTYKIN. Irina!

IRINA. What do you want?

CHEBUTYKIN. Come here, would you? *Venez ici.*

IRINA *goes and sits at the table.*

I can't do it without you.

IRINA *lays out the cards for patience.*

VERSHININ. Well, then. If we're not going to get any tea, let us at least refresh ourselves with a little philosophising.

TUSENBACH. By all means. What about?

VERSHININ. What about? Let us think for a moment about . . . well, for example, about life as it will be after we are gone, two or three hundred years from now.

TUSENBACH Well, I suppose that after we are gone, people will fly about in air balloons, and the cut of a jacket will be different, and maybe they'll discover a sixth sense and develop it. But life will remain the same – difficult, full of hidden mysteries, and happy. And a thousand years from now man will still be sighing, 'Oh, life is hard.' And yet at the same time he'll be just as afraid of death as he is now, he'll be just as reluctant to die.

VERSHININ (*after a moment's thought*). How can I put it? It seems to me that everything in this world must gradually change – is changing already, in front of our eyes. Two hundred years hence, three hundred years – a thousand, if you like – it's not a question of how long – but eventually a new and happy life will dawn. No part in this life shall *we* have, of course, but we are living for it now – working for it – yes, and suffering for it. We are creating it – and this alone is the purpose of our existence. This, if you like, is our happiness.

MASHA *laughs quietly.*

TUSENBACH. What's got into you?

MASHA. I don't know. All day today I've done nothing but laugh.

VERSHININ. I went to the same cadet school as you – I didn't go on to military academy. I read a lot, but I don't know how to choose my books, and I may be reading quite the wrong things. But for all that, the longer I live the more I want to know. I'm going grey, I'm nearly an old man already, but I know so little – oh, how little I know! All the same, the most important thing – the most real thing – that I think I do know, and know for sure. And how I should love to demonstrate to you that there is no happiness for us – must be none, will be none . . . We have simply to work and work, and happiness . . . that will be the lot of our remote descendants.

*Pause.*

Not me? Then at least my descendants, and their descendants after them.

> FEDOTIK *and* RODE *appear in the main room. They sit down and hum quietly, accompanying themselves on the guitar.*

TUSENBACH. According to you we can't even dream of happiness. But what if I am in fact happy?

VERSHININ. You're not.

TUSENBACH (*throws up his hands, claps them together, and laughs*). We plainly don't understand one another. Let me see, now, how can I convince you?

> MASHA *laughs quietly.*

(*Raising his finger to her.*) You laugh away! (*To* VERSHININ:) It's not just two or three hundred years – a million years from now, even, life will still be just the same as it's always been. It doesn't change; it remains constant; it follows its own laws – laws which have nothing to do with you, or which at any rate you'll never discover. The birds that fly south in the autumn – the cranes, for example – on and on they fly, and whatever lofty or petty thoughts they have fermenting inside their heads, on they will continue to fly. On and forever on, whatever philosophers they may have among them. Let them philosophise away to their heart's content, just so long as they go on flying.

MASHA. All the same, there is some point?

TUSENBACH. Some point ... Look, it's snowing. Where's the point in that?

> *Pause.*

MASHA. It seems to me that a man must have faith, or be seeking it, otherwise his life is empty, quite empty ... To live and not to know why the cranes fly, why children are born, why the stars are in the sky ... Either you know why you're alive or it's all nonsense, it's all dust in the wind.

*Pause.*

VERSHININ. All the same, it's sad one's youth has gone ...

MASHA. Gogol's right: 'Living in this world, my friends, is dull work!'

TUSENBACH. And I say: arguing with you, my friends, is uphill work! So boo to you.

CHEBUTYKIN (*reading the paper*). Balzac was married in Berdichev.

IRINA *hums quietly.*

I might put that down in my little book. (*Makes a note.*) Balzac was married in Berdichev. (*Reads his newspaper.*)

IRINA (*lays out patience. Absently*). Balzac was married in Berdichev.

TUSENBACH. The die is cast. (*To* MASHA:) You know, do you, that I've resigned my commission?

MASHA. So I heard. And no good do I see in that. I've no great love for civilians.

TUSENBACH. No matter ... (*Stands up.*) I'm not a handsome man – what sort of figure do I cut as a soldier? Not that it matters ... I'm going to work. For one day in my life at any rate I'm going to work so that I go home in the evening, fall into bed exhausted, and go straight to sleep. (*Moves away into the main room.*) Working people must sleep so soundly!

FEDOTIK (*to* IRINA). I went into that shop on Moscow Street today and bought you some coloured pencils. Also this penknife ...

IRINA. You've got used to treating me as a child, but I'm

grown up now, you realise ... (*Takes the pencils and the penknife. Joyfully.*) Oh, they're lovely!

FEDOTIK. And I bought a pocket-knife for myself ... Take a look at this ... one blade, two blades, three blades, this is for picking your ears, these are scissors, this is for cleaning your nails ...

RODE (*loudly*). Doctor, how old are you?

CHEBUTYKIN. Me? Thirty-two.

*Laughter.*

FEDOTIK. Now I'm going to show you a different patience. (*Lays out the cards.*)

*The samovar is brought in.* ANFISA *hovers around it.* NATASHA *enters shortly afterwards and also busies herself about the table. Enter* SOLYONY. *He makes his greetings to the company and sits down at the table.*

VERSHININ. What a wind, though!

MASHA. Yes, I'm sick of the winter. I can't even remember now what summer's like.

IRINA (*playing patience*). It's going to come out, I see. We shall get to Moscow.

FEDOTIK. On the contrary, it's not going to come out. The eight was on the two of spades, look. (*Laughs.*) So you won't get to Moscow.

CHEBUTYKIN (*reads the newspaper*). Manchuria. Smallpox rages.

ANFISA (*crossing to* MASHA). Masha, have your tea, dear. (*To* VERSHININ:) Here you are, colonel ... I'm sorry, dear, I've forgotten your name ...

MASHA. Bring it here, Nanny. I'm not going over there.

IRINA. Nanny!

ANFISA. Coming!

NATASHA (*to* SOLYONY). They understand, you know,

babies, they understand perfectly. 'Hello, Bobik!' I said.
'Hello, love!' And he gave me a kind of special look.
You think that's just a mother talking, don't you, but
no, not at all, I can assure you! He's a most unusual
baby.

SOLYONY. If that baby were mine, I'd fry him in a frying-
pan and eat him. (*Takes his glass of tea into the drawing-
room and sits down in the corner.*)

NATASHA (*covering her face with her hands*). So coarse! So
lacking in breeding!

MASHA. Happy the man who never notices whether it's
summer or winter. If I were in Moscow, I think I should
be indifferent to the weather . . .

VERSHININ. The other day I was reading the diary that
some French cabinet minister had kept while he was in
prison. He'd been convicted for his part in the Panama
Affair. With what delight, with what ecstasy, does he write
about the birds he can see through his cell window –
birds he'd never noticed before, in his days as a minister.
Now that he's at liberty again, of course, he notices the
birds no more than he did in the past. Nor will you notice
Moscow once you're living in it. Happiness is not for us
and never can be. All we can do is long for it.

TUSENBACH (*picks up a basket from the table*). Where are
the sweets?

IRINA. Solyony's eaten them.

TUSENBACH. The whole lot?

ANFISA (*serving tea*). Letter for you, dear.

VERSHININ. For me? (*Takes the letter.*) From my daughter.
(*Reads it.*) Yes, of course . . . (*To* MASHA:) If you'll excuse
me I'll just slip quietly away. I won't have any tea. (*Stands
up, agitated.*) It's the same old story . . .

MASHA. What? Or is it a secret?

VERSHININ (*quietly*). My wife has tried to poison herself

again. I must go. I'll get away without anyone noticing. It's all very unpleasant. (*Kisses* MASHA's *hand.*) My dear, my good and wonderful woman ... I'll slip quietly out through here ... (*He goes.*)

ANFISA. Where's he off to, then? I've just poured his tea ... The naughty man.

MASHA (*losing her temper*). Get away from me! Hanging around all the time – there's no rest from you ... (*Takes her cup of tea to the table.*) Silly old woman, I'm sick of you!

ANFISA. What are you in such a huff about? My sweet!

ANDREY (*off*). Anfisa!

ANFISA (*mimics him*). 'Anfisa!' He just sits in there ... (*She goes.*)

MASHA (*at the table in the main room, angrily*). Let me sit down, will you? (*Muddles the cards on the table.*) Taking up all the room with cards. Drink your tea!

IRINA. Masha, you're in a temper.

MASHA. Well, if I'm in a temper don't talk to me. Don't touch me!

CHEBUTYKIN (*laughing*). Don't touch her, don't touch ...

MASHA. You're sixty, but you might as well be six, the way you're always babbling on about God knows what.

NATASHA (*sighs*). My dear Masha, why do you use expressions like that in polite conversation? In good society, with your looks – I'll be quite frank, now – you could be simply enchanting, if it weren't for the language you use. *Je vous prie pardonnez-moi, Marie, mais vous avez des manières un peu grossierès.*

TUSENBACH (*suppressing his laughter*). May I ...? May I ...? I think there's some brandy there ...

NATASHA. *Il parait, que mon Bobik déjà ne dort pas,* he's woken up. My poor poppet's not very well today. I must go and look at him, do forgive me ... (*She goes.*)

IRINA. Where's the colonel gone?

MASHA. Home. Some extraordinary business with his wife again.

TUSENBACH (*goes over to* SOLYONY, *holding the brandy decanter*). You're always sitting on your own thinking about something, I can't imagine what. Come on, let's make it up. Let's have a glass of brandy.

*They drink.*

I shall probably have to play the piano all night. A lot of rubbish, most likely . . . Well, who cares?

SOLYONY. What do you mean, make it up? I haven't quarrelled with you.

TUSENBACH. You always give me the feeling that something has happened between us. You are an odd fish, I must say.

SOLYONY (*declaims*). I may be odd – but who's not odd,
Save fools alike as peas in pod? . . .
Aleko, be not angry!

TUSENBACH. Aleko? What, in Pushkin? I don't see what he's got to do with it . . .

*Pause.*

SOLYONY. When I'm alone with someone it's all right, I'm like anybody else. But in company I'm morose, I'm awkward, and, I don't know, I talk a lot of rubbish. All the same, I'm more honest, I'm more high-minded than a great many people. And I can prove it.

TUSENBACH. I often get angry with you because you keep picking on me in public. I can't help liking you, though, I don't know why. Anyway, who cares? – I'm going to get drunk tonight. Your health.

SOLYONY. And yours.

*They drink.*

I've never had anything against you, baron. But I have something of Lermontov's character. (*Quietly.*) I even look rather like him . . . Or so people tell me . . . (*Takes a perfume flask out of his pocket and pours some on to his hands.*)

TUSENBACH. I'm resigning my commission. *Basta!* For five years I've been thinking about it, and now at last I've made up my mind. I'm going to work.

SOLYONY (*declaims*). Aleko, be not angry . . . Forget, forget your longings and your dreams . . .

*As they talk,* ANDREY *enters quietly with his book and sits by the candle.*

TUSENBACH. I'm going to work . . .

CHEBUTYKIN (*coming into the drawing-room with* IRINA). And they entertained us in real Caucasian style – onion soup, followed by a *chekhartmá* of roast meat.

SOLYONY. *Cheremshá* isn't meat. It's ramson – it's a plant like our onion.

CHEBUTYKIN. No, my dear boy. *Chekhartmá* isn't an onion – it's a roast dish made from mutton.

SOLYONY. I tell you *cheremshá* is onion.

CHEBUTYKIN. And I tell you *chekhartmá* is mutton.

SOLYONY. And I tell you *cheremshá* is onion.

CHEBUTYKIN. I'm not going to argue with you. You've never been to the Caucasus and you've never eaten *chekhartmá*.

SOLYONY. I've never eaten it because I can't stand it. It smells like garlic.

ANDREY (*beseechingly*). That will do, now, gentlemen! I beg of you!

TUSENBACH. When are the mummers coming?

IRINA. Towards nine, they promised, so any time now.

TUSENBACH *begins to hum the music of a folk-song, 'Akh vy, seni'. He puts his arm round* ANDREY *and leads him in the dance that traditionally accompanies the song. First* ANDREY *and then* CHEBUTYKIN *take up both song and dance. Laughter.*

TUSENBACH (*kisses* ANDREY). Come on, Andryusha, let's drink together, and to hell with it! I'm going to call you Andryusha – you call me Nikolasha – and we'll drink together. And I'm coming with you, Andryusha, I'm coming to Moscow, I'm going to university.

SOLYONY. Which one? There are two universities in Moscow.

ANDREY. There's one university in Moscow.

SOLYONY. I tell you there are two.

ANDREY. There can be three, for all I care. The more the merrier.

SOLYONY. There are two universities in Moscow!

*Murmuring and hushing.*

There are two universities in Moscow – the old one and the new one. But if you don't care to listen, if you're going to be irritated by what I say, then I can perfectly well not speak. In fact I can go and sit in another room . . . (*Goes out through one of the doors.*)

TUSENBACH. Bravo, bravo! (*Laughs.*) Ladies and gentlemen, let the festivities commence – I'm going to sit down at the piano! He's a funny fellow, that Solyony . . . (*Sits down at the piano and plays a waltz.*)

MASHA (*waltzes by herself*). The baron's drunk, the baron's drunk, the baron's drunk again!

*Enter* NATASHA.

NATASHA (*to* CHEBUTYKIN). Doctor! (*Says something to him, then quietly goes out again.*)

CHEBUTYKIN *touches* TUSENBACH *on the shoulder and whispers something to him.*

IRINA. What's happening?

CHEBUTYKIN. Time we were going. I'll say goodbye.

TUSENBACH. Good night. We must be going.

IRINA. I'm sorry, but what about the mummers?

ANDREY (*embarrassed*). There won't be any mummers. The thing is, my dear, that Natasha says Bobik isn't entirely well, and therefore ... Anyway, I don't know, it doesn't matter to me either way.

IRINA (*shrugging*). Bobik's not well!

MASHA. Oh, God help us! If we're being thrown out we'll have to go. (*To* IRINA:) It's not Bobik that's sick – it's her ... In there! (*She taps her forehead.*) Little shop-keeper!

*ANDREY goes out through the righthand door into his own room.* CHEBUTYKIN *follows him. People make their farewells in the main room.*

FEDOTIK. What a shame! I was counting on spending the evening, but if the baby's ill then of course ... I'll bring him some toys tomorrow.

RODE (*loudly*). I had a good long sleep after dinner specially – I thought I should be dancing all night. It's only nine o'clock, you know.

MASHA. Let's go out into the street and talk for a moment. We'll decide what to do.

*People can be heard saying goodbye, and there is the sound of* TUSENBACH's *cheerful laugh. Everyone goes out.* ANFISA *and the* MAID *clear the table and put out the lights. The* NURSE *can be heard singing. Enter* ANDREY *quietly, in overcoat and hat, with* CHEBUTYKIN.

CHEBUTYKIN. Marrying – that's something I never got

around to, because my life has gone by like a flash of lightning. Also because I was madly in love with your mother, who had a husband already.

ANDREY. Never marry. Never – it's a bore.

CHEBUTYKIN. That may be, but think of loneliness. Philosophise away till you're black in the face, but loneliness is a terrible thing, dear boy ... Though when you come down to it, what does it matter?

ANDREY. Let's be off, then.

CHEBUTYKIN. What's the hurry? We've plenty of time.

ANDREY. I'm afraid my wife might stop me.

CHEBUTYKIN. Ah!

ANDREY. This time I'm not going to play. I'll just sit there for a bit. I don't feel too good ... What should I do about shortness of breath?

CHEBUTYKIN. Why ask me? I don't remember, dear boy. No idea.

ANDREY. Let's go through the kitchen.

*The doorbell rings, then it rings again. There is the sound of voices and laughter.* ANDREY *and* CHEBUTYKIN *go.*

IRINA (*enters*). What's going on out there?

ANFISA (*in a whisper*). It's the mummers!

*The doorbell rings.*

IRINA. Nanny, tell them there's no one at home. Say we're sorry.

*ANFISA goes.* IRINA *walks about the room, agitated and lost in thought. Enter* SOLYONY.

SOLYONY (*bewildered*). No one here ... Where are they all?

IRINA. Gone home.

SOLYONY. Odd. You're all on your own in here?

IRINA. All on my own.

*Pause.*

Goodbye.

SOLYONY. I lost my self-control just now, I forgot my manners. But you're not like all the rest of them. You're above them, you're pure, you can see the truth . . . You're the only one who can understand me. I'm in love – deeply and boundlessly in love . . .

IRINA. Goodbye. Do go.

SOLYONY. I can't live without you. (*Following her.*) Oh, my heart's delight! (*On the verge of tears.*) Oh, happiness! Sumptuous, magical, amazing eyes, the like of which I have never seen in any other woman . . .

IRINA (*coldly*). Stop! Please!

SOLYONY. This is the first time I have ever spoken my love for you, and I feel as if I were out of this world, as if I were on some other planet. (*Rubs his forehead.*) Anyway, what does it matter? Feelings obviously can't be forced . . . But happy rivals I will not have . . . I won't . . . I swear to you by all the saints, I'll kill any rival . . . You magical woman!

NATASHA *comes through, holding a candle.*

NATASHA (*looks first into one room, then into another, and goes past the door leading to her husband's room.*) Andrey's in there. He can go on reading. (*To* SOLYONY:) Forgive me, I didn't know you were here, I'm not dressed for visitors . . .

SOLYONY. That matters very little to me. Goodbye. (*He goes.*)

NATASHA. My poor dear girl, but you're tired! (*Kisses* IRINA.) You should have been in bed hours ago.

IRINA. Is Bobik asleep?

NATASHA. He's asleep, but he's very restless. Oh, by the way, my dear, there's something I've been meaning to say to you, only you've been out all the time, or else I've been busy . . . I think it's too cold and damp for Bobik with the nursery where it is. Now your room would be such a lovely one for a baby. My dear, will you move in with Olga for the time being?

IRINA (*not understanding*). Move where?

*A troika with bells can be heard approaching the house.*

NATASHA. You'll be in the same room as Olga, just for the time being, and Bobik will have your room. He's such a love! I said to him today, 'Bobik, you're mine! All mine!' And he looked at me with those funny little eyes of his.

*Doorbell.*

It must be Olga. She's terribly late.

*The* MAID *goes up to* NATASHA *and whispers in her ear.*

NATASHA. Protopopov? What a fool that man is! Protopopov's here – he's inviting me to go for a troika ride with him. (*Laughs.*) What strange creatures these men are . . .

*Doorbell.*

Somebody else arriving. I could go for a quick ten or fifteen minutes perhaps . . . (*To the* MAID.) Say I'll be down directly.

*Doorbell.*

The doorbell . . . That must be Olga . . . (*She goes.*)

*The* MAID *runs out.* IRINA *sits wrapped in thought. Enter* KULYGIN *and* OLGA, *followed by* VERSHININ.

KULYGIN. Well, bless my soul! I was told they were having company tonight.

VERSHININ. Odd. I only left half an hour ago, and they were waiting for the mummers . . .

IRINA. Everyone's gone.

KULYGIN. Has Masha gone, too? Where's she gone? And why is Protopopov waiting downstairs in a troika? Who is he waiting for?

IRINA. Don't ask me any questions . . . I'm too tired . . .

KULYGIN. Oh, Miss High and Mighty . . .

OLGA. The staff meeting has only just finished. I'm exhausted. Our headmistress is off sick, so at the moment I'm deputising for her. My head, my head's aching, oh, my head . . . (*Sits.*) Andrey lost two hundred rubles at cards yesterday . . . The whole town's talking about it . . .

KULYGIN. Yes, the meeting tired me, too. (*Sits.*)

VERSHININ. My wife took it into her head to give me a fright just now. She very nearly poisoned herself. Anyway, it's all sorted itself out, and I can breathe again . . . So, we have to go? Well, then, may I wish you all the best? (*To* KULYGIN:) Come on, let's you and I go on somewhere! I can't stay at home, I absolutely cannot . . . Come on!

KULYGIN. No, I'm too tired. (*Stands up.*) Tired, tired. My wife's gone home, has she?

IRINA. She must have.

KULYGIN. (*kisses* IRINA's *hand*). Goodbye, then. Tomorrow and the day after we can rest all day. Good night! (*Goes.*) I'd love some tea. I was counting on spending the evening in pleasant company and – oh, *fallacem hominum spem!* – the illusory hopes of men! Exclamation taking the accusative . . .

VERSHININ. I'll go on my own, then. (*He goes with* KULYGIN, *whistling.*)

OLGA. My head aches, my poor head . . . Andrey lost at cards . . . The whole town's talking . . . I'm going to bed.

(*Goes.*) Tomorrow I'm free ... Oh, heavens, how sweet that is! Free tomorrow, free the day after ... My head aches, oh, my poor head ... (*She goes.*)

IRINA (*alone*). They've all gone. No one here.

*An accordion plays in the street; the* NURSE *sings a song.*

NATASHA (*crosses the main room in fur coat and cap, with the* MAID *following her*). I'll be back in half-an-hour. I'm just going to have a bit of an outing. (*She goes.*)

IRINA (*left alone, falls into melancholy*). Moscow! Moscow! To Moscow!

CURTAIN

# Act Three

OLGA's room – now also IRINA's. *Beds left and right, surrounded by screens. It is past two o'clock in the morning. Offstage the alarm is being sounded for a fire which began much earlier. The household has plainly still not got to bed.* MASHA *is lying on a couch, dressed as usual in black. Enter* OLGA *and* ANFISA.

ANFISA. They're sitting in the hall downstairs now ... I said to them, 'Come upstairs,' I said, 'and then we can do something.' They just kept crying. 'It's Papa,' they said, 'we don't know where he is. Oh, please God he hasn't been burnt to death!' That's what they've got into their heads! There's some outside, too – and they've no clothes to their backs, neither.

OLGA (*takes clothes out of the wardrobe*). Here, take this grey dress ... And this one ... The jacket as well ... And take this skirt, Nanny ... Lord in heaven, what a thing to happen! The whole of Kirsanov Lane has burnt down, apparently ... Take this ... And this ... (*Tosses clothes into* ANFISA's *arms.*) The Vershinins had a terrible fright, poor things ... Their house very nearly got caught. They can stay the night here ... We can't let them go home ... And poor Fedotik! Everything he possessed – he's nothing left in the world ...

ANFISA. Olya, love, you'll have to call Ferapont or I'll never carry it all ...

OLGA (*rings*). We can ring but we shan't get anyone ... (*Through the doorway.*) Could you come here, please, anyone who's there!

*Through the open door can be seen a window red from*

*the glow of the fire. The sound of a fire brigade going past the house.*

What a nightmare! I'm so sick of it!

*Enter* FERAPONT.

Here, take these downstairs ... The Kolotilin girls are waiting down in the hall ... give the things to them. And give them this ...

FERAPONT. Right. In 1812 it was Moscow that was on fire. God bless us, weren't the French surprised!

OLGA. Off you go, then.

FERAPONT. Right. (*He goes.*)

OLGA. Nanny, dear, let them have it all. We don't need any of it – let them have the lot, Nanny, love ... I'm so tired – I can hardly stand ... We can't let the Vershinins go home ... The girls can sleep in the drawing-room, and the colonel downstairs with the baron ... Fedotik can go in with the baron, too, or else upstairs in the big living-room ... The doctor's drunk, horribly drunk – you'd think he'd picked tonight on purpose – we can't put anyone in with him. And Vershinin's wife in the drawing-room with the girls.

ANFISA (*exhausted*). Olyushka, my dear, don't turn me out! Please don't!

OLGA. Nanny, you're talking nonsense. No one's turning you out.

ANFISA (*lays her head on* OLGA's *breast*). Oh, my own one, oh, my precious, I toil away, I do my work ... But I'll get too feeble, and then they're all going to say: Out you go! But where will I go? Where can I go? Eighty years old. Eighty-one ...

OLGA. Just you sit down for a moment, Nanny, love ... You poor dear, you're worn out ... (*Sits her down.*) Have a rest, my love. You've lost all your colour!

*Enter* NATASHA.

NATASHA. They're saying they'll have to quickly set up a charity for the people who lost their homes in the fire. I think that's an excellent idea. We must always help the poor – it's the duty of the rich. Bobik and Sofochka are fast asleep, for all the world as if nothing had happened. We've got so many people in the house – wherever you go it's full. There's influenza in town at the moment – I'm worried the children might catch it.

OLGA (*not listening to her*). You can't see the fire from this room. It's quite peaceful in here . . .

NATASHA. Isn't it . . . I must be an absolute sight. (*In front of the mirror.*) People keep telling me I've put on weight . . . and it's not true! Not the slightest bit! Masha's asleep, though – she's exhausted, the poor love . . . (*To* ANFISA, *coldly.*) How dare you sit down in my presence! Get up! Get out!

ANFISA *goes. Pause.*

Why you keep that old woman on I can't understand!

OLGA (*taken aback*). I'm sorry, but *I* don't quite understand . . .

NATASHA. She's no use here. She's a peasant – she ought to be living in her village . . . It's just pampering them! I like a little order in the house! There shouldn't be people in the house we don't need. (*Looks at* OLGA's *face.*) My poor love, you're tired! Our headmistress is tired! When my Sofochka gets bigger and goes to school, though, I'm going to be so frightened of you.

OLGA. I'm not going to be headmistress.

NATASHA. You'll be the one they choose, Olechka. It's been decided.

OLGA. I shall decline. I can't do it . . . I haven't the strength.

(*Drinks water.*) You were so rude to Nanny just then . . .
I'm sorry, but I can't bear it . . . I thought I was going to
faint . . .

NATASHA (*alarmed*). I'm sorry, Olya, I'm sorry . . . I didn't
mean to upset you.

   MASHA *gets up, takes her cushion, and goes out angrily.*

OLGA. You do see, my dear . . . We had a peculiar upbring-
ing, perhaps, but I can't bear that sort of thing. It de-
presses me to see anyone treated like that, it makes me ill
. . . I just feel like giving up!

NATASHA. I'm sorry, I'm sorry . . . (*Kisses her.*)

OLGA. The slightest rudeness, a harshly spoken word, and
it upsets me . . .

NATASHA. I often say more than I should, it's quite true,
but, my dear, you must agree, she could live in her village.

OLGA. She's been with us for thirty years.

NATASHA. But she can't work now, can she! Either I don't
understand what you're saying, or you won't understand
what I'm saying . . . She's incapable of work, she does
nothing but sleep or just sit there.

OLGA. Let her just sit there.

NATASHA (*in surprise*). What do you mean, let her just sit
there? She's a servant, isn't she? (*Through her tears.*) I
don't understand you, Olya. I have a nanny and a wet-
nurse, we have a maid and a cook . . . What do we need
that old woman for? What do we want with her?

   *The alarm is sounded offstage.*

OLGA I've aged ten years in this one night.

NATASHA. We've got to come to an understanding, Olga.
School for you – home for me. You have your teaching –
I have the household to run. And if I say something about

the servants then I know what I'm talking about, I know
– what – I – am – talking about . . . And I want that
thieving old hag out of the house by tomorrow . . . (*Stamps
her foot.*) That old witch . . .! How dare people cross me
so! How dare they! (*Controlling herself.*) Because really, if
you don't move downstairs we shall be forever quarrelling.
It's frightful.

  *Enter* KULYGIN.

KULYGIN. Where's Masha? We ought to be getting home.
Apparently the fire's dying down. (*Stretches.*) It's only
the one block gone, but there was the wind, of course, and
for a start it looked as if the whole town was on fire. (*Sits.*)
I'm exhausted. Olechka, my dear . . . I often think if it
weren't for Masha I should marry you. You're a sweet kind
woman . . . I'm worn out. (*Cocks his ear.*)
OLGA. What?
KULYGIN. You'd think he'd done it tonight on purpose.
The doctor – he's gone on the spree, he's quite horribly
drunk. You'd think he'd absolutely picked the night!
(*Stands up.*) He's coming up here, I think . . . Can you
hear? Yes, he is . . . (*Laughs.*) Honestly, what a rascal . . .
I'm going to hide . . . (*Goes to the wardrobe and stands in
the corner.*) What a villain.
OLGA. He hasn't been drinking for two years, and now
suddenly he's up and drunk himself silly . . . (*Goes with
NATASHA away to the back of the room.*)

  *Enter* CHEBUTYKIN. *With perfectly steady gait, as if
  sober, he crosses the room, stops, looks round, then goes
  over to the washstand and begins to wash his hands.*

CHEBUTYKIN (*morosely*). To hell with the lot of them . . .
Lot the rot . . . They think I'm a doctor, they think I
know how to treat all the ailments under the sun, but I

know absolutely nothing – forgotten anything I ever knew
– don't remember a thing – absolutely nothing.

OLGA *and* NATASHA *go without his noticing.*

Well, to hell with them. Wednesday last I treated a woman
in town and she died, and it was my fault she died. Yes
. . . Twenty-five years back I knew a thing or two, but
now I can't remember anything. Not a thing. Maybe I'm
not even human – I just put on this appearance of having
arms and legs and head. Maybe I don't exist at all – I just
think I'm walking and eating and sleeping. (*Weeps.*) Oh,
if only I could be non-existent! (*Stops weeping. Morosely.*)
Well, I don't know . . . Day before yesterday there was
this conversation in the Mess. 'Shakespeare!' they go. 'Vol-
taire . . .' I haven't read a line of any of them – I just put a
look on my face as if I had. And the others did the same.
But the meanness of it! The shabbiness! And that woman
came into my mind, the one I finished off on Wednesday
. . . then everything else came back as well, and I felt as if
my whole soul was warped and soiled and ugly . . . And
off I went and started drinking . . .

*Enter* IRINA, VERSHININ, *and* TUSENBACH. TU-
SENBACH *is wearing new and stylish civilian clothes.*

IRINA. Let's sit down here for a moment. No one's going to
come in here.
VERSHININ. If it hadn't been for the military the whole
town would have gone up in flames. Sterling work! (*Rubs
his hands with pleasure.*) Sterling lads and sterling work!
KULYGIN (*going across to him*). What time is it?
TUSENBACH. Gone three already. It's getting light.
IRINA. Everyone's just sitting around in the big living-
room. No one's going. That precious Solyony of yours is

sitting there, too ... (*To* CHEBUTYKIN:) You should be getting to bed, doctor.

CHEBUTYKIN. Quite all right ... I thank you ... (*Combs his beard.*)

KULYGIN (*laughs*). He's got himself a little spifflicated, has our good doctor! (*Claps him on the shoulder.*) Sterling work! *In vino veritas*, as the ancients would have it.

TUSENBACH. People keep asking me to get up a concert in aid of the victims.

IRINA. Yes, but who'd be in it?

TUSENBACH. It could be managed, if that's what people want. Masha, for instance, is a wonderful pianist.

KULYGIN. Wonderful!

IRINA. She's forgotten it all. She hasn't played for three years now ... or is it four?

TUSENBACH. Absolutely no one in this town knows anything about music, not a soul, but I do, and I give you my word that Masha is a magnificent pianist – a gifted one, almost.

KULYGIN. Quite right, baron. I love Masha very much. She's a splendid woman.

TUSENBACH. But imagine being able to play so marvellously, and knowing at the same time that nobody, absolutely nobody, could appreciate it!

KULYGIN (*sighs*). Quite ... But would it be entirely suitable for her to take part in a concert?

*Pause.*

I don't know, you see. It might be perfectly all right. Our headmaster is a charming man, I must in all honesty say. Most charming, highly intelligent – but he does have very definite views ... It's nothing to do with him, of course, but all the same, I could have a word with him if you like ...

CHEBUTYKIN *picks up a china clock and examines it.*

VERSHININ. I got absolutely filthy at the fire. I can't imagine what I look like.

*Pause.*

I heard just in passing yesterday that they're thinking of some rather remote posting for our brigade. Some say the Kingdom of Poland, some reckon Siberia.

TUSENBACH. I heard the same thing. Well, the town will be deserted.

IRINA. We'll be leaving, too!

CHEBUTYKIN (*drops the clock, which breaks*). Smithereens!

*Pause. Everyone is upset and embarrassed.*

KULYGIN (*picking up the pieces*). Fancy breaking such a valuable object. Oh, doctor, doctor! Gamma minus for conduct!

IRINA. That was poor Mama's clock.

CHEBUTYKIN. Maybe it was ... So, all right, it was Mama's. Maybe I didn't break it, and it only seems I did. Maybe we only seem to exist, and in fact we aren't here at all. I don't know anything; there isn't anything anyone knows. (*Reaching the door.*) What are you staring at? Natasha's having a little love-affair with Protopopov, and you don't see it ... You just sit here and see nothing, and all the time Natasha's having a little affair with Protopopov ... (*He goes, humming to himself.*)

VERSHININ. So ... (*Laughs.*) How odd all this is, when you come to think about it!

*Pause.*

When the fire started I ran home as fast as I could, and the first thing I see is there's our house, safe and sound

and not in any danger. But there on the doorstep are my
two little girls – they've got nothing on but their shifts –
there's no sign of their mother – people rushing to and fro
– horses galloping – dogs running – and on the girls' faces
alarm, terror, entreaty – I don't know what; and at the
sight of those faces my heart contracted within me. God
in heaven, I thought, what more will these children have
to endure in life's long course? I snatched them up and I
ran and I kept thinking this same thought: what more will
they have to endure in this world!

*The sound of the alarm. Pause.*

I got here, and here's their mother, shouting and raging.

*Enter* MASHA *with her cushion. She sits down on the
couch.*

And as my little girls stood on the doorstep in their shifts,
and the street was red from the flames, and the noise was
terrifying, I found myself thinking that it must have been
rather like this many years ago when some enemy made a
surprise raid, and looted and burnt ... Still, when you
really come down to it, there's an enormous difference
between now and then. And when a little more time has
passed, two or three hundred years, say, they'll look back
on the life we lead now in just the same way, with just the
same mixture of horror and scorn. Everything about the
present time will seem awkward and clumsy and terribly
uncomfortable and outlandish. Oh, but what a life it's
going to be, surely, what a life! (*Laughs.*) Forgive me, I've
started to philosophise again. May I continue, though?
I've a terrible longing to philosophise – I'm in just the
mood for it.

*Pause.*

It's as if the whole world were still asleep. That's why I say: what a life it's going to be! All you can do is imagine it ... Here we are now with only three people like you in town; but in succeeding generations there will be more, and more, and ever more, until the day dawns when everything has come round to your way of thinking, and everyone has come round to your way of life; and then you in your turn will be relegated to the past, and there will arise people who are better than you ... (*Laughs.*) I'm in a rather peculiar mood today. Oh God, but I want to live! (*Begins to hum Prince Gremin's aria from 'Eugene Onegin', Act III, Scene 1 – 'To love must young and old surrender'.*)

MASHA. Trum-tum-tum ...

VERSHININ. Tum-tum ...

MASHA. Tra-ra-ra?

VERSHININ. Tra-ta-ta. (*Laughs.*)

*Enter* FEDOTIK.

FEDOTIK (*dances*). I've lost the lot! Gone up in smoke! I'm cleaned right out!

*Laughter.*

IRINA. How can you joke about it? Everything went?

FEDOTIK (*laughs*). The lot. I'm cleaned out. Nothing left. My guitar went, my photographic stuff, all my letters ... I'd got a little notebook to give you – that went, too.

*Enter* SOLYONY.

IRINA. No, please, go away. No one's allowed in here.

SOLYONY. Why is the baron, if I'm not?

VERSHININ. We must all go, in fact. How is the fire?

SOLYONY. Dying down, apparently. No, but I do find it

positively odd – why the baron and not me? (*Takes out his flask of scent and sprinkles himself.*)

VERSHININ. Trum-tum-tum?

MASHA. Trum-tum.

VERSHININ (*laughs. To* SOLYONY). Come on, we'll go down to the living-room.

SOLYONY. All right, then, I shan't forget this. What does the poem say?

> We could spell out the moral of this piece –
> But let us not provoke the geese.

(*Looking at* TUSENBACH.) Cheep, cheep, cheep ... (*He goes with* VERSHININ *and* FEDOTIK.)

IRINA. That wretched Solyony has fumigated the room ... (*wonderingly.*) The baron's asleep! Baron! Baron!

TUSENBACH (*waking up*). I'm tired, though ... A brick-works ... I'm not rambling – I am in fact shortly going to move away from here and start a job at a brickworks ... I've already had talks about it. (*To* IRINA, *tenderly.*) You're so pale, so lovely, so fascinating ... Your pale skin seems to brighten the dark air like light ... You're sad, you're discontented with life ... Oh, come away with me, come away and we can work together ...!

MASHA. Out you go, now.

TUSENBACH (*laughing*). Oh, you're here, are you? I can't see. (*Kisses* IRINA's *hand.*) Goodbye, then, I'll be going ... I look at you now and I remember how once upon a time, long, long ago, on your name-day, you were all bright and cheerful, and you talked about the joys of work ... And what a happy life I caught a glimpse of then! Where has it gone? (*Kisses her hand.*) You've tears in your eyes. Go to bed, it's getting light already ... another day's beginning ... If only I might devote my life to you!

MASHA. Out you go! Really ...

TUSENBACH. I'm going . . . (*He goes.*)

MASHA (*lying down*). Fyodor? Are you asleep?

KULYGIN. Um?

MASHA. You should be getting home.

KULYGIN. My dear Masha, my dear sweet Masha . . .

IRINA. She's exhausted. You should let her have a rest, Fedya.

KULYGIN. I'm going, I'm going . . . My lovely, splendid wife . . . I love you, my one and only . . .

MASHA (*angrily*). *Amo, amas, amat, amamus, amatis, amant.*

KULYGIN (*laughs*). No, truly, she's an amazing woman. I've been married to you for seven years, and it seems like yesterday. On my word of honour. No, truly, you're an amazing woman. I'm content, content, content!

MASHA. I'm bored, bored, bored . . . (*Sits up.*) And one thing I can't get out of my head . . . It's absolutely outrageous. It keeps nagging at me – I can't go on not mentioning it. I mean about Andrey . . . He's mortgaged this house to the bank, and his wife's got her hands on all the money. But in fact the house doesn't belong just to him – it belongs to all four of us! He must know that, if he's got a spark of decency in him.

KULYGIN. Masha, what do you want him to do? Poor Andrey owes money right, left, and centre, heaven help him.

MASHA. All the same, it's an outrageous way to behave. (*Lies down.*)

KULYGIN. You and I aren't poor. I work – I go off to school each day, then I give private lessons . . . A straightforward man, that's me. A plain, straightforward man . . . *Omnia mea mecum porto*, as they say – all I have I carry with me.

MASHA. I'm not in need of anything. I'm just outraged by the unfairness of it.

*Pause.*

Go on, then, Fyodor!

KULYGIN (*kisses her*). You're tired. Have a little rest for half-an-hour, and I'll sit up and wait for you at home. Off to sleep ... (*Moves.*) I'm content, content, content. (*He goes.*)

IRINA. How much lesser a man has our Andrey become, in fact, living with that woman. How the spark has gone out of him, how he's aged! Once upon a time he was working for a university chair; yesterday he was boasting about getting a seat at last on the local Executive Council. He's got a seat, and Protopopov's the head of it ... The whole town's talking, the whole town's laughing – he's the only one who doesn't know and can't see ... Now everyone goes running to the fire while he sits in his room and doesn't bat an eyelid. All he does is play his violin. (*Irritably.*) Oh, it's horrible, horrible, horrible! (*Weeps.*) I just can't bear any more ...! I can't, I can't ...!

*Enter* OLGA. *She tidies around her bedside table.*

(*Sobs loudly.*) Throw me away, throw me away, I can't go on ...!

OLGA. What is it? What's the matter? My love!

IRINA (*sobbing*). Where's it all gone? Where is it? Oh, heavens, heavens! I've forgotten it all, I've forgotten it ... It's all mixed up inside my head ... I can't remember the Italian for window, or ceiling ... I'm forgetting it all, day by day forgetting it, and life's going away, and it will never come back, never, and we shall never get to Moscow ... I see that now – we're not going ...

OLGA. My love, my love ...

IRINA (*controlling herself*). Oh, I'm so unhappy ... I can't work, I won't work. I've had enough! First I was in the telegraph office – now I work for the town council, and I loathe and despise everything they give me to do ... I'll be twenty-four next birthday, I've been working forever, and my brain's dried up, I've grown thin, I've grown old, I've grown ugly, and nothing out of it, nothing, no kind of satisfaction, and time's flying, and I keep feeling as if I'm getting further away from the life that's real and beautiful, further and further away, into some kind of bottomless pit. I'm in despair, and how I'm still alive, how I haven't killed myself before now, I really don't know . . .

OLGA. Don't cry, my little girl, don't cry . . . It hurts me to see you.

IRINA. I'm not crying, I'm not . . . Enough of that . . . There, now I've stopped crying. Enough . . . Enough!

OLGA. My love, I'm talking to you now as your sister, as your friend. If you'll take my advice you'll marry the baron!

　　IRINA *weeps quietly.*

After all, you respect him, you have great regard for him . . . He's not handsome, it's true, but he's a decent, worthwhile man . . . And anyway, women don't marry for love – they do it because it's their duty. That's what I think, at any rate, and I should marry without love. Anyone who proposed to me – I'd marry him, so long as he was someone worthwhile. Even if he was an old man I'd marry him . . .

IRINA. I kept waiting for us to be in Moscow. That's where I was going to meet the real one. I dreamt about him, I was in love with him . . . But it's turned out to be nonsense, just so much nonsense . . .

OLGA (*embraces her sister*). My love, my lovely sister, I do understand. When the baron left the service and came here in an ordinary suit I thought he was so plain that I actually started to cry . . . 'Why are you crying?' he asked.

What could I say? But if it were God's will for him to marry you, then I should be very happy. Because that's another matter, another matter entirely.

> NATASHA, *carrying a candle, crosses from the righthand door to the left in silence.*

MASHA (*sits*). She's roaming about as if she were the one who'd started the fire.

OLGA. You are a silly, Masha. Shall I tell you who's the biggest silly in our family? – It's you. I'm sorry.

> *Pause.*

MASHA. Dear sisters, I want to make confession. I think I shall die if I don't say it. I'm going to make my confession to you, then never to another soul ... I'm going to say it, this very minute. (*Quietly.*) It's my secret, but you both must know it ... I can't not say it ...

> *Pause.*

I'm in love, I'm in love ... I'm in love with that man ... The one you saw just now ... Oh, what's the use? – I'm in love with Vershinin ...

OLGA (*goes to her own corner behind the screens*). Stop that. I can't hear, in any case.

MASHA. But what can I do? (*Clutches her head.*) First of all I thought, What a strange man! Then I felt sorry for him ... then I began to be in love with him ... I began to be in love with his voice, and with the things he said, and with his misfortunes, and with his two little girls ...

OLGA (*behind the screen*). I can't hear. Whatever nonsense you're talking, I can't hear.

MASHA. Oh, you are a funny one, Olya! I'm in love – all right, so that's my fate. So that's my lot in life ... He loves me, too ... It's terrifying. Isn't it? Is it wrong?

(*Takes* IRINA *by the hand, and draws her nearer.*) Oh, my sweet ... Somehow we shall live our lives, whatever happens to us ... You read some novel and you think, that's all old stuff, everyone knows all that. But as soon as you fall in love yourself you realise that no one knows anything, and that we each have to solve our own lives ... My loves, my sisters ... I've confessed to you. Now I shall be silent ... Now I shall be like the madman in that story of Gogol's ... silence ... silence ...

*Enter* ANDREY, *followed by* FERAPONT.

ANDREY (*angrily*). What do you want? I don't understand.

FERAPONT (*in the doorway, unhurriedly*). If I've said it once I've said it a dozen times.

ANDREY. First of all you can address me as 'sir'! I do have a rank, you know, I do happen to be a member of the Council.

FERAPONT. Sir, it's the firemen, sir, they're asking please may they take their carts down to the river through the garden. Otherwise they have to keep going round – it's backbreaking.

ANDREY. Very well. Tell them, very well.

FERAPONT *goes*.

I'm sick of them. Where's Olga?

OLGA *comes out from behind the screen*.

You're the person I'm looking for. Give me the key to the cupboard, will you – I've lost mine. You know that little key you've got.

OLGA *silently gives him the key.* IRINA *goes to her own corner behind the screen.*

*Pause.*

What an enormous fire, though! It's begun to die down now. Damn it, he made me so cross, that man Ferapont. That was a stupid thing I said to him . . . Making him call me sir.

*Pause.*

Why don't you say something, then, Olya?

*Pause.*

It's time you stopped all this nonsense. It's time you stopped pouting about like that for no earthly reason. You're here, Masha. Irina's here. All right, then, let's have it out in the open, once and for all. What have you three got against me? What is it?

OLGA. Stop it now, Andryusha. We'll talk about it tomorrow. (*Becoming upset.*) What a torment this night has been!

ANDREY (*very embarrassed*). Don't get upset. I'm simply asking you, perfectly calmly: what is it you've got against me? Just tell me straight out.

VERSHININ (*off*). Trum-tum-tum!

MASHA (*stands up. Loudly*). Tra-ta-ta! (*To* OLGA:) Good night, Olga, God bless you. (*Goes behind the screen and kisses* IRINA.) Sleep well . . . Good night, Andrey. Do go away, now, they're exhausted . . . you can have it all out tomorrow . . . (*She goes.*)

OLGA. That's right, Andryusha – let's postpone it till tomorrow . . . (*Goes to her corner behind the screen.*) Time for bed.

ANDREY. I'll just say what I have to say and then I'll go. Forthwith . . . In the first place you've got something against Natasha, my wife – and this I've been aware of from the very day we got married. Natasha is a fine person – honest, straightforward, and upright – that's my opinion. I love and respect my wife – I respect her, you understand? – and I insist that others respect her, too. I say it again – she is an honest and upright person, and all your little marks of displeasure – forgive me, but you're simply behaving like spoilt children.

*Pause.*

Secondly, you seem to be angry that I'm not a professor, that I'm not a scientist. But I serve in local government, I am a member of the local Council, and this service I consider just as sacred, just as elevated, as any service I could render to science. I am a member of the local Council and proud of it, if you wish to know . . .

*Pause.*

Thirdly . . . I have something else to say . . . I mortgaged the house without asking your consent . . . To this I plead guilty, and indeed I ask you to forgive me . . . I was driven to it by my debts . . . thirty-five thousand . . . I don't play cards now – I gave it up long since – but the main thing I can say in my own justification is that you're girls, and you get an annuity, whereas I had no . . . well, no income . . .

*Pause.*

KULYGIN (*in the doorway*). Masha's not in here? (*Alarmed.*) Where is she, then? That's odd . . . (*He goes.*)

ANDREY. They're not listening. Natasha is an outstanding woman, someone of great integrity. (*Walks about in silence, then stops.*) When I got married I thought we were going to be happy . . . all going to be happy . . . But my God . . . (*Weeps.*) My dear sisters, my own dear sisters, don't believe me, don't trust me . . . (*He goes.*)

KULYGIN (*in the doorway, alarmed*). Where's Masha? She isn't in here, is she? Surprising thing. (*He goes.*)

  *The sound of the alarm; an empty stage.*

IRINA (*behind the screens*). Olya! Who's that banging on the floor?

OLGA. That's the doctor. He's drunk.

IRINA. No peace tonight.

  *Pause.*

  Olya! (*Looks out from behind the screen.*) Have you heard? They're taking the brigade away from us, they're posting them somewhere far away.

OLGA. It's only rumours.

IRINA. We shall be left all on our own if they go ... Olya!

OLGA. What?

IRINA. Dear Olya, I do have a lot of respect for the baron, I do have a great regard for him, he's a fine man, and I'll marry him, all right – only we must go to Moscow! We must – I implore you! There's nowhere like Moscow in the whole wide world! We must go, Olya! We must!


CURTAIN

# Act Four

*The old garden of the Prozorovs' house. A long avenue of fir-trees, at the end of which can be seen the river. On the further bank of the river is the forest. Right – the verandah of the house, with a table on which there are bottles and glasses; people have evidently just been drinking champagne. Noon. From time to time people go through the garden on their way from the road to the river; half a dozen soldiers go by in quick time. CHEBUTYKIN, in a genial mood which never abandons him throughout the act, is sitting in an armchair in the garden, waiting to be summoned. He is wearing a peaked military cap and carrying a stick. KULYGIN – wearing a decoration round his neck and no moustache – IRINA, and TUSENBACH are standing on the verandah seeing off FEDOTIK and RODE, who are coming down the steps. Both officers are in marching order.*

TUSENBACH (*embraces* FEDOTIK). You're a good man. We've got on so well together. (*Embraces* RODE.) One more for you, then . . . Goodbye, old friend.

IRINA. We'll see each other again.

FEDOTIK. No, we shan't. We never will.

KULYGIN. Who knows? (*Wipes his eyes and smiles.*) Now here I am starting to cry.

IRINA. We'll meet again one day.

FEDOTIK. What – in ten, fifteen years time? We'll scarcely recognise each other by then. We'll greet each other like strangers. (*Takes a photograph.*) Keep still . . . One last one.

RODE (*embraces* TUSENBACH). We'll never see each other again . . . (*Kisses* IRINA's *hand.*) Thank you for every-thing, thank you!

FEDOTIK (*with irritation*). Stand still, will you!

TUSENBACH. God willing, we'll meet again. Write to us, though. Be sure to write.

RODE (*looks round the garden*). Goodbye, trees! (*Calls.*) Hup-hup!

*Pause.*

RODE. Goodbye, echo!

KULYGIN. Who knows, you may get married over there in Poland . . . A little Polish wife to put her arms round you and whisper soft words in Polish! (*Laughs.*)

FEDOTIK (*glancing at his watch*). We've less than an hour in hand. Solyony's the only one from our battery who's travelling on the barge – the rest of us will be marching. Three batteries are leaving today in battalion order, and another three tomorrow – then peace and quiet will descend upon the town.

TUSENBACH. Also frightful boredom.

RODE (*to* KULYGIN). And your wife is where?

KULYGIN. Masha? In the garden.

FEDOTIK. We must say goodbye to her.

RODE. Goodbye, then! We must go, or I shall start crying . . . (*Quickly embraces* TUSENBACH *and* KULYGIN, *and kisses* IRINA's *hand.*) We've had a wonderful life here . . .

FEDOTIK (*to* KULYGIN). Something for you to remember me by . . . A notebook with its own little pencil . . . We'll go down to the river through here . . .

*They depart, both gazing about them.*

RODE (*calls*). Hup-hup!

KULYGIN (*calls*). Goodbye!

> FEDOTIK *and* RODE *meet* MASHA *away upstage and make their farewells. She goes off with them.*

IRINA. They've gone . . . (*Sits down on the bottom step of the verandah.*)

CHEBUTYKIN. They forgot to say goodbye to me.

IRINA. Did you remember to say goodbye to them?

CHEBUTYKIN. No, I forgot, too, somehow. Anyway, I shall be seeing them again shortly – I'm off tomorrow. Yes . . . One more day left, that's all. A year from now and I'll be getting my discharge. Then I'll come back here again and live out my time with you . . . Only one year left before my pension, one short year . . . (*Puts his newspaper in his pocket and takes out another one.*) I'm going to come and stay with you and be a completely reformed character . . . I'm going to become such a quiet little – I don't know – proper little, decorous little fellow . . .

IRINA. You ought to reform, though, my dear. You really ought to, one way or another.

CHEBUTYKIN. I know. I'm aware of that. (*Sings quietly.*)
    Ta-ra-ra boom-de-ay,
    Ta-ra-ra boom-de-ay . . .

KULYGIN. Incorrigible, the doctor! Quite incorrigible!

CHEBUTYKIN. Yes, I should have come to you for lessons. Made you my reform-master.

IRINA. Fyodor has shaved off his moustache. I can't bear to look!

KULYGIN. Why ever not?

CHEBUTYKIN. I'd tell you what you look like now, but it's beyond my powers of description.

KULYGIN. Come, come. This is the done thing, this is the *modus vivendi*. Our headmaster is clean-shaven, and I shaved, too, as soon as I became an inspector. No one likes it, but I don't care. I'm content. With or without a moustache, I'm equally content. (*Sits.*)

*At the end of the garden* ANDREY *wheels the baby, asleep, in its perambulator.*

IRINA. Doctor, dear, I'm terribly worried. You were there yesterday, weren't you, outside the theatre? Tell me what happened.

CHEBUTYKIN. What happened? Nothing. Lot of nonsense. (*Reads his newspaper.*) What does it matter?

KULYGIN. The story I heard is that Solyony and the baron met yesterday in the street outside the theatre . . .

TUSENBACH Do stop it! Really! (*Flaps his hand and goes off into the house.*)

KULYGIN. Anyway, that's where it was . . . Solyony began to pick on the baron, and the baron lost patience and made some slighting remark . . .

CHEBUTYKIN. I don't know. It's all nonsense.

KULYGIN. The tale is told of a Latin teacher in a seminary who wrote 'Tripe!' on a pupil's essay. 'Please, sir,' said the boy, 'does that mean it's good or bad, *tri-pe?*' He thought it was Latin, you see! (*Laughs.*) You can't help laughing. Apparently Solyony's in love with Irina, and he's conceived a great hatred for the baron . . . It's quite understandable. Irina's a very nice girl. She's like Masha, in fact – the same dreamy type. Only you have a more gentle nature, Irina. Though of course Masha has a very nice nature, too. I love her – Masha.

VOICES (*off, at the end of the garden*). Hulloo! Hup-hup!

IRINA (*shudders*). I don't know, I'm jumping at the slightest thing today.

*Pause.*

I've got everything ready – I'm sending my things off after dinner. The baron and I are getting married tomorrow, and it's tomorrow we're leaving for the brickworks. Then the very next day I shall be working in the school there, and a new life will be starting. Somehow God will give me strength! When I was taking the examination to be a teacher I actually cried for joy.

*Pause.*

The cart will be coming for our things very shortly . . .

KULYGIN. That's all very fine, but it's a little head-in-the-clouds, somehow. Just a lot of ideas, not quite down to earth. You have my sincerest good wishes, though.

CHEBUTYKIN (*emotionally*). My sweet and lovely girl, my precious . . . Up and away you've gone – there's no catching you. I've dropped behind, like a bird heading south that's got too old to fly. Fly on, my loves, fly on, and God go with you!

*Pause.*

Mistake, you know, shaving your moustache off.

KULYGIN. Don't keep on about it! (*Sighs.*) So the troops will be off today, and everything will go back to the way it was. They can say what they like – Masha is a fine upstanding woman. I love her very much, and I bless my lot in life . . . Odd how much one person's lot in life can differ from another's . . . In the excise department here there works one Kozyrev. He was at school with me, but he got himself thrown out of the fifth form because he simply could not grasp *ut* followed by a consecutive clause. Now he lives in terrible poverty – he's a sick man into the bargain – and whenever I run into him I say, 'Hello, consecutive *ut*!' 'Yes,' he says, 'exactly, it's all consecutive.' And he coughs . . . Whereas I've been lucky all my life, I'm a happy man, I even have the Order of St. Stanislaus, second class, and now I'm teaching others that famous consecutive *ut* in my turn. I'm a man of some intelligence, of course – more so than many – but that's not the secret of happiness . . .

*The sound of 'The Maiden's Prayer' being played on the piano inside the house.*

IRINA. The Maiden's Prayer. And tomorrow evening I shan't be hearing it – I shan't be coming face to face with Protopopov . . .

*Pause.*

He's sitting there in the drawing-room. He's even come today . . .

KULYGIN. Hasn't our headmistress arrived yet?

IRINA. Not yet. She has been sent for. If only you knew how hard it's been for me, living here alone without Olya . . . She's resident at the school, and she's the headmistress, so she's busy all day, while I'm on my own, I'm bored, I've nothing to do, and I hate the room I live in . . . So I simply decided – if I'm not destined to live in Moscow, then so be it. That's my lot in life. There's nothing to be done about it . . . Everything is in the hands of God, that's the truth of the matter. The baron proposed to me . . . So – I thought about it for a while, and I made up my mind to it. He's a good, kind man – in fact it's surprising how good and kind he is . . . And suddenly it was as if my heart had grown wings. My spirits rose, and I was seized again by the desire to work, to work . . . But then yesterday something happened, some mysterious thing came looming over me . . .

CHEBUTYKIN. *Tri-pe.* As the boy said. Nonsense.

NATASHA (*out of the window*). It's our headmistress!

KULYGIN. Our headmistress has arrived. Come on, then.

*He goes with* IRINA *into the house.*

CHEBUTYKIN (*reads the paper, singing quietly*).
            Ta-ra-ra boom-de-ay,
            Ta-ra-ra boom-de-ay . . .

MASHA *approaches; at the end of the garden* ANDREY
*wheels the perambulator.*

MASHA. So he's just quietly sitting here, is he? Just having
a little sit.

CHEBUTYKIN. What if I am?

MASHA (*sits*). Nothing . . .

*Pause.*

You were in love with my mother?

CHEBUTYKIN. Very much.

MASHA. And she with you?

CHEBUTYKIN (*after a pause*). That I don't remember.

MASHA. Is my one here? We had a cook once who called her
policeman that – my one. Is he here, my one?

CHEBUTYKIN. Not yet.

MASHA. When you snatch happiness in fits and starts and
bits and pieces the way I have, and then lose it again the
way I am, you find yourself getting gradually coarser and
more foul-tempered . . . (*Indicates her breast.*) It boils up
inside me here . . . (*Looking at her brother* ANDREY, *who is
wheeling the perambulator.*) Look at Andrey, our lovely
brother . . . All our hopes have foundered. Thousands of
people raised the great bell up, much toil and money
were expended, then suddenly it fell and shattered.
Suddenly, just like that, for no good reason. And so did
Andrey . . .

ANDREY. When are they going to quieten down a bit in the
house? Such a row.

CHEBUTYKIN. Won't be long. (*Looks at his watch.*) I've got
an old-fashioned striking watch . . . (*Winds the watch, and
it strikes.*) The first, second, and fifth batteries are leaving
on the dot of one . . .

*Pause.*

And me tomorrow.

ANDREY. Forever?

CHEBUTYKIN. Don't know. Might come back in a year's time. Though heaven knows . . . What does it matter?

*The sound of a harp and fiddle being played somewhere in the distance.*

ANDREY. The town's going to be deserted. It's like a candle being snuffed out.

*Pause.*

Something happened yesterday outside the theatre. Everyone's talking about it, but I don't know what it was.

CHEBUTYKIN. Nothing. A lot of nonsense. Solyony began picking on the baron, the baron flared up and insulted him, and the end of it was that Solyony felt obliged to challenge him to a duel. (*Looks at his watch.*) About time for it now, I think . . . Half-past twelve, in those woods you can see on the other side of the river . . . Bang bang (*Laughs.*) Solyony thinks he's Lermontov – he even writes verse. Well, a joke's a joke, but this will be his third duel.

MASHA. Will be whose third duel?

CHEBUTYKIN. Solyony's.

MASHA. What about the baron?

CHEBUTYKIN. What about the baron?

*Pause.*

MASHA. Everything's going round and round inside my head. I say they ought to be stopped, though. He could wound the baron – or kill him, even.

CHEBUTYKIN. The baron's a nice chap, but one baron more or less – what does it matter? Let them go ahead. It doesn't matter!

A VOICE (*calling, from beyond the garden*). Hulloo! Hup-hup!

CHEBUTYKIN. They're waiting. That's Skvortzov shouting. One of the seconds. He's sitting in the boat.

*Pause.*

ANDREY. If you want my opinion, taking part in a duel is quite straightforwardly immoral. So is attending one, even as a doctor.

CHEBUTYKIN. It only seems so . . . We're not here, there's nothing in the world, we don't exist, we only seem to exist . . . Anyway, what does it matter?

MASHA. That's right, talk, talk, talk, the whole day long . . . (*Makes a move to go.*) It's bad enough living in a climate like this – because it will be snowing before we know where we are – but to have to listen to these conversations into the bargain . . . (*Stopping.*) I'm not going into the house – I can't go in there . . . You'll tell me when Vershinin arrives . . . (*Goes along the avenue.*) The birds are flying south already . . . (*Looks up.*) Swans or geese . . . My loves, my happy loves . . . (*She goes.*)

ANDREY. Our house is going to be deserted. The officers will have gone, you'll have gone, my sister will have got married, and I shall be left alone in the place.

CHEBUTYKIN. What about your wife?

*Enter* FERAPONT *with some papers.*

ANDREY. A wife's a wife. She's honest, she's decent, she's – yes – good-hearted. But at the same time there's something in her that reduces her to the level of a little blind furry animal. She's certainly not a human being. I'm telling you all this because you're a friend, the only person I can open my heart to. I love Natasha, it's true, but sometimes she seems to me amazingly squalid, and

then I don't know where I am – I can't understand why I
love her so, or at any rate did love her . . .

CHEBUTYKIN (*stands up*). My friend, I'm leaving tomorrow
– we may never see each other again. So here is my
advice to you. Put on your cap, pick up your stick, and
walk out of here . . . Walk out and keep walking, without
so much as a backward glance. And the further you go
the better.

> SOLYONY *crosses the end of the garden with two other*
> *officers. Seeing* CHEBUTYKIN, *he turns towards him,*
> *while the other officers continue on their way.*

SOLYONY. It's time, doctor! Half-past twelve already.
(*Greets* ANDREY.)

CHEBUTYKIN. Coming. I'm sick of the lot of you. (*To*
ANDREY:) Andryusha, if anyone wants me, tell them I'll
be back directly . . . (*Sighs.*) Oh-oh-oh!

> ANDREY *goes.*

SOLYONY. The peasant had no time to gasp
            Before he felt the bear's hard clasp.
    (*They move off together.*) What's all that groaning for,
    Grandpapa?

CHEBUTYKIN. Mind your own business.

SOLYONY. Fit and well, are we?

CHEBUTYKIN (*angrily*). Fit as a flea.

SOLYONY. There's no need for Grandpapa to get excited. I
shan't overdo it. I shall just wing him like a woodcock.
(*Takes out his scent and sprinkles it over his hands.*) I've
used up a whole flaskful today, and still they smell. They
smell like a corpse.

> *Pause.*

Well, there we are . . . You remember Lermontov's poem?

'Rebelliously he seeks the storm,
As if in storms there promised peace . . .'

CHEBUTYKIN. That's right.

The peasant had no time to gasp.

Before he felt the bear's hard clasp. (*He goes with* SOLYONY.)

VOICES (*calling, off*). Hup-hup!

*Enter* ANDREY *and* FERAPONT.

FERAPONT. Will you sign the papers . . .

ANDREY (*irritably*). Get away from me! Get away! I beg of you! (*He goes with the perambulator.*)

FERAPONT. That's what papers are for, you know, to be signed. (*Goes away upstage.*)

*Enter* IRINA *and* TUSENBACH *in a straw hat.* KULYGIN *crosses the stage.*

KULYGIN (*calling*). Hulloo, Masha, hulloo!

TUSENBACH. There, by the look of it, goes the only man in town who's glad the troops are leaving.

IRINA. That's understandable.

*Pause.*

Our town's going to be deserted now.

TUSENBACH (*glancing at his watch*). My love, I shall be back directly.

IRINA. Where are you going?

TUSENBACH. I've got to go into town. I've got to . . . see some of my friends off.

IRINA. You're not telling the truth . . . Nikolai, why are you so preoccupied today?

*Pause.*

What happened yesterday outside the theatre?

TUSENBACH (*makes an impatient movement*). In an hour I shall be back, and with you again. (*Kisses her hands.*) My precious . . . (*Gazes into her face.*) Five years have gone by now since I first loved you, and still I can't get used to it, still you seem to grow more beautiful. Your hair . . . your eyes . . . Tomorrow I'm going to take you away, we're going to work, we're going to be rich, all my dreams will come true. You're going to be happy. Only one thing wrong with it all – just one. You don't love me!

IRINA. That's not within my control. I'll be your wife, I'll be your loyal and submissive wife, but there's no love there, and there's nothing I can do about that. (*Weeps.*) Not once in my life have I ever been in love! Oh, I've dreamt so much about love – dreamt about it for so long now, night and day. But my heart is like some priceless grand piano that's been locked up, and the key to it lost.

*Pause.*

You look anxious.

TUSENBACH. I didn't sleep all night. There's nothing terrible in my life, nothing I should be afraid of. It's just this lost key that torments me and gives me sleepless nights . . . Say something to me.

*Pause.*

Say something . . .

IRINA. What? Say what? What is there to say?

TUSENBACH. Anything.

IRINA. Stop, stop!

*Pause.*

TUSENBACH. Ridiculous how such silly little things can sometimes take on a sudden importance in your life, for no reason you can put your finger on. You laugh at them just as you always did, you think how absurd they are, and yet you go along with it all and feel you haven't the strength to stop. Oh, let's not talk about it! I feel cheerful. I look at these fir-trees, at these maples and birches, and it's as if I'm seeing them for the first time in my life. And everything's looking at me – with curiosity – waiting. Such lovely trees, and really, such a lovely life there ought to be around them!

VOICES (*off*). Hulloo! Hup-hup!

TUSENBACH. I must go, it's past time ... Here's a tree that's withered up, yet still it sways in the wind with the others. It will be like that with me, I think, if I should die. I shall still have a hand in life one way or another. Goodbye, my love ... (*Kisses her hands.*) Those papers you gave me are on the table in my room, underneath the calendar.

IRINA. I'll come with you.

TUSENBACH (*in alarm*). No, no! (*Quickly goes, then stops in the avenue.*) Irina!

IRINA. What?

TUSENBACH (*not knowing what to say*). I didn't have any coffee this morning. Will you tell them to make me some ... (*Quickly goes off.*)

IRINA *stands lost in her own thoughts, then goes away upstage and sits on the swing. Enter* ANDREY *with the perambulator.* FERAPONT *appears.*

FERAPONT. Look, they're not my papers, you know – they're official. It wasn't me that thought them up.

ANDREY. Oh, where is it, where has it gone, that past of mine, when I was young and clever and light of heart, when I thought and reasoned elegantly, when present and future were both alight with hope? Why, when we have still scarcely begun to live, do we become dull and grey and uninteresting and idle and indifferent and useless and unhappy . . .? Our town has been here for two hundred years, it's got a hundred thousand inhabitants, and not one of them who hasn't been exactly like all the others – not one, past or present, who's been ready to die for a cause – not one scholar, not one artist, nobody even faintly remarkable, who might have aroused envy, or some passionate desire to emulate him . . . They've just eaten, and drunk, and slept, and then died . . . The next lot have been born, and they in their turn have eaten, drunk, slept, and then, to avoid being stupified by boredom, they've introduced a little variety into their lives by vile scandal-mongering and vodka and cards and quibbling lawsuits; and the wives have deceived their husbands, while the husbands have turned a blind eye; and irresistibly this sordid influence has crushed the children, and the divine spark within them has guttered out, and they have become the same miserable, indistinguishable corpses as their mothers and fathers . . . (*To* FERAPONT, *angrily.*) What do you want?

FERAPONT. What? Oh, sign the papers.

ANDREY. I'm sick of the sight of you.

FERAPONT (*handing him the papers*). The doorman at the revenue office was telling me just now . . . In Petersburg last winter by all accounts, he said, they had two hundred degrees of frost.

ANDREY. The present is loathsome, but then when I think about the future – well, that's another story. It all becomes so easy and spacious; and in the distance there's a gleam of light – I can see freedom, I can see me and my children being freed from idleness, from roast goose and cabbage, from little naps after dinner, from ignoble sponging off others . . .

FERAPONT. Two thousand people froze to death, by all accounts. Everyone was terrified, he said. Either in Petersburg or in Moscow – I can't remember.

ANDREY (*seized by tender feeling*). My dear sisters, my wonderful sisters! (*On the verge of tears.*) Masha, my sister . . .

NATASHA (*at the window*). Who's that talking so loudly out here? Is it you, Andryusha? You'll wake Sofochka. *Il ne faut pas faire du bruit, la Sophie est dormée déjà. Vous êtes un ours.* (*Getting angry.*) If you want to talk, give the perambulator to someone else. Ferapont, take the perambulator from the master.

FERAPONT. Take the perambulator, right. (*Takes it.*)

ANDREY (*embarrassed*). I'm talking quietly.

NATASHA (*inside the window, petting her baby boy*). Bobik! Isn't Bobik a rascal now! Isn't Bobik a naughty boy!

ANDREY (*glancing at the papers*). All right, I'll look through them and sign whatever's necessary, and you can take them back to the Council . . .

> ANDREY *goes into the house, reading the papers.* FERAPONT *pushes the perambulator down to the end of the garden.*

NATASHA (*inside the window*). What's mama called, then, Bobik? There's a good boy! Who's that, then? That's Auntie Olya. Say, 'Hello, Auntie Olya!'

> *Enter two wandering musicians, a man and a girl, playing fiddle and harp.* VERSHININ, OLGA, *and* ANFISA *come out of the house and listen to them for a moment in silence.* IRINA *approaches.*

OLGA. Our garden is like a public highway – people come walking through, they come riding through. Nanny, give these people something . . .

ANFISA (*gives the musicians something*). Off you go, then, my dears, and God go with you.

*The musicians bow and go off.*

Poor wretches. It's not a full stomach makes them play. (*To* IRINA:) Hello, Irisha! (*Kisses her.*) Eh, child, but I'm having the time of my life! At the school, my precious, in the official Government living quarters, along with Olyushka. Appointed to me by the Lord in the fullness of my years. Sinner that I am, in all my born days I've never lived so . . . Great big apartment it is, and me with a room and a bed all to myself. And everything official from the Government. I wake up in the night – and oh my Lord, oh Mother of God, there's not a happier soul in all the world!

VERSHININ (*glances at his watch. To* OLGA). We shall be leaving directly. It's time for me to go.

*Pause.*

I should like to wish you all the best . . . Where's Masha?

IRINA. She's somewhere in the garden. I'll go and look for her.

VERSHININ. If you'd be so kind. I am pressed for time.

ANFISA. I'll go and look as well. (*Calls.*) Mashenka, hulloo! (*Goes off with* IRINA *to the end of the garden.*) Hulloo-oo! Hulloo-oo!

VERSHININ. All things come to an end sooner or later. Now it's our turn to part. (*Looks at his watch.*) The town has been giving us something in the style of a luncheon. We drank champagne, the mayor made a speech. I sat there eating and listening, but in spirit I was here, with all of you . . . (*Looks round the garden.*) I've grown accustomed to you all.

OLGA. Shall we ever see each other again?

VERSHININ. Probably not.

*Pause.*

My wife and the two girls will stay on here for a couple of months. Please, if anything should happen, if anything should be needed . . .

OLGA. Yes, yes, of course. Rest assured.

*Pause.*

By tomorrow there won't be a soldier left in town. It will all have become nothing but a memory. And for us, of course, a new life will be commencing.

*Pause.*

Nothing works out as we would have it. I didn't want to be headmistress, but headmistress I've nonetheless become. So there's no question of my living in Moscow . . .

VERSHININ. Anyway . . . Thank you for everything . . . Forgive me for anything I may have done wrong . . . I've talked a great deal – a very great deal, I'm afraid. Forgive me for that, too, and remember me kindly.

OLGA (*wipes her eyes*). Where has Masha got to?

VERSHININ. What else can I say to wish you farewell? What is there to philosophise about . . .? (*Laughs.*) Life is hard. To many of us it appears blank and hopeless, but we have to concede nonetheless that it is becoming steadily easier and brighter. And by all appearances the time is not far off when it will be quite cloudless. (*Looks at his watch.*) Time for me to be going, it really is! In days gone by the human race kept itself busy with wars. It filled out its life with campaigns and raids and conquests. But all that now has become a thing of the past, leaving behind a vast empty space which we for the time being lack the means to fill. But mankind seeks, and will of course find. Ah, speed the day!

*Pause.*

I tell you, if human industry could be complemented by education, and education by industry. (*Looks at his watch.*) Time for me to go, though . . .

OLGA. Here she comes.

*Enter* MASHA.

VERSHININ. I've come to say goodbye . . .

OLGA *goes off a little to one side so as not to hinder their farewells.*

MASHA (*looking into his face*). Goodbye . . . my love . . .

*A prolonged kiss.*

OLGA. Come on, now . . .

MASHA *sobs bitterly.*

VERSHININ. Write to me . . . my love, yes . . . Don't forget! Let me go . . . It's time . . . (*To* OLGA:) Take her, please, it really is . . . time . . . I'm late already . . . (*Shaken, he kisses* OLGA's *hands, then once again embraces* MASHA, *and quickly goes off.*)

OLGA. Come on, Masha! Stop it, now, my precious . . .

*Enter* KULYGIN.

KULYGIN (*in embarrassment*). Never mind, let her cry, let her cry . . . My dear Masha, my good, kind Masha . . . You're my wife, and I'm happy no matter what . . . I'm not complaining, I'm not reproaching you . . . Olga can be my witness to that . . . We'll go back to the same old way

of life we had before, and not a word will I breathe, not a
hint . . .

MASHA (*restraining her sobs*). On a far sea shore an oak
tree grows,

>  And from it hangs a golden chain . . .
>  And from it hangs a golden chain . . .

I'm going out of my mind . . .

>  On a far sea shore . . . an oak tree grows . . .

OLGA. Calm down, now, Masha . . . Calm down . . . Give
her some water.

MASHA. I've stopped crying.

KULYGIN. She's stopped crying . . . She's good, she's
kind . . .

*The sound of a shot, dull and distant.*

MASHA. On a far sea shore an oak tree grows,

>  And from it hangs a golden chain . . .
>  A golden cat forever goes . . . A talking cat . . .

I'm getting mixed up . . . (*Drinks water.*) A failed life . . .
Nothing left now that I want . . . I shall calm down in a
moment . . . Not that it matters . . . What is all this about
a far sea shore? Why have I got this phrase in my head?
My thoughts are getting all mixed up.

*Enter* IRINA.

OLGA. Calm down, Masha. There's a good girl . . . Let's go
inside, shall we?

MASHA (*angrily*). I'm not going in there. (*Sobs, but then
immediately stops.*) I've stopped going into that house –
I'm not going in now . . .

IRINA. Let's all sit down together for a moment, even if we
don't say anything. I am leaving tomorrow, after all . . .

*Pause.*

KULYGIN. Look what I took away from some little chap in the third form yesterday . . . (*Puts on a beard complete with moustache.*) I look like the German master . . . (*Laughs.*) Don't I? You have to laugh at some of these boys.

MASHA. You do look like that German.

OLGA (*laughs*). Yes, you do.

*MASHA weeps.*

IRINA. Come on, Masha.

KULYGIN. Very like him . . .

*Enter NATASHA.*

NATASHA (*to the maid*). What is it? Protopopov will sit with Sofochka for a bit, and Andrey can push Bobik. What a business children are . . . (*To* IRINA:) Irina, you're leaving tomorrow – it's such a shame. Stay a few more days, anyway, why don't you. (*Sees* KULYGIN *and cries out.*)

*KULYGIN laughs and takes off the beard.*

Honestly! You gave me a fright! (*To* IRINA:) I've got used to having you around. Don't think I'm going to find it easy to part with you. I shall have Andrey and that violin of his moved into your room – he can scrape away in there to his heart's content! And then in his old room we'll put Sofochka. She really is an amazing child! Such a poppet! Today she looked at me with eyes like this, and – 'Mama!'

KULYGIN. An admirable child, it must be said.

NATASHA. So tomorrow I shall be all on my own here. (*Sighs.*) The first thing I'm going to do is to have that avenue of fir-trees cut down, and then this maple here . . . It looks such a sight in the evening . . . (*To* IRINA:) My love, that belt doesn't suit you at all . . . Terrible taste . . . You need something a little brighter. And all round here

I'm going to have flowers planted – flowers and more flowers – and we shall have the scent . . . (*Sharply.*) Why is there a fork lying about on the seat out here? (*Goes into the house. To the* MAID.) Why is there a fork lying about on the seat out here, I want to know! (*Shouts.*) Be quiet!

KULYGIN. She's off!

*A band, off, plays a march. They all listen.*

OLGA. They're leaving.

*Enter* CHEBUTYKIN.

MASHA. Our men . . . our ones. So – fare them well! (*To her husband.*) We must go home . . . Where are my hat and shawl?

KULYGIN. I put them inside . . . I'll go and fetch them. (*Goes into the house.*)

OLGA. That's right, we can all go home now. It's time to be moving.

CHEBUTYKIN. Olga Sergeyevna!

OLGA. What?

*Pause.*

What?

CHEBUTYKIN. Nothing . . . I don't know how to say it to you . . . (*Whispers in her ear.*)

OLGA (*frightened*). It's not possible!

CHEBUTYKIN. I know . . . It's a nasty business . . . I've had enough, I don't want to say any more . . . (*With irritation.*) Anyway, what does it matter?

MASHA. What's happened?

OLGA (*puts her arms round* IRINA). A terrible day this is . . . My dear, I don't know how to say it to you . . .

IRINA. What? Tell me quickly, somebody – what is it? For the love of God! (*Weeps.*)

CHEBUTYKIN. There's been a duel. The baron was killed . . .

IRINA (*weeps quietly*). I knew it, I knew it . . .

CHEBUTYKIN (*sits on a garden seat upstage*). I've had enough . . . (*Takes a newspaper out of his pocket.*) Let them have their little cry . . . (*Sings quietly.*)

>            Ta-ra-ra boom-de-ay,
>            Ta-ra-ra boom-de-ay . . .

Doesn't matter, does it?

*The three sisters stand huddled against each other.*

MASHA. Oh, but listen to the band! They're leaving us. One has left us altogether – left us forever. We shall remain behind, on our own, to start our life again. We have to live . . . We have to live . . .

IRINA (*puts her head on* OLGA's *breast*). A time will come when people will understand what it was all for, what the purpose was of all this suffering, and what was hidden from us will be hidden no more. In the meantime, though, we have to live . . . we have to work, that's all, we have to work! Tomorrow I shall go on my way alone. I shall take up my teaching post, and devote my life to those who may have some use for it. It's autumn now. Soon winter will come and bring the first falls of snow, and I shall be working, I shall be working . . .

OLGA (*embraces both her sisters*). The band plays so bravely – you feel you want to live! Merciful God! Time will pass, and we shall depart forever. We shall be forgotten – our faces, our voices, even how many of us there were. But our sufferings will turn to joy for those who live after us. Peace and happiness will dwell on earth, and people living now will be blessed and spoken well of. Dear sisters, our life is not ended yet. We shall live!

And the band plays so bravely, so joyfully – another moment, you feel, and we shall know why we live and why we suffer ... If only we could know, if only we could know!

*The music grows quieter and quieter.* KULYGIN, *smiling cheerfully, brings* MASHA's *hat and shawl.* ANDREY *pushes the perambulator with* BOBIK *sitting in it.*

CHEBUTYKIN (*sings quietly*). Ta-ra ... ra ... boom-de-ay ... Ta-ra-ra boom-de-ay ... (*Reads his newspaper.*) Anyway, it doesn't matter. It doesn't matter.

OLGA. If only we could know, if only we could know!


CURTAIN

# The Cherry Orchard

*This translation* of The Cherry Orchard *was first staged by the* *National Theatre in the Olivier on 3 February 1978. The cast* *was as follows:*

| | |
|---|---|
| RANYEVSKAYA (Lyuba), *a landowner* | Dorothy Tutin |
| ANYA, *her daughter, aged 17* | Judi Bowker |
| VARYA, *her adopted daughter, aged 24* | Susan Fleetwood |
| GAYEV (Lenya), *Ranyevskaya's brother* | Robert Stephens |
| LOPAKHIN (Yermolay), *a businessman* | Albert Finney |
| TROFIMOV (Pyetya), *a student* | Ben Kingsley |
| SIMEONOV-PISHCHIK, *a landowner* | Terence Rigby |
| CHARLOTTA IVANOVNA, *the governess* | Helen Ryan |
| YEPIKHODOV, *the estate clerk* | Nicky Henson |
| DUNYASHA, *the chambermaid* | Susan Littler |
| FIRS, *the footman, an old man of 87* | Ralph Richardson |
| YASHA, *the young footman* | Derek Thompson |
| A PASSER-BY | Peter Needham |
| THE STATIONMASTER | Daniel Thorndike |

*Directed by* Peter Hall
*Designed by* John Bury
*Lighting by* David Hersey
*Music by* Harrison Birtwistle and Dominic Muldowney
*Dance by* Sally Gilpin

**The action takes place on Ranyevskaya's estate.**

*This revised translation of* The Cherry Orchard *was produced by Michael Codron at the Aldwych Theatre, London, on 24 October 1989, with the following cast:*

| | |
|---|---|
| DUNYASHA, *the chambermaid* | Abigail McKern |
| LOPAKHIN (Yermolai), *a businessman* | Bernard Hill |
| YEPIKHODOV, *the estate clerk* | Tom Watt |
| FIRS, *the footman* | Michael Gough |
| ANYA, *Ranyevskaya's daughter* | Miranda Foster |
| RANYEVSKAYA (Lyuba), *a landowner* | Judi Dench |
| CHARLOTTA IVANOVNA, *the governess* | Kate Duchêne |
| VARYA, *Ranyevskaya's adopted daughter* | Lesley Manville |
| GAYEV (Lenya), *Ranyevskaya's brother* | Ronald Pickup |
| SIMEONOV-PISCHIK, *a landowner* | Barry Stanton |
| YASHA, *the young footman* | John Dougall |
| TROFIMOV (Petya), *a student* | Nicholas Farrell |
| A PASSER-BY | Tom Hollander |
| THE STATIONMASTER | Stanley Page |
| THE POSTMASTER | Peter Sowerbutts |
| PARTY GUESTS | Kate Anthony |
| | Patricia Samuels |

*Directed by* Sam Mendes
*Designed by* Paul Farnsworth
*Lighting by* Mick Hughes
*Music by* Corin Buckeridge
*Association Producer* David Sutton

# Act One

*A room which is still known as the nursery. One of the doors leads to* ANYA's *room. Half-light, shortly before sunrise. It is May already, and the cherry trees are in blossom, but outside in the orchard it is cold, with a morning frost. The windows are closed.*

*Enter* DUNYASHA *with a candle, and* LOPAKHIN *with a book in his hand.*

LOPAKHIN. God be praised, the train's arrived. What time is it?

DUNYASHA. Nearly two o'clock. (*Extinguishes the candle.*) It's light already.

LOPAKHIN. So the train's how late? Two hours, at least. (*Yawns and stretches.*) Fine one I am. Complete fool. Came all the way here to go and meet them at the station, and then just dropped off while I was sitting there. It's a shame. You might have woken me.

DUNYASHA. I thought you'd gone. (*Listens.*) That sounds like them now.

LOPAKHIN (*listens*). No . . . Luggage to pick up, one thing and another . . .

  *Pause.*

She's lived abroad for five years – I don't know what she'll be like now . . . She's a fine woman. Easy, straightforward. I remember, when I was a boy of fifteen or so, my father – he kept a shop then in the village here – dead now, of course – he punched me in the face, and the blood started to pour out of my nose . . . For some reason we'd come into the yard here together, and he was drunk. It seems like yesterday. She was only young – such a slim young thing. She brought me in and she took me to the washstand in this room, in the nursery.

'Don't cry, my little peasant,' she says. 'It'll heal in time for your wedding . . .'

*Pause.*

My little peasant . . . it's true, my father was a peasant – and here am I in a white waistcoat and yellow shoes. Like a pig in a pastry-cook's . . . The only difference is I'm a rich man, plenty of money, but look twice and I'm a peasant, a real peasant . . . (*Leafs through the book.*) I was reading this book. Couldn't understand a word. Fell asleep over it.

*Pause.*

DUNYASHA. And the dogs, they haven't slept all night. They can sense that the mistress is coming.

LOPAKHIN. What's the matter with you, Dunyasha?

DUNYASHA. My hands are all of a tremble. I'm going to faint.

LOPAKHIN. Very tender plant, aren't you, Dunyasha? Dress like a lady, do your hair like one, too. Not the way, is it? You want to remember who you are.

*Enter* YEPIKHODOV *with a bouquet. He is wearing a jacket and highly polished boots that squeak loudly. As he comes in he drops the bouquet.*

YEPIKHODOV (*picks up the bouquet*). The gardener sent them. He says to put them in the dining-room. (*Gives the bouquet to* DUNYASHA.)

LOPAKHIN. And bring me some kvass.

DUNYASHA. Very good. (*Goes out.*)

YEPIKHODOV. Three degrees of frost this morning, and the cherry all in blossom. I can't give our climate my seal of approval. (*Sighs.*) Indeed I can't. It never knows how to lend a helping hand at the right moment. And I mean look at me – I bought myself these boots the day before yesterday, and they squeak so much, I mean it's quite impossible. I mean, put it like this – what should I grease them with?

LOPAKHIN. Leave off, will you? Pester, pester.

YEPIKHODOV. I don't know. Every day some disaster happens to me. Not that I complain. I'm used to it. I even smile.

*Enter* DUNYASHA. *She gives* LOPAKHIN *his kvass.*

YEPIKHODOV. I'll go, then. (*Stumbles against the table, which falls over.*) There you are ... (*As if exulting in it.*) You see what I'm up against! I mean, it's simply amazing! (*Goes out.*)

DUNYASHA. To tell you the truth, he's proposed to me.

LOPAKHIN. Ah!

DUNYASHA. I don't know *what* to say ... He's all right, he doesn't give any trouble, it's just sometimes when he starts to talk – you can't understand a word of it. It's very nice, and he puts a lot of feeling into it, only you can't understand it. I quite like him in a way, even. He's madly in love with me. He's the kind of person who never has any luck. Every day something happens. They tease him in our part of the house – they call him Disasters by the Dozen ...

LOPAKHIN (*listens*). I think they're coming.

DUNYASHA. They're coming! What's the matter with me? I've gone all cold.

LOPAKHIN. They are indeed coming. Let's go and meet them. Will she recognize me? Five years we haven't seen each other.

DUNYASHA (*in agitation*). I'll faint this very minute ... I will, I'll faint clean away!

*Two carriages can be heard coming up to the house.* LOPAKHIN *and* DUNYASHA *hurry out.*

*The stage is empty. Then there is noise in the adjoining rooms. Across the stage, leaning on his stick, hurries* FIRS, *who has gone to the station to meet the mistress. He is wearing ancient livery and a top hat. He is saying something to himself, but not a word of it can be made out. The noise offstage grows louder and louder.*

A VOICE (*off*). This way, look.

> *Enter* RANYEVSKAYA, ANYA, *and* CHARLOTTA IVANOVNA *who has a little dog on a lead. All three ladies are dressed for travelling:* VARYA *in an overcoat and shawl;* GAYEV, SIME-ONOV-PISHCHIK, LOPAKHIN, DUNYASHA *with a bundle and an umbrella,* SERVANTS *carrying things – they all go across the room.*

ANYA. This way. Mama, do you remember which room this is?

RANYEVSKAYA (*joyfully, on the verge of tears*). The nursery!

VARYA. So cold. My hands are quite numb. (*To* RANYEVSKAYA.) Your rooms – the white one and the mauve one – they've stayed just as they were, Mama.

RANYEVSKAYA. The nursery. My own dear room, my lovely room . . . I slept in here when I was a little girl. (*Weeps.*) And now I'm like a little girl again . . . (*Kisses her brother, then* VARYA, *then her brother once more.*) And Varya's just the same as before – she looks like a nun. And Dunyasha I recognize . . . (*Kisses her.*)

GAYEV. The train was two hours late. What do you think of that? What kind of standards do these people have?

CHARLOTTA (*to* PISHCHIK). My dog can eat nuts even.

PISHCHIK (*surprised*). Would you believe it!

> *They all go out except* ANYA *and* DUNYASHA.

DUNYASHA. We waited and waited . . . (*She takes off* ANYA'S *coat and hat.*)

ANYA. I didn't sleep on the way – I haven't slept for four nights . . . Oh, I'm completely frozen!

DUNYASHA. You went away in Lent, with snow on the ground still, and now look at it. Oh, my dear! (*Laughs and kisses her.*) I've waited and waited for you. My own precious! My heart's delight . . . ! I'm going to tell you at once – I can't contain myself another minute . . .

ANYA (*inertly*). Nothing else.

DUNYASHA. Yepikhodov – you know who I mean, the estate
clerk – just after Easter he proposed to me.

ANYA. Still on about the same old thing . . . (*Tidying her hair.*)
I've gradually lost all the pins . . .

*She is completely exhausted – unable to keep her balance, even.*

DUNYASHA. I don't know *what* to think. He's in love with me, so
in love with me!

ANYA (*looks into her room, tenderly*). My room, my windows, just
as if I'd never been away. I'll get up in the morning, I'll run out
into the orchard . . . Oh, if only I could get to sleep! I didn't
sleep all the way – I was worn out with worry.

DUNYASHA. The day before yesterday Mr. Trofimov arrived.

ANYA (*joyfully*). Petya!

DUNYASHA. He's sleeping in the bath-house – he's living out
there. He said he was afraid of being in the way. (*Looks at her
pocket watch.*) We ought to wake him up, but Miss Varya said
not to. Don't you go waking him, she says.

*Enter* VARYA, *with a bunch of keys on her belt.*

VARYA. Dunyasha, quick now – Mama's asking for coffee.

DUNYASHA. Very good. (*Goes out.*)

VARYA. Well, God be praised, you've got here, both of you.
You're home again, Anya. (*Cuddling her.*) My darling's come
home! My lovely's come home again!

ANYA. I've had a most terrible time.

VARYA. I can imagine.

ANYA. I set out from here in Holy Week. It was cold. Charlotta
talked the whole way – she kept showing me conjuring tricks.
Why on earth you saddled me with Charlotta . . .

VARYA. You couldn't have travelled alone, my darling. Not at
seventeen!

ANYA. Anyway, we get to Paris, and it's cold, it's snowing. My
French is terrible. Mama's living up on the fifth floor, and when
I arrive she's got people with her – Frenchmen, I don't know
who they were, and ladies, and some ancient Catholic priest

holding a prayer-book – and the air's full of tobacco smoke, and it's bleak and uncomfortable. And suddenly I felt sorry for Mama. I felt so sorry for her I put my arms round her and pressed her head against me and couldn't let go. After that Mama kept hugging me, and crying . . .

VARYA (*on the verge of tears*). Don't, don't . . .

ANYA. She'd already sold that villa she had outside Menton. She's nothing left, nothing. Nor have I – not a kopeck. We scarcely managed it here. And Mama doesn't understand! We'll sit down to dinner in a station restaurant, and she orders the most expensive item on the menu. Then she tips all the waiters a ruble each. Charlotta's the same. And Yasha has to be fed, too – it's simply frightful. You know Mama has this footman, Yasha. We brought him with us.

VARYA. I've seen the rogue.

ANYA. So what – have we paid the interest?

VARYA. How could we?

ANYA. Oh God, oh God . . .

VARYA. In August they're going to sell the estate off.

ANYA. Oh God . . .

LOPAKHIN (*looks in at the door, and moos*). M-e-e-e . . . (*Goes out.*)

VARYA (*through her tears*). Oh, I'd like to give him such a . . . (*Raises her fist threateningly.*)

ANYA (*embraces* VARYA – *quietly*). Varya, has he proposed?

> VARYA *shakes her head.*

Look, he loves you . . . Why don't you get things straight between you? What are you both waiting for?

VARYA. I'll tell you what I think – I think nothing's going to come of it. He's very busy, he hasn't got time for me – he doesn't even notice. Well, good luck to him, but I can't bear the sight of him. Everyone talks about our wedding, everyone keeps congratulating me, but in fact there's nothing there – it's all a kind of dream. (*In a different tone.*) You've got a bumble-bee brooch.

ANYA (*sadly*). Mama bought it. (*Goes into her room, and speaks cheerfully, childishly.*) And in Paris I went up in an air-balloon!

VARYA. Oh, my darling's come home! My lovely's come home again!

*DUNYASHA is back with the coffee-pot. She makes the coffee. VARYA stands by the door to ANYA's room.*

Oh, my darling, I go about the house all day in a dream. If we could just get you married to some rich man, then I could be easy in my mind. I could take myself off into a retreat, then to Kiev, to Moscow, and oh, I'd walk all round the holy places . . . I'd just keep walking and walking. The glory of it!

ANYA. The birds are singing in the orchard. What time is it now?

VARYA. It must be after two. Time for you to sleep, my darling. (*Going in to ANYA.*) The glory of it!

*Enter YASHA with a rug and travelling bag.*

YASHA (*crosses with delicacy*). All right to come through?

DUNYASHA. I shouldn't even recognize you, Yasha. You've changed so abroad!

YASHA. Mm . . . And who are you?

DUNYASHA. When you left I was so high . . . (*Indicates from the floor.*) Dunyasha. Fyodor Kozoyedov's daughter. You don't remember!

YASHA. Mm . . . Quite a pippin, aren't you? (*Looks round and embraces her. She screams and drops a saucer.*)

*Exit YASHA, swiftly.*

VARYA (*in the doorway, displeased*). Now what's going on?

DUNYASHA (*through her tears*). I've smashed the saucer . . .

VARYA. That's good luck.

ANYA (*coming out of her room*). We should warn Mama – Petya's here.

VARYA. I gave orders not to wake him.

ANYA (*reflectively*). Six years since Father died, and only a month later that Grisha was drowned in the river. My brother . . . Seven years old, and such a pretty boy. Mama couldn't bear it. She escaped – fled without so much as a backward glance . . . (*Shivers.*) I understand her so well, if only she knew!

*Pause.*

And Petya Trofimov was Grisha's tutor. He may remind her . . .

*Enter* FIRS, *in jacket and white waistcoat.*

FIRS (*goes to the coffee-pot, preoccupied*). The mistress will be taking it in here . . . (*Puts on white gloves.*) The coffee ready? (*To* DUNYASHA, *sternly.*) What's this, girl? Where's the cream?

DUNYASHA. Oh, my Lord . . . (*Rushes out.*)

FIRS (*busies himself about the coffee-pot*). Oh, you sillybilly! (*Mutters to himself.*) Come from Paris . . . The master went to Paris once . . . by post-chaise . . . (*Laughs.*)

VARYA. What are you going on about, Firs?

FIRS. What do you want? (*Joyfully.*) My lady has come home! I waited for her! I can die happy . . . (*Weeps with joy.*)

*Enter* RANYEVSKAYA, GAYEV, LOPAKHIN *and* SIMEONOV-PISHCHIK *who is wearing a tight-fitting, long-waisted coat in a fine material, and wide, Oriental-looking trousers.* GAYEV, *as he comes in, makes movements with his arms and trunk as if he were playing billiards.*

RANYEVSKAYA. How did it go? Let's see . . . Yellow into the corner. Then off the cushion into the middle pocket.

GAYEV. And screw back into the corner! There was a time, my sister, when you and I slept in this very room. And now I'm fifty-one already, strange as it seems.

LOPAKHIN. Yes, the time goes by.

GAYEV. Who?

LOPAKHIN. I say the time goes by.

GAYEV. It reeks of cheap scent in here, though.

ANYA. I'm going to bed. Good night, Mama. (*Kisses her mother.*)

RANYEVSKAYA. My beloved child. (*Kisses her hands.*) Are you pleased to be home? I don't think I shall ever manage to come down to earth.

ANYA. Good night, Uncle.

GAYEV (*kisses her face and hands*). The Lord guard and keep you. How like your mother you are! (*To his sister.*) Lyuba, at her age you were just like that.

> ANYA *gives her hand to* LOPAKHIN *and* PISHCHIK, *then goes out and closes the door behind her.*

RANYEVSKAYA. She's tired out.

PISHCHIK. It's a long way to go, no doubt about it.

VARYA (*to* LOPAKHIN *and* PISHCHIK). Well, then, gentlemen. Past two o'clock. Time to be saying goodbye.

RANYEVSKAYA (*laughs*). Varya, you're just the same as ever. (*Draws her close and kisses her.*) I'll drink my coffee, then we'll all go.

> FIRS *puts a cushion under her feet.*

Thank you, my dear. I've got into the coffee habit. I drink it day and night. Thank you, my dear old friend. (*Kisses* FIRS.)

VARYA. I must see if they've brought all the things. (*Exits.*)

RANYEVSKAYA. Is this really me sitting here? (*Laughs.*) I feel like leaping into the air and waving my arms about. (*Covers her face with her hands.*) Perhaps it's all a dream. Oh, but I love my country, God knows I do, I love it tenderly. I couldn't look out of the carriage window – I did nothing but weep. (*On the verge of tears.*) However, the coffee has to be drunk. Thank you, Firs, thank you, my dear. I'm so glad to find you still alive.

FIRS. The day before yesterday.

GAYEV. His hearing's going.

LOPAKHIN. I have to leave straight away, before five o'clock. I'm off to Kharkov. Such a shame. I just wanted to get a look at you, have a few words ... You're still as magnificent as ever.

PISHCHIK (*breathes hard*). You've grown even more lovely ... Dressed in Paris fashions ... I could throw caution to the winds.

LOPAKHIN. In the eyes of your sort – your brother here, for instance – I'm a boor, I'm a money-grubbing peasant, but I don't give a damn about that. The only thing I want is for you to trust me as you did before, to see your amazing, heart-breaking eyes looking at me the way they used to. Merciful God! My father was a serf, and your father and grandfather owned him. But you – yes, you were the one – you did so much for me once that I've forgotten all that, and I love you like my own flesh and blood ... more than my own flesh and blood.

RANYEVSKAYA. I can't sit still. I'm physically incapable ... (*Jumps up and walks about in a state of great emotion.*) I shall never survive this joy ... Laugh at me, I'm such a fool ... My bookcase, my own dear bookcase ... (*Kisses the bookcase.*) My dear old table.

GAYEV. Nanna died while you were away.

RANYEVSKAYA (*sits and drinks coffee*). Yes, God rest her soul. They wrote and told me.

GAYEV. And Anastasy died. Petrushka – you remember him? With the squint? He left me. Living in town now, working for the local police inspector. (*He takes a box of fruit-drops out of his pocket and sucks one.*)

PISHCHIK. My daughter Dashenka – she sends her best regards ...

LOPAKHIN. I want to tell you some very pleasant and cheering news. (*Glances at his watch.*) I shall be leaving very shortly, we haven't time for a proper talk ... I'll put it in two words, then. You know, of course, that your cherry orchard is to be sold to pay your debts – the sale is fixed for the twenty-second of August. But don't you worry yourself about it, my dear – sleep easy in your bed at night – there is a way out ... This is my plan. Now listen carefully. Your estate is only thirteen miles out of town; the railway has now come through right next to it; and if the cherry orchard and the land along the river are broken up into building lots and leased out as sites for summer cottages, then you will possess an income of – at the very least – twenty-five thousand rubles a year.

GAYEV. I'm sorry, but it's such nonsense!

RANYEVSKAYA (*to* LOPAKHIN). I don't entirely understand you.

LOPAKHIN. You will get from your leaseholders at the very minimum ten rubles a year per acre. And if you advertise it now, then I swear upon anything you like to name that by the autumn you won't have a single acre left – it will all have been taken up. In short – congratulations, you're saved. It's a marvellous position with this deep river. The only thing, of course, is that you need to tidy it up a bit. Remove all the old buildings, for example – like this house, which won't have any use now – and cut down the old cherry orchard.

RANYEVSKAYA. Cut it down? My dear, forgive me, but you don't understand. If there is one thing of any interest at all in this whole province – if there is even something rather remarkable – then it's our cherry orchard.

LOPAKHIN. There's only one thing remarkable about this orchard. It's very big. You only get a full crop every other year, and then there's nothing to do with it – no one buys it.

GAYEV. There's even a reference to this orchard in the encyclopaedia.

LOPAKHIN (*glances at his watch*). If we don't think of something, if we don't come to some decision, then on the twenty-second of August not only the cherry orchard but the whole estate will be sold at auction. So nerve yourselves! There is no other way out, I swear to you. None whatsoever.

FIRS. In the old days, forty, fifty years ago, they used to dry the cherries, they used to soak them, they used to pickle them, they used to make jam out of them, and year after year . . .

GAYEV. Do be quiet, Firs.

FIRS. And year after year they'd send off dried cherries by the cartload to Moscow and Kharkov. There was money then! And the dried cherries were soft and juicy and sweet and scented . . . They knew the recipe in those days.

RANYEVSKAYA. And what's happened to this recipe now?

FIRS. They've forgotten it. No one remembers it.

PISHCHIK (to RANYEVSKAYA). How was it in Paris, then? Did you eat frogs?

RANYEVSKAYA. I ate crocodiles.

PISHCHIK. Would you believe it!

LOPAKHIN. Up to now in the countryside we've had only the gentry and the peasants. But now a new class has appeared – the summer countrymen. Every town now, even the smallest, is surrounded with summer cottages. And we may assume that over the next twenty years or so our summer countryman will be fruitful and multiply exceedingly. Now he merely sits on his verandah and drinks tea, but you know it may come to pass that he'll put his couple of acres to some use, and start to cultivate them. And then this old cherry orchard of yours will become happy and rich and luxuriant . . .

GAYEV (exasperated). Such nonsense!

*Enter* VARYA *and* YASHA.

VARYA. Mama, there are two telegrams that came for you. (*Selects a key which clinks in the lock as she opens the antique bookcase.*) Here.

RANYEVSKAYA. From Paris. (*Tears up the telegrams without reading them.*) Paris is over and done with.

GAYEV. But, Lyuba, do you know how old this bookcase is? I pulled out the bottom drawer last week, and I looked, and there were some numbers burnt into the wood with a poker. This bookcase was built exactly one hundred years ago. What do you think of that? We could celebrate its centenary. It's an inanimate object, but all the same, whichever way you look at it, it's still a bookcase.

PISHCHIK (*in surprise*). A hundred years . . . Would you believe it!

GAYEV. Yes . . . Quite an achievement . . . (*Feels the bookcase.*) Dear bookcase! Most esteemed bookcase! I salute your existence, which for more than a hundred years now has been directed towards the shining ideals of goodness and of truth. For a hundred years your unspoken summons to fruitful labour has never faltered, upholding, (*on the verge of tears*) through all the generations of our family, wisdom and faith in a better future, and fostering within us ideals of goodness and of social consciousness.

Pause.

LOPAKHIN. Yes . . .

RANYEVSKAYA. You're the same as ever, Lenya.

GAYEV (*in some slight confusion*). In off into the righthand corner! Then screw back into the middle pocket!

LOPAKHIN (*glances at his watch*). Well, I must be on my way.

YASHA (*hands pills to* RANYEVSKAYA). Take your pills now, perhaps . . .

PISHCHIK. Dearest heart, you mustn't go taking medicines . . . there's neither harm nor charm in them . . . Give them here . . . Dear lady. (*Picks up the pills, tips them out on to his palm, blows on them, puts them into his mouth, and washes them down with kvass.*) There!

RANYEVSKAYA (*alarmed*). But you've gone utterly mad!

PISHCHIK. I've taken all the pills.

LOPAKHIN. There's a greedyguts!

Everyone laughs.

FIRS. When he was here at Easter he put away half a bucket of pickled cucumbers . . . (*Mutters.*)

RANYEVSKAYA. What's he going on about now?

VARYA. He's been muttering away like this for the last three years. We've got used to it.

YASHA. Old age, isn't it?

> CHARLOTTA IVANOVNA *crosses the stage, in a white dress. She is very thin and very tightly laced, with a lorgnette hanging from her belt.*

LOPAKHIN. Forgive me, I haven't had a chance to say hello to you. (*Tries to kiss her hand.*)

CHARLOTTA (*taking her hand away*). Let you kiss my hand, and next thing I know you'll be after my elbow, then my shoulder . . .

LOPAKHIN. Not having any luck today, am I?

> *Everyone laughs.*

Come on, then, show us a conjuring trick!

CHARLOTTA. No, I just want to go to bed. (*Goes out.*)

LOPAKHIN. Well, we'll meet again in three weeks time. (*Kisses* RANYEVSKAYA's *hand.*) So until then. (*To* GAYEV.) Goodbye. (*Exchanges kisses with* PISHCHIK.) Goodbye. (*Gives his hand to* VARYA, *then to* FIRS *and* YASHA.) I only wish I didn't have to go. (*To* RANYEVSKAYA.) If you come to a decision about the houses, let me know, and I'll get you fifty thousand on account. Think about it seriously.

VARYA (*angrily*). Oh, go *on*!

LOPAKHIN. I'm going, I'm going. (*Exits.*)

GAYEV. A boor – the man's a boor. Oh, *pardon* . . . Varya's going to marry him. He's Varya's intended.

VARYA. Uncle, please, don't start.

RANYEVSKAYA. Why, Varya, I shall be very happy. He's a good man.

PISHCHIK. A most – it has to be said – worthy man. And my Dashenka . . . she also says that, well, she says various things. (*Snores, but immediately wakes up again.*) But all the same, dear lady, if you could oblige me . . . with a loan of two hundred and forty rubles . . . The interest on my mortgage is due tomorrow . . .

VARYA (*alarmed*). No, no!

RANYEVSKAYA. I really do have nothing.

PISHCHIK. Well, it'll get itself found somehow. (*Laughs*.) I never lose hope. Here we are, I think to myself, everything's lost, I'm done for – but not at all, because lo and behold – the railway's come through my land, and . . . they've paid me. And by and by, you'll see, one day soon, something else will happen . . . There's two hundred thousand Dashenka's going to win – she's got a lucky ticket.

RANYEVSKAYA. The coffee's finished. We can go to bed.

FIRS (*brushes* GAYEV; *lecturing*). You've put the wrong trousers on again. What am I to do with you?

VARYA (*quietly*). Anya's asleep. (*Quietly opens a window*.) The sun's up already – it's not cold. Look, Mama – what marvellous trees they are! And oh, sweet heavens, the air! And the starlings are chattering!

GAYEV (*opens another window*). The orchard's all in white. You haven't forgotten, Lyuba? The way the long avenue there runs straight, straight, like a ribbon stretched taut, the way it shines on moonlit nights. You remember? You haven't forgotten?

RANYEVSKAYA (*looks out of the window at the orchard*). Oh, my childhood, my innocence! In this nursery I slept, from this room I looked out at the orchard, and happiness woke with me every morning. The orchard was just the same then, nothing has changed. (*Laughs with joy*.) All, all in white! Oh, my orchard! After dark foul autumn and cold cold winter, again you're young and filled with happiness, and not abandoned by the angels. If only the millstone could be lifted from my neck. If only I could forget my past!

GAYEV. Yes, even the orchard will be sold to meet our debts. Strange as it seems . . .

RANYEVSKAYA. Look – there's Mama, our own dead Mama, walking through the orchard . . . in a white dress! (*Laughs with joy*.) It's her.

GAYEV. Where?

VARYA. God save you, Mama.

RANYEVSKAYA. There's no one there. It just looked like it for a
moment. To the right, on the turning to the summer-house – a
tree bending under its blossom like the figure of a woman.

*Enter* TROFIMOV, *in a shabby student's uniform and spectacles.*

What an amazing orchard it is! The white masses of the
blossom, the pale blue of the sky . . .

TROFIMOV. Lyubov Andreyevna!

*She looks round at him.*

I'm just going to pay my respects to you, and then I'll go away
and leave you in peace. (*Ardently kisses her hand.*) I was told to
wait until morning, but I didn't have patience enough.

RANYEVSKAYA *gazes at him in perplexity.*

VARYA (*on the verge of tears*). It's Petya.

TROFIMOV. Trofimov. Petya Trofimov. I used to be Grisha's
tutor . . . Have I really changed so much?

RANYEVSKAYA *embraces him and weeps quietly.*

GAYEV (*embarrassed*). Come on, Lyuba. Come on, now.

VARYA (*weeps*). Petya, I did tell you to wait until tomorrow.

RANYEVSKAYA. My Grisha . . . my boy . . . Grisha . . . my
son . . .

VARYA. What can we do, Mama? It was God's will.

TROFIMOV (*softly, on the verge of tears*). There now . . . There,
now . . .

RANYEVSKAYA (*weeps quietly*). My boy died, my little boy was
drowned . . . Why? Why, my friend? (*More quietly.*) Anya's
asleep in there, and here am I talking at the top of my voice . . .
making a noise . . . What's this, Petya? Why have you lost your
looks? Why have you aged so?

TROFIMOV. You know what some old woman on a train the other
day called me? – 'That mangy-looking gentleman.'

RANYEVSKAYA. You were still only a boy before, just a nice

young student. Now you've got glasses, your hair's gone thin. You're surely not still a student? (*Goes to the door.*)

TROFIMOV. I should think I'm going to be a perpetual student. The Wandering Student, like the Wandering Jew.

RANYEVSKAYA (*kisses her brother, then* VARYA). Well, off to bed, then . . . You've aged, too, Leonid.

PISHCHIK (*follows her*). So, bedtime . . . Oh, my gout. I'll stay the night here, I think. (*To* RANYEVSKAYA.) And in the morning, dearest heart, if you would . . . two hundred and forty rubles . . .

GAYEV. Never gives up, does he?

PISHCHIK. Two hundred and forty rubles . . . I have to pay the interest on my mortgage.

RANYEVSKAYA. I have no money, my sweet.

PISHCHIK. I'll give it back, my dear. It's the most piffling sum.

RANYEVSKAYA. Well, all right. Leonid will give it to you. You give it to him, Leonid.

GAYEV. If it's up to me, he can whistle for it.

RANYEVSKAYA. What can we do? Just give it to him . . . He needs it . . . He'll give it back.

*Exeunt* RANYEVSKAYA, TROFIMOV, PISHCHIK *and* FIRS.

GAYEV, VARYA *and* YASHA *remain.*

GAYEV. My sister still hasn't got out of the habit of flinging her money around. (*To* YASHA.) Do go away, my dear good chap – you smell of chickens.

YASHA (*grinning*). And you're just the same as you always were.

GAYEV. Who? (*To* VARYA.) What does he say?

VARYA (*to* YASHA). Your mother's come from the village. She's been sitting in the servants' hall since yesterday waiting to see you.

YASHA. Well, good luck to her, then.

VARYA. Shameless, aren't you?

YASHA. What's the point. She could just as well have come tomorrow. (*Goes out.*)

VARYA. Mama's exactly the same as she was. She hasn't changed
at all. If it was up to her she'd have given everything away.
GAYEV. Yes . . .

*Pause.*

If for some disease a great many different remedies are proposed, then it means that the disease is incurable. I think, I
cudgel my brains – I have many remedies, a great many – and
what that means when you get down to it is that I haven't a
solitary one. It would be a good thing if we got an inheritance
from someone. It would be a good thing if we married Anya
to some very rich man. It would be a good thing if we went to
Yaroslavl and tried our luck with that aunt of ours, the countess.
She's very rich indeed, you know.

VARYA (*weeps*). If only God would help.

GAYEV. Don't howl. Aunt is very rich, but she doesn't like us. In
the first place, my sister married an ordinary lawyer instead of a
gentleman with property . . .

ANYA *appears in the doorway.*

She married a commoner, and the way she's behaved – well,
you couldn't say it was very virtuously. She's good, she's kind,
she's a splendid woman, I love her dearly, but however many
extenuating circumstances you think up, the fact has to be
faced: she is depraved. You can sense it in her slightest movement.
VARYA (*in a whisper*). Anya is standing in the doorway.
GAYEV. Who?

*Pause.*

Funny – I've got something in my right eye. I can't see properly. And on Thursday, when I was at the district court . . .

*Enter* ANYA.

VARYA. Why aren't you asleep, Anya?

ANYA. I can't get to sleep.

GAYEV. My pet. (*Kisses* ANYA's *face and hands.*) My child . . .
(*On the verge of tears.*) You're not my niece – you're my
angel. You're everything to me. Believe me. Trust me.

ANYA. I trust you, uncle. Everyone loves you, everyone looks up
to you . . . but, dear Uncle, you must be quiet, only be quiet.
What were you saying just then about my mother – about your
own sister? Why did you say that?

GAYEV. Yes, yes . . . (*Covers his face with her hand.*) Really, that
was terrible! God forgive me! And today I made a speech to
the bookcase . . . so stupid! And only when I'd finished did I
realize how stupid it was.

VARYA. It's true, Uncle dear, you must keep quiet. Just be quiet,
that's all.

ANYA. If you're quiet, you'll be calmer in yourself, too.

GAYEV. I am silent. (*Kisses their hands.*) Not a word. Just one
thing on a matter of business. On Thursday I was at the district court, and, well, a few of us there got talking about this
and that, one thing and another, and it seems it would be possible to arrange a loan against my note of hand to pay the bank
interest.

VARYA. If only the Lord would help!

GAYEV. On Tuesday I'll go and have another talk about it. (*To*
VARYA.) Don't howl. (*To* ANYA.) Your mother will have a
word with Lopakhin. He obviously won't refuse her. And you
– as soon as you've got your breath back you'll go to Yaroslavl
to see the countess, your great aunt. So we'll be operating from
three sides at once – and the job's as good as done. We shall
pay the interest, of that I'm convinced. (*Puts a fruit drop in his
mouth.*) I swear, upon my honour, upon whatever you like,
that the estate will not be sold! (*Excitedly.*) By my hope of
happiness I swear it! Here's my hand on it – call me a low, dishonourable fellow if I let it go to auction! By my whole being
I swear to you!

ANYA (*her calm mood has returned to her: she is happy*). What a good man you are, Uncle, what a good and clever man! (*Embraces him.*) Now I'm calm! Quite calm! I'm happy!

*Enter* FIRS.

FIRS (*to* GAYEV, *reproachfully*). What? Have you no fear before God? When are you going to bed?

GAYEV. Right now, right now. You go off. Don't worry about me, I'll undress myself. Well, night night, then, children. Details tomorrow, but now to bed. (*Kisses* ANYA *and* VARYA.) I am a man of the eighties. Not a period they speak well of these days, but I can tell you that I have suffered not a little in this life for my convictions. It's no accident that your ordinary peasant loves me. You have to know your peasant! You have to know how to . . .

ANYA. Uncle, you're off again!

VARYA. Dear uncle, just be quiet.

FIRS (*angrily*). Leonid Andreyich!

GAYEV. I'm coming, I'm coming . . . Off to bed, then. Cushion, cushion, and into the middle pocket! Clean as a whistle . . . (*Goes out, with* FIRS *trotting behind him.*)

ANYA. Now I'm calm. I don't want to go to Yaroslavl – I don't like our great aunt. But all the same I'm calm. Thanks to Uncle. (*Sits down.*)

VARYA. We must get some sleep. I'm off. One rather annoying thing happened while you were away, though. You know what used to be the servants' quarters? Well, of course, it's only the elderly servants who live there now: Yefimushka, Polya, Yevstigney, oh, yes, and Karp. Well, they began to let various riff-raff in to spend the night. I said nothing about it. Only then I hear they've been spreading a rumour to the effect that I've had them fed on nothing but dried peas. Out of meanness, do you see . . . And all this is Yevstigney's doing . . . Right, I think to myself. If that's the way you want it, then just you wait. So I send for Yevstigney . . . (*Yawns.*) He comes in . . .

What's all this, then, Yevstigney? I say to him . . . You're such a fool . . . (*Looks at* ANYA.) Anyechka . . . !

*Pause.*

Asleep . . . ! (*Takes* ANYA *by the arm.*) Off we go to bed, then . . . Off we go . . . ! (*Leads her.*) My poor precious has fallen fast asleep! Off we go . . .

*A long way away, beyond the orchard, a* SHEPHERD *plays on a reed pipe.*

TROFIMOV *crosses the stage, and stops at the sight of* VARYA *and* ANYA.

VARYA. Sh . . . She's asleep . . . asleep . . . Off we go, my own sweet precious.

ANYA (*quietly, half asleep*). So tired . . . I can still hear the harness bells . . . Uncle . . . dear Uncle . . . Mama and Uncle, too . . .

VARYA. Off we go, my own sweet love. Off we go . . .

*They go into* ANYA's *room.*

TROFIMOV (*moved*). My sunshine! My springtime!


**CURTAIN**

# Act Two

*The open fields. A wayside shrine – old, crooked, and long neglected. Beside it – a well, large slabs which were evidently once tombstones, and an old bench. A path can be seen leading to the Gayev estate. At one side rise the dark shapes of poplars; this is where the cherry orchard begins.*

*In the distance is a row of telegraph poles, and a long way away on the horizon a large town can just be made out, visible only in very fine, clear weather. The sun is just about to set.*

CHARLOTTA, YASHA *and* DUNYASHA *are sitting on the bench;* YEPIKHODOV *is standing beside it, playing the guitar. They are all in a reflective mood.*

CHARLOTTA *is wearing an old peaked cap. She has taken a gun off her shoulder and is adjusting the buckle on the sling.*

CHARLOTTA (*meditatively*). I haven't got proper papers – I don't know how old I am. So I always think of myself as being young. When I was a little girl Mama and my father used to go round all the fairs giving shows. Very good shows they were, too. And I'd turn somersaults and do all kinds of little tricks. And when Papa and Mama died, some German lady took me in and began to give me an education. So, all right, I grew up, and then I went to be a governess. But where I come from and who I am, I don't know. Who my parents were – whether they were even married or not – I don't know. (*Gets a cucumber out of her pocket and eats it.*) I don't know anything.

*Pause.*

I so long to talk to someone, but there's no one to talk to. I haven't got anyone.

YEPIKHODOV (*plays the guitar and sings*).

> What should I care for life's clamour,
> What for my friend or my foe . . .

How very agreeable it is to pluck at the strings of a mandoline!

DUNYASHA. That's not a mandoline – that's a guitar. (*Powders herself in a pocket mirror.*)

YEPIKHODOV. For the madman who's in love it's a mandoline. (*Sings.*)

> . . . Had I a passion requited
> Warming my heart with its glow?

YASHA *joins in.*

CHARLOTTA. Horrible way these people sing! Faugh! Like jackals howling!

DUNYASHA (*to* YASHA). All the same, how lovely to spend some time abroad.

YASHA. Yes, of course. I couldn't agree more. (*Yawns, and then lights a cigar.*)

YEPIKHODOV. Oh, absolutely. Everything abroad's been in full constitution for years.

YASHA. Obviously.

YEPIKHODOV. Here am I – I mean, I'm a grown man – I read – I read all sorts of important books – but what I can't make out is any I mean kind of movement of opinion when it comes to what I personally want in life. Put it this way – do I want to go on living, or do I want to shoot myself? I mean, I always carry a revolver on me, look. (*Shows the revolver.*)

CHARLOTTA. Done it. I'm off. (*Slings the gun on her shoulder.*) Yepikhodov, you're a genius. A terrifying genius. All the women ought to be mad about you. Brrr! (*Starts to go.*) These great brains – they're all such fools. I've no one to talk to. Alone, always alone, I haven't got anyone. And who I am and why I am remains a mystery . . . (*Goes unhurriedly off.*)

YEPIKHODOV. I mean, leaving everything else aside, I mean just taking my own case, and I'm not going to mince my words, but, really, fate has treated me quite relentlessly. I've been tossed around like a rowing-boat in a high sea. All right, let's say I'm talking nonsense. In that case, why, just to take one example, why, when I woke up this morning, why did I find, sitting there on my chest, this enormous spider? Like this. (*Demonstrates with both hands.*) All right, take another example. I pour myself some kvass, to have a drink, and there in the glass is something really profoundly horrible. I mean, a cockroach, for example.

*Pause.*

Have you read Buckle? The History of Civilization?

*Pause*

(*To* DUNYASHA.) If I might trouble you, I should appreciate the chance of a word or two.

DUNYASHA. Go on, then.

YEPIKHODOV. I should have been hopeful of having it in private. (*Sighs.*)

DUNYASHA (*embarrassed*). All right – only first fetch me my cloak. You'll find it by the cupboard. It's rather damp here.

YEPIKHODOV. Now I know what to do with my revolver . . . (*Takes his guitar and goes off playing it.*)

YASHA. Poor old Disasters! Between you and me, that man is a fool. (*Yawns.*)

DUNYASHA. Just so long as he doesn't go and shoot himself.

*Pause.*

I've got so nervy these days – I worry all the time. They took me into service when I was a little girl still. I've got out of the way of ordinary people's life now. Look at my hands – white as white, like a lady's. I've turned into someone all refined, someone terribly delicate and ladylike – I'm frightened of everything. It's dreadful being like this. And Yasha, if you deceive me, well, I don't know what would become of my nerves.

YASHA (*kisses her*). Real country pippin, aren't you? Of course, every girl's got to remember who she is. If there's one thing I hate more than anything else, it's a girl who doesn't know how to behave herself.

DUNYASHA. I'm absolutely passionately in love with you. Because you're an educated man – you can talk about anything.

*Pause.*

YASHA (*yawns*). Right . . . What I think is, if a girl's in love with someone then she's got no morals.

*Pause.*

Nice having a cigar in the open air . . . (*Listens.*) Someone coming . . . It's *them*.

DUNYASHA *impetuously embraces him.*

Go home as if you'd been down to the river for a swim – here, along this path. Otherwise you'll run into them and they'll think I've been seeing you. I'm not having that.

DUNYASHA (*coughs quietly*). Your cigar's given me a headache . . . (*Goes off.*)

YASHA *remains, sitting beside the shrine.*

*Enter* RANYEVSKAYA, GAYEV, *and* LOPAKHIN.

LOPAKHIN. It has to be settled once and for all – time won't wait. Look, it's a simple enough question. Do you agree to lease out the land for summer cottages or not? Answer me one word: yes or no? Just one word!

RANYEVSKAYA. Who's smoking some foul cigar? (*Sits.*)

GAYEV. It's very convenient now they've built the railway. (*Sits.*) We popped into town and had some lunch . . . Yellow into the middle pocket! I should have gone indoors first and had a quick game.

RANYEVSKAYA. You've still got time.

LOPAKHIN. Just one word! (*Pleading.*) Give me an answer!

GAYEV (*yawns*). Who?

RANYEVSKAYA (*looks into her purse*). There was a lot of money in here yesterday, and today there's hardly any. My poor Varya feeds everyone on milk soup to economize – she gives the old men in the kitchen nothing but dried peas, while I somehow just go on mindlessly spending . . . (*Drops the purse and scatters gold coins.*) And now it's gone everywhere . . . (*She is annoyed.*)

YASHA. Leave it to me – I'll do it. (*Picks up the coins.*)

RANYEVSKAYA. Would you, Yasha? And why did I go into town for lunch? That horrible restaurant of yours with the music playing, and the tablecloths smelling of soap . . . Why do you drink so much, Lenya? Why do you eat so much? Why do you talk so much? In the restaurant today you kept talking again – and it was all so rambling. The seventies, the Decadent movement. And who were you saying it all to? Fancy telling the waiters about the Decadents!

LOPAKHIN. Yes.

GAYEV (*waves his hand*). I'm incorrigible, that's obvious. (*To* YASHA, *irritated.*) What is it? You're perpetually dangling in front of my eyes.

YASHA (*laughs*). I can't hear your voice without wanting to laugh.

GAYEV (*to his sister*). Either he goes, or I do.

RANYEVSKAYA. Off you go, Yasha.

YASHA (*gives* RANYEVSKAYA *her purse*). Certainly. (*Scarcely restrains himself from laughing.*) This instant. (*Goes.*)

LOPAKHIN. Your estate is going to be bought by Deriganov. He's a very wealthy man. I gather he's coming to the sale in person.

RANYEVSKAYA. Where did you hear that?

LOPAKHIN. It's what they're saying in town.

GAYEV. Our aunt in Yaroslavl has promised to send something, but when and how much – that we don't know.

LOPAKHIN. What would it be? A hundred thousand? Two hundred thousand?

RANYEVSKAYA. Ten or fifteen thousand, and lucky if we get even that.

LOPAKHIN. Forgive me for saying this, but such frivolous people as you, such strange unbusinesslike people, I have never come across. You are told in plain language that your estate is being sold, and you simply do not understand.

RANYEVSKAYA. What can we possibly do? Tell us.

LOPAKHIN. I tell you every day. Every day I tell you exactly the same thing. The cherry orchard and the land along the river must be leased out for summer cottages – and it must be done now, as soon as possible – the sale is upon us! Get it into your heads! Just once make up your minds to have the houses and you will get money – as much money as you like – and you will be saved.

RANYEVSKAYA. Summer cottages – summer people – forgive me, but it's so squalid.

GAYEV. I agree entirely.

LOPAKHIN. I don't know whether to scream, or to burst into tears, or to fall down in a faint. I can't go on! You reduce me to despair! (*To* GAYEV.) You're an old woman!

GAYEV. Who?

LOPAKHIN. An old woman. You! (*Starts to go.*)

RANYEVSKAYA (*frightened*). No, don't go. Stay with us, my dear. I beg you. Perhaps we'll think of something.

LOPAKHIN. What is there to think of?

RANYEVSKAYA. Don't go, I implore you. It's more fun with you here, at any rate . . .

*Pause.*

I keep waiting for something to happen – as if the house were going to come down about our ears.

GAYEV (*deep in thought*). Red, cushion, and into the corner . . . Cushion, red, and into the corner . . .

RANYEVSKAYA. We have sinned, and sinned greatly . . .

LOPAKHIN. What are your sins, then?

GAYEV (*puts a fruit drop in his mouth*). They say I've wasted all my substance in fruit drops . . . (*Laughs.*)

RANYEVSKAYA. Oh, my sins . . . Always I've thrown money about like a lunatic, and I married a man who made nothing of his life but debts. My husband died of champagne – he was a terrible drinker – and my misfortune then was to fall in love with someone else. I gave myself to him, and it was just at that time – and this was my first punishment, it was like a club coming down on my head – my little boy . . . in the river here . . . my little boy was drowned, and I went away, went abroad, went utterly away, went meaning never to return, never to see this river again . . . I shut my eyes, ran blindly – and *he* after me . . . pitilessly, brutally. I bought a villa outside Menton, because *he* fell sick there, and for three years I knew no rest, neither by day nor by night. For three years he was an invalid – he drained my strength – my spirit broke. And last year, when the villa was sold to pay my debts, I went to Paris, and there he robbed me openly, he threw me aside, he took up with another woman. I tried to poison myself . . . So stupid, so shameful . . . And suddenly I yearned for Russia, for my homeland, for my daughter . . . (*Wipes her tears.*) Lord, Lord have mercy! Forgive me my sins! Don't punish me any more! (*Takes a telegram out of her pocket.*) I got this today from Paris . . . He begs my forgiveness, implores me to return . . . (*Tears the telegram up.*) There's a sound of music somewhere. (*Listens.*)

GAYEV. That's our famous Jewish orchestra. Do you remember? Four fiddles, flute, and double bass.

RANYEVSKAYA. It still exists? We ought to get them here somehow – we ought to arrange an evening.

LOPAKHIN (*listens*). I can't hear anything . . .
(*Sings quietly.*)

> *Money talks, so here's poor Russkies*
> *Getting Frenchified by Germans.*

(*Laughs.*) Very good play I saw last night. Very funny.

RANYEVSKAYA. There's nothing funny in the world. People shouldn't watch plays. They should look at their own selves a little more often. What grey lives they all lead. How much they say that should never be said at all.

LOPAKHIN. True. We live like complete fools, it has to be admitted.

*Pause.*

My father was a peasant. He was an idiot, he knew nothing, he taught me nothing, all he did was to take his stick to me when he was drunk. And when you get down to it, I'm just the same sort of stupid oaf myself. I've never learnt anything. I write such a foul hand I'm ashamed for people to see it. I'm a pig.

RANYEVSKAYA. What you need, my friend, is to get married.

LOPAKHIN. Yes . . . That's true.

RANYEVSKAYA. To Varya, why not? Our own Varya. She's a good girl.

LOPAKHIN. Yes.

RANYEVSKAYA. She came to me from simple people – she works the whole day long. But the main thing is, she loves you. Yes, and you've liked her for a long time now.

LOPAKHIN. Fair enough. I've nothing against it. She's a good girl.

*Pause.*

GAYEV. I've been offered a job in a bank. Six thousand a year. Have you heard about that?

RANYEVSKAYA. The idea! You just stay as you are.

*Enter* FIRS. *He has brought an overcoat.*

FIRS (*to* GAYEV). Now will you put it on, sir, if you please, or you'll be getting damp.

GAYEV (*puts on the coat*). Firs, my friend, you're a bore.

FIRS. No call for that, now. You went off this morning without a word. (*Examines him.*)

RANYEVSKAYA. You've aged, Firs, haven't you?

FIRS. What do you want?

LOPAKHIN. She says you've aged a lot!

FIRS. I've lived a long life. They were marrying me off before your Papa even arrived in the world. (*Laughs.*) And when the Freedom came, in sixty-one, I was already head valet. I didn't agree to have the Freedom – I stayed with the masters . . .

*Pause.*

And I remember, everyone was glad. But what they were glad about they didn't know themselves.

LOPAKHIN. Lovely it was before. At least they flogged you.

FIRS (*not having heard right*). Oh, my word, they were. The peasants belonged to the masters, and the masters to the peasants. Now it's all chippety-choppety – you can't make any sense of it.

GAYEV. Do be quiet for a moment, Firs. Tomorrow I have to go into town. I've been promised an introduction to a general who might put up something against my note of hand.

LOPAKHIN. Nothing's going to come of it, whatever you do. And you're not going to pay that interest, don't worry.

RANYEVSKAYA. He's living in a dream. There's no general.

*Enter* TROFIMOV, ANYA *and* VARYA.

GAYEV. Some more of us coming.

ANYA. It's Mama.

RANYEVSKAYA (*tenderly*). Here . . . here . . . my own darlings . . . (*Embracing* ANYA *and* VARYA.) If only you knew how much I love you both! Sit next to me – here . . .

*They all settle themselves down.*

LOPAKHIN. Our Wandering Student always seems to be wandering with the young ladies.

TROFIMOV. Mind your own business.

LOPAKHIN. He'll be fifty before he knows where he is, and still a student.

TROFIMOV. Why don't you leave off your stupid jokes?

LOPAKHIN. Not losing your temper, are you, O weird one?

TROFIMOV. Don't keep badgering me.

LOPAKHIN (*laughs*). All right, then, my dear sir. What do you make of me?

TROFIMOV. I'll tell you what I make of you, sir. You're a wealthy man – you'll soon be a millionaire. And just as there must be predatory animals to maintain nature's metabolism by devouring whatever crosses their path, so there must also be you.

*They all laugh.*

VARYA. Petya, I think it would be better if you told us about the planets.

RANYEVSKAYA. No, let's go on with the conversation we were having yesterday.

TROFIMOV. What was that about?

GAYEV. Pride.

TROFIMOV. We talked for a long time yesterday, but we never arrived at any conclusions. Human pride, in the sense you're using it, has some kind of mystical significance. And you may even be right, in your own fashion. But if we're going to talk about it in a down-to-earth way, without any fancy trimmings, then what sort of pride can there be – does the expression have any sense at all – if man is physiologically ill-constructed, if in the vast majority of cases he is crude and stupid and profoundly unhappy? We have to stop admiring ourselves. We have simply to work.

GAYEV. It makes no difference – you still die.

TROFIMOV. Who knows? And what does it mean – you die? Perhaps man has a hundred senses, and at death it's only the five we know of that perish, while the other ninety-five go on living.

RANYEVSKAYA. What a clever man you are, Petya!

LOPAKHIN (*ironically*). Oh, staggeringly.

TROFIMOV. Mankind is advancing, perfecting its powers. All the things that are beyond its reach now will one day be brought close and made plain. All we have to do is to work, to bend all our strength to help those who are seeking the truth. Here in Russia very few as yet are working. Most members of the intelligentsia, so far as I know it, are seeking nothing, neither the truth nor anything else. They're doing nothing – they're still incapable of hard work. They call themselves the intelligentsia, but they treat servants like children, and peasants like animals. They don't know how to study. They never do any serious reading. They understand next to nothing about art; science they merely talk about. They're all terribly serious people with terribly stern expressions on their faces. They all talk about nothing but terribly important questions. They all philosophize away. And right in front of their eyes the whole time there are workers living on filthy food and sleeping without pillows to their heads, thirty and forty to a room – and everywhere bugs, damp, stench, and moral squalor. And all the fine conversations we have are plainly just to distract attention from it all. Our own attention, and other people's, too. Show me – where are the crèches that everyone's always going on about – where are the reading-rooms? They're only in novels – they don't exist in reality. There's just filth and banality and barbarism. I have little love for all those serious faces; I fear those serious conversations. Better to be silent.

LOPAKHIN. Listen, I get up before five every morning, I work all the hours God gave, I'm constantly handling money – my own and other people's – and I can't help seeing what my fellow men are like. You've only got to start trying to do something to discover how few honest, decent people there are in the world. Sometimes, when I can't sleep, I think to myself: 'Lord, you gave us immense forests, boundless plains, broad horizons – living in it all we ought properly to be giants.'

RANYEVSKAYA. A lot of use giants would be. They're all right in fairy-tales. Anywhere else they're frightening.

YEPIKHODOV *crosses upstage, playing the guitar.*

(*Pensively.*) There goes Yepikhodov . . .

ANYA (*likewise*). There goes Yepikhodov . . .

GAYEV. The sun has set, ladies and gentlemen.

TROFIMOV. Yes.

GAYEV (*softly, as if declaiming*). O nature, wondrous nature! You shine with an everlasting radiance, beautiful and indifferent; you that we call Mother unite within yourself existence and death; you give life and you destroy it . . .

VARYA (*imploringly*). Uncle!

ANYA. You're doing it again!

TROFIMOV. You'd be better off potting yellow.

GAYEV. I am silent, I am silent.

*They all sit lost in thought. Silence. All that can be heard is* FIRS *muttering quietly. Suddenly there is a distant sound, as if from the sky: the sound of a breaking string – dying away, sad.*

RANYEVSKAYA. What was that?

LOPAKHIN. I don't know. Somewhere a long way off, in the mines, a winding cable has parted. But a long, long way off.

GAYEV. Perhaps a bird of some sort . . . something like a heron.

TROFIMOV. Or some kind of owl.

RANYEVSKAYA (*shivers*). Horrible, I don't know why.

*Pause.*

FIRS. It was the same before the troubles. The owl screeched, and the samovar moaned without stop.

GAYEV. Before what troubles?

FIRS. Before the Freedom.

*Pause.*

RANYEVSKAYA. Listen, my friends, we must be going. The night is drawing on. (*To* ANYA.) There are tears in your eyes. What is it, child? (*Embraces her.*)

ANYA. Nothing. Just tears. It doesn't matter.

TROFIMOV. There's someone coming.

A PASSER-BY *appears. He is wearing an overcoat and a stolen white peaked cap; he is slightly drunk.*

PASSER-BY. Begging your pardon – can I get through this way to the station?

GAYEV. Yes. Along this path.

PASSER-BY. Most profoundly grateful. (*Coughs.*) Wonderful weather . . . (*Declaims.*)

> My friend, my brother, weary, suffering, sad,
> Though falsehood rule and evil triumph,
> Take courage yet and let your soul be glad . . .

*Pause.*

> Go to the Volga. Hear again
> The song it sings, the song of groans –
> The litany of hauling men,
> Groaned from weary hearts and bones.
> Volga! All spring's melted snows,
> And still you cannot flood your plain
> As wide as this land overflows
> With all its people's sea of pain . . .

(*To* VARYA) Mademoiselle, spare a few kopeks for a starving Russian.

VARYA *is frightened, and cries out.*

LOPAKHIN (*angrily*). Now that's enough! There are limits!

RANYEVSKAYA (*hurriedly*). Wait . . . here you are . . . (*Looks in her purse.*) I've no silver . . . Never mind, here – ten rubles . . . (*Gives him a gold coin.*)

PASSER-BY. Most profoundly grateful. (*Goes off.*)

*Laughter.*

VARYA (*frightened*). I'm going in . . . Oh, Mama – at home there's nothing for the servants to eat, and you gave him ten rubles.

RANYEVSKAYA. What's to be done with me? – I'm so silly! When we get home I'll give you everything I've got. (*To* LOPAKHIN.) You'll lend me some more, won't you?

LOPAKHIN. Your humble servant.

RANYEVSKAYA. Ladies and gentlemen, it's time we were going. Oh, and Varya, while we were sitting here we quite made a match for you. So congratulations.

VARYA (*on the verge of tears*). Don't joke about it, Mama.

LOPAKHIN. Get thee to a nunnery, Ophelia-Ophoolia.

GAYEV. My hands are shaking – I've been missing my billiards.

LOPAKHIN. Nymph, in thy orisons be all my sins dismembered!

RANYEVSKAYA. Off we go, then. It's nearly time for supper.

VARYA. He gave me such a fright. My heart's simply pounding.

LOPAKHIN. Let me remind you, ladies and gentlemen: the cherry orchard will be coming up for sale on the twenty-second of August. Think about it! Think!

*They all go out except* TROFIMOV *and* ANYA.

ANYA (*laughing*). We ought to thank that tramp for frightening Varya. Now we're alone.

TROFIMOV. She's afraid you and I are suddenly going to fall in love with each other. She doesn't let us out of her sight for days at a time. What she can't get into her narrow mind is that we're above such things as love. Our whole aim – the whole sense of our life – is to avoid the petty illusions that stop us being free and happy. On, on, on! We are going to that bright star that blazes from afar there, and no one can hold us back! On, on, on! In step together, friends!

ANYA (*clasping her hands*). How beautifully you talk!

*Pause.*

It's wonderful here today.

TROFIMOV. Yes, amazing weather.

ANYA. What have you done to me, Petya? Why don't I love the cherry orchard like I used to? I loved it so tenderly. I thought there was nowhere finer on earth.

TROFIMOV. All Russia is our orchard. The earth is broad and beautiful. There are many marvellous places.

*Pause.*

Think for a moment, Anya: your grandfather, your great-grandfather – all your forebears – they were the masters of serfs. They owned living souls. Can't you see human faces, looking out at you from behind every tree-trunk in the orchard – from every leaf and every cherry? Can't you hear their voices? The possession of living souls – it's changed something deep in all of you, hasn't it. So that your mother and you and your uncle don't even notice you're living on credit, at the expense of others – at the expense of people you don't allow past the front hall . . . We're two hundred years behind the times at least. We still have nothing – no properly defined attitude to the past. We just philosophize away, and complain about our boredom or drink vodka. But it's only too clear that to start living in the present we have to redeem our past – we have to break with it. And it can be redeemed only by suffering, only by the most unheard-of, unceasing labour. You must understand that, Anya.

ANYA. The house we live in hasn't been ours for a long time now. I'm going to leave, I give you my word.

TROFIMOV. Throw the keys down the well, and go. Be free as the wind.

ANYA (*in delight*). You put it so beautifully!

TROFIMOV. Have faith in me, Anya! Have faith in me! I'm not thirty yet – I'm young – I'm still a student – but I've borne so much already! Every winter I'm hungry, sick and fearful, as poor as a beggar. And the places I've been to! The places where fate has driven me! And all the time, at every minute of the day and night, my soul has been filled with premonitions I can't explain or describe. I have a premonition of happiness, Anya. I can just see it now . . .

ANYA (*pensively*). The moon is rising.

*There is the sound of* YEPIKHODOV *still playing the same mournful song on his guitar. The moon rises. Somewhere over by the poplar trees* VARYA *is looking for* ANYA.

VARYA (*calling off*). Anya! Where are you?
TROFIMOV. Yes, the moon is rising.

*Pause.*

Here it is – happiness. Here it comes. Closer and closer. I can hear its footsteps already. And if we don't see it, if we never know its face, then what does it matter? Others will!

VARYA (*off*). Anya! Where are you?
TROFIMOV. There's that Varya again! (*Angrily.*) It's outrageous!
ANYA. Come on – let's go down to the river. It's nice there.
TROFIMOV. Come on, then.

*They start to go.*

VARYA (*off*). Anya! Anya!


**CURTAIN**

# Act Three

*The drawing-room, with an archway leading through into the ball-room. The chandelier is lit.*

*From an ante-room comes the sound of the Jewish orchestra mentioned in Act Two. Company has been invited for the evening. In the ballroom they are dancing the 'grand-rond'.*

SIMEONOV-PISHCHIK (*off*). Promenade à une paire!

> *The* COUPLES *emerge into the drawing-room – first* PISHCHIK *and* CHARLOTTA IVANOVNA, *second* TROFIMOV *and* RANYEVSKAYA, *third* ANYA *and the* POSTMASTER, *fourth* VARYA *and the* STATIONMASTER, *and so on.* VARYA *is quietly weeping, and wiping her eyes as she dances. In the last couple is* DUNYASHA. *They go round the room.*

PISHCHIK. Grand-rond balancez . . .! Les cavaliers à genoux et remerciez vos dames!

> FIRS, *wearing a tailcoat, brings the seltzer water on a tray.* PISHCHIK *and* TROFIMOV *come into the drawing-room.*

PISHCHIK. Blood-pressure – that's my trouble. I've had two strokes already, and I don't find dancing easy. But you know what they say – if you run with the pack you must wag your tail. I'm as strong as a horse. My late father, who was something of a humourist, God rest his soul, used to say the venerable tribe of Simeonov-Pishchik was descended from the horse that Caligula made consul . . . (*Sits down.*) But the snag is – no money! What do people say? – A hungry dog believes only in meat . . . (*Snores and immediately wakes up again.*) Same with me – can't think about anything but money.

TROFIMOV. It's true – there is something rather horse-like about you.

PISHCHIK. Well, that's all right . . . a horse is a good beast . . . a horse can be sold.

*There is the sound of billiards being played in the next room. VARYA appears in the archway to the ballroom.*

TROFIMOV (*teasing*). Madame Lopakhina! Madame Lopakhina!
VARYA (*angrily*). And who's this? The mangy-looking gentleman.
TROFIMOV. Yes, that's what I am – a mangy-looking gentleman. And proud of it!
VARYA (*reflecting bitterly*). Here we are, we've hired musicians – but what are we going to pay them with? (*Goes out.*)
TROFIMOV (*to* PISHCHIK). If all the energy you've expended during your life in the quest for money had gone on something else, you could have turned the world upside down by now.
PISHCHIK. Nietzsche – the philosopher – very great philosopher, very famous one – man of enormous intelligence – he claims in his books that it's all right to forge banknotes.
TROFIMOV. You've read Nietzsche, have you?
PISHCHIK. Well . . . my daughter Dashenka was telling me about him. Though with the position I'm in now, even if I started forging banknotes . . . I've got to pay three hundred and ten rubles the day after tomorrow . . . I've got hold of a hundred and thirty . . . (*Feels his pockets in alarm.*) The money's gone! I've lost the money! (*On the verge of tears.*). Where's the money? (*Joyfully.*) Here it is, in the lining . . . I'd quite come out in a sweat.

*Enter* RANYEVSKAYA *and* CHARLOTTA IVANOVNA.

RANYEVSKAYA (*hums a Caucasian dance, the lezghinka*). Why is Leonid taking so long? What can he be doing in town? (*To* DUNYASHA.) Dunyasha, ask the musicians if they'd like some tea.
TROFIMOV. The sale probably never took place.
RANYEVSKAYA. It wasn't the moment to have the band, it wasn't

the moment to get up a ball. Well, who cares? (*Sits down and hums quietly.*)

CHARLOTTA (*offers* PISHCHIK *a pack of cards*). Think of a card. Any card you like.

PISHCHIK. I've thought of one.

CHARLOTTA. Now shuffle the pack. Good. Give it to me, then, my dear monsieur Pishchik. *Ein, zwei, drei!* Now have a look and you'll find it in your side pocket.

PISHCHIK (*gets a card out of his side pocket*). The eight of spades – that's absolutely right! (*Amazed.*) Well, would you believe it!

CHARLOTTA (*to* TROFIMOV, *holding the pack in the palm of her hand*). The top card – quick – what is it?

TROFIMOV. I don't know . . . oh . . . the queen of spades.

CHARLOTTA. Right! (*To* PISHCHIK.) Well? The top card?

PISHCHIK. The ace of hearts.

CHARLOTTA. Right! (*Claps her hands, and the pack disappears.*) Marvellous weather we're having!

*A mysterious female voice answers, apparently from under the floor.*

VOICE. Oh, yes, wonderful weather!

CHARLOTTA. You are my heart's ideal!

VOICE. Yes, I've taken rather a fancy to you.

STATIONMASTER (*applauds*). Madame the ventriloquist! Bravo!

PISHCHIK (*amazed*). Would you believe it! Enchanting woman! I've absolutely fallen in love with you.

CHARLOTTA. In love? (*Shrugs her shoulders.*) Are you really capable of love? *Guter Mensch, aber schlechter Musikant.*

TROFIMOV (*claps* PISHCHIK *on the shoulder*). You're so much like a horse, you see . . .

CHARLOTTA. Your attention please. One more trick. (*Takes a travelling rug off one of the chairs.*) I have here a very fine rug, a very fine rug for sale. (*Shakes it.*) Who'll buy this very fine rug?

PISHCHIK (*amazed*). Would you believe it!

CHARLOTTA. *Ein, zwei, drei!* (*She has lowered the rug; now she quickly raises it.*)

> ANYA *is standing behind the rug. She curtseys, runs to her mother and embraces her, then runs back into the ballroom amid general delight.*

RANYEVSKAYA (*applauds*). Bravo, bravo . . .!

CHARLOTTA. Once more, now! *Ein, zwei, drei!* (*Raises the rug.*)

> VARYA *is standing behind the rug. She bows.*

PISHCHIK (*amazed*). Would you believe it!

CHARLOTTA. And that is the end of my show. (*Throws the rug at* PISHCHIK, *curtseys, and runs out into the ballroom.*)

PISHCHICK (*hurries after her*). What a witch, though! What a witch! (*Goes.*)

RANYEVSKAYA. And still no sign of Leonid. I don't understand what he could be doing in town for all this time. It must be over by now. Either the estate is sold, or else the sale never took place. What's the point of keeping us all in suspense?

VARYA (*trying to calm her*). Uncle has bought it – I'm sure of that.

TROFIMOV (*sarcastically*). Oh, of course he has.

VARYA. Great-aunt gave him authority to purchase it in her name, and to transfer the mortgage to her. It was all for Anya's sake. And, God willing, I'm sure Uncle will have done it.

RANYEVSKAYA. To buy this estate – and to buy it in her own name, because she doesn't trust us – your great-aunt sent fifteen thousand rubles – not enough even to pay the interest. (*Covers her face with her hands.*) Today my fate is being decided. My fate . . .

TROFIMOV (*teases* VARYA). Madame Lopakhina!

VARYA (*angrily*). The Wandering Student! They've thrown you out of university twice already.

RANYEVSKAYA. Why are you getting so cross, Varya? All right, he's teasing you about Lopakhin – but what of it? If you want to marry Lopakhin, then marry him. He's a good man, he's an interesting person. If you don't want to, then don't. Darling, no one's forcing you.

VARYA. I must tell you, Mama, that this is something I take very seriously. He's a good man, and I like him.

RANYEVSKAYA. Then marry him. Why wait? I don't understand.

VARYA. Mama dear, *I* can't propose to *him*. For two years now everyone's been talking to me about him. Everyone's been talking except him. He either says nothing or else makes a joke of it. I see why. He's busy making his fortune – he's no time for me. If only we had some money – just a little, a hundred rubles even – I'd throw up everything, I'd go away. I'd go into a nunnery.

TROFIMOV. The glory of it!

VARYA (*to* TROFIMOV). I thought students were supposed to have a little sense in their heads! (*In a gentle voice, with tears in her* (*eyes.*) Oh, but Petya, you've grown so ugly, you've aged so! (*To* RANYEVSKAYA, *no longer crying.*) It's just that I can't manage without things to do, Mama. Every minute of the day I must have something to do.

*Enter* YASHA.

YASHA (*scarcely restraining himself from laughing*). Yepikhodov's broken the billiard cue . . .! (*Goes out.*)

VARYA. What's Yepikhodov doing here? Who said he could play billiards? I simply don't understand these people. (*Goes out.*)

RANYEVSKAYA. Don't tease her, Petya. You can see, she's unhappy enough as it is.

TROFIMOV. She's very diligent, I must say that for her. Particularly at minding other people's business. All summer she's given me and Anya no peace. She's been frightened we were going to have some kind of romance. What's it to do with her?

Particularly since I've shown not the slightest sign of it – I'm not given to that sort of vulgarity. We're above such things as love!

RANYEVSKAYA. I suppose I must be beneath them. (*In great anxiety.*) Why isn't Leonid back? If only I knew whether the estate was sold or not. It seems such an incredible disaster that I just can't think – I can't keep control of myself . . . I could scream as I stand here . . . I could do something quite foolish. Save me, Petya. Talk to me about something, talk to me . . .

TROFIMOV. Does it make any difference whether the estate's been sold today or not? All that was finished with long ago – there's no way back – the path's grown over. Be calm now, my dear. Don't deceive yourself. Face up to the truth for once in your life.

RANYEVSKAYA. Yes, but what truth? You can see which is truth and which is falsehood, but I feel as if I'd gone blind – I can't see anything at all. You boldly settle all the great questions, but my love, isn't that because you're young, isn't that because you've never had to live a single one of those questions out? You look boldly forwards, but isn't that because you have the eyes of youth, because life is still hidden from them, so that you see nothing frightening in store? You're more daring than the rest of us, you're deeper, you're more honest – but think about it for a moment, be just a touch magnanimous in your judgment, take pity on me. After all, I was born here, my father and mother lived here, my grandfather . . . I love this house. Without the cherry orchard I can't make sense of my life, and if it really has to be sold, then sell me along with it . . . (*Embraces* TROFIMOV, *and kisses him on the forehead.*) And then this is where my son was drowned . . . (*Weeps.*) You're a good man, a kind man – have pity on me.

TROFIMOV. You know I sympathize with all my heart.

RANYEVSKAYA. Yes, but not said like that, not like that . . . (*Takes out her handkerchief, and a telegram falls on the floor.*)

There is such a weight upon my heart today, you can never know. All this noise here – my heart jumps at every sound – everything in me jumps. But to go away and be on my own – I can't, because as soon as I'm alone and surrounded by silence I'm terrified. Don't judge me, Petya. I love you as if you were my own child. I should have been glad to let you marry Anya – I truly should. Only, my precious boy, you must study, you must finish at university. It's so strange – you do nothing but get yourself tossed by fate from one place to the next. Isn't that true? Yes? And you must do something with your beard somehow to make it grow. (*Laughs.*) You are an absurd man!

TROFIMOV (*picks up the telegram*). I've no desire to be known for my looks.

RANYEVSKAYA. It's a telegram from Paris. Every day they come. One yesterday, another one today. That wild man – he's ill again, he's in trouble again. He begs my forgiveness, he implores me to come, and really I ought to go to Paris, I ought to be with him. You're pulling your stern face, Petya, but my dear, what can I do, what can I possibly do? He's ill, he's lonely and unhappy, and who'll look after him there, who'll keep him from making mistakes, who'll give him his medicine at the right time? And what's the point of hiding it or not talking about it? – I plainly love him. I love him, love him. He's a millstone round my neck – he'll take me to the bottom with him. But I love this millstone of mine – I can't live without it. (*Presses* TROFIMOV's *hand.*) Don't think harsh thoughts, Petya. Don't say anything to me. Don't speak.

TROFIMOV (*on the verge of tears*). Forgive me if I'm frank, please God forgive me, but listen – he's openly robbed you!

RANYEVSKAYA. No, no, no, you mustn't say things like that . . . (*Covers her ears.*)

TROFIMOV. Look, he's no good, and you're the only one who doesn't know it! He's a petty scoundrel, a nobody . . .

RANYEVSKAYA (*angry now, but restraining it*). You're twenty-six, twenty-seven years old, and you're still a schoolboy, you're still a fifth-former.

TROFIMOV. If you say so.

RANYEVSKAYA. It's time you were a man. At your age you must understand people who know what it is to love. You must know what it is yourself! You must fall in love! (*Angrily.*) Yes, yes! You're no more pure than I am! You're just a prig, a ridiculous freak, a monster . . .!

TROFIMOV (*in horror*). What is she saying?

RANYEVSKAYA. 'I'm above such things as love!' You're not above anything – you're merely what our Firs calls a sillybilly. Fancy not having a mistress at your age!

TROFIMOV (*in horror*). This is appalling! What is she saying? (*Rushes towards the ballroom, holding his head.*) Appalling . . . I can't cope with this, I shall have to go . . . (*Goes out, but immediately comes back.*) Everything is finished between us! (*Goes out into the anteroom.*)

RANYEVSKAYA (*calls after him*). Petya, wait! You absurd man! I was joking! Petya!

> *In the anteroom someone can be heard rushing downstairs, and then suddenly falling with a crash.* ANYA *and* VARYA *cry out, but then at once there is a sound of laughter.*

What's happening out there?

> ANYA *runs in.*

ANYA (*laughing*). Petya's fallen downstairs! (*Runs out.*)

RANYEVSKAYA. What a freak that Petya is . . .

> *The* STATIONMASTER *takes up a position in the middle of the ballroom.*

STATIONMASTER. The Scarlet Woman. A poem in six parts by Aleksey Konstantinovich Tolstoy. Part One.

> The merry rev'llers throng the hall;
> The lute plays sweet; the cymbals brawl;
> The crystal blazes; gold shines bright;

> While 'twixt the columns, rich brocades
> Hang swagged with finely broidered braids,
> And flowering shrubs anoint the night . . .

*People are listening to him, but from the anteroom come the sounds of a waltz, and the reading stops short. Everyone dances.* TROFIMOV, ANYA, VARYA *and* RANYEVSKAYA *emerge from the anteroom.*

RANYEVSKAYA. Now, Petya . . . Petya with the pure soul . . . Please forgive me. Shall we dance . . .? (*Dances with him.*)

*ANYA and VARYA dance.*

*Enter* FIRS. *He puts his stick next to the side door.* YASHA *has also entered, and is watching the dancing.*

YASHA. What's up with you, then, Grandad?

FIRS. I'm not right in myself. When we gave a ball in the old days we used to have generals dancing here, we had barons, we had admirals. Now we send for the postmaster and the station-master, and even them they're none too eager. I'm not as strong as I was. The old master, her grandfather, used to treat all our ailments with a dose of sealing-wax. I've been taking sealing-wax every day for twenty years or more. Maybe that's why I'm still alive.

YASHA. Real old bore, aren't you, Grandad? (*Yawns.*) Why don't you just drop dead?

FIRS. Oh, you . . . sillybilly. (*Mumbles.*)

TROFIMOV *and* RANYEVSKAYA *dance first in the ballroom, and then in the drawing-room.*

RANYEVSKAYA. *Merci.* I'm going to sit down for a moment. (*Sits.*) I'm quite tired out.

*Enter* ANYA.

ANYA (*excitedly*). Some man just came to the kitchen saying the cherry orchard's been sold.

RANYEVSKAYA. Sold? To whom?

ANYA. He didn't say. He's gone now. (*Dances with* TROFIMOV.)

*They both go out into the ballroom.*

YASHA. That was just some old man gossiping. Some stranger.

FIRS. And Leonid Andreyich still isn't here. He still hasn't come. He's wearing his light autumn coat, he'll go and catch cold. When will these young people learn?

RANYEVSKAYA. I shall die on the spot. Yasha, go and find out who it was sold to.

YASHA. What, from the old man? He left ages ago. (*Laughs.*)

RANYEVSKAYA (*with slight irritation*). What are you laughing at? What are you so pleased about?

YASHA. Very funny man, that Yepikhodov. Fatuous devil. Old Disasters by the Dozen.

RANYEVSKAYA. Firs, if the estate is sold, where will you go?

FIRS. Wherever you tell me to go.

RANYEVSKAYA. Why are you pulling that face? Are you ill? You could go to bed, you know.

FIRS. Oh, yes . . . (*Smiles.*) I go to bed, and who's going to wait on everyone, who's going to see to everything? There's only me to do the whole house.

YASHA (*to* RANYEVSKAYA). Madam, can I ask you a special favour? If you go to Paris again, please take me with you. I can't possibly stay here. (*Looking round and lowering his voice.*) I don't have to tell you – you can see it for yourself. It's an uneducated country, they're people without any morals. And then on top of that there's the boredom – and the food they give us in the kitchen, it's disgusting – and then there's Firs here wandering round all the time muttering away to himself. Take me with you! Please!

*Enter* PISHCHIK

PISHCHIK. You wonderful woman, may I beg just one thing? One tiny waltz? (RANYEVSKAYA *accompanies him.*) Enchanting

creature! All the same, I shall take a hundred and eighty
rubles off you . . . I will, you know . . . (*He dances.*) A hundred
and eighty tiny rubles . . .

*They have passed through into the ballroom.*

YASHA (*sings quietly*). 'And will you know just how my heart
beats faster . . .?'

*In the ballroom a figure in a grey top hat and check trousers
waves its arms and leaps about.*

VOICES (*off*). It's Charlotta Ivanovna! Bravo!
DUNYASHA (*who has stopped to powder her nose*). Miss told me to
dance because there are too many gentlemen and not enough
ladies, and now my head's spinning, my heart's pounding. And
the postmaster just told me something that quite took my breath
away.

*The music becomes quieter.*

FIRS. What did he tell you?
DUNYASHA. He said, You're like a flower.
YASHA (*yawns*). The ignorance of these people . . . (*Goes out.*)
DUNYASHA. Like a flower . . . I'm such a sensitive girl – I do
terribly love it when people say nice things to me.
FIRS. You'll have your head turned, you will.

*Enter* YEPIKHODOV.

YEPIKHODOV (*to* DUNYASHA). You've no wish to see me, have
you . . . As if I was some kind of insect. (*Sighs.*) Ah, life!
DUNYASHA. What do you want?
YEPIKHODOV. And you're right, no doubt, possibly. (*Sighs.*)
Though, of course, if you look at it from one point of view, then
I mean you have reduced me – and forgive me for saying this,
but I mean I'm not going to mince my words – you have reduced me to, well, let's put it like this, to a complete and utter
state of mind. I know what's in my stars – every day some dis-

aster happens – I've long been used to it – I look upon my fate now with a smile. I mean, you gave me your word, and although I . . .

DUNYASHA. Please, we'll talk about it later. Leave me in peace now. I'm busy dreaming. (*Plays with a fan.*)

YEPIKHODOV. Every day another disaster, and I mean, all I do is smile. Laugh, even.

*Enter* VARYA *from the ballroom.*

VARYA (*to* YEPIKHODOV). Are you still here? Have you no respect? (*To* DUNYASHA.) Out of here, Dunyasha. (*To* YEPIKHODOV.) First you play billiards and break the cue, and now you parade about the drawing-room as if you were a guest.

YEPIKHODOV. I'm not going to account for my behaviour to you, if I may say so.

VARYA. I'm not asking you to account for your behaviour. I'm telling you. All you do is wander about from place to place. You never get down to any work. We keep a clerk, but what for, heaven only knows.

YEPIKHODOV (*offended*). Whether I do any work or not – whether I wander about or eat or play billiards – these are questions that can only be judged by people older and wiser than you.

VARYA. You dare to talk to me like that! (*Flaring up.*) You dare! Are you trying to tell me I don't know what's right and wrong? Clear off out of here! This minute!

YEPIKHODOV (*cowering*). Kindly express yourself with more refinement.

VARYA (*beside herself*). Out of here! This instant! Out!

*He goes to the door, and she after him.*

Disasters by the Dozen – that's right! I want neither sight nor sound of you in here!

*YEPIKHODOV is by now out of the room.*

YEPIKHODOV (*off, behind the door*). I'll tell about you!

VARYA. Oh, coming back, are you? (*Seizes the stick that* FIRS *left beside the door.*) Come on, then . . . Come on . . . Come on . . . I'll show you . . . Are you coming? My word, you're going to be for it . . .! (*Raises the stick threateningly.*)

    *Enter* LOPAKHIN.

LOPAKHIN. Thank you kindly.

VARYA (*angrily and sarcastically*). Sorry! My mistake.

LOPAKHIN. That's all right. I'm touched to get such a warm welcome.

VARYA. Oh, please – think nothing of it. (*Goes away from him, then looks round and asks softly.*) I didn't hurt you, did I?

LOPAKHIN. No, no. Don't worry about it. I shall just have the most enormous bump, that's all.

VOICES (*off, in the ballroom*). Lopakhin's arrived! Lopakhin's here!

    *Enter* PISHCHIK.

PISHCHIK. As large as life . . . (*He and* LOPAKHIN *kiss.*) You smell of brandy, my dear fellow. And we're making merry here as well.

    *Enter* RANYEVSKAYA.

RANYEVSKAYA. Is it him . . .? (*To* LOPAKHIN.) Why so long? Where's Leoníd?

LOPAKHIN. He arrived with me – he's just coming . . .

RANYEVSKAYA (*alarmed*). So what happened? Did they hold the sale? Speak!

LOPAKHIN (*confused, afraid to reveal his joy*). The sale ended just on four o'clock. We missed the train – we had to wait till half-past nine. (*Sighs heavily.*) Ouf! My head's rather going round . . .

    *Enter* GAYEV. *In his left hand he is carrying his purchases; with his right he is wiping away his tears.*

RANYEVSKAYA. Lenya! Lenya!, what happened? (*Impatiently in tears.*) Quickly, for the love of God . . .

GAYEV (*gives her no reply except a flap of the hand; to* FIRS, *weeping*). Here, take these . . . anchovies, Crimean herrings . . . I haven't eaten anything all day . . . Oh, what I've been through!

*The door into the billiard room is open; the click of balls can be heard.*

YASHA (*off*). Seven and eighteen!

*GAYEV's expression changes; he is no longer weeping.*

GAYEV. I'm horribly tired. Help me change, will you, Firs? (*Goes off to his room by way of the ballroom, with* FIRS *after him.*)

PISHCHIK. What happened at the sale? Tell us!

RANYEVSKAYA. Is the cherry orchard sold?

LOPAKHIN. It is.

RANYEVSKAYA. Who bought it?

LOPAKHIN. I did.

*RANYEVSKAYA is utterly cast down; if she were not standing beside the armchair and the table she would fall.* VARYA *takes the keys off her belt, throws them on the floor in the middle of the room, and goes out.*

I bought it! One moment . . . wait . . . if you would, ladies and gentlemen . . . My head's going round and round, I can't speak . . . (*Laughs.*) We got to the sale, and there was Deriganov – I told you he was going to be there. All your brother had was fifteen thousand, and Deriganov straightway bid the mortgage plus thirty. I thought, all right, if that's the way things are, and I got to grips with him – I bid forty. Him – forty-five. Me – fifty-five. So he's going up in fives, I'm going up in tens . . . Well, that was that. I bid the mortgage plus ninety, and there it stayed. So now the cherry orchard is mine! Mine! (*He gives a shout of laughter.*) Great God in heaven – the cherry orchard is mine! Tell me I'm drunk – I'm out of my mind – tell me it's all an illusion . . . (*Stamps his feet up and down.*) Don't laugh at me!

If my father and grandfather could rise from their graves and see it all happening – if they could see me, their Yermolay, their beaten, half-literate Yermolay, who ran barefoot in winter – if they could see this same Yermolay buying the estate . . . The most beautiful thing in the entire world! I have bought the estate where my father and grandfather were slaves, where they weren't allowed even into the kitchens. I'm asleep – I'm imagining it – it's all inside my head . . . (*Picks up the keys, smiling tenderly.*) She threw down the keys – she wants to demonstrate she's no longer mistress here. (*Jingles the keys.*) Well, it makes no odds.

*The sound of the band tuning up.*

Hey, you in the band! Play away! I want to hear you! Everyone come and watch Yermolay Lopakhin set about the cherry orchard with his axe! Watch the trees come down! Summer cottages, we'll build summer cottages, and our grandchildren and our great-grandchildren will see a new life here . . . Music! Let's have some music!

*The music plays.* RANYEVSKAYA *has sunk down on to a chair and is weeping bitterly.*

(*Reproachfully.*) Why, why, why didn't you listen to me? My poor dear love, you won't bring it back now. (*In tears.*) Oh, if only it were all over. If only we could somehow change this miserable, muddled life of ours.

PISHCHIK (*takes him by the arm, speaks with lowered voice*). She's crying. We'll go next door and let her be on her own. Come on . . . (*Takes him by the arm and leads him out towards the ballroom.*)

LOPAKHIN. What's all this? Let's hear that band play! Let's have everything the way I want it! (*Ironically.*) Here comes the new landlord, the owner of the cherry orchard! (*Accidentally bangs into an occasional table, and almost overturns the candelabra.*) I can pay for it all! (*Goes out with* PISHCHIK.)

*There is no one in either ballroom or drawing-room except*
RANYEVSKAYA, *who sits crumpled and weeping bittterly.*
*The music plays quietly.*

ANYA *and* TROFIMOV *hurry in.* ANYA *goes up to her mother*
*and kneels before her.* TROFIMOV *remains by the archway into*
*the ballroom.*

ANYA. Mama . . .! You're crying, Mama? Dear Mama, sweet,
kind, beautiful Mama – I love you and bless you. The cherry
orchard's sold, it's lost and gone – that's true. But don't cry,
Mama. You still have life in front of you. You still have a
generous heart and a pure soul . . . We'll go away, love, you
and me, we'll go away from here, we'll go away. We'll plant a
new orchard, lovelier still, and when you see it you'll
understand. And your heart will be visited by joy, a quiet, deep,
joy like evening sunlight, and you'll smile again, Mama! Come,
love! Come . . .!

**CURTAIN**

# Act Four

*The same as Act One.*

*There are no curtains at the window, and no pictures. A little furniture remains, stacked up in one corner, as if for a sale. You can feel the emptiness.*

*Upstage, and by the door leading to the outside, are stacked suitcases, bundles made up for a journey, etc.*

*The door on the left is open, and the voices of* VARYA *and* ANYA *can be heard from beyond.* LOPAKHIN *stands waiting.* YASHA *is holding a tray of glasses filled with champagne.*

*In the anteroom* YEPIKHODOV *is packing a box. From upstage off can be heard a hum of voices – the peasants who have come to say farewell.*

GAYEV (*off*). Thank you, men. Thank you.

YASHA (*to* LOPAKHIN). The peasants have come to make their farewells. They're a decent enough lot, if you want my opinion. They're just not very bright.

*The hum of voices dies away.*

*Enter through the anteroom* RANYEVSKAYA *and* GAYEV. *She is not weeping, but she is pale and her face is trembling. She cannot speak.*

GAYEV. Lyuba, you gave them your purse! You mustn't do things like that! You really must not!

RANYEVSKAYA. I couldn't help it! I simply couldn't help it!

*They both go out.*

LOPAKHIN (*following them to the doorway*). May I humbly

propose a farewell drink? I didn't think to bring any from town, and I could only find one bottle at the station. Come on – have a drink!

*Pause.*

What – don't you want to? (*Moves away from the door.*) If I'd known I wouldn't have bought it. Well, I shan't have any, either.

YASHA *carefully places the tray on a chair.*

You might as well have a drink yourself, then, Yasha.

YASHA. To all those departing! And to all those staying behind. (*Drinks.*) This isn't real champagne, I can tell you that.

LOPAKHIN. Eight rubles a bottle.

*Pause.*

Cold as hell in here.

YASHA. They haven't lit the stoves today. Who cares? We're leaving. (*Laughs.*)

LOPAKHIN. What?

YASHA. Sheer pleasure.

LOPAKHIN. October out there, but the sun's shining, the air's still. It's like summer. Good building weather. (*Glances at his watch, and goes to the door.*) Please bear in mind, ladies and gentlemen, you've only forty-six minutes before the train goes! That means we have to leave for the station in twenty minutes. Do make a little haste, now.

*Enter* TROFIMOV *from outside, wearing an overcoat.*

TROFIMOV. Just about time to go, isn't it? The carriages are here. Heaven knows where my galoshes are. They've vanished. (*Through the doorway.*) Anya, I haven't got my galoshes! I can't find them!

LOPAKHIN. I have to go to Kharkov – I'll be travelling on the same train as the rest of you. That's where I'm staying all winter. I've just been loafing around all this time with you people, going out of my mind with nothing to do. I can't get by without work. I don't know what to do with my hands. They look strange just hanging around like this. They look as if they belonged to somebody else.

TROFIMOV. Well, in a minute we'll be leaving, and you'll be resuming your valuable labours.

LOPAKHIN. Have a glass.

TROFIMOV. I won't, thank you.

LOPAKHIN. So, you're off to Moscow now?

TROFIMOV. Yes, I'm going into town with them. Then tomorrow morning, on to Moscow.

LOPAKHIN. So what, none of the professors been giving their lectures? All waiting for you to arrive, are they?

TROFIMOV. No business of yours.

LOPAKHIN. How many years now have you been at university?

TROFIMOV. Oh, think up something a bit newer than that. That's an old one – old and feeble. (*Looks for his galoshes.*) Listen, we shall probably never see each other again, so allow me to give you one piece of advice as a farewell present. Don't keep waving your arms about! Break yourself of this habit of gesticulating. And all this business of building summer cottages, then calculating that eventually the people who rent them will turn into landlords themselves – that's also a form of arm-waving. All the same, I can't help liking you. You've got fine, sensitive fingers, like an artist's. You've got a fine, sensitive soul, too.

LOPAKHIN (*embraces him*). Goodbye, then, old son. Thanks for everything. Here – just in case you need it – have some money for the journey.

TROFIMOV. What for? I don't need it.

LOPAKHIN. Look, you haven't got any!

TROFIMOV. Yes, I have. Thank you. I got some for a translation I did. Here, in my pocket. (*Anxiously.*) But what I haven't got is my galoshes!

VARYA (*from the next room*). Take your junk away, will you? (*Throws out on to the stage a pair of galoshes.*)

TROFIMOV. Why are you so cross, Varya? Oh, but these aren't
my galoshes!

LOPAKHIN. I planted nearly three thousand acres of poppy this
spring, and I've made a clear forty thousand rubles on it. But
when my poppy was in bloom – what a picture! So here I am,
I'm telling you, I've made forty thousand, and I'm offering you
a loan because I've got it there to offer. Why turn up your nose?
I'm a peasant . . . I'm not going to tie it up in pink ribbon for
you.

TROFIMOV. Your father was a peasant, and mine was a
dispensing chemist, and from that follows absolutely nothing at
all.

LOPAKHIN *takes out his note-case.*

Leave it, leave it . . . Offer me two hundred thousand if you
like, and I still wouldn't take it. I'm a free man. And everything that you all value so highly and dearly – all of you, rich
men and beggars alike – it hasn't the slightest power over me.
It's just so much thistledown, drifting in the wind. I can manage without you – I can go round the side of you. I'm strong
and proud. Mankind is marching towards a higher truth, towards a higher happiness, as high as ever may be on this earth,
and I am in its foremost ranks!

LOPAKHIN. And you'll get there, will you?

TROFIMOV. I shall get there.

*Pause.*

Either get there, or else show others the way.

*From the distance comes the sound of an axe thudding against a
tree.*

LOPAKHIN. Well, then, goodbye, old lad. Time to go. We turn
up our noses at each other, you and me, but life goes on regardless. When I'm at work – and I can work long hours and never
tire – then my thoughts run easier, and I feel I know why I
exist. And how many people are there in Russia, my friend, who
exist and never know the reason why? Well, it makes no odds –

it doesn't stop the world going round. I'm told her brothe. 's found a job – in a bank, apparently – six thousand a year. On. he'll never stick at it, of course – he's bone idle.

ANYA (*in the doorway*). Mama says will they please not sta... cutting down the orchard until she's gone.

TROFIMOV. For heaven's sake – how could anyone have so littl tact? (*Goes out through the anteroom.*)

LOPAKHIN. I'll see to it, I'll see to it . . . It's quite true – the. people . . . (*Goes out after him.*)

ANYA. Has Firs been sent off to the hospital?

YASHA. I told them this morning. I assume they sent him off.

ANYA (*to* YEPIKHODOV, *who is crossing the room*). Ask them, will you, please, if they've taken Firs to the hospital.

YASHA (*offended*). I told Yegor this morning. What's the point asking ten times over?

YEPIKHODOV. The aged Firs, in my considered opinion, is past repair. It's not a hospital he needs – it's gathering to his fathers. And I can only envy him. (*Puts down the suitcase he is carrying on top of a hat-box, and crushes it.*) Of course! Of course! I knew I was going to do that! (*Goes out.*)

YASHA (*mockingly*). Poor old Disasters!

VARYA (*outside the door*). Have they taken Firs to hospital?

ANYA. Yes, they have.

VARYA. Why didn't they take the letter to the doctor?

ANYA. It'll have to be sent on after him, then. (*Goes out.*)

VARYA (*from the next room*). Where's Yasha? Tell him, will you, his mother's come. She wants to say goodbye to him.

YASHA (*flaps his hand*). Oh, they'll drive me to drink.

DUNYASHA *all this while has been busying herself about things; now that* YASHA *is alone she goes up to him.*

DUNYASHA. If only you'd just give me a glance, Yasha. You're going away . . . abandoning me . . . (*Weeps and throws herself on his neck.*)

YASHA. What's all the crying for? (*Drinks champagne.*) Six days from now I'll be in Paris again. Tomorrow we'll be getting on board that express and we'll be away like smoke. I can't believe it. *Vive la France* . . .! Not my style, this place. I can't live here, there's no help for it. I've seen all I want to see of ignorance – I've had my fill of it. (*Drinks champagne.*) So what's there to cry about? Behave yourself properly, then you won't cry.

DUNYASHA (*powders herself, looking in a little mirror*). You will write to me from Paris, won't you? I loved you, you know, Yasha – I loved you so much! I'm terribly tender-hearted, Yasha!

YASHA. They're coming. (*Busies himself about the suitcases, humming quietly.*)

   *Enter* RANYEVSKAYA, GAYEV, ANYA *and* CHARLOTTA IVANOVNA.

GAYEV. We ought to be going. We haven't much time in hand. (*Looking at* YASHA.) Who is it smelling of herrings?

RANYEVSKAYA. Another ten minutes, and we'll get into the carriages . . . (*Glances round the room.*) Farewell, dear house. Farewell, old grandfather house. The winter will go by, spring will come, and then soon you won't be here – they'll be pulling you down. So many things these walls have seen! (*Fervently kisses her daughter.*) My treasure, you're radiant – your eyes are sparkling like two diamonds. You're pleased, then? Very pleased?

ANYA. Very pleased. There's a new life beginning, Mama!

GAYEV (*cheerfully*). Absolutely – everything's all right now. Before the cherry orchard was sold we were all frightfully upset, we were all suffering. And then, as soon as the question had been finally settled, and no going back on it, we all calmed down, we got quite cheerful even . . . Here am I, I'm an old hand when it comes to banks – and now I'm a financier . . . yellow into the middle pocket . . . and Lyuba, you look better somehow, you really do.

RANYEVSKAYA. Yes. My nerves are better, it's true.

*She is helped into her overcoat and hat.*

I'm sleeping well. Take my things out, will you, Yasha. It's time to go. (*To* ANYA.) My own little girl, we'll see each other again soon. When I get to Paris I'll be living on the money your great-aunt in Yaroslavl sent to buy the estate – hurrah for her! But it won't last long.

ANYA. Mama, you'll come back soon, soon . . . won't you? I'm going to study and take my examinations – and then I'm going to work, I'm going to help you. Mama, you and I are going to read all sorts of books together. We will, won't we? (*Kisses her mother's hands.*) We'll read in the autumn evenings, read lots and lots of books, and a marvellous new world will open up before us . . . (*Lost in her dreams.*) Come back, Mama . . .

RANYEVSKAYA. I will, my precious. (*Embraces her.*)

*Enter* LOPAKHIN. CHARLOTTA *quietly hums a tune.*

GAYEV. Charlotta's happy – she's singing!

CHARLOTTA (*picks up a bundle that looks like a swaddled infant*). My little baby! Off to bye-byes now . . .

INFANT (*cries*). Wah! Wah!

CHARLOTTA. Hush, my pretty one! Hush, my darling boy!

INFANT. Wah! Wah!

CHARLOTTA. Poor little thing! (*Tosses the bundle back where it came from.*) So you'll try to find me a place, will you, please? I can't manage otherwise.

LOPAKHIN. We'll find something for you, never you fear.

GAYEV. They're all leaving us. Varya's going away . . . Suddenly no one needs us any more.

CHARLOTTA. I've nowhere to live in town. I shall have to go farther afield. (*Hums.*) But what do I care?

*Enter* PISHCHIK.

LOPAKHIN. Well, of all the world's wonders . . . !

PISHCHIK (*out of breath*). Oh, let me get my breath back . . . such a state . . . my dear good people . . . water, some water . . .

GAYEV. After money, is he? No good looking at me . . . I shall depart from temptation. (*Goes out.*)

PISHCHIK. Long time since I was in this house . . . wonderful woman . . . (*To* LOPAKHIN.) And you're here . . . Very pleased to catch you . . . Man of enormous intelligence . . . Here . . . Take this . . . Four hundred rubles . . . Eight hundred still to come . . .

LOPAKHIN (*shrugs in bewilderment*). It's like a dream . . . Where on earth did you get it?

PISHCHIK. Wait . . . Hot . . . Most extraordinary thing. Some Englishmen arrived – found some kind of white clay in my land . . . (*To* RANYEVSKAYA.) And four hundred for you . . . You amazing, wonderful woman . . . (*Gives her the money.*) The rest later. (*Drinks the water.*) Someone was just telling me – young man on the train – apparently there's some great philosopher who recommends jumping off the roof. 'Jump!' he says – and apparently that's the whole problem in life. (*In amazement.*) Would you believe it! Some more water . . .

LOPAKHIN. Who were these Englishmen?

PISHCHIK. I gave them a twenty-four year lease on the section with the clay in it . . . But forgive me, I can't stay now . . . I've got to gallop . . . Go and see old Znoykov . . . And Kardamonov . . . I owe money to all of them . . . (*Drinks.*) Your very good health . . . I'll look in on Thursday . . .

RANYEVSKAYA. We're just moving into town – and tomorrow I'm going abroad.

PISHCHIK. What? (*Alarmed.*) What's this about moving into town? So that's why I can see all this furniture . . . all these suitcases . . . Well, there we are . . . (*On the verge of tears.*) There we are . . . People of the most tremendous intelligence, these Englishmen . . . There we are . . . Be happy . . . God give you strength . . . There we are, then . . . To everything in this world there is an end . . . (*Kisses* RANYEVSKAYA's *hand.*) And

if one day the rumour reaches you that the end has come for
me, then remember this old . . . this old horse, and say: 'Once
on this earth there was a certain Simeonov-Pishchik . . . God
rest his soul . . .' Most remarkable weather . . . Yes . . . (*Exits
in great confusion, but at once returns and speaks from the doorway.*
Dashenka sends her regards! (*Goes out.*)

RANYEVSKAYA. We could even be going now. I'm leaving with
two things still on my mind. One is poor Firs. (*Glances at her
watch.*) We could wait another five minutes . . .

ANYA. Mama, Firs has been taken to hospital. Yasha did it this
morning.

RANYEVSKAYA. My other worry is Varya. She's used to rising
early and doing a day's work. Now she has nothing to do all
day she's like a fish out of water. Poor soul, she's grown thin
and pale, she's forever weeping . . .

*Pause.*

(*To* LOPAKHIN.) As you well know, I dreamt of . . . seeing her
married to you, and everything appeared to be pointing in that
direction. (*Whispers to* ANYA, *who motions to* CHARLOTTA,
*whereupon both of them go out.*) She loves you – you like her –
and why you seem to avoid each other like this I simply do not
know. I don't understand it.

LOPAKHIN. I don't understand it myself, I have to admit. It's
all very strange. If there's still time, then I'm ready – here and
now, if you like. Let's get it over with, and *basta*. I have a
feeling I'll never propose once you've gone.

RANYEVSKAYA. Splendid. It'll only take a minute, after all. I'll
call her in at once.

LOPAKHIN. We've even got champagne, appropriately enough.
(*Looks at the glasses.*) Empty. Someone's drunk the lot.

YASHA *coughs.*

Well, that really is lapping it up.

RANYEVSKAYA (*animatedly*). Wonderful. We'll go out of the room. Yasha, *allez!* I'll call her . . . (*Through the doorway.*) Varya, leave all that and come here. Come on! (*Goes out with* YASHA.)

LOPAKHIN (*looks at his watch*). Yes . . .

*Pause.*

*There is stifled laughter and whispering outside the door. Finally* VARYA *comes in.*

VARYA (*looks round the room at some length*). That's strange. I can't find it anywhere . . .

LOPAKHIN. What are you looking for?

VARYA. I packed it myself and I can't remember where.

*Pause.*

LOPAKHIN. Where are you off to now, then?

VARYA. Me? To the Ragulins. I've agreed to keep an eye on the running of the house for them. Well, to be housekeeper.

LOPAKHIN. That's in Yashnevo, isn't it? What, about forty-five miles from here?

*Pause.*

Well, here we are, no more life in this house . . .

VARYA (*examining things*). Where is it . . .? Or perhaps I packed it in the trunk . . . No, no more life in this house. Never again.

LOPAKHIN. And I'm off to Kharkov now . . . on this train, in fact. Lot of business to do. I'm leaving Yepikhodov in charge here. I've taken him on.

VARYA. Really?

LOPAKHIN. This time last year we had snow already, if you remember. Now it's calm and sunny. The only thing is the cold. Three degrees of frost.

VARYA. I didn't look.

*Pause.*

Anyway, our thermometer's broken . . .

*Pause.*

A VOICE (*through the door from outside*). Where's Lopakhin?

LOPAKHIN (*as if he has been expecting this call for some time*). Coming! (*Goes rapidly out.*)

*VARYA, now sitting on the floor, lays her head on a bundle of clothing, and sobs quietly. The door opens and RANYEVSKAYA cautiously enters.*

RANYEVSKAYA. What?

*Pause.*

We must go.

VARYA (*she has already stopped crying; wipes her eyes*). Yes, Mama, dear, it's time. I'll get to the Ragulins today provided we don't miss that train . . .

RANYEVSKAYA (*through the doorway*). Anya, get your things on!

*Enter ANYA, followed by GAYEV and CHARLOTTA IVANOVNA. GAYEV is wearing an overcoat with a hood.*

*The SERVANTS and CARRIERS foregather. YEPIKHODOV busies himself about the things.*

Well, then, I think we can finally be on our way.

ANYA (*joyfully*). On our way!

GAYEV. My friends! My dear good friends! Leaving this house forever, can I stand silent, can I refrain from saying a word of farewell, from giving expression to those feelings that now invade my whole being . . .?

ANYA (*imploringly*). Uncle!

VARYA. Dear uncle, don't!

GAYEV (*gloomily*). Off the cushion and into the middle . . . I am silent.

*Enter* TROFIMOV, *followed by* LOPAKHIN.

TROFIMOV. What are we waiting for, then? It's time to go!

LOPAKHIN. Yepikhodov, my coat!

RANYEVSKAYA. I'm going to stop here for one more minute. It's as if I'd never really seen before what the walls in this house were like, what the ceilings were like. And now I look at them avidly, with such a tender love.

GAYEV. I remember, when I was six years old, sitting up on this windowsill on Trinity Sunday and watching my father go to church.

RANYEVSKAYA. Have all the things been taken out?

LOPAKHIN. I think the lot. (*To* YEPIKHODOV, *as he puts on his overcoat.*) Have a look, though, see if everything's all right.

YEPKHODOV (*in a hoarse voice*). Don't worry – leave it to me!

LOPAKHIN. Why are you talking in that sort of voice?

YEPIKHODOV. Just drinking some water, and I swallowed something.

YASHA (*contemptuously*). The ignorance of these people . . .

RANYEVSKAYA. We shall depart, and not a living soul will remain behind.

LOPAKHIN. All the way through until the spring.

VARYA (*pulls an umbrella out of one of the bundles in a way that looks as if she were raising it threateningly :* LOPAKHIN *pretends to be frightened*). What? What are you doing . . .? It never even entered my head.

TROFIMOV. Ladies and gentlemen, we must get into the carriages. It really is time! The train will be arriving any minute!

VARYA. Here they are, Petya – your galoshes, next to this suitcase. (*In tears.*) And what dirty galoshes they are . . .

TROFIMOV (*putting on the galoshes*). Off we go, then!

GAYEV (*in great confusion, afraid of bursting into tears*). The train . . . the station . . . In off into the middle, off the cushion into the corner . . .

RANYEVSKAYA. Off we go!

LOPAKHIN. Are we all here? No one left behind? (*Locks the side door on the left.*) The things are all stacked in here, we must lock up. Right, off we go!

ANYA. Farewell, old house! Farewell, old life!

TROFIMOV. Hail, new life! (*Goes with* ANYA.)

> VARYA *looks round the room and goes out without hurrying.* YASHA *and* CHARLOTTA *go out with her little dog.*

LOPAKHIN. So, until the spring. Out you go, all of you ... Goodbye! (*Goes out.*)

> RANYEVSKAYA *and* GAYEV *are left alone together. As if they have been waiting for this, they throw themselves on each other's necks and sob quietly, restraining themselves, afraid of being overheard.*

GAYEV (*in despair*). My sister, my sister ...

RANYEVSKAYA. Oh my dear orchard, my sweet and lovely orchard! My life, my youth, my happiness – farewell! Farewell!

ANYA (*off, calling cheerfully*). Mama!

TROFIMOV (*off, cheerfully and excitedly*). Hulloooo ...!

RANYEVSKAYA. One last look at the walls ... the windows ... This is the room where our poor mother loved to walk ...

GAYEV. My sister, my sister ...!

ANYA (*off*). Mama!

TROFIMOV (*off*). Hulloooo ...!

RANYEVSKAYA. We're coming!

> They go out.

> The stage is empty. There is the sound of all the doors being locked, and then of the carriages departing. It grows quiet. Through the silence comes the dull thudding of the axe. It sounds lonely and sad. Steps are heard.

> From the door on the right comes FIRS. He is dressed as always, in jacket and white waistcoat, with his feet in slippers. He is ill.

FIRS (*goes to the door and tries the handle*). Locked. They've gone. (*Sits down on the sofa.*) They've forgotten about me. Well, never mind. I'll just sit here for a bit . . . And I dare say he hasn't put his winter coat on, he's gone off in his autumn coat. (*Sighs anxiously.*) I never looked to see. When will these young people learn? (*Mutters something impossible to catch.*) My life's gone by, and it's just as if I'd never lived at all. (*Lies down.*) I'll lie down for a bit, then . . . No strength, have you? Nothing left. Nothing . . . Oh you . . . sillybilly . . . (*Lies motionless.*)

*A sound is heard in the distance, as if from the sky – the sound of a breaking string, dying away, sad.*

*Silence descends, and the only thing that can be heard, far away in the orchard, is the thudding of the axe.*

**CURTAIN**

# A Note on the Translation

This is not a complete collection of Chekhov's plays. I thought it inappropriate to include *Wild Honey*, my version of his first, untitled play, because I extensively reshaped and rewrote the original text, whereas the translations in this volume are all entirely straight – as close to the original as I can make them. They are also intended for production, and if you are asking actors and directors to commit themselves to a text you must first be committed to it yourself. I have therefore included only those plays which I felt I could translate up to this standard. I have omitted the weaker one-act plays. (In a separate volume, entitled *The Sneeze*, I have trimmed the four one-act plays included here and supplemented them with adaptations of some of Chekhov's stories to make up a complete evening.) I have also omitted *The Wood Demon*, which is of great interest academically as an early version of *Uncle Vanya*, but of little theatrically since all the best material in it appears to vastly greater effect in the latter play.

I hesitated for much longer over *Ivanov*. This is a play which has been quite frequently produced, and found to be of dramatic interest. It has notable champions. Ronald Hingley believes it to be not only an improvement upon its predecessor, the untitled play, but finer than *The Seagull*, which he thinks has been 'overrated in general esteem'. The late Dr Simon Behrman, a physician with a close interest in Chekhov, wrote to me urging its value, more plausibly, as a classic acccount of depression, and as a symptom of Chekhov's own depressed state of mind. It does indeed have a characteristically depressive lack of energy and action. When we first meet the wretched Ivanov in Act One he is already in low spirits and racked by guilt, and he continues so to the end of the play, when he shoots himself. At no point does he undergo any development or even variation of mood, except at the end of Act Two, when Sasha declares her love for him. At this he 'gives a peal of happy laughter' and has a vision of a new life starting. But this altered state lasts for only some twenty-five seconds, by my calculation, before he realises with horror that they are being watched by his wife, and relapses into guilt and inertia, never to re-emerge.

It is impossible not to compare him as a character with Platonov, in the earlier, untitled play, who also betrays his wife, and who also falls victim to guilt and melancholy. But Platonov goes through a hundred moods. His spirits soar as well as plummet. He has moments of ridiculous hope, is self-deceiving as well as self-knowing, has impossible ideals, feels love and malice and friendship as well as despair and emptiness; and is, above all, *changed* by the events of the play. The characters around Ivanov make a poor contrast, too, with the figures around Platonov. Ivanov's wife has an interesting history – she has renounced her Jewish faith to marry him and been rejected by her family in consequence – but remains dramatically a helpless victim, unlike Platonov's wife, who suffers a similar marital humiliation, but who refuses to be patronised by her repenting but unreforming husband. Ivanov's new love, Sasha, is a pale figure beside the two women who pursue Platonov. All the other characters are dismissed, with an impatience and high-handedness that come oddly from Chekhov, as grasping, dishonest, philistine, drunken, slothful, or priggish. I may be as blind as it seems to me Hingley is to the virtues of the untitled play and *The Seagull*, but, however many times I reread the original, I do not see how to make a translation of this material which I can expound to a director and defend to a cast.

Any translator of Chekhov must be painfully aware of the very large number of other versions of these plays which have been made over the years, and also of Chekhov's own hostility to the whole idea of being translated – 'I can't stop them, can I? So let them translate away; no sense will come of it in any case.' All the earlier English versions, so far as I know, have been made either by people who could read the original but who had no experience in writing plays, or by English dramatists who knew the original only through the literal version of a collaborator, or through the published editions, combined often with a mysterious inner certainty about what Chekhov was saying, or what he ought to have been saying if only he had been more like themselves. My only qualification for trying again is that I happen both to know Russian and to write plays. Translating a play is rather like writing one. The first principle, surely, is that each line should be what that particular character would have said at that particular moment if he had been a native English-speaker. This involves inhabiting that character, or trying to, as intimately as if he were one's own. The second basic principle, it seems to me, is that every line must be as immediately comprehensible as it was in the original; there are no footnotes in the theatre, and no turning back to a previous page.

Practical difficulties arise in applying these principles, particularly with familiar references to matters that are unfamiliar to a modern English audience. I have expanded some of these, and cut others. The hardest problems are caused by the many literary allusions. They are all explained in the detailed notes on the individual plays that follow. I have dealt with them in various ways in the text. Some of them are inessential, and would in any case be obscure to a modern Russian audience, and these I have felt free to cut. But most of them are both essential to the sense and, to a Russian, current coin, burnished with use. I have done my best with these, but there is no way of catching that well-worn familiar shine.

The other general problem is that of names. Russsians address each other and refer to each other sometimes by their surnames (Voynitzky, say), sometimes by a combination of given name and patronymic (Ivan Petrovich, to take the same familiar character), just occasionally by the patronymic alone, and often by a diminutive of the given name (in this case Vanya), or by any one of a bewildering range of its variants (Ivasha, Isha, Ishuta, Iva, Vanyukha, Vanyusha, Vanyura, Vanuta, to name but a few allotropes of this same single name), or even, among the educated classes before the Revolution, by its French equivalent (Vanya's mother calls him Jean). English-speaking actors have great difficulties with these shifting clouds of unpronounceable syllables. So do English-speaking audiences, who neither understand the implication of the different combinations nor remember which characters they belong to. To transliterate them blindly would clearly be a breach of my second principle (immediate comprehensibility) – and also, I think, of my first. These characters must all become native English-speakers, and native English-speakers do not attempt foreign words and names. I have therefore simplified ruthlessly. This changes the feel of some relationships, particularly between servants and their masters.

The transliteration itself is another problem. Where mine is inconsistent, or departs from usual practice, it is because I have simplified it to make it easier for actors to get a reasonable approximation to the original sound. Rigidity can in any case produce nonsense. The surname of the Baron in *Three Sisters*, for example, was clearly transliterated into the Cyrillic from a German original, 'Tusenbach'. Elisaveta Fen recovers it into Latin script in her translation as 'Toozenbakh', which is like the translating machine that is supposed to have put 'Out of sight, out of mind' into Japanese and recovered it into English as 'Invisible, insane.' Other translators go to the opposite extreme, and put given names into English. Never 'Vanya', for some reason – I know of no translation entitled *Uncle Jack* – but in the same play Ronald Hingley gives 'Helen Serebryakov' and 'Michael Astrov'. Why not Tony Chekhov, in that case? And why should Russians be the only people to enjoy the advantage of anglicisation? Why not Charles Marx and Henry Ibsen? John-James Rousseau and Leonard from Vinci? Nor do I see any reason for imposing male surnames on the women. Why should Ranyevskaya and Sereb-ryakova have to become Mrs Ranyevsky and Mrs Serebryakov any more than Mrs Warren and Mrs Tanqueray should have to be introduced to Russian audiences as Warrena and Tanqueraya? I am also baffled by the habit that some critics and others have of referring to *Madame* Ranyevskaya and *Madame* Arkadina. They are not Frenchwomen, and are nowhere in the original given French honorifics.

I have used the new and authoritative 30-volume *Complete Collected Works and Letters* throughout. I had already translated *Three Sisters* and *The Cherry Orchard* before I could lay my hands on Volumes 12 and 13, which contain the plays, and I have revised my versions of these with the help of the very copious and thorough notes in this edition, upon which I have drawn extensively throughout. I have also made a number of changes in these last two plays as a result of the experience gained in translating the earlier ones. It took me a long time, for example, to work out the state an English-speaker would be in when he was speaking *skvoz' slyozy* – literally 'through tears' – in view of Chekhov's insistence that the people who do this are not crying. It took me even longer to find out that when a watchman can be heard 'knocking' in the garden at night he is doing it (to warn off intruders) with a *kolotushka* – a kind of mallet – against a piece of wood.

I should like to thank the National Theatre, which commissioned the first of these translations, *The Cherry Orchard*, and so started me off on the whole enterprise. I am also grateful to the various producers who first commissioned the other three translations, even though the original productions were all aborted. I had valuable help and advice from Nelya Yevdokimova in Moscow, Zoya Anderson in London and Dr Anthony Stokes in Oxford, and was saved from a number of blunders and misreadings by looking at various earlier published translations. Dr Donald Rayfield, Professor of Russian and Georgian at Queen Mary and Westfield College, and one of the world's most distinguished and original Chekhov scholars, has very generously made a considerable number of suggestions for corrections and improvements to the two earlier editions of this book, and they are incorporated here. If anyone were to make a line-by-line comparison he would discover that Prof Rayfield has extracted me from at least half-a-dozen small but shameful errors.

I hope that, with the help of all this and in spite of all that, these versions have something of the feel of the original. The naturalness and simplicity of Chekhov's style have been noted before. His characters' speech often has another elusive quality, too – a certain glancing eloquence which seems to catch very precisely the truth in their hearts. Translations sometimes fail to convey this transparency, this sense of looking straight through the words into the people who utter them. The intense pleasure of translating these plays is that it brings one close both to their strong and subtle construction and to the people who inhabit them – closer, I suspect, than any performance in the theatre ever will. It's only Chekhov himself who eludes one still.

The vaudevilles present relatively few difficulties. I have taken some liberties, though, with *The Evils of Tobacco*. However quickly and cynically Chekhov claimed to have written his short plays, he took considerable care over correcting and improving them in the various published editions through which they subsequently went. He lavished particular care upon *Tobacco*. Even if he spent only two-and-a-half hours, as he claimed, on the original version, he must have spent many times more than that on the later ones. Over the years the piece went through six major revisions. The last of them was almost at the end of this life, in 1902, when he was writing *The Cherry Orchard*. This was so radical that he claimed the result as an entirely new play, and indeed the whole tone of the piece, if not the substance, has certainly changed considerably by this time. By the sixth edition the comedy has largely drained away, and left the hapless Nyukhin without the snuff-taking that presumably first gave him his name (Sniff), but with a confession of despair now as stark and unconcealed in its way as Uncle Vanya's or Andrey Prozorov's. I have restored some of the humour of the earlier versions. Although I have used the final edition of 1902 as the basis, and Nyukhin still reaches his direct confession of despair at the end, we are obliged first of all, as we were in Chekhov's earlier versions, to perceive the man's wretchedness for ourselves through his efforts to conceal it.

I have also slightly truncated *Swan Song*. In the original the old actor performs not only the various extracts from Shakespeare given here, but also a speech from *Boris Godunov* and some lines from another work of Pushkin's, his great epic poem *Poltava*. The play goes on to end with Chatsky's bitter farewell to Moscow at the end of Griboyedov's *Woe from Wit*. Once again the play was subject to rewriting, and in earlier editions ended with all or part of the *Othello* quotation: while in the original story from which the play was taken the old actor is led miserably off to his dressing room at the end without ever demonstrating his vanished greatness at all. I have reverted to the *Othello* ending. The Shakespeare on its own seems a perfectly adequate demonstration of Svetlovidov's past glories, and while the Pushkin and the Griboyedov would be as familiar to Russians as the Shakespeare is to us I can see no way of making them even recognisable to an English audience. Chekhov plainly felt that the Shakespeare (in translation) would present no difficulty to Russians. Whether this disparity is a testimony to the universality of English drama or to the parochialism of English audiences I do not know.

Most of the literary allusions in *The Seagull*, fortunately from a translator's point of view, are to Shakespeare again, and clearly identified as such by the characters who make them. I have in fact added an extra line of Shakespeare. In the original, Arkadina slips into playing the closet scene from *Hamlet* with Konstantin because in Russian Gertrude's speech begins 'My son.' I have made her start with a line of Gertrude's from the play scene as an alternative way in. But there are one or two Russian allusions that should be mentioned. Sorin, in Act Three, goes into town to get away for a little from what he calls, in the original, 'this gudgeon's life'. I have slightly reorganised this to make it at any rate clear to non-anglers that gudgeon live in the mud on the river-bottom. But I can find no way to suggest the literary background of the allusion, which is to the fish in Saltykov-Shchedrin's chilling fable *The Wise Gudgeon*. Saltykov's gudgeon, terrified of being eaten by a pike or crushed by a crab, digs a hole in the mud and hides himself in it, only to emerge to snatch his food when everything else is asleep and then to rush back in terror, unable ever to fulfil his natural function in life by marrying and having children. 'And in this way,' says Saltykov, 'the wise gudgeon lived a hundred years and more. And all the time he trembled and he trembled. Neither friends nor relations did he have; he neither went to see anyone nor did anyone come to see him. He never played cards, nor drank strong drink, nor smoked tobacco, nor chased after pretty girls – only trembled and thought the one same thought: "God be praised, I seem to be alive!"' This is the picture of Sorin's life that the original would suggest to a Russian audience. The danger that terrifies the poor gudgeon most, incidentally, is the prospect of being caught by an angler and turned into fish soup – a fate which Sorin avoided but which one might think Nina did not.

Konstantin, in Act Four, refers to the mad miller in *The Water Sprite*. This is the fragment of a verse-drama by Pushkin about a miller's daughter who is made pregnant and abandoned by a prince. She throws herself into the millstream, whereupon her father becomes demented with grief, and declares that he is the raven of the locality. The drowned girl herself becomes a water-sprite, and seems to be on the point of getting her revenge when the fragment ends. The parallel with Nina and Trigorin is obvious.

There is another quotation, or what appears to be a quotation, that I have not been able to identify. Arkadina's line in Act One, given here as 'Come, then, away, ill-starred old man,' appears in Russian to be metrical in form and poetic in vocabulary and word-order. I assume it is a line from some part which Arkadina has played, and indeed in an earlier draft of the act she goes on to add: 'In some play or other it says: "Come to your senses, old man!"' Arkadina's line in Act Two, given here as 'I am troubled in my soul', also looks suspiciously poetic in the original. I have consulted a number of sources and a number of Russian friends without success. The lines may well be from forgotten plays, or even entirely fictitious. On the other hand there may be a little more meaning to be gleaned here.

Chekhov gives precise references for all the songs that Sorin and Dorn sing to themselves. I have retained the titles of only the two which may still be familiar. The others, which have disappeared into the mists of time and would be entirely unfamiliar even if disinterred from the archives, I have reduced to unspecified humming.* On the other hand I have slightly expanded Dorn's reference to Jupiter's anger in Act One to reconstruct the classical saying to which it alludes.

I have followed the Complete Collected Works in restoring the cuts and changes demanded by the censor. Potapenko, the friend who was ironically (see Introduction) charged with shepherding the text through the process of censorship, reported to Chekhov that there were unexpected difficulties. 'Your Decadent looks with indifference upon his mother's love affairs, which is not allowed by the censor's rules.' The censor himself later wrote to Chekhov direct to remove all doubt about what he wanted done. 'I have marked a number of places in blue pencil,' he explained, 'in addition to which I think I should make clear that I had in mind not so much the expressions themselves as the general sense of the relations established by these expressions. The point is not the cohabitation of the actress and the writer, but the calm view taken of this state of affairs by her son and her brother.' Negotiations dragged on throughout the summer of 1896, with Chekhov making some changes and Potapenko making others. After one suggested alteration, in a letter to Potapenko, Chekhov added in exasperation: 'Or whatever you like, even a text from the Talmud.' In the first printed text of the play, in journal form in December 1896, which was not subject to theatrical censorship, Chekhov reverted to his original version. It is true that in all the subsequent book editions he used the censored text; but these were published with the assurance on the title-page that the plays they

*The songs both in *The Seagull* and the other plays now *have* been disinterred by Donald Rayfield, in a paper he presented to the 1987 Chekhov Colloquium in Cambridge. Prof Rayfield makes it clear that they all ironically underline and counterpoint the text, but there is no way I can see of giving this practical effect in production.

contained had been 'passed unconditionally by the censorship for production.' The changes are small and of no very great significance, but there seems no possible reason now for not using the text that Chekhov himself plainly wanted.

There is a double irony, as things turned out, in Konstantin's allusion to the censorship in the first act – one intended by Konstantin and another added by circumstance. I have slightly expanded the reference, to make it comprehensible while leaving it oblique (Russian audiences, of course, have more experience in reading between the lines). Konstantin explains his premature departure from university by likening himself to an item which has failed to appear in the press 'owing to circumstances beyond the editor's control'. Chekhov had the same difficulty with Trofimov in *The Cherry Orchard* – how to explain that someone had been expelled from university for his political activities. It was impossible to get a direct reference to this past the censor – but not, apparently, a reference to the process of censorship itself.

I have cut some of the French variants of personal names in *Uncle Vanya*. 'Hélène' is too remote from 'Yelena' for English ears to make the connection fast enough. I have, however, retained Maria Vasilyevna's 'Alexandre' for 'Alexander' and 'Jean' for Vanya, which do seem in some way characteristic of her abstraction from the muddy realities of Russian rural life.

The Ostrovsky play that Astrov refers to in Act One, when he is looking for his cap to leave, is *The Girl without a Dowry*. Paratov, the reckless, dashing cad who has broken the heart of the girl in the title, and who is just about to break it again, introduces himself to Karandyshev, her pusillanimous fiancé, in the words that Astrov quotes – 'a man with large moustaches and small abilities.' Astrov has presumably prompted himself to think of Ostrovsky by what he has muttered just before this, which is a quotation from a character in another of Ostrovsky's plays, *Wolves and Sheep*. In its original context it is an incoherent protestation of ignorance from a timid aunt when she is interrogated by the despotic local matriarch about whether her niece already has a suitor. The point of the line in its original context is its comical incoherence, but out of that context it is so elliptical as to be meaningless, and I have cut it. Astrov is quoting again in Act Two when he talks to Sonya about Yelena's beauty. The line comes from Pushkin's poem, *The Tale of the Dead Princess and the Seven Bogatyrs*. This is the same story as Snow White and the Seven Dwarfs (though the *bogatyrs* with whom Pushkin's princess finds refuge are not dwarfs but the warrior-heroes of Russian folk-tales), and the line is adapted from what the mirror says to the wicked stepmother after she has disposed of her rival. To make this clear I have modified it to refer to its more familiar equivalent in Grimm. There is plainly an ironical parallel between the mirror's telling the stepmother about the stepdaughter's beauty, and Astrov's telling the stepdaughter about the stepmother's.

There is another literary reference which I have cut, as having no point but its familiarity, and no familiarity in translation (probably none today even in Russian). When Vanya in Act One describes Serebryakov writing in his study from morning until far into the night he adds in the original a quotation from a satire upon odes by one I.I. Dmitrievich (1760–1837), which in translation would run roughly:

> We rack our brains and crease our brow,
> And scribble odes and more odes yet.
> But not the smallest hint of praise
> Do either odes or author get.

I have also, for similar reasons, cut the words of the song that Astrov sings in the middle of the night, in Act Two, and his reference, later in the same scene, to his Feldscher's idiosyncratic pronunciation. I have made a slight change in the wonderful scene in the same act where Yelena and Sonya are reconciled. What they do in the original is drink *Brüderschaft*, and what they thereby resolve to be to each in future, of course, is *ty*, the second person singular. I have made another small change in Act Four, when

Telegin in the original describes Vanya's attempt to shoot Serebryakov as 'a subject worthy of Aivazovsky's brush'. Aivazovsky was a nineteenth-century painter who was most celebrated for his marine studies, though he also painted a number of battle scenes, and it may be these that Telegin has in mind. He produced some six thousand works, but not even this impressive productivity will make his name meaningful to a modern English audience.

I regret any pain caused by the demolition of two landmarks familiar to generations of English audiences. 'Missed again!' or something like it is a funnier line than Chekhov's, but fails to capture an important part of the sense. What Vanya says in the original is 'A *promakh* again?!'. A *promakh* is not just a miss; it is any kind of mistake or false move, and surely (see Introduction) refers to more than just the two shots. Then there is the question of Telegin's nickname. This is given in every translation I have come across as 'Waffles'. The Russian, *Vaflya* does indeed mean a waffle, but Telegin is given the name, as he explains, because of his pockmarked appearance. I can find no grounds for believing that 'Waffles' in English suggests the after-effects of smallpox. It sounds comfortably like an English nickname, it is true, but its implications are surely all wrong. To modern English ears it might indicate a taste for meaningless verbiage; nearer the time, according to Partridge, a waffles (low, 1904) was 'a loafer, a sauntering idler'. Telegin's speech becomes confused when he is upset, but he doesn't waffle. He is idle, certainly, but his idleness is not sauntering – it goes with his abnegation, humility, and saintly devotion to the ideals of love and marriage. I can think of no English nickname that suggests pockmarks. And even if a suitable English equivalent did exist, there would surely be something odd about applying it to a Russian. A lot of English nicknames sound embarrassing enough attached to Englishmen; applied to Russians, nursery locutions such as 'Waffles', 'Boofy', 'Bingo', etc., seem as bogus as spats and co-respondent shoes. The only possible proceeding with '*Vaflya*,' it seemed to me in the end, was to leave it out. I have made do with the occasional diminutive, and shifted Telegin's reference to his pockmarks into his earlier remarks about his 'unprepossessing appearance'.

In the original, Serebryakov is planning to use the money left over from the sale of the estate to buy a modest dacha 'in Finland'. Finland was at the time, of course, a grand duchy of the Russian Empire, and it seems at first sight mysterious why Serebryakov should want to live in the countryside there if he can't stand the countryside anywhere else in Russia. Its attraction, though, as Ronald Hingley has grasped in his translation, was no doubt that the Finnish frontier was only twenty miles from St Petersburg, and I have stolen Hingley's solution.

I have left one line as opaque as it is in the original. It comes in the scene where Astrov is telling Sonya that there is no light in the distance for him because there is no one he loves. In describing his life he says that he is 'ceaselessly pummelled by fate'. He offers no details, and to English ears it sounds the kind of thing that Russians tend to say in plays. Sometimes, however, they say them with very specific meaning. The phrase recalls Ranyevskaya's complaint to Trofimov, the 'Wandering Student' in *The Cherry Orchard*, that 'you do nothing but get yourself tossed by fate from one place to the next', and Trofimov's problem (see Introduction), like Konstantin's in *The Seagull*, was his political activity – while Chekhov's was getting any reference to this past the censor. Does Astrov have similar views and similar problems? I know of no external evidence to support this interpretation, but one has always to be prepared for the lines between the lines in Russian texts. In a Soviet play I translated (*Exchange*, by Trifonov) a character says of his grandfather simply that he has 'recently returned to Moscow'. I remember how foolishly over-suspicious I felt when I asked Trifonov if the absence of any reference to where he had returned *from* could possibly imply that it had been exile, or the camps. I also remember how naïve I felt when I saw his surprise that I should have to ask, since it was already there in black and white, as he saw it, clearly stated in good plain Russian.

Chekhov did in fact start on the Solomon project which he at one stage discussed with Suvorin as an alternative to the early versions of *Vanya*, and the following fragment, found among his papers, suggests how different it would have been. The metaphysical anguish which the king expresses in this monologue appears to derive not from the figure of wealth and wisdom in Chronicles but from the author of Ecclesiastes. The ascription to Solomon in the first verse of Ecclesiastes ('The words of the Preacher, the son of David, king in Jerusalem') was once taken literally, but is now thought to be conventional. The book is now considered to be the work of a much later author, and its wonderful melancholy Epicurean charm more Hellenistic than Judaic.

SOLOMON (*alone*). O, how dark life is! No night in all its blackness when I was a child struck such terror into me as does my unfathomed existence. My God, to my father David Thou gavest but the gift of bringing words and sounds together as one, of singing and praising Thee with plucked strings, of sweetly weeping, of wresting tears from the eyes of others and of finding favour with beauty; but to me why gavest Thou also a languishing spirit and unsleeping hungry thought? Like an insect born out of the dust I hide in darkness, and trembling, chilled, despairing, fearful, see and hear in all things a fathomless mystery. To what end does this light of morning serve? To what end does the sun rise from behind the Temple and gild the palm-tree? To what end is the beauty of women? Whither is yonder bird hastening, what is the meaning of its flight, if it and its fledglings and the place to which it hurries must like me come to dust? O, better I had never been born, or that I were a stone to which God had given neither eyes nor thoughts. To weary my body for the night I yesterday like a common workman dragged marble to the Temple; now the night is come, and I cannot sleep . . . I will go and lie down again . . . Forses used to tell me that if one imagines a flock of sheep running and thinks hard about it then one's thoughts will dissolve and sleep. This will I do . . . (*Exit.*)

I have expanded a few references in *Three Sisters* which might

otherwise have been unfamiliar – to Dobrolyubov and the Panama
Affair, for example – and have tried to suggest the way in which
Masha and Vershinin, at their parting, address each other for the
first time (in our hearing, at any rate) by the intimate *ty*. But the
real difficulties in this play are (once again and more than ever) the
literary allusions. I have completed quotations where necessary to
make internal sense, but cannot give them the air of familiarity
they should have. The lines that Masha gets on the brain ('On a far
seashore an oak tree grows . . .') are the opening of the Prologue
to Pushkin's *Ruslan and Ludmilla;* a magical invocation of the
world of fairy-tales, introducing the story of Ruslan's attempts to
recover his abducted bride. Solyony's lines, 'The peasant had no
time to gasp/Before he felt the bear's hard clasp,' are from
Krylov's fable *The Peasant and the Workman*, about a peasant who
is saved from a bear when a workman manages to hit it on the
head with an axe, and who then complains that this has ruined the
value of the bear's skin. Solyony returns to Krylov in Act Three
with, 'We could spell out the moral of the piece/But let us not
provoke the geese,' which is the end of a fable about a flock of
geese being driven to market who stand on their dignity because of
their noble descent, from the sacred geese who saved the Capitol
in Rome. 'Not teasing the geese' has become a Russian common-
place.

Solyony also quotes Chatsky, the hero of Griboyedov's *Woe
from Wit* – 'I may be odd – but who's not odd,/Save fools alike as
peas in pod?' – then goes straight on with a reference to Aleko.
Aleko is the hero of Pushkin's poem *The Gypsies*, a high-born
youth who falls in love with a Gypsy girl, is accepted into her
family, and then murders both her and her lover when she proves
unfaithful. The relevance to Solyony's own nature is obvious,
though the words he seems to be quoting do not actually occur in
the original. Lermontov, Solyony's idol, so admired the poem that
he used it as the basis of a libretto for an opera. The lines that
Solyony quotes in the last act ('Rebelliously he seeks the storm,/As
if in storms there promised peace . . .') are from *The Sail*,
probably Lermontov's most famous poem, and indeed one of the

most celebrated evocations in any literature of the lonely defiance of the Romantic hero.

Masha quotes (or slightly misquotes) from two of Gogol's stories. 'Living in this world, my friends, is dull work,' is Gogol's reflection (though in the original he says nothing about living) as he leaves the little town of Mirgorod in the rain and mud of autumn at the end of *How Ivan Ivanovich quarrelled with Ivan Nikiferovich,* the story of how two former friends have grown old and grey in the lawsuit which has arisen after one of them called the other a gander. 'Silence . . . silence . . .' is from *The Memoirs of a Madman.* Or more precisely, 'Never mind, never mind . . . silence,' which is what the wretched government clerk in the story tells himself every times he thinks of the unattainable charms possessed by the daughter of the head of his department.

Chebutykin's lines in Act One ('For love and love alone/Was man put in his earthly home') are the start of an aria in an old and forgotten comic opera, *The Werewolves.* In a letter to Stanislavsky, Chekhov says that the song from which Chebutykin sings a snatch as he goes off in Act Three ('Won't you deign to eat this date . . .') comes from an operetta whose title he has forgotten, and I have reduced it to unspecified humming. Donald Rayfield, in his paper on the songs in Chekhov's plays, suggests that operetta underlies the whole structure of *Three Sisters.* The plot, he says, mimics that of *The Geisha,* a popular operetta version, first produced in 1896, of the *Madam Butterfly* story.

In Act Four Chebutykin keeps singing the first two lines from the chorus of *Ta-ra-ra boom-de-ay.* In the American original the chorus consists simply of this same nonsense phrase repeated four times over, and until I read Prof Rayfield's paper I had supposed that Chebutykin's version ('*Tarara boombiya/Sizhy na tumbe ya,*' where the second line means literally 'I sit on a kerbstone') was his own abstracted improvisation, which led me to provide a no less offhand couplet to translate it. Prof Rayfield points out that Chebutykin is singing the standard Russian version of the song, which, instead of repeating the first line, turns to melancholy introspection. (It continues: '*I gor'ko plachu ya/Chto malo znachu ya'* – 'And I weep bitterly/That I'm of little significance.') I have reluctantly decided that the least obtrusive solution is to return to the original words.

Vershinin, in the same act, begins to sing 'To love must young and old surrender,' the magnificent bass aria from the last act of *Eugene Onegin*, in which Prince Gremin tells Onegin that the tempests of love are beneficial both to the man in the flower of youth and to the 'grizzled, hardened warrior'. The parallel with Vershinin's own feelings is obvious; Gremin tells Onegin how dreary his life has been until Tatyana appeared, 'and like a ray of sunlight in the midst of my unhappiness gave me life and youth, youth and happiness.' Tchaikovsky's libretto here is a curious reversal of Pushkin's original, where the unnamed prince who has married Tatyana makes no comment on the success of the match. In the passage that starts with the same line Pushkin is discussing not the prince's love for Tatyana but Onegin's – and his view of late love is very different from Tchaikovsky's. The effects of love upon the young, he says, are as beneficial as spring storms. But in late life it comes like the storms of autumn, that 'turn the meadows into marsh, and strip bare the woods around'.

One of the minor puzzles of the play is exactly what game Masha and Vershinin are playing with their little private conversation in Act Three that goes 'Trum-tum-tum . . . – Tum-tum . . . – Tra-ra-ra? – Tra-ta-ta.' It may (or may not) help elucidate it to know that it was apparently based on an incident that occurred in February 1896 in the restaurant of the Slavyansky Bazar in Moscow when, according to a pseudonymous eye-witness, an unnamed actress who later played Masha (and who many have been the Yavorskaya with whom Chekhov had already had an affair the year before) made her feelings plain to him as follows:

'Tra-ta-ta,' she said, laughing.
'What's that?'
'Tra-ta-ta!'
'Are you in love?'

She gave a loud laugh, shrugged her shoulders and shook them
hard, then, raising her voice, declaimed:
'Tra-ta-ta . . .'
'Indeed! But how has he so captivated you?'
She laughed even more, leaned over the back of the chair, and
as if breathless with passion, her eyes narrowed, and with a
catch in her voice, said almost quietly:
'Tra-ta-ta . . .'

Chekhov laughed heartily, apparently, and promised to use it.

Another considerable problem is finding consistent equivalents
for the many recurring words and phrases. The hardest – and
most ubiquitous – is *vsyo ravno* and its variants, which I have
rendered as 'It doesn't matter' (see Introduction). 'It's all the
same' would be closer, but is less capable of being adapted to all
the different situations in which it occurs. The effect of repetition
must, I think, in a play where it is used so consciously, take
precedence over exactitude.

In *The Cherry Orchard* I have teased out *vyechniy studyent* (see
Introduction), and attached a date to the emancipation of the
serfs, which would have been as firmly located in Russian minds
as (say) the Second World War in ours. I have supplied what
Chekhov merely specifies in a stage-direction, the first few lines of
Alexei Tolstoy's marvellously bad poem *The Scarlet Woman*, which is
about a Judaean courtesan who boasts that she will subdue Jesus with
one of her irresistible looks, and instead is herself subdued by John
the Baptist with one of his.

Rather more hesitantly, I have supplied some of the lines to
which the Passer-by alludes only cryptically in the original. The
speech as written is merely: 'My brother, my suffering brother
. . . go out to the Volga; whose groans . . .?' The first half is a
misquotation from an indifferent poem by Nadson, whom I
suspect, from references in the letters, Chekhov despised. The
second comes from what seems to me a rather magnificent poem
by Nekrasov, *Reflections on the Gateway to a Great House*. It

changes the nature of the scene to have the Passer-by recite several lines, but the two poems do parallel a lot of what Trofimov says, and it is clearly in breach of my second principle of translation (immediate comprehensibility) to have a man come on and say, 'Go out to the Volga; whose groans . . .?' It may also be relevant in understanding this scene that the word for 'Passer-by', *prokhozhy*, meant in Siberian usage at that time someone who was tramping the roads to escape from prison or exile. Chekhov must have come across this usage on his journey to Sakhalin, though whether he intended any part of that sense here I do not know.

Before Chekhov rewrote Act Two after the opening in Moscow (see Introduction) Charlotta did not appear in the scene at the beginning of the act, and Trofimov did not have his two speeches at the end, where he asks Anya to have faith in him, and sees happiness coming with the rising moon. Instead the act began with a scene between Trofimov and Anya:

YASHA *and* DUNYASHA *are sitting on the bench.* YEPIKHODOV *is standing beside it.* TROFIMOV *and* ANYA *come along the path from the estate.*

ANYA. Great-aunt is all alone in the world – she's very wealthy. She's no love for Mama. The first few days I was there I found it very hard – she didn't say much to me. Then she cheered up and started to laugh. She promised to send the money – she gave me and Charlotta some for the journey. Oh, but it's a horrible feeling, being the poor relation.

TROFIMOV. It looks as if there's someone here already . . . Sitting on the bench. Let's go on, then.

ANYA. I was away from home for three weeks. I started to pine most dreadfully.

TROFIMOV *and* ANYA *go out.*

Then Dunyasha says 'All the same, how lovely to spend some time abroad . . .' After Ranyevskaya's line, 'Perhaps we'll think of something,' the original text continued:

VARYA *and* CHARLOTTA IVANOVNA *come along the path from the estate.* CHARLOTTA *is wearing a man's suit, and is carrying a gun.*

VARYA. She's a sensible, well-brought-up girl, and nothing can happen, but all the same she shouldn't be left alone with a young man. Supper at nine o'clock. Make sure you're not late.

CHARLOTTA. I'm not hungry. (*Hums quietly.*)

VARYA. It doesn't matter. You must be there for appearances' sake. Look, they're sitting over there, on the bank.

VARYA *and* CHARLOTTA IVANOVNA *go out.*

And at the end of the act, after Anya's line: 'You put it so beautifully!' the scene originally continued:

TROFIMOV. Sh . . . Someone's coming. It's that Varya again! (*Angrily.*) It's outrageous!

ANYA. Come on – let's go down to the river. It's nice there.

TROFIMOV. Come on, then.

ANYA. The moon will be rising soon.

ANYA *and* TROFIMOV *go out. Enter* FIRS, *then* CHARLOTTA IVANOVNA. FIRS *mutters away as he looks for something on the ground near the bench. He strikes a match.*

FIRS. Oh, you sillybilly!

CHARLOTTA (*sits down on the bench and takes off her peaked cap*). Is that you, Firs? What are you looking for?

FIRS. The mistress has lost her purse.

CHARLOTTA (*searches*). Here's her fan. And here's her handkerchief – it smells of perfume. (*Pause.*) There isn't anything else. She's perpetually mislaying things. She's mislaid her life, even. (*Hums quietly.*) I haven't got proper papers – I don't know how old I am. So I think of myself as being young . . . (*Puts the cap on* FIRS, *who sits motionless.*) Oh, I love you, my dear sir! (*Laughs.*) *Ein, zwei, drei!* (*Takes the cap off* FIRS *and puts it on herself.*) When I was a little girl, Mama and my father used to go round all the fairs . . .

And she gives what is now the opening speech of the act, down o, 'I don't know anything'. Then:

FIRS. When I was twenty, twenty-five years old, I was going along one day with the deacon's son and the cook, Vasily, and just here, on this stone, there was a man sitting . . . a stranger – belonged to someone else – we didn't know him . . . For some reason I got scared, and I went off, and after I'd gone the other two set on him and killed him . . . he'd got money on him.

CHARLOTTA. So? *Weiter!* Go on!

FIRS. So then along came the law, and they started to question us. They took the pair of them away . . . they took me, too. I was two years in jail . . . Then that was that, they let us go. It was a long while back. (*Pause.*) I can't remember it all.

CHARLOTTA. An old man like you – it's time for you to die. (*Eats the cucumber.*)

FIRS. Eh? (*Mutters to himself.*) So there they were, they all went along together, and there they stopped . . . Uncle jumped down from the cart . . . he picked up the sack . . . and inside that sack was another sack. And he looks, and there's something going twitch! twitch!

CHARLOTTA (*laughs quietly*). Twitch, twitch! (*Eats the cucumber.*)

> *Someone can be heard walking quietly along the path and quietly playing the balalaika. The moon rises. Somewhere over by the poplars* VARYA *is looking for* ANYA.

VARYA (*calling off*). Anya! Where are you?

*Curtain.*

# The Pronunciation of the Names

The following is an approximate practical guide. In general, all stressed a's are pronounced as in 'far' (the sound is indicated below by 'aa') and all stressed o's as in 'more' (they are written below as 'aw'). All unstressed a's and o's are thrown away and slurred. The u's are pronounced as in 'crude'; they are shown below as 'oo'. A y at the beginning of a syllable, in front of another vowel, is pronounced as a consonant (i.e., as in 'yellow', not as in 'sky').

## The Evils of Tobacco

> Nyukhin – *Nyookh*een
> Natalya Semyonovna – Na*taa*lya Sem*yawn*ovna

## Swan Song

> Svetlovidov (Vasily Vasilich) – Svetlo*veed*ov ( Va*see*li Va*seel*eech)
> Nikita Ivanich (Nikitushka) – Nee*keeta* Ee*vaan*eech (Nee*keet*ooshka)
>
> Petrushka – Pe*troosh*ka
> Yegorka – Ye*gawr*ka

## The Bear

> Popova (Yelena Ivanovna) – *Pawp*ova (Yel*yayna* Ee*vaan*ovna)
> Smirnov (Grigory Stepanovich) – Smeer*nawf* (Gree*gawr*i Ste*paan*oveech)
> Luka – *Look*a

Dasha – *Daash*a
Gruzdyov – Groozd*yawf*
Korchagin – Kor*chaag*een
Kuritzin – *Koo*ritzin
Matuzov – Ma*too*zov
Nikolai – Neeko*lie*
Pelageya – Pela*gaya*
Semyon – Sem*yawn*
Vlasov – *Vlaas*ov
Yaroshevich – Yaro*shay*veech

## The Proposal

Chubukov (Stepan Stepanovich) – Choobooka*wf* (Ste*paan*
  Ste*paan*oveech)
Natalya Stepanovna – Na*talya* Ste*paan*ovna
Lomov (Ivan Vasilyevich) – *Lawm*ov (Ee*vaan*
  Va*seely*eveech)

Maruskin – Ma*roo*skin

## The Seagull

Arkadina (Irina) – Aar*kaad*eena (I*ree*na)
Konstantin (Kostya) – Konstan*teen* (*Kaw*stya)
Sorin (Petrusha) – *Saw*reen (Pe*troo*sha)
Nina – *Nee*na
Shamrayev – Sham-*rye*-yev
Polina – Po*lee*na
Masha – *Maa*sha
Trigorin (Boris Alekseyevich) – Triga*wree*n (*Boree*s
  Alek*say*eveech)
Dorn (Yevgeni) – Dawrn (Yev*gay*ni)
Medvedenko (Semyon) – Medved*yenk*o (Sem*yawn*)
Yakov – *Yaak*ov

Chadin, Pashka – *Chaad*een, *Paash*ka
Gogol – *Gawg*ol

Grokholsky – Grok*hawl*sky
Izmailov – Iz-*my*-lov
Kharkov – *Khaar*kov
Krechinsky – Kre*cheen*sky
Mama – *Maam*a
Matryona – Matr*yawn*a
Molchanovka – Mol*chaa*novka
Nekrasov – Ne*kraas*sov
Papa – *Paap*a
Poltava – Pol*taav*a
Sadovsky – Sa*dawv*sky
Silva – *Seel*va
Slavyansky Bazar – Sla*vyań*sky Ba*zaar*
Suzdaltzev – *Sooz*daltzev
Tolstoy – Tol*stoy*
Turgenyev – Toor-*gain*-yev
Yeletz – Ye*letz*

## Uncle Vanya

Serebryakov – Se-re-bra-*kawf*
Yelena – Yel*yay*na
Sonya – *Sawn*ya
Maria Vasilyevna – Mar*eey*a Va*seel*yevna
Vanya – *Vaan*ya
Astrov – *Aas*trov
Telegin (Ilya Ilich, Ilyusha) – Tel*yay*gin (Eel*ya* Eel*yeech*,
    Eel*yoosh*a)
Marina – Mar*een*a

Batyushkov – *Baat*yooskhov
Dostoyevsky – Dosto*yev*sky
Ivan Ivanich – Ee*vaan* Ee*vaan*ich
Kharkov – *Khaar*kov
Kursk – Koorsk
Malitzkoye – *Maal*-itz-ko-ye
Mama – *Maam*a

Papa – *Paap*a
Pavel Alekseyevich – *Paav*el Alek*say*evich
Turgenev – Toor-*gain*-yev
Yefim – Ye*feem*

## Three Sisters

Andrey Prozorov (Andryusha) – An*dray Prawz*orov
(An*dryoosh*a)

Natasha – Na*taash*a

Olga (Olga Sergeyvna, Olyushka, Olyechka) – *Awl*ga
(*Awl*ga Ser*gay*evna, *Awl*yooshka, *Awl*yechka)

Masha (Maria, Mashenka) – *Maash*a (Mar*eea*, *Maash*enka)

Irina (Irinushka, Irisha) – I*reen*a (I*reen*ooshka, I*reesh*a)

Kulygin (Fyodor, Fyedya) – *Kool*igin (*Fyaw* – dor, *Fye* –
dya – both in two syllables, not three)

Vershinin – Ver*sheen*in

Tusenbach (Nikolai, Nikolasha) – *Tooz*enbakh (Niko*lie* –as
in 'lie' meaning 'untruth' – Niko*laash*a)

Solyony – Sol*yawn*y

Chebutykin (Ivan Romanich) – Chebo*otik*in (Ee*vaan*
Ro*maan*ich)

Fedotik – Fe*daw*tik

Rode – *Rawd*e

Ferapont – Fera*pawnt*

Anfisa – An*fees*a

Aleko – Al*yek*o
Basmannaya – Bas*maan*naya
Berdichev – Ber*deech*ev
Bobik – *Baw*bik
Dobrolyubov – Dobro*lyoob*ov
Gogol – *Gawg*ol
Kirsanov – Keer*saan*ov
Kolotilin – Kolo*teel*in
Kozyrev – *Kawz*irev
Krasny – *Kraas*ny

Lermontov – *Lair*montov
Mama – *Maam*a
Nemetzkaya – Ne*metz*kaya
Novo-Devichi – *Nawv*o-*Devi*chi
Papa – *Paap*a
Protopopov – Proto*paw*pov
Saratov – Sa*raat*ov
Skvortzov – Skvort*zawf*
Sofochka – *Saw*fochka
Testov – *Test*ov

## The Cherry Orchard

Ranyevskaya (Lyuba, Lyubov Andreyevna) – Ran*yevs*kaya
    (*Lyoob*a, Lyoo*bawf* An*dray*evna)
Anya, Anyechka – *Aan*ya, *Aan*yechka
Varya – *Vaar*ya
Gayev (Leonid Andreyich, Lenya) –
    *Guy*-(as in Fawkes)-yev, *Len*ya, Leo*need* An*dray*ich)
Lopakhin (Yermolay) – Lo*paak*heen (Yermo*lie* – as in 'lie'
    meaning 'untruth')
Trofimov (Petya) – Tro*feem*ov (*Pet*ya)
Simeonov-Pishchik – Sim*yawn*ov-*Peesh*-cheek
Charlotta Ivanovna – Shar*lawt*a Eev*aan*ovna
Yepikhodov – Yepi*khawd*ov
Dunyasha – Doon*yaash*a
Firs – Fierce
Yasha – *Yaash*a

Anastasy – Anas*taas*y
Dashenka – *Daash*enka
Deriganov – Deri*gaan*ov
Grisha – *Greesh*a
Kardamonov – Karda*mawn*ov
Karp – Kaarp
Kharkov – *Khaar*kov
Kozoyedov (Fyodor) – Kozo*yed*ov (*Fyaw* – dor – two
    syllables, not three)

Lopakhina – Lo*paakh*ina
Mama – *Maam*a
Petrushka – Pe*troosh*ka
Polya – *Pawl*ya
Ragulin – Ra*gool*in
Tolstoy (Aleksey Konstantinovich) – Tol*stoy* (Aleks*ay*
    Konstan*teen*ovich)
Yaroslavl – Yaro*slaavl*
Yashnevo – *Yaash*nevo
Yefimushka – Ye*feem*ooshka
Yegor – Ye*gawr*
Yevstigney – Yevstig*nay*
Znoykov – *Znoy*kov

Methuen Drama also publish separate paperback editions of each of Chekhov's four masterpieces in the Theatre Classics series, all translated and introduced by Michael Frayn:

The Cherry Orchard
ISBN 0–413–39340–2

The Seagull
ISBN 0–413–42140–6

Three Sisters
ISBN 0–413–52450–7

Uncle Vanya
ISBN 0–413–15950–7


Also available, translated and adapted by Michael Frayn, are:

The Sneeze
(The Sneeze; The Alien Corn; The Bear; The Evils of Tobacco;
The Inspector-General; Swan Song; The Proposal; Plots)
ISBN 0–413–42490–1

Wild Honey
ISBN 0–413–55160–1

*Methuen Modern Plays*

*include work by*

| | |
|---|---|
| Jean Anouilh | Stephen Lowe |
| John Arden | Doug Lucie |
| Margaretta D'Arcy | John McGrath |
| Peter Barnes | David Mamet |
| Brendan Behan | Patrick Marber |
| Edward Bond | Arthur Miller |
| Bertolt Brecht | Mtwa, Ngema & Simon |
| Howard Brenton | Tom Murphy |
| Simon Burke | Peter Nichols |
| Jim Cartwright | Joseph O'Connor |
| Caryl Churchill | Joe Orton |
| Noël Coward | Louise Page |
| Sarah Daniels | Luigi Pirandello |
| Nick Dear | Stephen Poliakoff |
| Shelagh Delaney | Franca Rame |
| David Edgar | David Rudkin |
| Dario Fo | Willy Russell |
| Michael Frayn | Jean-Paul Sartre |
| Paul Godfrey | Sam Shepard |
| John Guare | Wole Soyinka |
| Peter Handke | Theatre de Complicite |
| Jonathan Harvey | Theatre Workshop |
| Declan Hughes | Sue Townsend |
| Terry Johnson | Timberlake Wertenbaker |
| Barrie Keeffe | Victoria Wood |